THE PSYCHOLOGY OF JURIES

THE PSYCHOLOGY OF JURIES

Edited by Margaret Bull Kovera

American Psychological Association • Washington, DC

Published by
American Psychological Association
750 First Street, NE
Washington, DC 20002
www.apa.org

To order
APA Order Department
P.O. Box 92984
Washington, DC 20090-2984
Tel: (800) 374-2721; Direct: (202) 336-5510
Fax: (202) 336-5502; TDD/TTY: (202) 336-6123
Online: www.apa.org/pubs/books
E-mail: order@apa.org

In the U.K., Europe, Africa, and the Middle East, copies may be ordered from
American Psychological Association
3 Henrietta Street
Covent Garden, London
WC2E 8LU England

Typeset in Goudy by Circle Graphics, Inc., Columbia, MD

Printer: Bang Printing, Brainerd, MN
Cover Designer: Mercury Publishing Services, Inc., Rockville, MD

Library of Congress Cataloging-in-Publication Data

Names: Kovera, Margaret Bull, 1966- editor.
Title: The psychology of juries / edited by Margaret Bull Kovera.
Description: Washington, DC : American Psychological Association, [2017] | Includes bibliographical references and index.
Identifiers: LCCN 2016037883 | ISBN 9781433827044 | ISBN 1433827042
Subjects: LCSH: Jury—United States—Decision making. | Jury—United States.—Psychological aspects.
Classification: LCC KF8972 .P79 2017 | DDC 347.73/752019—dc23 LC record available at https://lccn.loc.gov/2016037883

British Library Cataloguing-in-Publication Data
A CIP record is available from the British Library.

Printed in the United States of America
First Edition

http://dx.doi.org/10.1037/0000026-000

To Craig Kovera: my husband, my best friend, and my biggest fan.

CONTENTS

CONTRIBUTORS

Brian H. Bornstein, PhD, Department of Psychology, University of Nebraska–Lincoln

Dennis Devine, PhD, Department of Psychology, Indiana University—Purdue University, Indianapolis

Theodore Eisenberg, JD, Cornell University Law School, Ithaca, NY

Hiroshi Fukurai, PhD, Department of Sociology, University of California, Santa Cruz

Valerie P. Hans, PhD, Cornell University Law School, Ithaca, NY

William Hirst, PhD, Department of Psychology, New School for Social Research, New York, NY

Jennifer S. Hunt, PhD, Department of Psychology, Buffalo State College, The State University of New York, Buffalo

Norbert L. Kerr, PhD, Department of Behavioral and Organizational Sciences, Claremont Graduate University, Claremont, CA; School of Psychology, University of Kent, Canterbury, United Kingdom; and Department of Psychology, Michigan State University, East Lansing

Jonathan J. Koehler, PhD, Northwestern Pritzker School of Law, Chicago, IL

Margaret Bull Kovera, PhD, John Jay College of Criminal Justice and the Graduate Center, City University of New York, New York

Daniel A. Krauss, JD, PhD, Department of Psychology, Claremont McKenna College, Claremont, CA

Sanja Kutnjak Ivković, PhD, SJD, School of Criminal Justice, Michigan State University, Lansing

Lora M. Levett, PhD, Department of Sociology and Criminology & Law, University of Florida, Gainesville

Joel D. Lieberman, PhD, Department of Criminal Justice, University of Nevada–Las Vegas

John B. Meixner, Jr., JD, PhD, Law Clerk for Judge Gerald E. Rosen of the United States District Court for the Eastern District of Michigan

Jaihyun Park, PhD, Department of Psychology, Baruch College and the Graduate Center, City University of New York, New York

Jennifer K. Robbennolt, JD, PhD, College of Law, University of Illinois, Champaign

Mary R. Rose, PhD, Department of Sociology, University of Texas, Austin

Charles B. Stone, PhD, Department of Psychology, John Jay College of Criminal Justice and the Graduate Center, City University of New York, New York

Christina A. Studebaker, PhD, Master of Legal Studies, ThemeVision LLC, Indianapolis, IN

PREFACE

I have always been an avid reader. As a child, I could often be found reading while I was walking, brushing my teeth, eating my meals, or doing just about any other activity. When I was in eighth grade, my parents were called into my principal's office because I had been surreptitiously (or so I thought) reading novels in band and algebra classes. Legal thrillers, especially courtroom dramas, featured prominently in my reading list back then and still do. Growing up reading these books, I thought I wanted to be a litigator. That was until I spent the summer between my sophomore and junior years in college at Northwestern working at one of the big law firms in Chicago. A summer of typing memos written by summer interns and doing paralegal work for corporate business deals, not to mention the condescending treatment of the secretaries by the other staff, was not what I had envisioned when reading those courtroom dramas. The experience convinced me that law school was not something that I wanted to pursue.

Yet, returning to Northwestern for my junior year, I enrolled in a psychology and law class, taught by Larry Heuer—then a postdoc at Northwestern's business school and now a professor at Barnard College—and first encountered empirical research on jury decision making. I carried the textbook around with me, much like I did those novels when I was a child, reading about studies in which researchers were seeking answers to important questions about whether juries functioned as they should. Could they operate free from bias? Could they disregard inadmissible evidence? Could they understand the instructions that they were given by the judge? Some juries were tasked with deciding whether people would die for the crimes they had committed. Could they do so fairly? Were they competent to make the decisions that the law required of them? It seemed to me that these were fundamental questions of great consequence because these decision-making bodies had the power to deprive citizens of their freedom and potentially their lives. Knowing that they could do so fairly and competently was crucially important. I was hooked and have been studying juries ever since.

I was not alone. Thousands of studies have been conducted on jury decisions and behavior. But as years passed, and I developed from an emerging jury scholar to an editor of *Law and Human Behavior*, serving as a gatekeeper for what jury research was published, I noticed a concerning trend. Although I was seeing many conference presentations and reading many manuscript submissions describing jury research, I was often underwhelmed. In my opinion, jury researchers were often spending valuable time and resources investigating questions that were not important, either theoretically or practically. And as an editor, I noted that there were great disagreements among reviewers of jury research about what types of methods were appropriate for studying the questions under consideration.

When I took a systematic look at how jury research was faring in the review process at *Law and Human Behavior*, my fears were confirmed. Between January 2005 and mid-August 2014, although submitted articles were more likely to address some aspect of jury decision making or behavior than any other topic, research on juries was accepted at less than half of the rate of research on other topics. For some reason, jury research was not faring well in the review process. Although it is possible that reviewers of jury research have higher standards for publication and presentation than reviewers in any other area of social science and law, it is more likely that reviewers judge jury research using the same criteria on which other papers are judged: (a) does the paper make a significant contribution to the literature (i.e., is the research question important?) and (b) are there methodological limitations of the research? It is possible that the higher rejection rate for jury research may be the result of fundamental disagreements among scholars about what questions are important to ask and what methods are appropriate to use when collecting data to answer those important questions.

One night over dinner, I expressed my concerns to Chris Meissner, then program director of the Law and Social Science Program at the National Science Foundation (NSF). He remarked that he and his colleagues also were finding that many proposals for research to study jury decision making were not surviving the review process. Chris encouraged me to seek funding from NSF for a conference on the future of jury research, at which leading law and psychology scholars could come together to discuss the types of questions jury scholars might ask to move the field forward and tackle the ongoing controversy about the desirability of different methodological features in the research used to test those questions. With funding from NSF, 29 jury scholars, including law professors, sociologists, criminologists, and psychologists, convened at John Jay College of Criminal Justice, the City University of New York (CUNY), to have those discussions. This volume is the culmination of the discussions that began at that conference but have continued to evolve over time. I hope that our contributions to this volume inspire those who read them to tackle new and important research questions with as much methodological rigor as they can muster.

I am grateful for the financial support for the conference provided by NSF under Grant Number SES-1155352. Any opinions, findings, and conclusions or recommendations expressed in this material are those of the authors and do not necessarily reflect the views of NSF. I am also grateful for the logistical support provided by the Office for the Advancement of Research at John Jay College—CUNY. Most of all, I am profoundly thankful to the scholars who spent their valuable time traveling to New York City to spend a day and a half pondering possible directions in which jury scholars might take their research and to those who collected their thoughts more formally into the contributions that appear in this volume. Special thanks go to Jennifer Robbennolt, who agreed to step in and complete Ted Eisenberg's chapter when he passed away suddenly. Ted's influence on the field is evident in this volume, and his contributions to the future of jury research will be sorely missed. And as always, I am indebted to Hope and Craig Kovera for their patience with me when working on this book took time that I would rather have been spending with them.

THE PSYCHOLOGY OF JURIES

INTRODUCTION: AN OVERVIEW

MARGARET BULL KOVERA

> Trial by jury is the most rational and effective method for discovering the truth.
>
> —Sir John Fortescue, *On the Laws and Governance of England*

> I consider [trial by jury] as the only anchor, ever yet invented by man, by which a government can be held to the principles of its constitution.
>
> —Thomas Jefferson to Thomas Paine

These statements represent long-held beliefs that trial by jury is the superior method for the resolution of disputes, both between the government and its citizens and between citizens. The jury was deemed so important by the founders of the United States of America that the right to a jury was guaranteed in three of the 10 amendments that constitute the Bill of Rights to the Constitution. Juries serve as an important check against government officials who might try to overreach with their authority (Amar, 1991). For example, the Fifth Amendment provides for grand juries that are drawn from among the citizenry to inquire into charges brought by prosecutors against other citizens and that have the power to determine that there is insufficient evidence for a prosecution to proceed. The criminal jury, a right guaranteed under the Sixth Amendment, has the power to acquit a defendant who they believe is being prosecuted with unreliable or manufactured evidence or to acquit when they believe the law broken is unconstitutional. And the Seventh

http://dx.doi.org/10.1037/0000026-001
The Psychology of Juries, M. B. Kovera (Editor)

Amendment guarantees the right to a civil jury. Even amendments that do not specifically mention juries implicate them (Amar, 1991). For example, the Fourth Amendment protection against unlawful search and seizure is enforced through juries who are the ultimate arbiters of whether a search was reasonable and lawful. In sum, the jury serves as a powerful mechanism for protecting citizens from improper governmental influence.

Because of the centrality of the jury to many of the protections afforded to U.S. citizens under the Constitution and the Bill of Rights, it is crucial to understand whether the jury functions as it is intended. Are juries fair and impartial? Do they follow the law as it is given to them? Do they properly evaluate the evidence before them? If the answer to these questions is no, then it is also important to evaluate the effectiveness of any safeguards or procedural innovations that might improve the function of the jury.

Perhaps it is not surprising, given the importance that the founders placed on the jury in the U.S. Constitution, that the jury—as it operates in the United States at least—has received considerable scholarly attention, initially from legal scholars but more recently from social scientists. After the publication of Kalven and Zeisel's (1966) *The American Jury*, there was an explosion of research on the jury. The Web of Science Social Science Citation Index database lists over 3,700 articles on the topic of jurors or juries and the PsycINFO database contains abstracts for almost 3,900 articles on the topic. However, as we shall see in one of the chapters to come, the publication rate of jury research has slowed in recent years, at least at one of the major scholarly outlets for this type of research. Indeed, a scan of the reference lists for the chapters contained in this volume suggests that much of the influential work on jury decision making and behavior was conducted decades ago.

Why has the volume of jury research—at least research that has been published in high-quality scholarly outlets—seemingly slowed to a trickle? Some scholars have complained about the variability in the methodological quality of the research produced on jury behavior. Others have bemoaned the seemingly limited impact that this voluminous jury scholarship has had on judicial decision making, raising questions about whether jury scholars are asking important or inconsequential research questions and whether they are using appropriate methods to study jury behavior and decision making. There is no question that to pass muster in the peer-review process it is essential that an investigation tackles important questions using the most appropriate methods for answering those questions.

In the interest of reinvigorating jury scholarship, this volume collects the thoughts of a number of esteemed jury scholars in response to two general questions: What are some important areas of inquiry that have been overlooked by jury researchers, and what methods should researchers rely on when studying those questions? For anyone interested in how juries make decisions and whether they do so competently, these scholars have provided comprehensive reviews of the literature addressing these questions. For consumers of jury scholarship, including legal practitioners, there are helpful principles for understanding how best to evaluate the quality of jury research. For both the new and more established jury scholar, the authors have also illustrated new areas of inquiry that are ripe for empirical investigation. There are enough novel questions within the covers of this book to keep many laboratories bustling for years to come.

The structure of the book reflects these two motivating questions, with a set of chapters devoted to each question. In Part I (consisting of Chapters 1–6), authors identify important, yet understudied, topics at the intersection of psychology and law, review what research is currently available on the topics, and then suggest new sets of research questions that would advance the field theoretically or practically (and sometimes both). Specifically, the first two chapters suggest new avenues for research that emphasize the importance of studying the jury as a group rather than a collection of individual jurors. In Chapter 1, Lora M. Levett and Dennis Devine—two scholars who have a particular interest in group processes in jury settings—describe a decision-making model that integrates earlier work on group processes in social influence with a psychological model of individual juror decision making (Devine, 2012). The first half of the model describes how jurors use the evidence they hear during trial to create narrative explanations or stories about how trial-related events likely occurred. The second half of the model describes how the jury chooses which of the jurors' stories to endorse. In Chapter 2, cognitive psychologists William Hirst and Charles B. Stone review research that challenges legal assumptions that deliberation serves to correct errors in individual jurors' memories of the trial evidence and the law.

The remaining chapters in Part I each address an important area of inquiry related to jury decision making and functioning that needs further attention from jury scholars. In Chapter 3, Christina A. Studebaker—a respected trial consultant and jury scholar—argues that previous research has neglected an examination of the myriad ways attorneys influence the trial process, consequently influencing juror decisions. The bulk of the chapter provides the reader with many examples of legal practice strategies that are ripe for empirical investigation, reviewing whatever limited research is available and suggesting new avenues for research.

In Chapter 4, Jennifer S. Hunt reviews the existing literature on the effects of race, ethnicity, and culture as they relate to jury decisions and behavior. She proposes a research agenda for studying the effects of race and ethnicity on targets (e.g., defendants, victims) and subjects (i.e., jurors), as well as examining the variability of behavior that occurs within different racial and ethnic groups and evaluating interventions designed to reduce the racial and ethnic disparities currently manifested in the jury system.

In Chapter 5, two renowned law professors, Jennifer K. Robbennolt and the late Theodore Eisenberg, ask us to consider the benchmarks we are using to evaluate jury competence. Robbennolt and Eisenberg note that although one benchmark for jury competence is whether they arrive at decisions that are similar to those rendered by judges, there are relatively few areas in which researchers have directly compared judge and juror decision making (with the exception of decisions about damage awards in civil cases); the authors call on scholars to rectify this deficit.

In Chapter 6, Valerie P. Hans, Hiroshi Fukurai, Sanja Kutnjak Ivković, and Jaihyun Park remind us that many countries are developing systems of lay participation, which share some features of the U.S. jury system (e.g., lay jurors, deliberation) but have different characteristics as well, including mixes of professional and lay judges and nonbinding decisions by lay participants. The authors describe the characteristics of these systems and novel—at least in the context of traditional jury research—methods for examining the types of comparative questions that have arisen as a function of these emerging jury systems across the globe.

In Part II (consisting of Chapters 7–10), a number of prominent jury scholars answer the second guiding question: Should researchers place a greater value on ecological or external validity than on internal validity when designing and evaluating jury research? In other words, should we emphasize conducting studies that emulate real juries as much as possible (ecological validity) in the hope that this will increase the generalizability (external validity) of our studies, or should we be more concerned with conducting tightly controlled experimental studies that allow for causal conclusions based on the results (internal validity)?

In Chapter 7, Jonathan J. Koehler and John B. Meixner, Jr. argue that researchers' methodological choices to emphasize one type of validity over another should be governed by the goals of the research, with research intended to support theory development properly emphasizing internal validity at the expense of ecological or external validity. However, if the research has more applied goals, the authors argue that researchers should be certain to design studies that have high ecological validity.

Similarly, in Chapter 8, Daniel A. Krauss and Joel D. Lieberman argue for more realistic participant samples, more standardized and realistic stimuli, increased stimulus sampling, and better collaboration with legal scholars to improve the methods of jury researchers. However, they present empirical evidence from a survey of editors and editorial board members of journals that publish jury research that suggests that these respondents—who influence what types of jury research are published in high-impact psychology and law journals—may be relatively unconcerned with whether jury simulation research has high ecological validity.

In Chapter 9, Brian H. Bornstein updates his analysis of the validity of jury research (Bornstein, 1999), noting new trends that have emerged since that article was published, including a reduction in the number of articles addressing jury issues, fewer studies using undergraduate participants, and more studies using videotaped stimuli and deliberation. Although he concludes that the verisimilitude of jury research is increasing overall, he notes that simulations have not improved on one important dimension, the consequentiality of the decisions made by participants.

In Chapter 10, the final chapter of Part II, Mary R. Rose uses an empirical approach to test an assumption of many jury scholars who argue for increased verisimilitude in jury simulations, specifically that courts and legal practitioners will not accept findings from jury simulations that are low in ecological validity. Her analyses suggest that instead of dismissing jury research findings because of low verisimilitude, courts rely on simulation studies when they support procedural changes that justices want to make but dismiss them when they support making changes to policy that they find undesirable.

In Part III, the final chapter and a conclusion provide a synthesis of the book's themes, both suggesting that there are times in which the research question lends itself to particular jury methods, and they make recommendations for future directions for research. In Chapter 11, Norbert L. Kerr, an esteemed jury scholar who notably contributed significantly to developing theory about jury decision making and to addressing pressing practical concerns about jury competence, provides us with a swan song—his advice, based on his 40-year career studying jury behavior, for what jury researchers should and should not do when designing research. His thoughts mirror the structure of this book in that his list of dos and don'ts for jury researchers addresses how to choose important research questions and the methodologies used to test those questions.

In the concluding chapter, I end the volume with a synthesis of the recommendations for choosing important research questions and appropriate research methods to test those questions. Both sets of choices likely rest on whether the goals of the researcher are weighted toward developing basic theory about jury decision making or toward addressing more applied concerns. I identify three areas of inquiry that would benefit from future attention from jury researchers, providing readers with a road map for how to produce influential research that is both theoretically and practically interesting and methodologically sound.

REFERENCES

Amar, A. R. (1991). The Bill of Rights as a constitution. *The Yale Law Journal, 100*, 1131–1210. http://dx.doi.org/10.2307/796690

Bornstein, B. H. (1999). The ecological validity of jury simulations: Is the jury still out? *Law and Human Behavior, 23*, 75–91. http://dx.doi.org/10.1023/A:1022326807441

Devine, D. J. (2012). *Jury decision making: The state of the science*. New York: New York University. Press.

Kalven, H., & Zeisel, H. (1966). *The American jury*. Boston, MA: Little, Brown.

I

IMPORTANT BUT UNDERSTUDIED TOPICS IN JURY RESEARCH

1

INTEGRATING INDIVIDUAL AND GROUP MODELS OF JUROR DECISION MAKING

LORA M. LEVETT AND DENNIS DEVINE

Despite considerable scientific study, scholars have yet to formulate a unified theory of jury decision making that accounts for both the predeliberation preferences of individual jurors and the collective deliberation process. Researchers have focused primarily on input–output variables in jury deliberation (such as using predeliberation preference distributions to predict final verdicts; e.g., Davis, 1973; Davis, Kerr, Atkin, Holt, & Meek, 1975) or specific aspects of the deliberation process (e.g., Hastie, Penrod, & Pennington, 1983; Stasser, Kerr, & Bray, 1982). The goal of this chapter is to advance our understanding of jury decision making by identifying, integrating, and extending existing theoretical models relevant to juror and jury decisions. In the first half, we review models of juror and jury decision making and the social dynamics of the deliberation process. In the second half, we present a unified multilevel theory that integrates juror and jury decision making.

Both authors contributed equally to this work; authorship was randomly determined.

http://dx.doi.org/10.1037/0000026-002
The Psychology of Juries, M. B. Kovera (Editor)

MODELS OF JUROR DECISION MAKING

Most literature on jury and juror decision making focuses on individual jurors' decisions. Researchers have traditionally conceptualized individual jurors' decisions using mathematical or explanation-based models (Hastie, 1993). Mathematical models treat jurors interchangeably, using formal equations to represent how the typical juror weights various pieces of evidence to render a verdict. In explanation-based models, jurors' experiences and knowledge play a role in their generation of a rich verbal account of trial-relevant events and chosen verdict.

Mathematical Models of Juror Decision Making

The most popular mathematical models are the Bayesian, algebraic, and stochastic process models (Hastie, 1993). A full review of these models is not possible given the scope of this chapter (for a more thorough review, see Devine, 2012; Hastie, 1993). Generally, these models rest on the assumption that at any given time (e.g., the beginning, middle, and end of the trial) jurors make decisions using the cognitive equivalent of a single mental "meter" that represents jurors' beliefs in the probability the defendant committed the crime. Jurors begin a trial with some initial belief in the defendant's guilt based on preconceived notions, personal values, and/or the judge's instructions. Jurors then adjust that belief throughout the trial (Hastie, 1993).

According to these models, jurors identify pieces of evidence with probative value, assign weight to each piece, combine the weighted pieces, and use the result to adjust their belief in the defendant's guilt. At the end of trial, jurors compare their final beliefs in the defendant's guilt to their personal thresholds for conviction and choose the verdict that best corresponds. Unlike the other mathematical models, stochastic process models allow for a range of possible verdicts in a probabilistic fashion to account for the unknowable and/or unpredictable aspects of jury decision making (e.g., the impact of extralegal information).

Although similar in their use of formal equations, mathematical models vary in the calculation of how evidence is parsed, weighted, and combined with jurors' previous belief in the defendant's guilt. The Bayesian model involves an equation based on probability theory that multiplicatively combines jurors' weights of the evidence with the jurors' a priori belief in the probability the defendant is guilty (Hastie, 1993). Algebraic models presume that pieces of evidence are weighted and combined in an additive fashion to arrive at a value indicative of the defendant's likely guilt.

Mathematical models also vary with regard to whether and when jurors will cease to update the mental meter with any further evidence. According to the Bayesian model, for example, if the mental meter reaches the extreme probabilities of 0 or 1, the meter will stop and new information will not be incorporated (Hastie, 1993). According to stochastic process models, jurors evaluate evidence throughout trial until a critical event occurs (e.g., the introduction of particularly convincing evidence), and the critical event freezes the meter. In contrast, the mental meter does not freeze in algebraic models at any point throughout the trial.

Research has shown support for the various mathematical models (e.g., Kerr, 1978; Moore & Gump, 1995). The primary criticism of these models is that using a single mental meter to describe how jurors make a decision at trial is too simplistic; in reality, the process is more multidimensional and has to account for more than just that evidence presented at trial (Hastie, 1993). For example, before finding a defendant guilty, the judge typically instructs jurors that each element of a particular crime must be satisfied beyond a reasonable doubt. This instruction implies that multiple mental meters may be at work, but existing mathematical models do not speak to how those meters would operate separately or in combination (Hastie, 1993).

The Story Model of Juror Decision Making

Whereas the mathematical models focus on predictive efficacy with regard to juror decisions, the story model of juror decision making has been lauded as the most descriptively accurate way to explain how jurors make decisions (Pennington & Hastie, 1988, 1992, 1993). The premise of this model is that jurors actively engage in the decision-making process, arrange the evidence into a narrative format, and use the resulting "story" to determine the verdict. According to the story model, this process takes place in three steps.

Story Construction

The first step, story construction, begins when a juror first learns of a case and may continue throughout the trial process and even into deliberation. During this step, jurors construct the story using trial evidence, their personal knowledge about similar types of events, and knowledge about what makes a complete story (Pennington & Hastie, 1993). Thus, jurors actively engage in arranging the pieces of evidence in story-like fashion to help make sense of the case. Each story consists of hierarchical units termed *episodes*, which are series of events that include persons, with motives or intentions, who take actions that have consequences. Organizing episodes into the story hierarchy reflects jurors' weighing the value of the episode.

Trial evidence is often presented in a disconnected format, meaning that jurors often hear about events out of the chronological order in which they occurred. For example, an eyewitness to a crime might take the stand after the coroner has testified as to the cause of the victim's death. In addition, witnesses typically testify in a question–answer format that does not allow for elaboration or explanation as to why certain events occurred (Pennington & Hastie, 1993). Given the disconnected nature of trial evidence, the stories jurors create (and episodes that make up the stories) may be incomplete. Thus, jurors may use their own personal experiences and knowledge to fill in the blanks in their stories (Pennington & Hastie, 1993).

Stories may vary from juror to juror given their wide variety of personal experiences or interpretations of the evidence (Pennington & Hastie, 1993). In addition, individual jurors may create multiple stories that could account for various interpretations of evidence. If multiple stories arise, the story model posits three factors to explain how jurors choose the best story: coverage, coherence, and uniqueness (Pennington & Hastie, 1993). Stories high in coverage account for a large amount of the trial evidence. If the story is consistent (i.e., it does not contradict itself or other evidence the juror believes), plausible (i.e., realistic), and complete (i.e., it contains all the necessary story elements), the story is likely to be high in coherence. Stories higher in coverage and coherence are more likely to be chosen as the best story. If only one story emerges as high in coverage and coherence, that story is considered high in uniqueness, the third factor. However, if more than one story is high in coverage and coherence, it compromises the uniqueness of either story. Any story is less likely to be endorsed because it is low in uniqueness.

Learning Verdict Options

The second stage of the story model involves jurors learning the verdict options (Pennington & Hastie, 1993). This is a difficult task given that jurors are typically instructed about possible verdict options only at the end of trial. Jurors do not always learn the applicable law successfully (Diamond & Levi, 1996; Reifman, Gusick, & Ellsworth, 1992). Jurors also may have preconceived notions about what constitutes certain verdict options that interfere with their ability to learn the actual law that applies to the case (Smith, 1991).

Story Mapping

In this final stage, jurors map their preferred story onto the possible verdict options and determine which one best matches the story (Pennington & Hastie, 1993). Jurors' confidence in a verdict is determined by the story's certainty factors (coverage, coherence, and uniqueness) and how well the verdict option matches the story (Pennington & Hastie, 1993). In criminal trials, if the best story favors the prosecution, jurors use judges' instructions about the standard of proof to determine whether their confidence in the story exceeds the threshold required for a conviction. If the threshold is not met, the juror should render a verdict of not guilty. The story model explains jurors' individual decisions in a variety of cases, including rape (Olsen-Fulero & Fulero, 1997), sexual harassment (Huntley & Costanzo, 2003), and murder (Behl, Kienzle, & Levett, 2013; Pennington & Hastie, 1993). In addition, the story endorsed by jurors at the end of trial mediates the relationship between evidence and verdict (Behl et al., 2013; Huntley & Costanzo, 2003; Pennington & Hastie, 1993). However, what the story model lacks (as do all the other individual models of juror decision making) is an explanation of how individual verdicts are combined into a group verdict during deliberation.

MODELS OF JURY DECISION MAKING

Traditional work examining jury decision making is primarily mathematical in nature, using an input–output approach to predict final jury verdicts based on the distribution of jurors' individual verdict preferences prior to deliberation (Hastie et al., 1983; Penrod & Hastie, 1979). The best predictor of the jury's verdict is the number of jurors favoring it before deliberation (Devine, Clayton, Dunford, Seying, & Pryce, 2001; Kalven & Zeisel, 1966). Although there are several formal models that map the jury's decision based on these verdict preferences (see Devine, 2012, for a review), the social decision scheme (SDS) model (Davis, 1973) and several subsequent offshoots have been used frequently to study the decisions of juries (Devine, 2012). As a class, these stochastic models account for how the diverse preferences of a group are reconciled; these models have successfully predicted jury decisions in numerous studies (e.g., Davis, Tindale, Nagao, Hinsz, & Robertson, 1984; Kerr, Niedermeier, & Kaplan, 1999).

The SDS model is based on the distribution of the initial verdict preferences of the group members and a set of decision schemes (or rules) that are designed to capture the implicit social process by which individual preferences are combined into a collective decision. The distribution of preferences is represented by a matrix of all possible combinations of predeliberation verdict preferences—in a six-person jury (6,0), (5,1), (4,2), (3,3), (2,4), (1,5), and (0,6)—and the number of juries with each combination of preferences. Then, decision rule(s) or scheme(s) are used to combine the preferences into a consensus (Davis, 1973). Various predictions yielded by each decision rule can be tested against data from mock or real juries to see which decision rule fits best. Across many studies, the best-supported decision scheme is one in which two thirds or more of a jury initially agree on a particular verdict; this verdict will most likely be the final jury verdict (Stasser, Kerr, & Davis, 1989). Whether a majority is successful also in part depends on the verdict favored by the majority. In keeping with giving the benefit of the doubt to the defendant, the strongest majorities are those that favor acquittal, especially if jurors are more divided at the beginning of deliberation (Devine et al., 2001; MacCoun & Kerr, 1988).

Other mathematical models of jury decision making have relied on probability distributions or Bayesian algorithms to understand how individual preferences combine into a single group decision (Penrod & Hastie, 1979). These models have examined the effect of various procedural variables on decision making (e.g., changing jury size or decision rule). Other researchers have used computer simulations that account for the probability that the majority will increase in size as the number of straw polls in deliberation occurs (Penrod & Hastie, 1979). Thus, some models have not only accounted for the initial verdict preferences of individual jurors but have also accounted for a small number of aspects of the deliberation process.

Aside from accounting for variables such as the number of straw polls, SDS-inspired researchers have largely ignored the deliberation process and the possibility that deliberation variables may mediate the relationship between individual verdict preferences of jurors and group verdict. However, several studies have indicated the deliberation process can change the jury's final decision (Diamond, 1997; Salerno & Diamond, 2010). In one study, although the initial verdict-preference distribution predicted final verdict, adding variables that captured what was said during deliberation almost doubled the amount of variance explained in final group verdicts (Hastie, Schkade, & Payne, 1999).

Other critiques of mathematical models of juror decision making also apply to the group input–output models—namely, that the mathematical models simplify a more multifaceted, complicated process, and although they predict probable outcomes, they do not elucidate the process the jury undergoes when reaching a decision or the conditions under which the less probable outcome will occur. Moreover, the mathematical models rest largely on the assumption that jurors have a predeliberation preference at the beginning of deliberation; however, that assumption is not always true. In one study, 20% of jurors reported they entered deliberation without a clear verdict preference, and 38% of jurors chose numbers near the mid-point of a continuous scale when asked to indicate which side they favored prior to deliberation (Hannaford-Agor, Hans, Mott, & Munsterman, 2002). Even though including undecided jurors does not change the predictive ability of the SDS model (Kerr & MacCoun, 2012), mathematical models do not account for how or why undecided jurors ultimately adopt a verdict during deliberation.

Further, information that may be important to understanding the quality of the decision is omitted in most group models. For example, the SDS-based models yield a probable verdict outcome. However, because the process is not addressed, we do not know whether all the jury members actually agree with the verdict (which may indicate a higher quality decision) or whether the verdict is a product of jurors agreeing with each other merely to end the deliberation. Thus, an explanation-based model of jury decision making that accounts for the deliberation process should account for social psychological variables that could influence the deliberation process as well as the input–output variables traditionally accounted for in mathematical models.

Group Dynamic Variables in Deliberation

Social psychological literature provides a plethora of information about how groups make decisions that might explain how jurors attempt to persuade one another during deliberation or how jury dynamics may affect the success of their persuasive efforts. Persuasion in groups takes place through either normative or informational processes (Deutsch & Gerard, 1955; Kaplan & Miller, 1987). Jurors who change their opinions because of normative influence publicly change their minds during deliberation but privately retain their original opinions (Kaplan & Miller, 1987; Moscovici & Lage, 1976). Conversely, jurors who change their minds because of informational influence both publicly and privately change their opinions during deliberation because of information or data presented by other jurors (Deutsch & Gerard, 1955).

Whether deliberating jurors change their opinion because of normative or informational influence may depend on whether others on the jury share their opinion. Social psychological research gives insight into the type of influence likely resulting from deliberating factions. If the majority prevails, normative influence may be the major source of influence in the deliberation (Moscovici & Lage, 1976; Moscovici & Personnaz, 1980). If the minority prevails, informational influence may be the major source of influence (Moscovici & Lage, 1976; Moscovici & Personnaz, 1980). However, minority jurors successfully persuade majority jurors at greater rates than the minority and majority literature has suggested (Diamond, Rose, & Murphy, 2006). Other aspects of the group dynamics in deliberation may help explain this discrepancy.

For example, the likelihood that jurors will change their verdict preference in deliberation may vary with the social sharedness of the information (i.e., the extent to which preferences and opinions are shared among group members; Kameda, Takezawa, Tindale, & Smith, 2002). Presumably, the information embraced by the majority in a deliberation is higher in social sharedness than information embraced by the minority. If so, minority jurors may be likely to conform to the majority opinion because the story they endorse lacks social sharedness. Thus, minority jurors in these circumstances may be more susceptible to normative influence than are majority jurors. However, if the majority of jurors are supporting the same verdict for different reasons (i.e., if they have each endorsed different stories that happen to support the same verdict), the social sharedness of information in that majority is lower than the social sharedness of information in a majority who endorse the same story. Thus, a majority with information high in social sharedness, rather than a majority with information low in social sharedness, should be more likely to influence a minority.

Integrating Story Variables Into the Group's Decision-Making Process

For jurors to agree on a particular verdict, they have to agree (at least publicly) on a similar story. The collective process jurors engage in during deliberation may be similar to the story-building process they engage in on an individual level—deciding on a sequence of events that accounts for the trial evidence and incorporates the collective jury's unique experiences and beliefs, using the certainty principles to evaluate the potential stories, agreeing on the various verdict options, and then mapping the agreed-on story to the possible verdict options to render a decision. Previous researchers have reported that deliberating jurors use processes similar to the story model (Hastie et al., 1999), and some research could be reinterpreted using the story model as a basis for understanding what happened during deliberation (Holstein, 1985).

To explore how story variables might apply in the group process, we present a reanalysis of the Holstein study accounting for possible story variables. In this study, the author coded 48 jury deliberations for the presence of *schematic interpretations*, which were defined as any attempt by a juror to provide an explanation of what happened during the incident in question (Holstein, 1985). Applying a story model lens, the schematic interpretations could be thought of as individual jurors' stories, based on the evidence and jurors' unique experiences. Across the 48 deliberations, jurors presented 15 different schematic interpretations of the evidence (with an average of 2.3 per deliberating jury). Further, jurors consistently reframed their own schematic interpretations to match those presented by others, suggesting that the story creation process is extended to deliberation, with jurors engaging in discussion to create a collective story. As the number of schematic interpretations proffered in a jury increased, so did the likelihood the jury would hang (Holstein, 1985). Reframed in terms of the story model, it is likely that the uniqueness of any one story was compromised by the presentation of multiple coherent stories high in coverage. Thus, confidence in any one story was low and the likelihood of choosing one particular story decreased with the number of unique stories presented.

Given the small sample of deliberations in Holstein's (1985) study, it is hard to generalize from these data. The study does, however, provide suggestive evidence that the story model might operate in deliberations in a manner not accounted for in current models of jury deliberation. Combining the story model variables with group dynamic variables provides testable hypotheses about different group dynamic effects that could facilitate development of a comprehensive, explanation-based theory of jury decision making.

A MULTILEVEL THEORY OF JURY DECISION MAKING

The multilevel theory of jury decision making (Devine, 2012) integrates decision making on two levels—the individual juror and the jury as a collective—via two separate but linked models. The theory follows from a systematic review of the scientific literature and is based on the following premises: (a) jurors are not interchangeable commodities—individual differences matter; (b) jurors create narrative explanations from the evidence as opposed to using a more abstract algorithmic decision process; (c) jurors use any and all case-related information they deem relevant; (d) deliberation represents a complex social influence process; and (e) majority factions within a jury usually succeed in obtaining their preferred verdicts—but not always. In essence, the director's cut model addresses the formation and evaluation of stories by individual jurors prior to deliberation, whereas the story sampling model covers decisions made by juries as a whole. The final product of the juror-level director's cut model—the stories preferred by individual jurors—serves as the starting point for the jury-level story sampling model. Figure 1.1 presents a consolidated representation of the theory's fundamental propositions.

The Director's Cut Model of Juror Decision Making

According to the director's cut model, jurors evaluate trial-related information like a film director uses video footage to create a movie. Similar to a director arranging scenes to form a cohesive "final cut," jurors assemble facts into an explanatory narrative in an effort to account for what they know (and believe) about the case. The director's cut model builds on some of the core concepts in the story model but goes beyond it, fleshing out the role of individual differences and providing a different cognitive mechanism for the evaluation of potential stories.

Story Beginnings

According to the director's cut model, jurors begin forming mental representations of a case as soon as they learn about it, potentially before

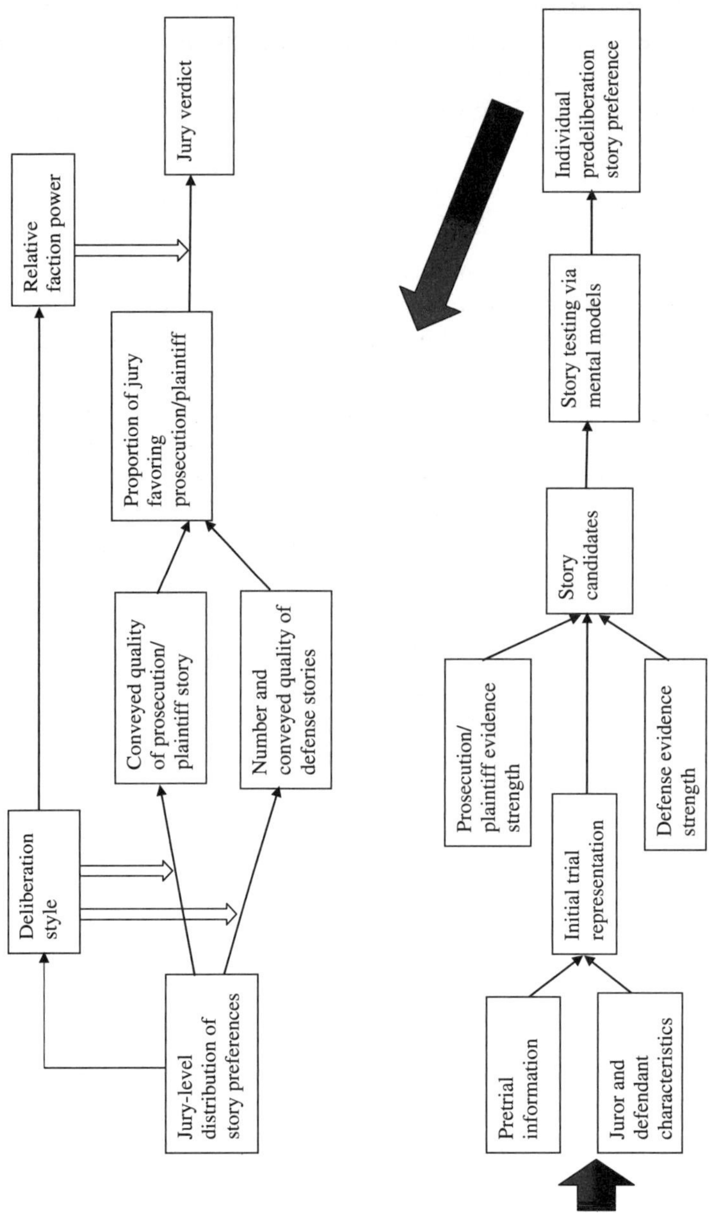

Figure 1.1. Multilevel theory of jury decision making.

they ever set foot in the courtroom. Jurors usually have little or no advance knowledge of the case they decide, but for highly publicized trials they may have seen one or more reports in the media. Pretrial publicity typically casts defendants in a negative light and has a reliable biasing effect on perceived culpability (Steblay, Besirevic, Fulero, & Jimenez-Lorente, 1999), likely by being incorporated into jurors' initial mental representation of the trial. Once in the courtroom, jurors learn the type of case to be decided, and this information contributes to the emerging mental representation via the activation of prototypic features associated with the case (Finkel & Groscup, 1997; Smith, 1991). Jurors will be familiar with various types of cases via their personal experience and exposure to the media, and learning the nature of the case at hand may yield implicit assumptions about the motives of the participants, the sequence of events, and the consequences of actions (Smith & Studebaker, 1996). Information activated via association with the case type likely remains in subsequent representations unless contradicted later by the evidence.

Jurors' scripts and stereotypes are a product of their life experiences, which in turn may be associated with their personal characteristics (Devine, 2012). In particular, four juror characteristics are modest predictors of verdict preference (Devine & Caughlin, 2014): (a) race, (b) gender (for some types of crime), (c) socioeconomic status (SES), and (d) trust in the legal system. In essence, defendants are more likely to be viewed as culpable by jurors who are (a) of a different race than the defendant; (b) female, when the crime involves sexual assault or child abuse; (c) high SES; or (d) high in legal system trust. Certain defendant characteristics may also trigger assumptions and beliefs about culpability, specifically, (a) SES, (b) prior criminal history, (c) physical attractiveness, and (d) in-court display of emotion (Devine, 2012; Devine & Caughlin, 2014). In effect, jurors may associate certain personal characteristics with legal wrongdoing—being poor, unemployed, homeless, and uneducated (i.e., low SES); having a criminal record; being physically unattractive; and having little or no sympathy for victims. To summarize, some jurors may be more likely to have stereotypes of lawbreakers that contain certain prototypical characteristics, and some defendant characteristics may be present in nearly all jurors' stereotypes of lawbreakers (e.g., Jones & Kaplan, 2003).

In addition to what jurors learn about a case pretrial and the presumptions they consciously or subconsciously make, information comes in the form of opening statements made by the attorneys. Attorneys make opening statements in almost every jury trial and with good reason—their words may have a considerable impact on jurors' initial mental representations of the trial. Opening statements typically provide an overview of the case from each side's perspective and often include specific factual assertions. Jurors are instructed not to treat opening statements as evidence, but they may be unable to tag this information reliably and set it aside if it is never substantiated during the trial.

In sum, jurors will create an initial mental representation of trial-related events using information gleaned from several sources—case-related media reports, cognitive schemata related to case types and criminals, and the attorneys' opening statements. The initial representation is rarely equivalent to a fleshed-out story, though, in that is missing the evidence.

Story Construction: Prosecution/Plaintiff. There are notable differences between the prosecution in a criminal trial and the plaintiff in a civil trial, but both shoulder the burden of proof. What constitutes persuasive evidence? Given jurors' predilection for stories, we theorize that strong evidence for the instigating side (i.e., prosecution or plaintiff) is a function of three characteristics of a narrative explanation: scope, credibility, and singularity.

Scope concerns the richness of the evidence and the degree to which it can yield a full explanation of the defendant's culpability. It includes the level of precision associated with the actions of principal actors, the extent to which their motives or mind-sets are clear, and the consequences of their actions—even when one or more of those elements is not legally relevant. Scope is not concerned with the degree to which the evidence satisfies the legal criteria for finding the defendant culpable, but rather how well it supplies jurors with a complete story.

Credibility concerns the trustworthiness or believability of the major elements in the instigator's story. Factual assertions by witnesses should be accepted as true unless they are (a) offered by a witness who is not seen as believable, (b) incompatible with the jurors' beliefs about how the world works, or (c) disputed by one or more trusted sources. In other words, factual assertions are likely incorporated into jurors' mental representations unless the source of the assertion lacks credibility. When multiple trusted sources disagree on a factual assertion, jurors may resolve the dilemma by choosing to believe the more trusted individual source, the assertion supported by the greater number of trusted sources, or the use of some other mechanism.

Singularity refers to the extent to which the prosecution/plaintiff's evidence converges on one story. Singularity is lower to the extent that more notable facts cannot be made to fit in a single story; it is higher when the evidence converges neatly and there are no leftover pieces. Jurors' desire for singularity represents a potential divergence between human nature and the requirements of the law. Mathematical models of juror decision making predict that more facts supporting the prosecution/plaintiff story will always lead to a higher probability of a juror preferring conviction, but the director's cut model suggests that additional facts are problematic if they cannot be merged into a single convincing narrative. Thus, more is not necessarily better when it comes to the prosecution/plaintiff's evidence.

Although these three features of the director's cut model overlap to some extent with the three certainty principles identified in the story model, there are some differences. First, scope, credibility, and singularity in the director's cut model describe what makes for strong evidence provided by the prosecution or plaintiff, whereas coverage, coherence, and uniqueness in the story model are mechanisms for choosing among story alternatives. A fundamental premise of the director's cut model is that jurors use another cognitive mechanism (i.e., mental modeling) to evaluate story alternatives. Further, although coverage and scope are essentially the same, the story model contains a construct (i.e., coherence) not featured in the director's cut model, whereas the latter includes a construct (i.e., credibility) not found in the story model. Finally, uniqueness in the story model is a function of how many story options exist, whereas singularity in the director's cut model concerns the extent to which leftover evidence cannot be accounted for by the prosecution/plaintiff's primary story.

Defense Story Construction. The defense in a jury trial has a choice of strategies when it comes to stories: Present an alternative version of events that counters (i.e., contradicts) the other side's story, identify multiple stories that are plausible, and suggest the correct one cannot be determined, or try to show the story offered by the prosecution/plaintiff is simply not correct without specifying any alternative version of events. Accordingly, several major types of alternative stories can be offered: (a) wrong defendant, (b) wrong actions, (c) wrong mind-set, and (d) wrong consequences.

The first type of alternative story maintains the defendant was not present and/or involved in the alleged illegal activity (i.e., *wrong defendant*). Stories of this type claim the defendant was misidentified as the perpetrator, and they may involve an alibi. Alternative stories of the *wrong actions* type acknowledge the defendant's presence and/or involvement but assert the defendant did not commit the illegal activity. Stories from these first two categories are likely to involve mistaken or lying eyewitnesses, inaccurate scientific test results, or nefarious police behavior (e.g., framing the defendant). In contrast, if there is certainty regarding the perpetrator's identity and actions, alternative stories will likely come from the latter two categories that focus on what the defendant was thinking (i.e., *wrong mind-set*) or what actually resulted (i.e., *wrong consequence*). Wrong mind-set stories acknowledge the defendant's culpable actions but assert those actions were unintentional (e.g., an accident), misconceived or misdirected, provoked in some way, or justifiable (e.g., self-defense). Wrong consequence stories assert that no injury or harm resulted from the defendant's actions or a different type of harm resulted than what was claimed, and thus the victim is malingering or exaggerating.

A few comments are in order about the alternative story possibilities. First, the nature of the case will constrain the viable alternative stories in a given trial, and the facts of the case will make some alternatives more plausible than others. Second, jurors likely vary in their receptivity to different types of alternative stories on the basis of their personal characteristics. For example, jurors who have had negative experiences with the legal system may be more willing to believe the police would tamper with evidence in the interests of securing a conviction. Third, other things being equal, all jurors may be more receptive to some types of alternative stories than others. In particular, jurors may prefer alternative stories that deny the defendant's presence or involvement as opposed to those that acknowledge the defendant's role in illegal activity. Fourth, jurors might be more receptive to alternative stories that involve one mistake or lying witness as opposed to multiple mistakes or a conspiracy involving several deceptive individuals simply because these latter stories may seem inherently more convoluted and implausible. Finally, a frequent legal strategy for the defense, poking holes in the prosecution/plaintiff story, leaves much to be desired from a psychological perspective in that it fails to offer what jurors really want—a compelling explanation of what actually happened.

Story Evaluation: Assessing the Options

How do jurors choose between the prosecution/plaintiff story and an alternative story offered (or implied) by the defense? A fundamental premise of the director's cut model is that jurors construct mental models to provide an overall test of story likelihood. Mental models have considerable empirical support (Johnson-Laird, 2006; Wyer, 2007) and may serve as the primary cognitive mechanism for evaluating stories. Different mental models can be generated and evaluated on the basis of different sets of factual premises, and the perceived likelihood of a story is expected to be a function of how well its corresponding mental model can represent a particular version of events.

Mental models can exist in a text-based *propositional modality* or an image-based *visual modality*, with their form in any given situation depending in large part on the task at hand and the modality of relevant information (Johnson-Laird, 1983, 2006). Given a general human reliance on the visual sense, many mental models created by jurors are probably based on the visual modality. Visual mental models are essentially cognitive simulations of some event or sequence of events based on beliefs about the way the world operates (e.g., how a car skids through an intersection or a body falls off a building). Jurors can evaluate potential stories by constructing a corresponding mental model based on a set of factual premises and then imagining the outcome when reality-based rules are applied. For instance, a juror might create a mental model to envision a fight between the defendant and victim, a traffic accident caused by driver inattention, or a burglar's entry into a home via a second-floor window. Inability to create a satisfactory mental model for a story should lead to the story's rejection, whereas generation of a viable mental model for a story should increase its perceived plausibility.

When it comes to choosing among rival stories, jurors may prefer simpler stories and those that involve dispositional attributions for the actions of focal individuals (e.g., the defendant). Simpler stories are probably more attractive than complex stories in that they have fewer probabilistic elements and should be easier to simulate with mental models. Jurors also likely prefer stories that portray human action as being attributable to dispositional tendencies because people tend to attribute the behavior of others to stable, internal motives. Particularly when violent behavior is involved, a desire to see consistency and intention in the actions of others may lead jurors to favor innately stories in which the defendant is viewed as a bad or evil person.

At the conclusion of the trial, jurors can be classified into one of four categories. Some jurors may believe the prosecution/plaintiff story has a high likelihood of being true—these jurors could be called *believers*. Other jurors, *doubters*, may believe a particular alternative story is more likely. Still other jurors may see multiple stories as viable and actively consider the options; these jurors could be referred to as *mullers*. Finally, other jurors, the *puzzlers*, may be unable to identify any satisfactory story. Thus, heading into deliberation, some jurors have a preferred story in mind, some are pondering the merits of multiple stories, and some are struggling just to identify any coherent story.

The Story Sampling Model of Jury Decision Making

The crux of the story sampling model is that deliberation is an iterative sharing process in which jurors search collectively for a compelling story to account for the evidence. Individual jurors exert informational influence by sharing various types of spoken contributions, and factions exert normative influence in proportion to their perceived size, leadership, and story-related agreement. Which type of influence is more important in any given deliberation depends on the deliberation style adopted by the jury, but majority factions usually succeed.

Sampling Juror Contributions

Most existing models of jury decision making focus on the relationship between an initial distribution of member verdict preferences and the jury's ultimate verdict but have little to say about the underlying process by which juries arrive at their decisions. In contrast, two models of group decision making address the dynamics of discussion (Stasser, 1988; Stasser & Vaughan,

1996). As depicted in these models, discussion is a mechanism for sampling the inputs of group members from the pool of task-relevant information they collectively possess. Applied to juries, deliberation amounts to a process in which the jury samples the spoken contributions of individual jurors. Spoken contributions can come in the form of isolated statements, factual assertions, preferred verdicts, and explanatory stories.

Jurors do not contribute equally to the discussion during deliberation (Devine, 2012). Four characteristics of jurors pertinent to speaking during deliberation are (a) extraversion, (b) gender, (c) SES, and (d) need for cognition. In particular, jurors who speak more during deliberation tend to be male and have higher levels of need for cognition, extraversion, and SES (Hastie et al., 1983; Shestowsky & Horowitz, 2004; York & Cornwell, 2006). In addition, forepersons tend to be inordinately participative and influential (Diamond & Casper, 1992; Hastie et al., 1983).

A premise of the story sampling model is that the frequency of different types of spoken contributions is inversely related to their informational influence on other jurors. At the base of the pyramid—least influential but most common—are *isolated statements*. These include scattered thoughts or observations that jurors have about different aspects of the trial, as well as various questions they pose to other jurors. Less frequent but more influential are *factual assertions* about what is true in the context of the case. These assertions are not necessarily true but are represented as such by the speaker and have some basis in reality. Examples include repeating a factual statement made by a witness, expressing a belief about the occurrence of some event, or inferring some action must have taken place. Factual assertions thus represent the building blocks of potential stories. Another type of spoken contribution is the *preferred verdict*. This category consists of statements that directly or indirectly convey the juror's opinion about the appropriate decision. These statements may come on the heels of one or more factual assertions, but at other times the speaker's reasoning may be far from obvious or missing entirely.

At the top of the pyramid, *stories* are theorized to be the least common but most influential type of spoken contribution during deliberation. A story represents a juror's attempt to provide a narrative explanation of the events at issue in the trial. Stories will vary regarding their comprehensiveness, with a *complete* story accounting fully for the defendant's motives, intentions, actions, and consequences, in contrast to a *partial* story that has only some of those elements. Stories also differ regarding how consciously accessible they are and the extent to which they can be articulated. Stories in the mind (or *cognitive* stories) likely diverge to some extent from *conveyed* stories that are shared aloud because of "slippage"—something lost in translation—in the form of omissions, confusing syntax, poor word choice, interruptions, and the like. In other words, the stories that jurors have in their heads are not necessarily the ones they communicate to others. Complete conveyed stories are likely to be rare but potentially influential—particularly when offered by a high-status juror. Indeed, the persuasive articulation of an alternative story may help to explain those times when the majority's preference is not the jury's ultimate verdict.

The Role of Deliberation Style

Deliberation essentially involves the sampling of individual juror contributions, but juries can approach their task in different ways (Hastie et al., 1983). When the jury adopts a *verdict-driven style*, straw polls are often used to gauge the degree of consensus within a jury, but they also expose the size of different factions within the jury and facilitate application of normative pressure. Verdict-driven deliberations may amount to a battle of the factions, with discussion featuring a disproportionately large number of preferred verdict statements and relatively few factual assertions. Complete stories may not emerge immediately, but they probably have more impact the earlier they are conveyed. Jurors who are undecided heading into deliberation—the mullers and puzzlers—may take a backseat during the discussion, listening to the believers and doubters and hoping to be convinced by something they hear. As such, the first compelling story offered may prove decisive in a verdict-driven deliberation.

In contrast, deliberation should play out quite differently when juries use an *evidence-driven style*. Relative to verdict-driven deliberations, evidence-driven deliberations should feature more factual assertions and fewer verdict preference statements. Conveyed stories are probably less frequent, especially early on, and more likely to emerge in a piecemeal fashion. One phenomenon that may occur in a pure evidence-driven deliberation is the construction of a jury-level story. Facts are likely to be established during deliberation the same way they are in everyday life—by being asserted and not contested. During deliberation, jurors may accept as true—implicitly or explicitly—any uncontested factual assertion. Each additional reference to the assertion may then further increase jurors' confidence in its truth. This implicit, iterative process highlights the importance of wording because descriptive terms included in the original assertion may eventually be treated as factual as well. As the facts are established, they take their place in an emerging narrative framework and serve as premises for other factual assertions.

At some point, the fact-determination process will be interrupted or terminated, and one or more jurors will attempt to articulate a story based on the collectively determined facts. This is probably a critical moment in an evidence-driven deliberation because subtle nuances in the form of framing and word choice associated with the initial articulation of the jury's story may be decisive for cases in which the evidence is somewhat ambiguous. Alternative stories based on the same facts may be offered at this time as well. The remaining discussion may take on some characteristics of a verdict-driven deliberation, but the more cooperative and congenial atmosphere of an evidence-driven deliberation should minimize normative influence relative to verdict-driven juries. Indeed, the construction of a jury-level story may coincide with those times when jurors report taking only one unanimous vote at the end of deliberation, essentially ratifying the straightforward implications of the jury's collective story.

Little is known about what causes juries to adopt different deliberation styles, but verdict-driven deliberation styles may be more likely when the evidence clearly favors one side (i.e., very weak or very strong) or when the trial is relatively straightforward with few facts in dispute. In other words, a verdict-driven approach should be more attractive when most jurors enter deliberation with a high degree of confidence in a particular story. Jurors may expect other jurors to think the same way and believe a quick vote will reveal this to be true.

Determinants of Influence and Verdict Choice

Jurors' final verdict preferences are a function of both informational influence and normative influence (Deutsch & Gerard, 1955). Informational influence arises, in part, from factual assertions but primarily from conveyed stories. A particular juror's informational influence is viewed as a multiplicative function of conveyed story quality and prestige. *Conveyed story quality* is defined as the degree to which a juror contributes to the articulation of a story. This contribution need not occur all at once nor necessarily involve the articulation of a complete story. A conveyed story can range from a single factual assertion to a complete story. *Prestige* refers to how highly a juror is thought of by others in the jury and is likely to be a function of several factors, including SES, case-specific expertise, and formal role within the group (e.g., foreperson). The determinants of a juror's prestige are expected to combine in an additive fashion, whereas informational influence is viewed as a multiplicative function of story quality and prestige such that the impact of jurors' conveyed story quality depends on their prestige within the jury. In essence, complete stories offered by high-status jurors should have the most impact on other jurors' thinking.

Normative influence during deliberation, in contrast, arises from the perception of verdict-favoring factions. According to the story sampling model, a faction's normative influence is a function of its power. *Faction power* is a multiplicative combination of its apparent size, the effectiveness of its leadership, and the degree of story agreement among its members. *Apparent faction size* refers to the perceived number of jurors who support a particular verdict. In many instances, the apparent size of a verdict faction will correspond closely to its actual size—but not always. Apparent and actual faction size should be closest when juries take many polls, particularly in the open, allowing jurors to determine not only the size of each faction but also which individuals are in each one. *Faction leadership* refers to the degree to which someone within the faction is willing and able to speak for its members and advocate their viewpoint.

Critical leadership tasks include articulating key factual assertions, offering and defending faction-preferred stories, and refuting points made by members of opposing factions. Faction leaders should be most effective when they are extraverted, high in prestige, and good speakers and when they possess some case-relevant knowledge (or perceived to possess it). Two or more individuals may lead a faction, but how successfully this can be done depends on how well the would-be leaders can coordinate their efforts. *Story agreement* reflects the extent to which the members of a verdict faction are in accord with respect to their preferred narrative explanation of the evidence. The normative power of a faction should be weaker when factions include subgroups that adhere to different stories (or variants) even though they favor the same verdict. Serious and salient disagreement among faction members should make it difficult to present a united front that facilitates the application of conformity pressure. The relationship among the three components of faction power is presumed to be multiplicative—meaning that if any component is low, the faction's normative influence will also be relatively low. Factions should be most powerful when perceived as large, effectively led, and united in their belief of the preferred story.

Which type of influence will have more impact in any given jury trial likely depends on the deliberation style adopted by the jury. When an evidence-driven style is adopted, informational influence should be the primary determinant of the jury's final verdict. When a verdict-driven style is adopted, jury verdicts will likely be determined by both informational and normative influence. Accordingly, the informational influence associated with individual jurors should be a strong predictor of the jury's verdict when an evidence-driven style is used, whereas faction power should be the better predictor when a verdict-driven style is used. When a majority faction exists initially within the jury, its preferred verdict will usually be the jury's eventual verdict (Devine et al., 2001; Hannaford-Agor et al., 2002; Kalven & Zeisel, 1966). However, the story sampling model identifies several circumstances that may increase the likelihood of a minority faction's preferred verdict becoming the jury's final verdict—that is, a reversal of the majority's initial preference. These circumstances include (a) the existence of a relatively large minority faction, (b) consensus within the minority faction regarding the underlying story, (c) strong minority faction leadership, (d) disagreement within the majority faction regarding the underlying story, (e) weak or nonexistent majority faction leadership, (f) adoption of an evidence-driven deliberation style or private polling that obscure the contours of the majority faction, and (g) the availability of a compromise verdict option. These circumstances should individually increase the likelihood of reversal and may interact as well. Indeed, given the established rarity of reversals, a combination of circumstances may be necessary for there to be much chance of reversing the initial majority.

Of course, there will also be times when there is no clear majority faction within the jury. This could occur when the jury is split evenly between two verdict options (i.e., guilty vs. not guilty; liable vs. not liable) or there are more than two verdict options. The latter scenario will most often arise when criminal juries are given the option to convict on a lesser charge (e.g., manslaughter or murder), but other nontraditional *compromise verdict* options implying reduced culpability will sometimes be available as well (e.g., guilty but mentally ill). The defining feature of a compromise verdict is a more central position on a continuum of culpability—somewhere between the two traditional options. Compromise verdicts should be more likely when there is no majority faction within the group (i.e., no faction has more than a plurality) or the factions have roughly the same power. They may be especially likely when the actions of defendants are not in dispute but their mind-sets are. Juries may be most likely to hang when there is no strong majority faction and no compromise verdict options are available.

Defendants often face multiple charges in criminal cases, and the same jury usually decides them all. The limited research available suggests juries spend the majority of their time discussing the first charge and much less time on successive charges (Tanford & Penrod, 1986). The story sampling model provides a straightforward explanation for these findings in postulating that juries try to arrive at a single story that explains all trial-related events. In reaching their initial verdict, jurors will fashion a story that, along with its associated factual premises, constrains subsequent decisions. The perceived implications of the story may be so obvious that jurors see little or no need to discuss the evidence further before deciding on any remaining charges. Extensive discussion after deciding the first charge may be limited to situations in which the defendant is accused of many disparate actions or salient conflicts exist among the stories favored by majority-faction jurors even though they lead to the same verdict.

Summary of the Director's Cut and Story Sampling Models

The multilevel theory of jury decision making consists of two linked models operating at different levels: individual jurors and collective juries.

The director's cut model specifies individual difference variables that affect juror information processing, identifies key aspects of prosecution/plaintiff evidence and different types of defense stories, and incorporates a cognitive mechanism for evaluating stories. Essentially, jurors construct an initial mental representation of a trial based on what they learn from the media and in the courtroom, as well as information from memory activated via scripts and stereotypes. They then update their initial representations as they hear evidence and use mental models to assess the likelihood of stories that might explain the evidence. According to the story sampling model, deliberation is an information-sampling process involving informational and normative influence to varying degrees. A key premise of the model is that informational influence comes primarily from conveyed stories whereas normative influence arises from the existence of verdict-favoring factions within the jury. Factions are theorized to have greater normative power to the extent they are perceived as large, well led, and united on a story. Informational influence is predicted to be the primary determinant of jury verdicts when the jury uses an evidence-driven style; normative influence is expected to be decisive when a verdict-driven style is adopted.

FUTURE RESEARCH DIRECTIONS

Our purpose was to review existing models of juror and jury decision making and offer a unified theory that integrates and extends them. Devine (2012) identified 13 testable hypotheses stemming from the director's cut model and 11 that follow from the story sampling model. Here we highlight a smaller set of propositions that can be empirically tested in the course of integrating individual and group level models of juror and jury decision making.

First, the deliberation style adopted by the jury should affect the number, timing, and completeness of stories shared during deliberation such that an evidence-driven style (vs. a verdict-driven style) will yield fewer conveyed stories and they will emerge later in the deliberation. Further, deliberation style should affect the likely success of a minority faction and the type of influence that accounts for opinion change in deliberation. Use of a verdict-driven deliberation style versus an evidence-driven style should increase the likelihood that a majority faction will be successful because it will more quickly highlight the contours of opposing factions and allow the majority faction to exert greater normative influence. Conversely, there may be more opportunity for the minority faction to exert informational influence on the majority faction and achieve a reversal verdict when the jury adopts an evidence-driven style.

Second, faction power should moderate the relationship between the number of jurors favoring the prosecution's (or plaintiff's) story and the jury's final verdict. Specifically, there should be a positive relationship between the number of "believers" and conviction (or liability) when the majority faction is relatively strong and the minority faction is relatively weak. Conversely, there should be a smaller—but still positive—relationship when the majority faction is fairly weak and the minority faction is fairly strong.

Third, instances of "reversal" in which the jury's final verdict is not consistent with an initial verdict-preferring majority should be more likely if the majority faction is (a) relatively small (or at least perceived as such), (b) without a clear leader, or (c) lacking unanimity with regard to the particular story preferred by its members. In addition, reversal verdicts should be more likely when (d) the minority faction is well led and (e) minority faction members agree on their preferred story. That is, the uniqueness or social sharedness of the story endorsed by each faction may help predict when a minority faction is likely to be successful; if the majority faction endorses the same verdict but various stories (vs. if the majority faction shares a story), a minority faction that shares the same story may be more likely to be successful.

If nothing else, this chapter stands as testament to the idea that deliberation is important but also complex, with many moving parts. There is much left to learn before we can fully account for the decisions of jurors and juries, but the benefits of an improved understanding are worth the effort it will require. Derivation of a multilevel theory that connects and extends existing level-specific models will be important for guiding the process, interpreting its results, and ultimately predicting how the jury will render a verdict.

REFERENCES

Behl, J. D., Kienzle, M. R., & Levett, L. M. (2013, November). *A test of the story model of juror decision making.* Paper presented at the American Criminology Society Meeting, Atlanta, GA.

Davis, J. H. (1973). Group decision and social interaction: A theory of social decision schemes. *Psychological Review, 80,* 97–125. http://dx.doi.org/10.1037/h0033951

Davis, J. H., Kerr, N. L., Atkin, R. S., Holt, R., & Meek, D. (1975). The decision processes of 6- and 12-person mock juries assigned unanimous and two-thirds majority rules. *Journal of Personality and Social Psychology, 32,* 1–14. http://dx.doi.org/10.1037/h0076849

Davis, J. H., Tindale, R. S., Nagao, D. H., Hinsz, V. B., & Robertson, B. (1984). Order effects in multiple decisions by groups: A demonstration with mock juries and trial procedures. *Journal of Personality and Social Psychology, 47,* 1003–1012. http://dx.doi.org/10.1037/0022-3514.47.5.1003

Deutsch, M., & Gerard, H. B. (1955). A study of normative and informational social influences upon individual judgement. *The Journal of Abnormal and Social Psychology, 51*, 629–636. http://dx.doi.org/10.1037/h0046408

Devine, D. J. (2012). *Jury decision making: The state of the science*. New York: New York University Press.

Devine, D. J., & Caughlin, D. E. (2014). Do they matter? A meta-analytic investigation of individual characteristics and guilt judgments. *Psychology, Public Policy, and Law, 20*, 109–134. http://dx.doi.org/10.1037/law0000006

Devine, D. J., Clayton, L. D., Dunford, B. B., Seying, R., & Pryce, J. (2001). Jury decision making: 45 years of empirical research on deliberating groups. *Psychology, Public Policy, and Law, 7*, 622–727.

Diamond, S. S. (1997). Illuminations and shadows from jury simulations. *Law and Human Behavior, 21*, 561–571. http://dx.doi.org/10.1023/A:1024831908377

Diamond, S. S., & Casper, J. D. (1992). Blindfolding the jury to verdict consequences: Damages, experts, and the civil jury. *Law and Society Review, 26*, 513–563. http://dx.doi.org/10.2307/3053737

Diamond, S. S., & Levi, J. N. (1996). Improving decisions on death by revising and testing jury instructions. *Judicature, 79*, 224–232.

Diamond, S. S., Rose, M. R., & Murphy, B. (2006). Revisiting the unanimity requirement: The behavior of the non-unanimous civil jury. *Northwestern University Law Review, 100*, 201–230.

Finkel, N. J., & Groscup, J. L. (1997). Crime prototypes, objective versus subjective culpability, and a commonsense balance. *Law and Human Behavior, 21*, 209–230. http://dx.doi.org/10.1023/A:1024830413404

Hannaford-Agor, P. L., Hans, V. P., Mott, N. L., & Munsterman, G. T. (2002). *Are hung juries a problem?* Retrieved from http://www.ncsc-jurystudies.org/What-We-Do/~/media/Microsites/Files/CJS/What%20We%20Do/Are%20Hung%20Juries%20A%20Problem.ashx

Hastie, R. (1993). Algebraic models of juror decision processes. In R. Hastie (Ed.), *Inside the juror: The psychology of juror decision making* (pp. 84–115). http://dx.doi.org/10.1017/CBO9780511752896.006

Hastie, R., Penrod, S. D., & Pennington, N. (1983). *Inside the jury*. http://dx.doi.org/10.4159/harvard.9780674865945

Hastie, R., Schkade, D. A., & Payne, J. W. (1999). Juror judgments in civil cases: Effects of plaintiff's requests and plaintiff's identity on punitive damage awards. *Law and Human Behavior, 23*, 445–470. http://dx.doi.org/10.1023/A:1022312115561

Holstein, J. A. (1985). Jurors' interpretations and jury decision making. *Law and Human Behavior, 9*, 83–100. http://dx.doi.org/10.1007/BF01044291

Huntley, J. E., & Costanzo, M. (2003). Sexual harassment stories: Testing a story-mediated model of juror decision-making in civil litigation. *Law and Human Behavior, 27*, 29–51. http://dx.doi.org/10.1023/A:1021674811225

Johnson-Laird, P. N. (1983). *Mental models: Towards a cognitive science of language, inference, and consciousness*. Cambridge, MA: Harvard University Press.

Johnson-Laird, P. N. (2006). *How we reason*. New York, NY: Oxford University Press.

Jones, C. S., & Kaplan, M. F. (2003). The effects of racially stereotypical crimes on juror decision-making and information-processing strategies. *Basic and Applied Social Psychology, 25*, 1–13. http://dx.doi.org/10.1207/S15324834BASP2501_1

Kalven, H., Jr., & Zeisel, H. (1966). *The American jury*. Chicago, IL: University of Chicago Press.

Kameda, T., Takezawa, M., Tindale, R. S., & Smith, C. M. (2002). Social sharing and risk reduction: Exploring a computational algorithm for the psychology of windfall gains. *Evolution and Human Behavior, 23*, 11–33. http://dx.doi.org/10.1016/S1090-5138(01)00086-1

Kaplan, M. F., & Miller, C. E. (1987). Group decision making and normative versus informational influence: Effects of type of issue and assigned decision rule. *Journal of Personality and Social Psychology, 53*, 306–313. http://dx.doi.org/10.1037/0022-3514.53.2.306

Kerr, N. L. (1978). Severity of prescribed penalty and mock jurors' verdicts. *Journal of Personality and Social Psychology, 36*, 1431–1442. http://dx.doi.org/10.1037/0022-3514.36.12.1431

Kerr, N. L., & MacCoun, R. (2012). Is the leniency asymmetry really dead? Misinterpreting asymmetry effects in criminal jury deliberation. *Group Processes & Intergroup Behavior, 15*, 585–602. http://dx.doi.org/10.1177/1368430212441639

Kerr, N. L., Niedermeier, K. E., & Kaplan, M. F. (1999). Bias in jurors vs. bias in juries: New evidence from the SDS perspective. *Organizational Behavior and Human Decision Processes, 80*, 70–86. http://dx.doi.org/10.1006/obhd.1999.2855

MacCoun, R. J., & Kerr, N. L. (1988). Asymmetric influence in mock jury deliberation: Jurors' bias for leniency. *Journal of Personality and Social Psychology, 54*, 21–33. http://dx.doi.org/10.1037/0022-3514.54.1.21

Moore, P. J., & Gump, B. B. (1995). Information integration in juror decision making. *Journal of Applied Social Psychology, 25*, 2158–2179. http://dx.doi.org/10.1111/j.1559-1816.1995.tb01831.x

Moscovici, S., & Lage, E. (1976). Studies in social influence: III. Majority versus minority influence in a group. *European Journal of Social Psychology*, 6, 149–174. http://dx.doi.org/10.1002/ejsp.2420060202

Moscovici, S., & Personnaz, B. (1980). Studies in social influence: V. Minority influence and conversion behavior in a perceptual task. *Journal of Experimental Social Psychology, 16*, 270–282. http://dx.doi.org/10.1016/0022-1031(80)90070-0

Olsen-Fulero, L., & Fulero, S. M. (1997). Commonsense rape judgments: An empathy–complexity theory of rape juror story making. *Psychology, Public Policy, and Law, 3*, 402–427. http://dx.doi.org/10.1037/1076-8971.3.2-3.402

Pennington, N., & Hastie, R. (1988). Explanation-based decision making: Effects of memory structure on judgment. *Journal of Experimental Psychology: Learning, Memory, and Cognition, 14*, 521–533. http://dx.doi.org/10.1037/0278-7393.14.3.521

Pennington, N., & Hastie, R. (1992). Explaining the evidence: Tests of the story model for juror decision making. *Journal of Personality and Social Psychology, 62*, 189–206. http://dx.doi.org/10.1037/0022-3514.62.2.189

Pennington, N., & Hastie, R. (1993). The story model for juror decision making. In R. Hastie (Ed.), *Inside the juror: The psychology of juror decision making* (pp. 192–222). http://dx.doi.org/10.1017/CBO9780511752896.010

Penrod, S., & Hastie, R. (1979). Models of jury decision-making: A critical review. *Psychological Bulletin, 86*, 462–492. http://dx.doi.org/10.1037/0033-2909.86.3.462

Reifman, A., Gusick, S. M., & Ellsworth, P. C. (1992). Real jurors' understanding of the law in real cases. *Law and Human Behavior, 16*, 539–554. http://dx.doi.org/10.1007/BF01044622

Salerno, J. M., & Diamond, S. S. (2010). The promise of a cognitive perspective on jury deliberation. *Psychonomic Bulletin & Review, 17*, 174–179. http://dx.doi.org/10.3758/PBR.17.2.174

Shestowsky, D., & Horowitz, L. M. (2004). How the need for cognition scale predicts behavior in mock jury deliberations. *Law and Human Behavior, 28*, 305–337. http://dx.doi.org/10.1023/B:LAHU.0000029141.46850.fb

Smith, V. L. (1991). Prototypes in the courtroom: Lay representations of legal concepts. *Journal of Personality and Social Psychology, 61*, 857–872. http://dx.doi.org/10.1037/0022-3514.61.6.857

Smith, V. L., & Studebaker, C. A. (1996). What do you expect? The influence of people's prior knowledge of crime categories on fact-finding. *Law and Human Behavior, 20*, 517–532. http://dx.doi.org/10.1007/BF01499039

Stasser, G. (1988). Computer simulation as a research tool: The DISCUSS model of group decision making. *Journal of Experimental Social Psychology, 24*, 393–422. http://dx.doi.org/10.1016/0022-1031(88)90028-5

Stasser, G., Kerr, N. L., & Bray, R. M. (1982). The social psychology of jury deliberations: Structure, process, and product. In N. L. Kerr & R. M. Bray (Eds.), *The psychology of the courtroom* (pp. 221–256). New York, NY: Academic Press.

Stasser, G., Kerr, N. L., & Davis, J. H. (1989). Influence processes and consensus models in decision-making groups. In P. Paulus (Ed.), *Psychology of group influence* (2nd ed., pp. 279–326). Hillsdale, NJ: Erlbaum.

Stasser, G., & Vaughan, S. (1996). Models of participation during face-to-face unstructured discussion. In E. Witte & J. H. Davis (Eds.), *Understanding group behavior: Consensual action by small groups* (Vol. 1, pp. 165–192). Mahwah, NJ: Erlbaum.

Steblay, N. M., Besirevic, J., Fulero, S. M., & Jimenez-Lorente, B. (1999). The effects of pretrial publicity on juror verdicts: A meta-analytic review. *Law and Human Behavior, 23*, 219–235. http://dx.doi.org/10.1023/A:1022325019080

Tanford, S., & Penrod, S. (1986). Jury deliberations: Discussion content and influence processes in jury decision making. *Journal of Applied Social Psychology*, *16*, 322–347. http://dx.doi.org/10.1111/j.1559-1816.1986.tb01144.x

Wyer, R. S., Jr. (2007). Principles of mental representation. In A. Kruglanski & E. T. Higgins (Eds.), *Social psychology: Handbook of basic principles* (2nd ed., pp. 285–307). New York, NY: Guilford Press.

York, E., & Cornwell, B. (2006). Status on trial: Social characteristics and influence in the jury room. *Social Forces*, *85*, 455–477. http://dx.doi.org/10.1353/sof.2006.0150

2

THE EFFECTS OF COLLABORATIVE REMEMBERING ON TRIAL VERDICTS

WILLIAM HIRST AND CHARLES B. STONE

One critical way by which the legal system can prevent inaccurate decisions on the part of the jury is to better understand the mnemonic dynamics underlying jury deliberation. Jurors are faced with the task of moving from the evidentiary phase of a trial, in which a vast array of evidence is presented, often without any coherent order to the presentation, to deliberation and a subsequent consensus around a particular verdict, guided in large part by their recollection of the presented evidence. The courts are largely reluctant to use mnemonic technology to aid jurors in recollecting the presented evidence. To be sure, jurors can ask for "read-backs," in which the judge reads back to the jury part of the transcript. But read-backs are limited to small segments of the testimony. Moreover, a written transcript is rarely handed over to the jury. Audio or video recordings of the trial are also not supplied. Moreover, 29% of the federal courts and 31% of state

http://dx.doi.org/10.1037/0000026-003
The Psychology of Juries, M. B. Kovera (Editor)

courts do not permit note taking (Mize, Hannaford-Agor, & Waters, 2007). In instances in which note taking is allowed, the jurors are cautioned not to rely too heavily on their notes. In other words, during deliberation, jurors must depend on their memory of what was presented in the evidentiary stage of the trial, not some form of external record. The reluctance of U.S. courts to allow jurors to use mnemonic aids reflects a long-standing assumption. Indeed, the U.S. courts have largely assumed that the collaborative nature of remembering during deliberation will lead to more accurate and complete recollections than might be expected if remembering occurred in isolation or with the help of mnemonic technology. For instance, reflecting the court's general mistrust in mnemonic technology, even for something as straightforward as a written transcript, *U.S. v. Montgomery* (1998) offered the following as possible jury instructions:

> I [the judge] want you to bear in mind that the testimony at trial is the evidence, not the transcripts. The transcript is not authoritative. If you remember something different from what appears in the transcript, your collective recollection is controlling. In other words, the transcripts may not serve as a substitute for the collective memories of the jury. (p. 9)

Despite the courts' resistance to technology and, in particular, their staunch support for the reliability of human collective memory, the extant evidence from psychological studies of collaborative remembering suggests that this reliance on collaborative remembering as a path to accurate memory is misplaced. Collaborative remembering can (a) block members of the group from remembering something that they might remember on their own, (b) lead to the spread of misleading information, and (c) induce collective forgetting (see Hirst & Echterhoff, 2012, for a review). Rather than producing a more accurate and complete memory, collaboration can lead to inaccurate and incomplete memories. Although none of this work has directly examined collaborative remembering during jury deliberation, the extant literature suggests that jurors may be able to build a consensus story around the collective memory emerging during deliberation, but this story could be incomplete and inaccurate.

In this chapter, we focus on how conversational influences during jury deliberation may shape the memories jurors have of the trial and, in turn, their verdicts. In particular, we examine whether jury deliberation hinders the construction of a coherent rendering of the evidence that is shared across jurors and whether the resulting rendering fully captures the presented evidence. However, before delving into the mnemonic consequences of collaborative remembering, let us first consider the standard model for how jurors reach a decision, the story model.

THE STORY MODEL

Although there is every reason to believe that the mnemonic effort on the jury's part during deliberation is as collaborative as the decision making itself, the standard account of the memory that jurors form of the evidence is an individually oriented story (see Devine, 2012; Hastie & Pennington, 2000; Pennington & Hastie, 1991, 1992, 1993). According to the story model, jurors individually weave together a story from the presented evidence, using their general, pretrial knowledge to provide the connective tissue necessary for the story to be both coherent and complete (Pennington & Hastie, 1991, 1992, 1993). Following their story construction, jurors match the choices available to them (often presented by the judge as, e.g., "guilty" or "not guilty") with their constructed story to arrive at a verdict.

Although the story model captures a critical aspect of the memory processes jurors undergo, it does not engage the collaborative process of remembering occurring during the deliberation. Story construction can, and in many instances does, occur before deliberation. As a result, jurors might begin deliberation with different stories. In such instances, the deliberation itself could be construed as an attempt to construct, from these disparate stories, a consensus story and from this newly constructed, consensus story arrive at a verdict (Pennington & Hastie, 1991, 1992, 1993). Jurors might begin a deliberation with a story, or the beginnings of a story, but during deliberation they and their fellow jurors may recall evidence that leads them to revise their story. In the end, if the jury is to arrive at a verdict, there has to be a consensus around a single story or, at least, related stories.

THE STORY MODEL AND JURY DELIBERATION

What is remembered during deliberation has an effect on the final verdict. To be sure, when there is a clear majority in predeliberation opinions, the final verdict will reflect the majority opinion 90% of the time (Kalven & Zeisel, 1966). In these instances, deliberation probably does not change the memories jurors have of the evidence. However, many cases only come to trial when the evidence is ambiguous. In such instances, there may not be a clear majority of strongly held opinions before deliberation, and predeliberation attitudes will not predetermine the outcome of the deliberation (Salerno & Diamond, 2010). Jurors often retrospectively report that they formed their opinions during the deliberation (Hannaford-Agor, Hans, Mott, & Munsterman, 2002). Finally, what individual jury members remembered after deliberation determines, in part, their judgment (Pritchard & Keenan, 1999, 2002). None of this research, however, investigated the collective memory of juries, by which we mean a consensus memory that juries, as a whole, might form and subsequently guide their jury-wide verdict.

Although these findings underscore the importance of deliberation in shaping verdicts in many instances, "we know fairly little about how individual preferences are translated into a group decision" (Bornstein & Greene, 2011, p. 65). Stasser (1988) filled in some of this gap by adapting his bias sampling model of collaborative remembering to jury deliberation. During deliberation, he averred, jurors sample their memory and, in doing so, refresh information that might not have been readily accessible for other jurors and introduce new information other jurors might not have encoded during the evidentiary phase of the trial. Although this model treats jurors' preferred verdict as a weighted sum (or average) of the information they have available in memory following deliberation, one could just as easily assert that jurors construct a story around available memories. What Stasser's adaptation adds is a model of how memories might become available during deliberation.

One of the strengths of this extension of the story model is that it nicely captures a critical point about the effects of deliberation: Deliberation affects the outcome of a trial, in part, because some evidence is discussed during the deliberation and, by implication, other evidence is not. As a result, the deliberation itself can alter the cognitive accessibility of the evidence presented during trial both at later points in the deliberation and when making the final judgment. Critically, this change in accessibility could reshape the stories that the jurors bring to the deliberation—in content, coherence, and coverage—and thereby affect the final verdict. Stasser's (1988) bias sampling model, however, does not fully encompass what is known about conversations and memory.

For instance, the model Stasser (1988) offered suggests that the collaborative remembering that occurs during deliberation will only benefit memory by refreshing previously forgotten memories or introducing evidence that some jurors might never have encoded. These putative benefits are probably what motivated, in part, the Ninth Circuit to insist that jurors trust their collective memory over the written transcript (*U.S. v. Montgomery*, 1998). Yet extensive evidence has suggested that collaborative remembering is not so straightforward, nor is the effect on participants' memory as limited as this description suggests. The evidence that examines jury deliberation is extremely limited, so generalization from the extant research done in nonjury contexts must proceed cautiously. Nevertheless, the extant evidence on conversation remembering underscores the need to consider the collaborative nature of remembering during jury deliberation.

In what follows, we discuss the different mnemonic consequences of collaborative remembering and their implications for jury deliberation. Although there are no doubt advantages to remembering jointly, we focus here on the disadvantages, in large part, as a corrective to the apparent sanguine view of the courts. In doing so, we emphasize how collaborative remembering blocks the full potential of jurors to remember the presented evidence, how one juror can implant false memories in other jurors, and how the selective remembering of most collaborative attempts at recounting can induce forgetting, sometimes in ways that can prove detrimental.

THE DOWNSIDE OF COLLABORATIVE REMEMBERING

The literature has revealed several possible disadvantages of collaborative remembering. Next, we review the empirical research on these disadvantages, as well as their application to jury deliberation.

Collaborative Inhibition

Empirical Findings

One might expect that when several people study material and then get together to recall it jointly, they would benefit from the group effort. One person might remember something that another might have forgotten, thereby refreshing their memory. Or *cross-cueing* may occur. That is, a recollection on the part of one member of the collective effort could trigger a related memory, thereby bringing to mind, for the group, a memory that would not have been remembered if the group had not come together in the first place. In many instances, as the Ninth Circuit opined (*U.S. v. Montgomery*, 1998), groups will remember more than any individual might remember, but the effect is not as strong as the court seemed to believe.

However, there are limits on how much a group will remember. If one sums all the memories of, say, four individuals when left to their own devices, this "nominal score" will usually be higher than the recall evidenced by four individuals who discussed said memories as a group, a result referred to as *collaborative inhibition*. The difference can often be quite dramatic. For example, in some instances, the collaborative group can recall as much as 16% less than the nominal group (Weldon, Blair, & Huebsch, 2000).

Collaborative inhibition is not simply the result of social loafing, though that no doubt might occur during collaborative remembering (Weldon et al., 2000). Rather it appears to arise because retrieval strategies that might be effective for one group member are blocked by the retrieval of memories by other group members. Different group members might organize the previously studied or experienced information in different ways. Thus, there are different effective retrieval strategies for the different members of the group.

As one member of the group pursues her strategy, it may lead to a direction in the collaborative remembering that is discordant with what might be the best retrieval strategies for other group members. Consequently, a group will remember less than the sum of what individual members might be capable of remembering alone. The claim for collaborative inhibition goes beyond Stasser's (1988) assertion that members of a group are more likely to recount shared memories, rather than uniquely held memories. It suggests that collaboration can block or impair the retrieval of both uniquely held memories and shared memories.

In support of the retrieval blockage hypothesis, collaborative inhibition is more likely to occur if researchers manipulate the experimental procedure to ensure that each member organizes that material differently before the group recounting (Barber & Rajaram, 2011). Alternatively, when experimenters instruct and direct participants to study and organize the to-be-remembered material in similar ways, collaborative inhibition disappears (Barber, Rajaram, & Fox, 2012; Finlay, Hitch, & Meudell, 2000). Although the phenomenon of collaborative inhibition is extremely robust, it is less likely to be found with intimate couples than with strangers, presumably because intimate couples are more likely to organize new information in a similar manner (Harris, Keil, Sutton, Barnier, & McIlwain, 2011). Finally, it disappears when two experts are studying the same material; airline pilots do not exhibit collaborative inhibition when jointly recounting simple or complex flight situations (Meade, Nokes, & Morrow, 2009).

As for cross-cueing, intuitively, one would assume that one benefit that groups achieve when jointly remembering is their ability to have one member trigger another member to remember something that he would not remember on his own. If participants' mnemonic organizations are similar, then a mnemonic cue offered by one of the participants is likely to elicit a memory for that person. For example, when airline pilots discussed flight situations, they did not exhibit collaborative inhibition because, most likely, they have similar mnemonic organizations of the information; thus, effective mnemonic cues for one should be effective for all of the pilots. That is, a collaborative facilitation effect should occur (Meade et al., 2009). Similarly, a number of psychologists working with long-term couples find effective cueing (Harris et al., 2011).

We are concerned here, of course, about instances in which group members possess different mnemonic representations, the more common instance for criminal cases coming to trial. One could argue that cross-cueing should also be effective in this situation. Anderson and Pichert (1978) examined the way different perspectives shaped memories of the same story. They built on Bartlett's (1932) long-standing observation that people remember schema-consistent information better than schema-inconsistent information.

Participants read a story about two people inspecting a house. In one condition, the title suggested that the people were burglars "casing the joint." In the other condition, the title suggested that the protagonists of the story were real estate agents. Not surprisingly, in a subsequent memory test, those in the burglar condition remembered details of the story related to burglary (e.g., what was in the jewelry box or what paintings were on the wall). The participants in the real estate condition remembered details relevant to buying a house (e.g., the condition of the furnace or the deteriorating state of the plaster on the wall). Immediately following the memory test, the experimenter indicated that he had read the wrong title, that the story, for instance, was not about burglars, as the participant had previously been informed, but about real estate agents. The experimenter then asked the participants to indulge him and recall the story once again, knowing this new information. Now, participants remembered the previously unrecalled schema-inconsistent information.

Those who believe that cross-cueing should play a large role in collaborative remembering, even when representations differ, essentially adopt the conclusion Anderson and Pichert (1978) did from their results: that schemata guide not just the way people memorize material but also how they remember it. As a result, group recounting should provide a means of guiding retrieval in ways that would not be present when remembering in isolation. Just as offering a new title allowed Anderson and Pichert to elicit seemingly forgotten memories, so also might a person's recollection in a group elicit seemingly forgotten memories from other group members, even those group members with disparate representations.

The empirical evidence, however, indicates that cross-cueing in group recountings is notoriously difficult to detect. If group members possess different mnemonic representations, then both cross-cueing and collaborative inhibition may occur. As a result, these effects may cancel each other out at the group level. As memory improves with cross-cueing, it declines with collaborative inhibition and vice versa. This interaction does not mean that the end result is a washout. Collaborative inhibition seems to be the stronger effect, in that it is usually observed in acts of collaborative remembering. Cross-cueing is less prolifically observed.

Application to Jury Deliberation

Collaboration, it would seem, may allow juries to remember more of the evidence presented during a trial than one might expect if one examined the recollections of a lone juror in isolation, but it hardly guarantees a complete recollection, one of the criteria on which to evaluate the story an individual—or a jury—constructs around the presented evidence. Indeed, the retrieval blockage model indicates that what is remembered by a jury during deliberation will inevitably be incomplete. This problem would not arise if jurors entered the deliberation with similar mnemonic representations—that is, to use the language of the story model, similar stories. But, as we noted, most cases that come to trial are contested and the defense and prosecutor usually present distinctive stories to the jurors. Consequently, collaborative inhibition is more likely to be the rule rather than the exception.

The problem is exacerbated because of the composition of juries. At least in the United States, the defendant is to be judged by his peers. The U.S. justice system is designed to ensure that a jury reflects the wide range of backgrounds and diversity of those eligible to serve on a jury (however, such attempts are not always successful; see, for example, Rose, 1999). Thus, the possibility of distinctive mnemonic representations across jurors is high, thereby increasing the probability of collaborative inhibition. In addition, the situation gets even worse because of jury size. Although the evidence is scant, what does exist suggests that collaborative inhibition increases with the size of the group (Walther et al., 2002). However, Saks and Marti (1997) found that larger juries discuss the facts of a trial more accurately and recall more facts relative to smaller juries. These results concerning juries are contrary to what one might expect from the research on collaborative remembering, which suggests that the size of the jury should, if anything, work against a complete recounting and, in doing so, diminish one's faith in a larger jury's final verdict.

How do we reconcile the differences between work in social memory research and those of Saks and Marti (1997)? First, Saks and Marti included only two studies, and, recently, Mukhopadhaya (2003) presented contrary findings. Second, and more important, Saks and Marti measured "amount recalled" post-deliberation. Thus, the mnemonic benefit of deliberation occurred after the discussion was completed, which, rather than contradicts, dovetails nicely with the literature on social memory (see, e.g., Finlay et al., 2000). A more pertinent measure would involve what is actually recounted during the deliberation because this is where social memory research has suggested that the recounting on the part of the jurors should be selective and incomplete.

As we have indicated, cross-cueing does not supply a way around the documented costs of collaboration. One might expect that jurors would cue each other to remember the evidence presented during trial, but at least according to the experimental studies we reviewed, for groups of strangers, effective cross-cueing is rare (but see Congleton & Rajaram, 2011). Of course, there may be much more at stake in a jury deliberation than in the experimental studies of collaborative remembering. Jurors may work harder at finding an effective cue. At present, however, the relevant research does not exist to justify such a claim.

Postevent Misinformation and Social Contagion

Empirical Findings

Probably the most widely applied finding in the psychology of memory to the legal systems has been the postevent misinformation effect. Established in the pioneering work of Elizabeth Loftus (1981; see Loftus, 2005, for a review), this effect has been most widely applied when considering the reliability of eyewitness testimony (see Loftus, 2013, for a review). In the standard experiment on the postevent misinformation effect, participants are shown a slide show of a traffic accident, for instance, in which a stop sign is seen at the intersection. A postevent (post–slide show presentation) narrative is then presented, which covers the same material but now specifies that there was a yield sign at the intersection. In a subsequent memory test of the original slide show, participants will often falsely recognize that the intersection contained a yield rather than a stop sign. The importance of the reliability of eyewitness testimony is straightforward: Discussions with other eyewitnesses, police, and even attorneys and court officials can implant misleading information and thereby have deleterious effects on the witness's memory for the crime (Loftus, 2013). A number of studies have reported success at implanting not just details, but entire events (Loftus & Pickrell, 1995). There is even recent evidence suggesting that a therapist or a police officer may even be able to implant a memory of committing a crime, when none, in fact, actually occurred (Shaw & Porter, 2015).

Although not originally studied in free-flowing conversations, recent work has shown that the postevent misinformation effect can be found in more naturalistic settings. When false memories are implanted in the context of a simple conversation, the implantation is often referred to as *social contagion*, though, in what follows, we use the terms *postevent misinformation effect* and *social contagion* interchangeably. In a fairly controlled setting, participants studied complex pictures and then, in pairs, recalled the content of the slides (Meade & Roediger, 2002). The social exchange was constrained because pairs systematically took turns remembering details. One member of the pair was a confederate, who intentionally recollected misleading information. The confederate was successful in implanting this misleading information, demonstrating the misinformation effect in a conversation, albeit a restricted one. Koppel, Wohl, Meksin, and Hirst (2014) demonstrated social contagion in the context of a free flowing conversation. In this study, participants individually studied slightly different versions of the same story and then jointly recounted the story. In a subsequent individual memory test, participants often falsely recalled the misinformation supplied by the other participant.

Social contagion does not occur whenever false information is introduced. False memories will be implanted about 30% of the time (Lindsay, Hagen, Read, Wade, & Garry, 2004). The level of contagion can be increased if the source of the misinformation is considered an expert (Brown, Coman, & Hirst, 2009; Dodd & Bradshaw, 1980; Smith & Ellsworth, 1987). Alternatively, warnings about the unreliability of a source can diminish the level of social contagion (Echterhoff, Groll, & Hirst, 2007; Muller & Hirst, 2010, 2014).

Application to Jury Deliberation

Whereas the work on the postevent misinformation effect and social contagion has led courts to instruct jurors about the fallibility of eyewitness testimony (see Loftus, 2013, for a review), no one has considered its impact on jury deliberation. We are not concerned here about intentionally misleading information presented during the evidentiary stage of the trial. If this occurred, the opposing attorney or the judge would no doubt raise objections. Rather, our concern is the introduction of false memories during deliberation. The unreliability of memory ensures that such false recollections have a reasonable probability of emerging during a jury deliberation, especially if the trial is complex. If one juror falsely recollects the presented evidence, this false memory has a 30% chance of being implanted in at least one other juror's memory. But will the false memory become incorporated into the collective memory of the jury? Such a collective memory is unlikely to be established with a single utterance of a false memory. It may have a 30% chance of being implanted in one juror's memory, but the probability of it being implanted in all 12 jurors is substantially smaller.

Moreover, the larger the jury, the less likely social contagion will occur, in that the more people there are in a group, the more likely it is that someone will object to an inaccurate recollection (Saks & Marti, 1997; Walther et al., 2002). This possibility would be true for ordinary conversations, but it is especially the case for jury deliberation. Although people often do not correct the mnemonic errors of others in everyday life, there is, as we have noted, a great deal at stake in a jury deliberation. It is likely that one of 12 jurors will object to incorrectly recollected evidence, especially if he or she feels that it will affect the final verdict. The possibility of a misleading recollection of one juror spreading across a jury as a whole, then, seems unlikely. But we caution that this is merely speculative at this point, in part, because jurors often incorrectly remember jury instructions, even following deliberation (Reifman, Gusick, & Ellsworth, 1992). These errors, however, may persist because the instructions may not figure prominently in the deliberations. For errors to be corrected, there have to be discussions about the errors. Although the issue of group size and memory correction has been studied outside the context of the jury system, no one to date has applied these findings to a judicial setting.

Retrieval-Induced Forgetting

Empirical Findings

There is growing evidence that selective retrieval, which no doubt occurs during jury deliberation, can also induce forgetting (Anderson, Bjork, & Bjork, 1994). This *retrieval-induced forgetting* (RIF) can account not only for the forgetting observed in tests of memory subsequent to a conversational interaction but also, at least in part, for collaborative inhibition. Selective retrieval on the part of one participant in a conversation will induce forgetting in other participants, making the forgotten item unlikely to be recalled as the conversation proceeds. Inasmuch as it affects both the person undertaking the remembering (i.e., the speaker) as well as those listening to the remembering, it can also lead to collective forgetting (Stone, Barnier, Sutton, & Hirst, 2010).

The phenomenon of RIF was first studied as a within-individual effect, using word pairs—a far step removed from the conversational interactions of a jury. In the original study of *within-individual retrieval-induced forgetting* (WI-RIF; Anderson et al., 1994), participants studied category-exemplar word pairs (e.g., fruit–apple, fruit–orange, vegetable–broccoli, vegetable–pea) and then received retrieval practice for half of the items from half of the categories (e.g., fruit–apple). On a final recall test, participants attempted to recall the originally studied exemplars. This experimental design yields three types of items: Rp+, practiced items from a practiced category (e.g., fruit–apple); Rp–, nonpracticed items from a practiced category (e.g., fruit–orange); and Nrp, nonpracticed items from a nonpracticed category (e.g., all of the vegetables). RIF occurs when the selective retrieval of practiced items (Rp+) induces forgetting of unpracticed, related items (Rp–) relative to unpracticed, unrelated items (Nrp)—that is, when Rp– < Nrp.

WI-RIF cannot be accounted for by decay alone. According to the most widely accepted account, as participants retrieve the practice item, they inhibit competing responses (i.e., the related items; Levy & Anderson, 2002). This inhibition lingers so that the inhibited items are harder to remember than the uninhibited ones (i.e., the unrelated items).

Along with colleagues, we have extended WI-RIF into a social context, what we have referred to as *socially shared retrieval-induced forgetting* (SS-RIF). In a typical experiment (e.g., Cuc, Koppel, & Hirst, 2007), two participants read a story and then jointly recount it. A final memory test followed. Critically, the joint recounting in many of the experiments involved free-flowing conversations (e.g., Stone, Barnier, Sutton, & Hirst, 2013). It should be noted that in some experiments, the exchange is one way. For instance, people listen to another person selectively recall the previously studied material rather than actively participate in jointly recounting the material with this person. In those instances in which a free-flowing conversation is used, the joint recounting is transcribed and coded for mentioned and unmentioned material from the original story, along with a note as to when a participant served as speaker or listener. This coding yields a record of Rp+, Rp–, and Nrp items when a participant was a speaker and when he or she was a listener. The standard RIF pattern (Rp– < Nrp) is found for both speakers and listeners in the final recall of each participant.

SS-RIF emerges because listeners concurrently, albeit covertly, retrieve with the speaker (e.g., Cuc et al., 2007; Hirst & Echterhoff, 2012; Stone et al., 2010; Stone, Barnier, et al., 2013). (We use the terms *speaker* and *listener* here and elsewhere because we are chiefly concerned with free-flowing conversations.) With this concurrent, covert retrieval, the listener retrieves the same material as the speaker and, hence, according to the principle of RIF, should be more likely to forget memories related to what the speaker recalled than to forget unrelated memories. SS-RIF differs from WI-RIF in that SS-RIF is optional. Listeners do not have to retrieve concurrently with a speaker, whereas speakers are, by definition, obligated to retrieve. Inasmuch as people are cognitive misers (Kahneman, 2013) and retrieval is effortful, the fact that listeners do, in many instances, concurrently retrieve is noteworthy.

Researchers have explored the conditions under which SS-RIF might be expected. If people are cognitive misers, they should concurrently retrieve only when motivated to do so (see also Echterhoff, Higgins, & Levine, 2009). In some instances, listeners may be epistemically motivated: The more the listener mistrusts the speaker's memory, for instance, the more likely he or she will be to retrieve concurrently so as to assess the accuracy of a speaker's utterances. SS-RIF occurred when listeners were instructed to monitor for the accuracy of what the speaker recollected, but not the fluidity (Cuc et al., 2007). Moreover, SS-RIF increased if listeners mistrusted the speaker and decreased if they trusted her or him (Koppel et al., 2014).

This latter finding is interesting in that it involves a pattern quite opposite from what is found in experiments on social contagion. In both instances, epistemic motives play a role, but with different consequences. As noted in the social contagion section earlier, social contagion is more likely if the source of the misleading information is an expert or trustworthy, less likely if the source is untrustworthy. The standard explanation involves the phenomenon of source monitoring (Johnson, Hashtroudi, & Lindsay, 1993). In some studies by Loftus and colleagues, participants saw the stop sign in the slide show and then heard about a yield sign in the postevent narrative (see, e.g., Loftus, 1979). When asked whether a stop sign or a yield sign was featured in the slide show, participants had difficulty remembering which sign was in which presentation. That is, they have difficulty monitoring the source of a memory. When listening to an untrustworthy source, individuals are more likely to make the effort to monitor the source of the information and, as a result, exhibit less of a postevent misinformation effect or social contagion.

In the case of SS-RIF, epistemic motives produced less concurrent retrieval and hence less SS-RIF. If listeners trust the speaker's memory, they should not make an effort to retrieve concurrently, thereby diminishing the prospect of SS-RIF. If they do not trust the speaker's memory, they should make the effort to retrieve concurrently. In the case of social contagion, the epistemic motive diminished the negative effects of social interaction on memory; in the case of SS-RIF, it increased it. Trusted or not, the speaker will have an effect on the listener; only the nature of the effect will change.

Relational motives also govern the strength of SS-RIF. Here the assumption is that listeners are more likely to retrieve concurrently if they feel socially related to the speaker. In such situations, they want to "relive" the experience with the speaker. In support of this claim, when listeners were more aware that there was an author behind a communication, either by listening to the speaker tell a story about himself or seeing a picture of the speaker, the more likely SS-RIF occurred (Fagin & Hirst, 2015). SS-RIF was not observed if a participant merely read a written communication without any information about its source (as is often the case when people read an instruction manual). Coman and Hirst (2015) offered another example of relational motives by exploring the effect of group membership on SS-RIF. Princeton students first studied a story and then listened to an audio recording of a young person selectively recalling the story. The recording was paired with a photograph and background information. SS-RIF was found when the speaker was identified as a Princeton student but not when he or she was identified as a Yale student. We do not suspect that the Princeton participants thought the Princeton or Yale student speaker was more or less credible. Rather, they were more likely to see themselves as related to the Princeton speaker (see also Barber & Mather, 2012).

SS-RIF does not occur only if one does not trust a person or if one wants to relate to him or her. Although concurrent retrieval takes effort, it probably occurs in most social exchanges of memories, including conversations. First, the relation between the source of information (speaker) and the recipient of the information (listener) can be minimal and still produce SS-RIF (Fagin & Hirst, 2015). Second, epistemic motives involve trust in the memory of the source, not the source himself or herself. Mnemonic trust and relatedness need not be negatively correlated. Conversational influences on memory may be, if you like, the default, even if concurrent retrieval requires effort. Indeed, in another context we have argued that social and conversational influences may be adaptive, in that they promote the formation of collective memories, a desirable outcome for creatures as social as humans (see, e.g., Hirst, 2010). Epistemic and relational motives may accentuate or diminish the strength of these default influences.

Of course, there may be instances in which listeners do more than simply concurrently retrieve with the speaker; they may fill in what the speaker leaves unmentioned (Chan, McDermott, & Roediger, 2006). However, such retrieval requires effort. It may require effort to retrieve concurrently with a speaker, but it requires even more effort to bring to mind a memory the speaker did not mention. When would a listener be sufficiently motivated to make this additional effort? The evidence suggests that it occurs when listeners feel their social identity is threatened (Coman, Stone, Castano, & Hirst, 2014). But, in many cases, the rapid exchange in most communicative settings, including conversations, create conditions that make such motivated recall difficult, because short gaps between exchanges often provide little time for an extensive mnemonic search (Hirst & Echterhoff, 2008). Importantly, SS-RIF can influence future attitudes and decisions. It affects decisions about medical treatments (Coman, Coman, & Hirst, 2013), how confident people are in their autobiographical memories (Stone, Luminet, & Hirst, 2013), the extent to which individuals dehumanize outgroup members (Coman et al., 2014), and political attitudes (Coman & Hirst, 2012).

Application to Jury Deliberation

Few studies have explicitly examined SS-RIF during jury deliberation (e.g., Haque & Stone, 2015). A main issue in examining SS-RIF is whether the way a conversation among jurors unfolds at any point during deliberation influences what is subsequently remembered during the deliberation. Coman and Hirst (2012) had pairs of participants first individually study arguments for or against euthanasia and then individually watch a presentation that selectively presented only issues in favor of euthanasia. In a subsequent conversation, the paired participants failed to discuss those items from the original arguments that were unmentioned in the selective presentation and related to what was mentioned. That is, they demonstrated SS-RIF not in a subsequent memory test but a subsequent conversation. Moreover, in a memory test that followed the conversation, SS-RIF was more pronounced in a manner that could be directly traced to the selective forgetting in the conversation. Thus, the selective remembering that occurs at the beginning of jury deliberation may have strong consequences for the way the jury talks about the evidence as the deliberation proceeds and for the collective memory that emerges out of the deliberation.

These considerations suggest that those jurors who begin the discussion can have a profound effect on the jury's collective memory. One individual, referred to by some researchers as the *dominant narrator*, often dominates conversational remembering (Cuc, Ozuru, Manier, & Hirst, 2006). In Cuc et al.'s (2006) study, the collective memory formed as a result of the conversation reflected the pre-conversational memories of the dominant narrator. The conversations examined in this study, however, were brief. Moreover, the researchers did not examine the effect of early conversational exchanges on later exchanges. Nevertheless, the collective memory of a conversing group does not necessarily reflect a blending of the discussants' memories equally.

One person, then, can shape the conversation and, in doing so, reinforce some memories, but also induce forgetting of other memories. This memory-shaping jury member might be the juror who begins the deliberation. Inasmuch as juries are not instructed as to how their discussion should unfold, the rules of conversational exchange a jury establishes might have a dramatic effect on the collective memory they form and, as a result, the verdict they render.

In addition, selective remembering of a category of information, as specified in the story model of jury decision making, should—and does—induce forgetting for unmentioned information from this category (Haque & Stone, 2015). For example, one category of the story model is "consequences." When two people discussed previously studied evidence with the instructions to imagine that they were jurors trying to arrive at a verdict, mentioning some previously studied consequences, while leaving others unmentioned, led to greater forgetting for the unmentioned ones. Selective remembering in a jury setting can result in selective forgetting.

The effects of SS-RIF on jurors' memories and their verdicts are not confined to jury deliberation. Both prosecutor and defense offer closing statements, representing the story each lawyer wants the jurors to take into the deliberation. Inasmuch as they reflect the perspective of the prosecutor and defense on the presented evidence, they are inevitably selective. Wohl and Hirst (2015) examined the effect of closing statements on the memory of "mock jurors" and the effect of these memory shifts on the verdict. Participants first learned of the evidence presented in a trial and then saw videotapes of both the prosecutor's and the defense's closing statement, without rebuttal. Selective remembering of both prosecutor and defense produced SS-RIF, mainly for evidence related to the character of the defendant (Wohl & Hirst, 2015). This SS-RIF, in turn, affected the verdict participants offered. When prosecutorial evidence related to character was forgotten, it increased the chance of a not guilty verdict. When defense character evidence was forgotten, it increased the chance of a less confidently held verdict.

CONCLUDING REMARKS

The study of remembering during jury deliberation is in its infancy. There are many reasons for this previous inattention to the collective memory of jury members, but chief among them is that students of memory have only begun to study seriously the effects of conversation on memories in the last decade or so. The present chapter, then, represents an attempt to relate this maturing literature to the particular instance of jury deliberation. What should be clear is that courts' faith in the "wisdom of the crowd" may need calibration. At least with respect to what a jury remembers, the work on conversational remembering and memory suggests that, although conversations at times can promote a more complete and reliable recollection of the evidence presented during the trial, they can also lead to both selective remembering and selective forgetting, which might detrimentally affect the verdict. This claim is based on what is known about conversational remembering in general terms rather than conversations taking place in a jury deliberation.

Clearly, this extension is speculative and has to be verified with future research specifically aimed at exploring the mnemonic effects of conversations during jury deliberation. For example, does an initial discussion of facts that suggests a guilty verdict induce forgetting for facts suggesting a verdict of not guilty, thereby making it unlikely for these latter facts to emerge even as the deliberation proceeds? If such an extension is valid, the work on conversations and memory raises serious concerns for the legal system. One way to avoid such deleterious effects might be through jury instructions and management. Presently, these do not take into account the relevant literature on conversations and memory. In fact, the courts seem to believe that conversations among multiple individuals should provide a means by which to overcome the limitations of individual memory. Researchers—and the legal system—have to begin to take seriously the impact juries' deliberation has on the way jurors remember the evidence and the way these memories become collective and, in turn, affect their subsequent verdict.

REFERENCES

Anderson, M. C., Bjork, R. A., & Bjork, E. L. (1994). Remembering can cause forgetting: Retrieval dynamics in long-term memory. *Journal of Experimental Psychology: Learning, Memory, and Cognition, 20*, 1063–1087. http://dx.doi.org/10.1037/0278-7393.20.5.1063

Anderson, R. C., & Pichert, J. W. (1978). Recall of previously unrecallable information following a shift in perspective. *Journal of Verbal Learning & Verbal Behavior, 17*, 1–12. http://dx.doi.org/10.1016/S0022-5371(78)90485-1

Barber, S. J., & Mather, M. (2012). Forgetting in context: The effects of age, emotion, and social factors on retrieval-induced forgetting. *Memory & Cognition, 40*, 874–888. http://dx.doi.org/10.3758/s13421-012-0202-8

Barber, S. J., & Rajaram, S. (2011). Exploring the relationship between retrieval disruption from collaboration and recall. *Memory, 19*, 462–469. http://dx.doi.org/10.1080/09658211.2011.584389

Barber, S. J., Rajaram, S., & Fox, E. B. (2012). Learning and remembering with others: The key role of retrieval in shaping group recall and collective memory. *Social Cognition, 30*, 121–132. http://dx.doi.org/10.1521/soco.2012.30.1.121

Bartlett, F. C. (1932). *Remembering*. New York, NY: Cambridge University Press.

Bornstein, B. H., & Greene, E. (2011). Jury decision making: Implications for and from psychology. *Current Directions in Psychological Science, 20*, 63–67. http://dx.doi.org/10.1177/0963721410397282

Brown, A. D., Coman, A., & Hirst, W. (2009). The role of narratorship and expertise in social remembering. *Social Psychology, 40*, 119–129. http://dx.doi.org/10.1027/1864-9335.40.3.119

Chan, J. C. K., McDermott, K. B., & Roediger, H. L., III. (2006). Retrieval-induced facilitation: Initially nontested material can benefit from prior testing of related material. *Journal of Experimental Psychology: General, 135*, 553–571. http://dx.doi.org/10.1037/0096-3445.135.4.553

Coman, A., & Hirst, W. (2012). Cognition through a social network: The propagation of induced forgetting and practice effects. *Journal of Experimental Psychology: General, 141*, 321–336. http://dx.doi.org/10.1037/a0025247

Coman, A., & Hirst, W. (2015). Social identity and socially shared retrieval-induced forgetting: The effects of group membership. *Journal of Experimental Psychology: General, 144*, 717–722. http://dx.doi.org/10.1037/xge0000077

Coman, A., Stone, C. B., Castano, E., & Hirst, W. (2014). Justifying atrocities: The effect of moral-disengagement strategies on socially shared retrieval-induced forgetting. *Psychological Science, 25*, 1281–1285. http://dx.doi.org/10.1177/0956797614531024

Coman, D., Coman, A., & Hirst, W. (2013). Memory accessibility and medical decision-making for significant others: The role of socially shared retrieval-induced forgetting. *Frontiers in Behavioral Neuroscience, 7*(72). http://dx.doi.org/10.3389/fnbeh.2013.00072

Congleton, A. R., & Rajaram, S. (2011). The influence of learning methods on collaboration: Prior repeated retrieval enhances retrieval organization, abolishes collaborative inhibition, and promotes post-collaborative memory. *Journal of Experimental Psychology: General, 140*, 535–551. http://dx.doi.org/10.1037/a0024308

Cuc, A., Koppel, J., & Hirst, W. (2007). Silence is not golden: A case for socially shared retrieval-induced forgetting. *Psychological Science, 18*, 727–733. http://dx.doi.org/10.1111/j.1467-9280.2007.01967.x

Cuc, A., Ozuru, Y., Manier, D., & Hirst, W. (2006). On the formation of collective memories: The role of a dominant narrator. *Memory & Cognition, 34*, 752–762. http://dx.doi.org/10.3758/BF03193423

Devine, D. J. (2012). *Jury decision making: The state of the science*. New York: New York University Press.

Dodd, D. H., & Bradshaw, J. M. (1980). Leading questions and memory: Pragmatic constraints. *Journal of Verbal Learning & Verbal Behavior, 19*, 695–704. http://dx.doi.org/10.1016/S0022-5371(80)90379-5

Echterhoff, G., Groll, S., & Hirst, W. (2007). Tainted truth: Overcorrection for misinformation influence on eyewitness memory. *Social Cognition, 25*, 367–409. http://dx.doi.org/10.1521/soco.2007.25.3.367

Echterhoff, G., Higgins, E. T., & Levine, J. M. (2009). Shared reality: Experiencing commonality with others' inner states about the world. *Perspectives on Psychological Science, 4*, 496–521. http://dx.doi.org/10.1111/j.1745-6924.2009.01161.x

Fagin, M., & Hirst, W. (2015). *Relational motives and socially shared retrieval-induced forgetting: The role of author's presence in acts of communication*. Manuscript in preparation.

Finlay, F., Hitch, G. J., & Meudell, P. R. (2000). Mutual inhibition in collaborative recall: Evidence for a retrieval-based account. *Journal of Experimental Psychology: Learning, Memory, and Cognition, 26*, 1556–1567. http://dx.doi.org/10.1037/0278-7393.26.6.1556

Hannaford-Agor, P. L., Hans, V. P., Mott, N. L., & Munsterman, G. T. (2002). *Are hung juries a problem?* Williamsburg, VA: National Center for State Courts.

Haque, F., & Stone, C. B. (2015). *Collaboratively crafting a story (model): The mnemonic and decision-making consequences of socially shared retrieval-induced forgetting within jury deliberations*. Manuscript in preparation.

Harris, C. B., Keil, P. G., Sutton, J., Barnier, A. J., & McIlwain, D. J. F. (2011). We remember, we forget: Collaborative remembering in older couples. *Discourse Processes, 48*, 267–303. http://dx.doi.org/10.1080/0163853X.2010.541854

Hastie, R., & Pennington, N. (2000). Explanation-based decision making. In T. Connolly, H. R. Arkes, & K. R. Hammond (Eds.), *Judgment and decision making: An interdisciplinary reader* (pp. 212–228). New York, NY: Cambridge University Press.

Hirst, W. (2010). A virtue of memory: The contribution of mnemonic malleability to collective memory. In P. A. Reuter-Lorenz, K. Baynes, G. R. Mangun, & E. A. Phelps (Eds.), *The cognitive neuroscience of the mind: A tribute to Michael. S. Gazzaniga* (pp. 139–154). http://dx.doi.org/10.7551/mitpress/9780262014014.003.0100

Hirst, W., & Echterhoff, G. (2008). Creating shared memories in conversation: Towards a psychology of collective memory. *Social Research, 75*, 183–216.

Hirst, W., & Echterhoff, G. (2012). Remembering in conversations: The social sharing and reshaping of memories. *Annual Review of Psychology, 63*, 55–79. http://dx.doi.org/10.1146/annurev-psych-120710-100340

Johnson, M. K., Hashtroudi, S., & Lindsay, D. S. (1993). Source monitoring. *Psychological Bulletin*, *114*, 3–28. http://dx.doi.org/10.1037/0033-2909.114.1.3

Kahneman, D. (2013). *Thinking, fast and slow*. New York, NY: Farrar, Straus & Giroux.

Kalven, H., & Zeisel, H. (1966). *The American jury*. Chicago, IL: University of Chicago Press.

Koppel, J., Wohl, D., Meksin, R., & Hirst, W. (2014). The effect of listening to others remember on subsequent memory: The roles of expertise and trust in socially shared retrieval-induced forgetting and social contagion. *Social Cognition*, *32*, 148–180. http://dx.doi.org/10.1521/soco.2014.32.2.148

Levy, B. J., & Anderson, M. C. (2002). Inhibitory processes and the control of memory retrieval. *Trends in Cognitive Sciences*, 6, 299–305. http://dx.doi.org/10.1016/S1364-6613(02)01923-X

Lindsay, D. S., Hagen, L., Read, J. D., Wade, K. A., & Garry, M. (2004). True photographs and false memories. *Psychological Science*, *15*, 149–154. http://dx.doi.org/10.1111/j.0956-7976.2004.01503002.x

Loftus, E. F. (1979). The malleability of human memory. *American Scientist*, *67*, 312–320.

Loftus, E. F. (1981). Mentalmorphosis: Alterations in memory produced by the mental bonding of new information to old. In J. Long & A. Baddeley (Eds.), *Attention and performance IX* (pp. 417–434). Hillsdale, NJ: Erlbaum.

Loftus, E. F. (2005). Planting misinformation in the human mind: A 30-year investigation of the malleability of memory. *Learning & Memory*, *12*, 361–366. http://dx.doi.org/10.1101/lm.94705

Loftus, E. F. (2013). 25 years of eyewitness science . . . Finally pays off. *Perspectives on Psychological Science*, 8, 556–557. http://dx.doi.org/10.1177/1745691613500995

Loftus, E. F., & Pickrell, J. E. (1995). The formation of false memories. *Psychiatric Annals*, *25*, 720–725. http://dx.doi.org/10.3928/0048-5713-19951201-07

Meade, M. L., Nokes, T. J., & Morrow, D. G. (2009). Expertise promotes facilitation on a collaborative memory task. *Memory*, *17*, 39–48. http://dx.doi.org/10.1080/09658210802524240

Meade, M. L., & Roediger, H. L., III. (2002). Explorations in the social contagion of memory. *Memory & Cognition*, *30*, 995–1009. http://dx.doi.org/10.3758/BF03194318

Mize, G. E., Hannaford-Agor, P., & Waters, N. L. (2007). *The state-of-the-states survey of jury improvement: A compendium report*. Williamsburg, VA: National Center for State Courts.

Mukhopadhaya, K. (2003). Jury size and the free rider problem. *Journal of Law Economics and Organization*, *19*, 24–44. http://dx.doi.org/10.1093/jleo/19.1.24

Muller, F., & Hirst, W. (2010). Resistance to the influences of others: Limits to the formation of a collective memory through conversational remembering. *Applied Cognitive Psychology*, *24*, 608–625. http://dx.doi.org/10.1002/acp.1572

Muller, F., & Hirst, W. (2014). Remembering stories together: Social contagion and the moderating influence of disagreements in conversations. *Journal of Applied Research in Memory and Cognition, 3*, 7–11. http://dx.doi.org/10.1016/j.jarmac.2013.12.002

Pennington, N., & Hastie, R. (1991). A cognitive theory of juror decision making: The story model. *Cardozo Law Review, 13*, 519–557.

Pennington, N., & Hastie, R. (1992). Explaining the evidence: Tests of the story model for juror decision making. *Journal of Personality and Social Psychology, 62*, 189–206. http://dx.doi.org/10.1037/0022-3514.62.2.189

Pennington, N., & Hastie, R. (1993). A theory of explanation-based decision making. In G. A. Klein, J. Orasanu, R. Calderwood, & E. C. Zsambok (Eds.), *Decision making in action: Models and methods* (pp. 188–201). Westport, CT: Ablex.

Pritchard, M. E., & Keenan, J. M. (1999). Memory monitoring in mock juries. *Journal of Experimental Psychology: Applied, 5*, 152–168. http://dx.doi.org/10.1037/1076-898X.5.2.152

Pritchard, M. E., & Keenan, J. M. (2002). Does jury deliberation really improve jurors' memories? *Applied Cognitive Psychology, 16*, 589–601. http://dx.doi.org/10.1002/acp.816

Reifman, A., Gusick, S. M., & Ellsworth, P. C. (1992). Real jurors' understanding of the law in real cases. *Law and Human Behavior, 16*, 539–554. http://dx.doi.org/10.1007/BF01044622

Rose, M. R. (1999). The peremptory challenge accused of race or gender discrimination? Some data from one county. *Law and Human Behavior, 23*, 695–702. http://dx.doi.org/10.1023/A:1022393506784

Saks, M. J., & Marti, M. W. (1997). A meta-analysis of the effects of jury size. *Law and Human Behavior, 21*, 451–467. http://dx.doi.org/10.1023/A:1024819605652

Salerno, J. M., & Diamond, S. S. (2010). The promise of a cognitive perspective on jury deliberation. *Psychonomic Bulletin & Review, 17*, 174–179. http://dx.doi.org/10.3758/PBR.17.2.174

Shaw, J., & Porter, S. (2015). Constructing rich false memories of committing crime. *Psychological Science, 26*, 291–301. http://dx.doi.org/10.1177/0956797614562862

Smith, V. L., & Ellsworth, P. C. (1987). The social psychology of eyewitness accuracy: Leading questions and communicator expertise. *Journal of Applied Psychology, 72*, 294–300. http://dx.doi.org/10.1037/0021-9010.72.2.294

Stasser, G. (1988). Computer simulation as a research tool: The DISCUSS model of group decision making. *Journal of Experimental Social Psychology, 24*, 393–422. http://dx.doi.org/10.1016/0022-1031(88)90028-5

Stone, C. B., Barnier, A. J., Sutton, J., & Hirst, W. (2010). Building consensus about the past: Schema consistency and convergence in socially shared retrieval-induced forgetting. *Memory, 18*, 170–184. http://dx.doi.org/10.1080/09658210903159003

Stone, C. B., Barnier, A. J., Sutton, J., & Hirst, W. (2013). Forgetting our personal past: Socially shared retrieval-induced forgetting of autobiographical memories. *Journal of Experimental Psychology: General, 142*, 1084–1099. http://dx.doi.org/10.1037/a0030739

Stone, C. B., Luminet, O., & Hirst, W. (2013). Induced forgetting and reduced confidence in our personal past? The consequences of selectively retrieving emotional autobiographical memories. *Acta Psychologica, 144*, 250–257. http://dx.doi.org/10.1016/j.actpsy.2013.06.019

U.S. v. Montgomery, 150 F.3d 983, 999–1000 (1998).

Walther, E., Bless, H., Strack, F., Rackstraw, P., Wagner, D., & Werth, L. (2002). Conformity effects in memory as a function of group size, dissenters and uncertainty. *Applied Cognitive Psychology, 16*, 793–810. http://dx.doi.org/10.1002/acp.828

Weldon, M. S., Blair, C., & Huebsch, P. D. (2000). Group remembering: Does social loafing underlie collaborative inhibition? *Journal of Experimental Psychology: Learning, Memory, and Cognition, 26*, 1568–1577. http://dx.doi.org/10.1037/0278-7393.26.6.1568

Wohl, D., & Hirst, W. (2015). *Socially shared retrieval-induced forgetting in mock juries: An examination of the role of closing arguments in criminal trials*. Manuscript in preparation.

3

INTEGRATING CONCEPTS OF TRIAL ADVOCACY INTO JUROR DECISION-MAKING RESEARCH

CHRISTINA A. STUDEBAKER

Empirical research conducted over the past 60 years in the field of juror and jury decision making has provided valuable information about various factors that can influence jurors' and juries' verdict decision making (for substantive reviews, see Devine, 2012; Devine, Clayton, Dunford, Seying, & Pryce, 2001; Hastie, 1993). For the most part, these factors have concerned trial participant characteristics (e.g., race and other demographic characteristics of the defendant, demographic characteristics and personality characteristics of jurors), case characteristics (e.g., expert testimony, scientific evidence, eyewitness evidence), and legal procedures (e.g., jury instructions, judicial admonitions to disregard inadmissible evidence, juror note taking). A category of factors that has not been extensively explored to date concerns aspects of legal practice. Psycholegal research on juror decision making in the adversarial justice system has largely overlooked the influence of a key component of the system—namely, adversaries.

http://dx.doi.org/10.1037/0000026-004
The Psychology of Juries, M. B. Kovera (Editor)

To determine a verdict, jurors must evaluate the evidence and then apply the jury instructions to the evidence. There is reason to believe that jurors appropriately base their decisions largely on the evidence rather than extralegal factors (Visher, 1987). The evidence, of course, is not one sided or neutral. Evidence consists of testimony from witnesses called by each side, and witness testimony results from direct examination and cross-examination conducted by attorneys on each side of the case. In addition, the attorneys for each side begin and end the case with opening statements and closing arguments containing case themes and interpretations of the evidence designed to favor their respective side. Clearly, opposing viewpoints are part of every case that goes to trial, and, in their attempts to persuade the trier(s) of fact, the attorneys on each side emphasize and bolster the evidence that favors their side as well as attack and minimize evidence that does not favor their side. As stated in a leading text on trial advocacy:

> A lawyer's goal at trial is to persuade the fact finder. Certainly one hopes that this may be achieved primarily as a result of the accuracy of the evidence, the integrity of the witnesses, the clarity of the communication, and the rightness of the cause. It would be naive, however, to suggest that the lawyer's skills do not play a part in convincing a judge or jury to enter a favorable verdict. (Lubet, 2004, p. 15)

One way attorneys influence jury verdicts is through jurors' perceptions of the attorneys themselves. Attorneys perceived by jurors to be credible, competent, and prepared can increase the likelihood of their case being perceived favorably (Diamond, Casper, Heiert, & Marshall, 1996; Hoolihan, 2014; Wood, Sicafuse, Miller, & Chomos, 2011). In addition to, and arguably more important than, the influence of the attorneys themselves is the influence of various techniques and strategies used by attorneys during trial. Note that the quote in the preceding paragraph refers to "the lawyer's skills" rather than "the lawyer." Another way to think about that is the distinction between "advocacy" and "the advocate."

In this chapter, I discuss the general topic of trial advocacy methods and how our understanding of juror and jury decision making would benefit from incorporating more research on advocacy methods. I first introduce a categorization scheme of commonly researched topics in the field of juror and jury research, which helps highlight gaps in the research conducted to date, specifically in the area of trial advocacy methods. A review of a handful of studies that have examined advocacy methods illustrates the valuable contributions this research provides to a more comprehensive understanding of the decision-making task faced by jurors and how they handle it. I then consider some of the challenges and obstacles of conducting research on advocacy methods, provide some recommendations for how to address those challenges, and offer some thoughts on specific research topics that would help us begin to fill important gaps in our understanding of the influence of trial advocacy methods on juror decision making.

HOW RESEARCH IS ORGANIZED

The paucity of research on advocacy methods may not be obvious at first because perceptions of the research landscape can be influenced by how research is categorized. At a general level, researchers distinguish between basic (or theoretical) research and applied research. Applied research is not necessarily separate from basic research, and some juror and jury decision-making studies may be considered to be both applied and basic research. However, the vast majority of juror and jury decision-making research is categorized as applied research because in one way or another it addresses real-world issues encountered by individuals in the process of potentially being selected to serve as jurors or in the process of carrying out their duties as jurors. Researchers who focus on the distinction between basic and applied research might believe that the scope of juror and jury decision-making research is sufficient because it can all be applied to real-world issues and problems. However, this view of research can overlook gaps in the research and, therefore, in our understanding. Just because research examines real-world issues does not mean that the research has adequately addressed the complexity of the real world.

Alternative ways of categorizing juror and jury decision-making research provide a more detailed view of the field and can highlight certain gaps in our knowledge. For example, applied research is often evaluated in terms of its ecological validity as well as internal and external validity (Bornstein, 1999; Bornstein & McCabe, 2005; Breau & Brook, 2007; Wiener, Krauss, & Lieberman, 2011). Consequently, juror and jury research studies are sometimes categorized according to whether the research was conducted in the field or the laboratory (e.g., Devine, 2012; Studebaker & Penrod, 1997). Another way to categorize juror and jury decision-making research is according to its primary goal. For example, the focus of some research in the field has been jury reform, with an eye toward examining legal procedures and alternative procedures that might help jurors or juries perform their task better (for overviews, see Ellsworth, 1999; Hans & Albertson, 2003). This category of research might be described as prescriptive, with the goal of recommending policy or procedure changes believed to improve the juror or jury decision-making process and/or outcomes. Other research has focused on testing and developing information-processing models and theories of juror decision making (e.g., Kerr, 1993; Ostrom, Werner, & Saks, 1978; Pennington & Hastie, 1986, 1991; Schum & Martin, 1982). Often, the main goal of this type of research is to better describe and explain the social–cognitive process by which jurors carry out the unique task of evaluating evidence presented through adversarial presentations and then determining a verdict.

Another basis on which juror decision-making studies can be categorized is the type of independent variable(s) examined. A benefit of this sort of categorization is that it allows a more direct comparison of variables that come into play in real-world juror decision making and variables that have been examined in juror decision-making research. Table 3.1 summarizes four general categories of independent variables that have been examined in juror decision-making research: (a) participant characteristics (e.g., Devine & Caughlin, 2014; Mazzella & Feingold, 1994; Sommers & Ellsworth, 2000), (b) case characteristics (e.g., Bottoms, Golding, Stevenson, Wiley, & Yozwiak, 2007; Krauss & Sales, 2001; Steblay, Besirevic, Fulero, & Jimenez-Lorente, 1999), (c) legal procedures (e.g., Heuer & Penrod, 1994; Horowitz & Bordens, 1990; Smith, 1991), and (d) trial advocacy characteristics (e.g., Diamond, Rose, Murphy, & Meixner, 2011; Spiecker & Worthington, 2003; Williams, Bourgeois, & Croyle, 1993). The participant characteristics category can be further separated into subcategories that pertain to jurors, victims/plaintiffs, defendants, and attorneys. The case characteristics category includes variables pertaining to particular types of evidence or cases. The legal procedures category includes procedures dictated by the justice system. These variables might differ across cases (e.g., the use of a six-person vs. 12-person jury), but the procedure used in any particular trial is either dictated by a formal rule or determined by the court. The use of any of these formal procedures in real-world cases is a function of the justice system and is not intended to favor systematically one side or the other. The trial advocacy category includes methods that an attorney can control and use with the intent of persuading jurors in favor of the attorney's client.

Table 3.1 includes examples of topics that fall within each of the proposed research categories and that have been empirically studied. The nature of some topics might allow them to fall into more than one category. For example, research on injury severity might be categorized as research examining a victim characteristic or a case characteristic. Additional possible research topics that have not yet been empirically studied will be discussed in more detail later. If a primary goal of the field of juror and jury decision-making research is to achieve a detailed and complete understanding of juror decision-making processes, including empirical examination of trial advocacy methods is essential. In the next section, I review some research findings on this variable.

TABLE 3.1
Categorization of Juror Decision-Making Research Topics by Types of Independent Variables

Independent variable category	Sample topics that have been empirically researched
Participant characteristics	
Juror characteristics	Demographics
	Personality factors and individual differences (e.g., need for cognition)
	Preexisting case relevant attitudes and beliefs
	Prior jury service
Victim/plaintiff characteristics	Demographics
	Credibility
	Injury severity
	Special subcategory of research on child witnesses
Defendant characteristics	Demographics
	Physical attractiveness
	Credibility
	Competency
	"Deep pockets"
	Prior convictions or other character evidence
Attorney characteristics	Demographics
Case characteristics	Expert testimony
	Scientific evidence
	Confession evidence
	Eyewitness testimony
	Pretrial publicity (e.g., amount, content, presentation medium)
	Nature of the injury
Justice system procedures	Standard of proof
	Decision rule
	Jury instructions (e.g., language/reading level, timing)
	Admonitions
	Juror note taking
	Juror question asking
	Pretrial publicity (e.g., court remedies)
	Bifurcation
	Damages caps
Trial advocacy methods	"Stealing thunder"
	Leading cross-examination questions
	Cross-examination of expert witnesses
	Presentation of character evidence
	Framing of damage award requests
	Opening statement tactics (including demonstrative/visual evidence)

Note. This listing is not intended to be exhaustive. It is intended to be illustrative and to further clarify the types of research topics that fall within each of the proposed research categories.

EFFECTS OF TRIAL ADVOCACY METHODS

A brief overview of empirical studies of trial advocacy methods helps to illustrate the type of contributions provided by this research. For example, researchers have shown that evidence presentation can influence jurors' perceptions of evidence, which can consequently affect key case decisions, including final verdicts. To be more specific, researchers interested in methods of minimizing the influence of damaging evidence about a witness tested the effects of a tactic referred to as *stealing thunder*, which consists of the witness or the witness's attorney presenting the damaging information before it is presented by opposing counsel (Dolnik, Case, & Williams, 2003; Williams et al., 1993). The stealing thunder strategy reduced the negative impact of damaging evidence about the defendant in a criminal trial and about an expert witness for the plaintiff in a civil trial. Specifically, use of this strategy resulted in a significantly higher probability of a verdict favorable to the side for which the target witness testified, significantly higher ratings of target witness convincingness, and significantly higher honesty ratings of the attorney who called the target witness. Subsequent research revealed that the stealing thunder strategy was effective, at least in part because mock jurors perceived the incriminating evidence as less damaging when it was presented by the witness before it was presented by opposing counsel (Dolnik et al., 2003). However, the positive effects of this strategy were negated when opposing counsel pointed out the tactic to the mock jurors.

Another trial advocacy method that has been empirically examined is cross-examination. For example, Kassin, Williams, and Saunders (1990) examined the strategy of using leading questions during the cross-examination of a witness. Specifically, mock jurors heard an attorney ask two questions of an opposing expert witness during cross-examination that implied something negative about the expert's reputation (i.e., "Isn't it true that your work is poorly regarded by your colleagues?" and "Hasn't your work been sharply criticized in the past?"). On average, mock jurors who heard these leading cross-exam questions provided significantly lower ratings of the expert's honesty, believability, competence, and persuasiveness than jurors who did not hear the leading questions. Furthermore, the negative effect of the leading questions on the expert's perceived credibility occurred even when the expert responded to the questions in the negative or when an objection by the opposing attorney (i.e., the attorney representing the side the expert was testifying on behalf of) was sustained.

Kovera and her colleagues (Austin & Kovera, 2015; Kovera, Levy, Borgida, & Penrod, 1994) conducted additional research on the cross-examination of expert witnesses, focusing on the cross-examination of psychological experts testifying about issues such as eyewitness testimony and interviewing child sex abuse victims. This research has shown that expert testimony about experimental studies is often more difficult for jurors to comprehend and recall than expert testimony based on anecdotal or case study evidence. Consequently, cross-examination intended to highlight shortcomings of experiments on which an expert is basing her or his opinions was most effective when the cross-examination included questions that educate jurors about basic criteria met by valid scientific studies.

Other researchers have examined whether the presentation of character evidence in criminal trials is an effective trial strategy. In one study, testimony by a character witness about a defendant's positive personality characteristics followed by cross-examination about specific bad acts by the defendant resulted in more negative judgments of the defendant than when no character evidence was presented (Hunt & Budesheim, 2004). There was no backlash against the defendant when the character witness for the defense was followed by a prosecution rebuttal witness (whose testimony was limited to general personality characteristics), rather than cross-examination of the character witness about specific bad acts by the defendant. Other research that examined the impact of evidence about the defendant's previous convictions found mixed results (Honess & Mathews, 2012). Whereas some mock jurors perceived the introduction of evidence about a defendant's previous convictions as an unfair tactic, jurors who engaged in heuristic processing of evidence were more likely to associate evidence of a defendant's previous conviction with higher confidence in the defendant's guilt in the present trial.

In the arena of civil trials, the strategy of basing damage award requests on lump sum requests versus different dollar/time quantifications has been examined (McAuliff & Bornstein, 2010). Interestingly, this preliminary study found that mock jurors awarded larger verdicts when the plaintiff requested a lump sum of $175,000 or $10/hour for 2 years (equivalent to $175,000) than when the plaintiff requested $7300/month or did not request any specific amount. Although this counterintuitive finding raises more questions than it answers about how jurors perceive damage award requests and determine final awards, the research still contributes to the field because it revealed gaps in our understanding of juror decision making.

The thing to note about these studies is that the experimental conditions within each examined essentially the same evidence. The difference among conditions in each study involved how the evidence was presented and how those differences in presentation affected mock jurors' perceptions of the case. Of course, advocacy techniques are used in opening statements and closing arguments as well as in the presentation of evidence. One empirical study of opening statements examined the effect of the prosecutor's response to a promise the defense attorney made in the opening statement that was not fulfilled by the later evidence (Pyszczynski, Greenberg, Mack, & Wrightsman, 1981). When the prosecutor failed to highlight that the defense attorney's promise was not fulfilled, the defendant was acquitted more often than when the prosecutor alerted the mock jurors in the government's closing argument that the defense attorney failed to fulfill the promise about the evidence in the opening statement.

These examples illustrate the breadth of topics that fall within the research category of trial advocacy methods. To date, however, substantially less research has been conducted on trial advocacy methods than on topics that fall under the categories of participant or case characteristics or legal system procedures. Expanding the breadth of juror decision-making research topics by conducting more research on trial advocacy methods would benefit the field of juror and jury decision making by enhancing our knowledge and increasing the relevance of the research to those outside the research field (e.g., attorneys, judges, policymakers).

WHY IS THERE NOT MORE RESEARCH ON TRIAL ADVOCACY METHODS?

One possible reason for the dearth of research on trial advocacy methods is the tendency for research to cluster around topics that have already received attention. Any particular research study typically raises questions about mediating and moderating variables as well as whether similar findings would be obtained in different geographical locations, with different materials, and/or with different research participants, eventually resulting in a collection of studies on a particular topic. The advantage of this sort of clustering is that a more complete understanding of a topic is obtained, depending on the amount, breadth, and quality of research. However, a disadvantage of this sort of clustering is that it often results in gaps in our knowledge of juror decision making. The challenge for any scientific field is to increase continually both the depth and breadth of knowledge in the field.

Another possible reason for less juror decision-making research on questions concerning trial advocacy methods than questions related to participant characteristics, case characteristics, and justice system procedures is that many psycholegal researchers have limited knowledge about the practice of law. The less familiar researchers are with what attorneys do in the course of litigation and preparing for trial, the more difficult it will be for those researchers to identify relevant research questions about legal practice and propose reasonable methods by which to gather data on those questions. Becoming familiar with the realities of legal practice takes time and effort, and training in the theory and methods of psycholegal research does not necessarily educate researchers about various ways to network and build relationships with attorneys and other legal professionals to develop this familiarity. The challenge for researchers of juror and jury decision making is to become familiar with various trial advocacy, or what lawyers may refer to as *legal practice*, methods and the reasons litigators use them and to acquire an understanding of relevant psychological theories and skills to conduct valid and reliable research.

A third possible reason for the lack of juror decision-making research to date on questions concerning trial advocacy methods is that researchers may fear that studying factors related to trial advocacy will cause them to be perceived as advocates or that they will become advocates. However, studying advocacy does not make one an advocate any more than studying bystander apathy makes one apathetic or studying psychopathy makes one a psychopath. Rather, developing a comprehensive understanding of juror decision making requires that all aspects of the decision-making task be empirically examined, including the use of various techniques designed to increase the plausibility and/or persuasiveness of certain information.

WHY IS TRIAL ADVOCACY RESEARCH IMPORTANT?

Researching trial advocacy methods is worthwhile because trial advocacy permeates the majority of information presented at trial. Although the judge decides what evidence can be admitted and the issues the jury has to decide, the trial attorneys have a primary role in many aspects of a case, including presenting opening statements and closing arguments, questioning witnesses, and introducing demonstrative exhibits designed to illustrate and highlight particular evidence. Through each of these legal procedures, attorneys use various techniques to advocate for their clients. Figure 3.1 illustrates the trial phases in which attorneys play a primary role.

Furthermore, the rules that govern attorney conduct require that when a lawyer is in the role of advocate, she or he "zealously asserts the client's position under the rules of the adversary system" (American Bar Association, 2016, para. 2). Consequently, in addition to lawsuits resulting from the opposing sides having different views of the evidence and conclusions to be drawn from it, it is possible that advocacy can result in the opposing attorneys and parties having further polarized views of a case. Cases involving parties and attorneys with the most polarized viewpoints are the ones that are most likely to proceed to trial and that jurors are asked to resolve. For example, in civil lawsuits in which the plaintiff is seeking monetary damages, the further apart the parties' valuation of the case is, the less likely it is that the parties will be able to successfully negotiate a pretrial settlement. In both

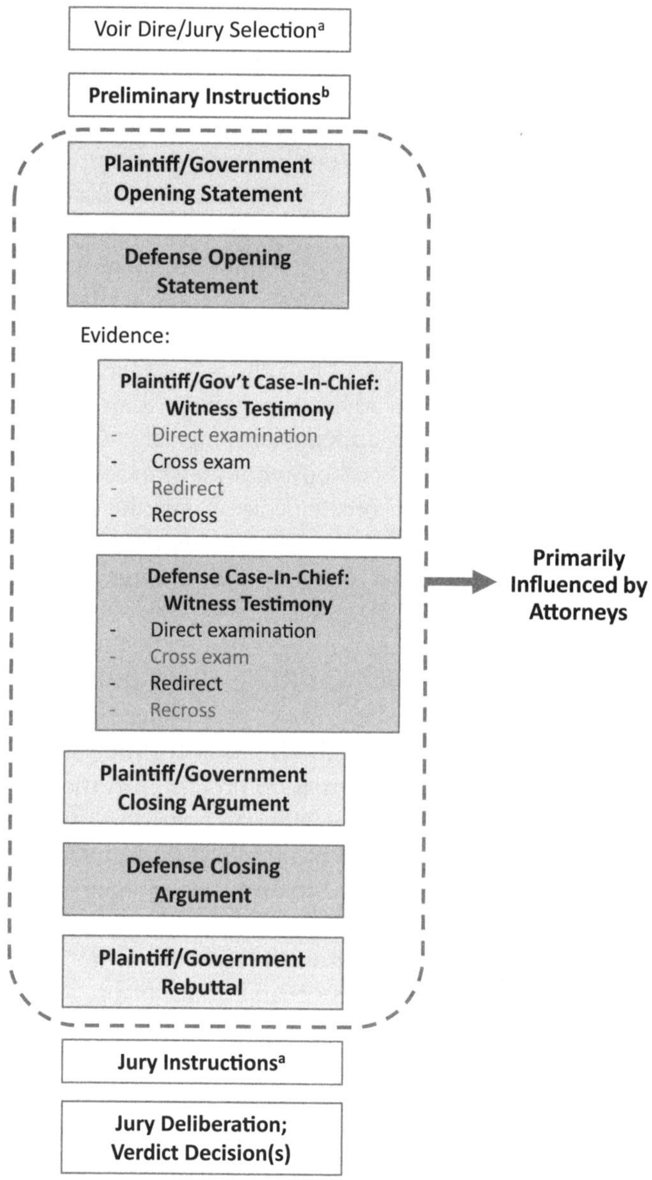

Figure 3.1. Steps in a jury trial.
[a]Attorneys can also play a role in voir dire and the drafting of preliminary and final jury instructions. The extent of the attorneys' role in these court procedures compared with that of other court professionals such as the judge and/or bailiff varies and is often determined by the presiding judge. [b]Preliminary instructions are instructions the judge gives to the jury at the beginning of some trials. Preliminary instructions may be used in either criminal or civil trials, or they may not be used at all. The purpose of preliminary instructions is to give the jury some "ground rules" for understanding the case they are about to hear.

criminal and civil cases, when opposing sides are able to reach a certain level of agreement about a case before trial, the case can be resolved without going to trial.

Trials are about persuasion. According to Lubet (2004), "persuasion is the trial lawyer's input designed to influence the judge or jury's output" (p. 31). Although the attorneys on each side of a case have the same set of facts, they present those facts in different ways. Trial attorneys highlight the facts favorable to their side, minimize or discredit facts unfavorable to their side, and present arguments and case themes throughout the trial that integrate all the evidence in a way they hope will persuade the jurors to find in favor of their side. Trial attorneys look to the aspects of trial over which they can exert some control to persuade jurors. Attorneys devote a great deal of time and energy developing the advocacy methods they will use in a case. Empirically examining the effect of those methods on juror decision making will provide a more comprehensive understanding of the decision-making processes of jurors. In addition, many advocacy methods are trial tactics to which the opposing side can respond with a countertactic. Research that examines the extended use of tactics and countertactics is essential to understanding juror decision making.

EXAMPLES OF TRIAL ADVOCACY METHODS THAT CAN BE EMPIRICALLY EXAMINED

Given that many psycholegal researchers have limited familiarity with particular advocacy methods that lawyers sometimes use in the course of litigation, a brief overview of some of these advocacy methods and some examples of research questions associated with them may be helpful in sparking further discussion and research on such issues.

Organizational Structure of Trial Information

One of the biggest challenges for litigators is to take a large amount of information, which often may be complex and sometimes may be associated with events spanning months or even years, and simplify it for the jurors. Techniques used to reduce the amount of information jurors must contend with (or at least remember) include identifying a handful of key themes and supplying jurors with an organizational structure that incorporates those themes and the supporting evidence. Organizational structures can be applied to a case at various levels, including the overall case (e.g., ordering of witnesses), the opening statement, the order of questions asked of any particular witness, and the closing argument.

The story model of juror decision making has been of interest to many psycholegal researchers as a method used by jurors to process trial information, presumably because of trial attorneys' frequent use of case "stories" and the model's potential to explain how jurors make verdict decisions. Empirical research that has compared mock juror verdicts in a case when the evidence was presented in story order (i.e., in chronological order as the events unfolded in the case) versus witness order has shown that mock jurors rated evidence presented in story order as stronger than the same evidence when presented in witness order (Pennington & Hastie, 1988). Researchers have traditionally defined a trial story, or narrative, as the presentation of case-related events and evidence in the temporal order in which they occurred, accompanied by descriptions of various parties' goals, actions, and consequences (see Pennington & Hastie, 1986). In the context of litigation strategy, the term *story* is often used to refer to a specific set of case themes that is emphasized by one side. Attorneys on each side of a case often create different stories based on the same set of evidence. For example, imagine a civil case in which a plaintiff claims the injury he sustained after using Company A's product is because Company A failed to warn users of dangers posed by the product when used for its intended purpose. The plaintiff may organize his case around case themes such as "Company A is greedy" and "Company A puts profits ahead of customer safety." In contrast, the defense case might be organized around a theme such as "The accident would have been avoided if the plaintiff had used the care and common sense that a reasonable person in his situation would have used."

When a case is complex or involves a great deal of evidence, a case story that simply presents events in chronological order might be limited in its ability to help jurors remember, effectively organize, and make sense of the evidence. Consequently, attorneys often use other methods of organizing trial information that may not be stories in the traditional sense but are designed with the intent to reduce the effort jurors must expend to track and remember the information. In addition to making the jurors' task easier, attorneys may decide to use other organizational structures because of the persuasive impact or the emotional reactions they believe such techniques will produce. Alternative "trial story" organizational structures include

- focusing on a key person or event and providing information that emanates from that focal point;
- grouping information by topic rather than by witness or chronologically;
- starting with the conclusion and then going backward in time;
- starting with an explanation of why the case is being litigated and the questions the jurors will be asked to answer followed by

information relevant to how they will answer them (see writings and talks by Simon Sinek, such as http://www.ted.com/talks/simon_sinek_how_great_leaders_inspire_action);

- ordering information strategically so that the strongest evidence and arguments are presented first and last and the weakest information is presented in the middle; and
- using a dramatic arc structure that incorporates emotion and includes exposition, rising action, climax, falling action, and then denouement (see writings and talks by Paul Zak, such as http://www.youtube.com/watch?v=q1a7tiA1Qzo).

Research that describes and categorizes various organizational or story structures would provide a good foundation for further research on how alternative organizational formats affect juror decision making. This research would likely begin with the task of collecting trial transcripts and trial stories from in-court observation and/or interviewing attorneys. This line of research could then be developed to examine the effect of different organizational structures (applied at the macro level in the overarching case story and key case themes, as well as more micro-level case components such as the opening statement and outlines for individual witness examinations) on measures such as jurors' attention, later recall of evidence and arguments, emotional reactions, and perceptions of attorneys, the parties, and other witnesses.

Over time, empirical research on various types of case stories or organizational structures might provide answers to questions such as whether there are particular characteristics associated with what jurors perceive as good or effective stories and whether there is an optimal number of themes to include in a story. Identifying standards of effectiveness against which themes can be judged is one potential line of research. For example, it has been proposed that for a case theme to be effective it has to be (a) able to be communicated easily, (b) memorable, (c) able to be applied to the case at a holistic level rather than to only subparts of the case, and (d) targeted at the jurors you have to persuade rather than the jurors that already favor your side (Broda-Bahm, 2008). Each of these standards presents one or more empirical questions. Other questions that could be examined include the effectiveness of defense stories that simply deny the plaintiff or prosecution story (e.g., "The plaintiff's evidence is purely circumstantial" or "The government cannot meet its burden of proof") compared with those that provide an alternative narrative or what might be referred to as a *counterscript*. Further research could explore how jurors process information when the opposing sides present competing stories.

In addition to the overall organizational structure of the case, attorneys also plan the order of questions they will ask of individual witnesses. One of the challenges faced by attorneys is how to deal with testimony that is likely to be perceived unfavorably for their side. One possible approach is to order information so that the unfavorable information is presented in the middle of the case (in terms of overall witness order) and/or in the middle of witness examination. Does this method work? If the unfavorable information is embarrassing or salient in some other way, perhaps jurors would be more likely to notice and remember it regardless of where in the trial it is presented. If so, the timing and context of where the information occurs in an argument or examination may not significantly affect memory for the information. Furthermore, if jurors perceive an attempt on the part of a witness or attorney to bury a bad fact, does this negatively affect credibility? Can the other side effectively counter an attempt to bury bad evidence by highlighting that evidence in their presentation—for example, by presenting it early or late in their presentation? All of these questions can and should be examined empirically.

Different organizational structures may also be more effective at different times in a trial depending on the task faced by jurors at the time. For example, a story structure may be more helpful and persuasive in the opening statement when jurors are unfamiliar with a case. At this point, a story structure might enhance jurors' attention and memory and may be an effective means for communicating alleged motivations and goals of key individuals in a case. In comparison, a legal-expository structure may be more persuasive in closing argument when jurors have been presented all the evidence in a case and face the task of applying the jury instructions to the evidence to determine a final verdict. Spiecker and Worthington (2003) examined the use of narrative and legal-expository organizational structures by the plaintiff and defense in opening and closing statements in a breach of contract case and found that, in terms of final responsibility apportionment and damage award decisions, the plaintiff benefited most from a mixed-format approach consisting of an opening statement in a narrative format and a closing argument in a legal-expository format. Interestingly, the most effective strategy for the defense involved a legal-expository format in both the opening statement and closing argument. Why would the plaintiff and defense differ in terms of the organizational approach that was most effective? Perhaps it is due, at least in part, to jurors' expectations about the type of argument each side will present. For example, perhaps jurors expect the defense to simply refute the plaintiff's evidence or arguments rather than present its own story. The fact that the plaintiff has the burden of proof may also play some role. If different organizational structures differ in effectiveness because of jurors' expectations, incorporating some measure of jurors' expectations into models of juror decision making may help improve the power of those models to explain accurately the juror decision-making process and predict final case beliefs and verdict decisions.

Repetition of Information

A technique that attorneys sometimes use to emphasize the importance of certain information is to devote more time to that information in the opening statement, witness questioning, and closing argument or to repeatedly address that information across witnesses as well as in opening statement and closing argument. This technique is based on the belief that the more times something is mentioned, the more likely it is that jurors will understand it, perceive it as important, believe it, and remember it (Lubet, 2004; Schwarz, 2004; Weaver, Garcia, Schwarz, & Miller, 2007). Empirical data are needed to test each of those beliefs. In addition, this technique has the possibility of backfiring, especially if it is overused. For example, repetition may lose effectiveness, assuming for the moment that the technique is at least somewhat effective, as the number of information items repeated increases. Even if only one or two items or case themes are repeated, are there possible negative effects of over-repetition such as boredom, reduced attention, or dislike of the attorney using the technique?

If one side uses the technique of repetition, can the other side negate possible positive effects of that repetition by use of countertechniques? In *The Jury Expert*, an online publication of the American Society of Trial Consultants, one consultant (Kellerman, 2013) proposed the following technique to counter opposing counsel's use of repetition to assert "a claim that in fact was unproven but *seems* to be a truthful fact because of the repetition" ("Turning Truthiness and Falsiness Into Nothingness," para. 3):

- label the tactic the opposing attorney is using as *repeating*,
- explain why the tactic may appear truthful but in reality is false,
- point out the weakness of evidence supporting the opposing attorney's claim or the complete lack of its presentation at trial,
- describe the opposing counsel's use of repetition as an attempt at distraction ("The opposing attorney is hoping you won't notice he or she has no evidence to support his or her claim and to refute ours"),
- warn jurors to put their guard up against the tactic ("Every time the opposing attorney repeats the claim, ask yourself 'where is the proof?'"), and
- provide your evidence ("Here is why he or she can't provide that evidence, because we've proven that ______").

What is the effect of this countertechnique on jurors' perceptions of the evidence, attorneys, and parties? Do each of the steps outlined contribute to the intended effect? Are there other countertechniques that might be used to address the technique of repetition by opposing counsel? These are all empirical questions, and results of well-designed and well-conducted research studies examining these questions will provide important answers and further our knowledge and understanding.

Gap Questions

Witnesses sometimes omit details in their testimony due to fatigue, anxiety, or some strategic decision. Sometimes the missed details, or *gaps*, are not important and other times they are. Examples of some types of information that would be considered important and that might be intentionally or accidentally left out of testimony include details concerning a defendant's whereabouts at a particular time that provide part of the defendant's alibi for an alleged crime, information relevant to the calculation of damages, and information relevant to an element of the legal claims that must be proven (Lubet, 2004). When an attorney notices gaps in the testimony provided by an opposing witness during direct examination, he or she might decide to ask the witness about those points on cross-examination, believing that the identification of gaps in the witness's testimony will negatively affect the witness's credibility in the eyes of the jurors. However, this technique has the potential to backfire.

The witness who faces these types of gap questions on cross-examination has the opportunity to fill in the gaps. Consequently, if the witness maintains a calm demeanor and answers the questions competently, the credibility of the witness might increase rather than decrease. Some attorneys recommend omitting any gap questions from cross-examination and instead highlighting gaps in the testimony of opposing witnesses only during closing argument. Waiting until closing argument to point out gaps in a witness's testimony, however, could be risky. Jurors sometimes fill in gaps in evidence on their own (Smith & Studebaker, 1996). Longer amounts of time between a witness's incomplete testimony and closing arguments may be associated with a higher likelihood that jurors would fill in evidence gaps before the closing arguments. It is also possible that gaps in witness testimony influence juror verdict decisions differently depending on the witness. Gaps in the testimony of government or plaintiff witnesses may be more likely to result in jurors concluding that the burden of proof has not been met, therefore, increasing the likelihood of a defense verdict. In contrast, gaps in the testimony of defense witnesses may be more likely to result in jurors concluding that the defense did not sufficiently defend against the claims. Empirical examination of the influence of gaps in testimony, whether attorneys ask gap questions as part of cross-examination, and a witness's responses to gap questions would provide important contributions to our knowledge of juror decision making.

Arousal of Juror Emotion

Trials can evoke a range of emotions in jurors. For example, jurors may feel sympathy for a plaintiff because of physical, financial, or emotional harm the plaintiff has experienced. Actions of corporate or criminal defendants that are alleged to have caused harm to others can arouse feelings of anger or disgust on the part of jurors. In addition, learning about danger associated with unsafe products or criminal acts in their community can cause jurors to be fearful. In addition to emotional reactions that might result from neutral presentations of evidence, emotional reactions of jurors might be amplified due to the way attorneys present case themes and arguments. A relatively recent book by trial consultant David Ball and attorney Don Keenan (2009) is devoted to teaching plaintiff attorneys how to arouse jurors' fear by developing case themes based on the idea that the defendant's behavior unnecessarily endangered the safety of the plaintiff as well as the safety of the larger community. Recommended strategies for countering this technique include educating jurors about plaintiff counsel's use of the technique, educating jurors about the realistic complexity of decisions faced by the defendant, and incorporating some humor into the trial (Bennett, 2009; Broda-Bahm, 2013), yet there is no empirical evidence that these strategies are effective.

Although the role of juror emotion in juror decision making has received some attention (see Bright & Goodman-Delahunty, 2006; Feigenson & Park, 2006; Semmler & Brewer, 2002), the use of emotion as an advocacy technique has received little empirical attention. In addition to the development of arguments and case themes intended to influence juror emotional reactions in ways that increase or decrease persuasion by one side or the other, trial attorneys can incorporate demonstrative evidence and exhibits into trial presentations that may have stronger influences on juror emotions than witness testimony alone. Empirical research designed to examine the role of various emotional reactions (e.g., anger, sympathy, fear) on juror decision making would contribute to our overall understanding of juror decision making. In addition, empirical research that examines emotional reactions to visual information including photographs and videos (e.g., day-in-the-life videos) and demonstrative exhibits (which are not evidence) would also add to our knowledge. Another empirical question is whether jurors' memory for, and evaluation of, witness testimony differs when the testimony is accompanied by visual information that provokes an emotional response compared with the same witness testimony presented without visual information.

Research on techniques to diffuse or minimize emotion would also contribute to our understanding of juror decision making. When attorneys suspect that jurors' emotional reactions are associated with unfavorable perceptions of their case, they may attempt to minimize or change those emotions or attribute the emotions to a different source that may alter their attributions of blame. An important contribution of research on trial advocacy techniques designed to influence jurors' emotional reactions one way or another will be a better understanding of how juror emotions mediate or moderate verdict decision making.

A COMMENT ON DEPENDENT MEASURES

Empirical research on juror and jury decision making routinely includes dependent measures of final verdicts and damage awards. Other measures such as witness credibility, persuasiveness ratings, or strength-of-evidence ratings are also sometimes included. To measure the influence of advocacy methods on juror decision-making processes and outcomes, a collection of dependent measures that allows for an examination and comparison of jurors' perceptions of each side of the case is called for. These dependent measures include

- strength-of-evidence ratings (overall for each side/party as well as ratings of individual evidence items),
- verdict shifts over time (across witnesses, over the course of direct examination and cross-examination),
- credibility ratings of attorneys and witnesses on each side,
- memory measures such as recall or recognition of evidence items that allow assessment of the amount and overall accuracy of information remembered,
- interpretation of (ambiguous) evidence items to determine whether the interpretation tends to favor one side or the other,
- methods of filling information gaps (e.g., do the "fillers" tend to favor one side or the other, or are they neutral?), and
- cognitive organizational structures such as overarching case narratives.

The decision-making task faced by jurors is often difficult. As stated earlier, the cases that end up going to trial rather than settling before trial are those that are likely to involve the most polarized views of the evidence, despite the fact that both sides have to deal with the same set of evidence. In addition, the cases that go to trial and that jurors must decide may be more likely to be evenly matched in terms of the strength of evidence and arguments expected to be presented by each side. In addition, jurors are likely to have both rational and emotional reactions to the evidence presented. Consequently, jury decision-making research that includes multiple measures of jurors' reactions to a case in addition to final verdicts can provide a more comprehensive understanding of the juror decision-making process.

LEARNING ABOUT LEGAL PRACTICE AND TRIAL ADVOCACY

In the course of their training on research methods, social science researchers in the field of juror and jury decision making often receive little information about how attorneys prepare for and conduct litigation. Some ways that researchers can become more familiar with litigation procedures in general as well as specific advocacy methods include the following:

- Observe real trials. Many students become interested in juror and jury decision making because of movies, television shows, or other popular media. But the trial procedures and litigation methods described in popular media can be inaccurate or atypical. Observing a variety of real trials can help researchers begin to separate fact from fiction and to become more familiar with various advocacy methods that raise empirical questions related to juror and jury decision making. Trials are public hearings, and members of the public are allowed to observe. With certain limited exceptions, each step of the judicial process is open to the public. Individuals who wish to observe a court in session may go to the courthouse, check the court calendar, and watch a proceeding (for more information on observing trials in federal court, see http://www.uscourts.gov/FederalCourts/UnderstandingtheFederalCourts/FederalCourtsAndThePublic.aspx).
- Read books, Internet articles, blogs, and other sources that provide information about trial advocacy techniques. Attorneys share information about litigation and trial advocacy methods in many resources that are available to the public. In addition to books and articles designed to help attorneys develop and fine-tune their litigation skills, video tutorials and seminars can be found online. Another source of information that focuses on advocacy methods designed to improve the clarity and persuasiveness of evidence is *The Jury Expert*, an online publication of the American Society of Trial Consultants (see http://www.thejuryexpert.com).
- Talk to, and more importantly listen to, litigation attorneys. Seek out opportunities to hear litigation attorneys talk about preparing for trial and going to trial. You might be able to attend a talk at a local bar association meeting or a continuing legal education seminar. You could also invite an attorney with litigation experience to give a guest lecture to social science researchers or to be part of a symposium or panel at a social science conference. Through personal connections or networking, you can seek out opportunities to speak one-on-one with

attorneys. When you hear attorneys talk about litigation, listen to how they talk about cases, trial strategy, and the aspects of litigation over which they do and do not have control. Learn to translate the ideas and concepts communicated by attorneys so that you can speak about them in social science research terms as well as legal terms.

- Talk to people who work closely with litigation attorneys (i.e., paralegals and trial consultants). Making contact with litigation attorneys can be challenging because of their busy schedules and demands on their time. Other people who have experience preparing for litigation include paralegals and trial consultants. These groups also have professional association meetings and educational seminars that researchers can attend.

Juror and jury decision making have many unique features compared with other types of decision making, not the least of which is the adversarial presentation of evidence and arguments by opposing attorneys. Yet, adversarial methods have received relatively little attention in empirical studies of juror and jury decision making. This limits our understanding of juror and jury decision making and the circumstances that may significantly increase the likelihood of an erroneous or impermissibly biased verdict decision. The empirical examination of adversarial methods is an important part of working to improve jurors' and juries' abilities to make fair decisions in the cases submitted to them.

REFERENCES

American Bar Association. (2016). *Model rules of professional conduct: Preamble and Scope*. Retrieved from http://www.americanbar.org/groups/professional_responsibility/publications/model_rules_of_professional_conduct/model_rules_of_professional_conduct_preamble_scope.html

Austin, J. L., & Kovera, M. B. (2015). Cross-examination educates jurors about missing control groups in scientific evidence. *Psychology, Public Policy, and Law, 21*, 252–264. http://dx.doi.org/10.1037/law0000049

Ball, D., & Keenan, D. (2009). *Reptile: The 2009 manual of the plaintiff's revolution*. New York, NY: Balloon Press.

Bennett, M. (2009). *Lizards don't laugh*. Retrieved from http://www.blog.bennettandbennett.com/2009/11/lizards-dont-laugh.html

Bornstein, B. H. (1999). The ecological validity of jury simulations: Is the jury still out? *Law and Human Behavior, 23*, 75–91. http://dx.doi.org/10.1023/A:1022326807441

Bornstein, B. H., & McCabe, S. G. (2005). Jurors of the absurd? The role of consequentiality in jury simulation research. *Florida State University Law Review, 32*, 443–467.

Bottoms, B. L., Golding, J. M., Stevenson, M. C., Wiley, T. R. A., & Yozwiak, J. A. (2007). A review of factors affecting jurors' decisions in child sexual abuse cases. In M. P. Toglia, D. J. Read, D. F. Ross, & R. C. L. Lindsay (Eds.), *The handbook of eyewitness psychology: Vol 1. Memory for events* (pp. 509–543). Mahwah, NJ: Erlbaum.

Breau, D. L., & Brook, B. (2007). "Mock" mock juries: A field experiment on the ecological validity of jury simulations. *Law & Psychology Review, 31*, 77–92.

Bright, D. A., & Goodman-Delahunty, J. (2006). Gruesome evidence and emotion: Anger, blame, and jury decision-making. *Law and Human Behavior, 30*, 183–202. http://dx.doi.org/10.1007/s10979-006-9027-y

Broda-Bahm, K. (2008). Getting beyond the catchy phrase and creating a trial theme that truly works. *The Jury Expert*. Retrieved from http://www.thejuryexpert.com/2008/07/getting-beyond-the-catchy-phrase-and-creating-a-trial-theme-that-truly-works/

Broda-Bahm, K. (2013). Taming the reptile: A defendants' response to the plaintiff's revolution. *The Jury Expert*. Retrieved from http://www.thejuryexpert.com/2013/11/taming-the-reptile-a-defendants-response-to-the-plaintiffs-revolution/

Devine, D. J. (2012). *Jury decision making: The state of the science*. New York: New York University Press.

Devine, D. J., & Caughlin, D. (2014). Do they matter? A meta-analytic investigation of individual characteristics and guilt judgments. *Psychology, Public Policy, and Law, 20*, 109–134. http://dx.doi.org/10.1037/law0000006

Devine, D. J., Clayton, L. D., Dunford, B. B., Seying, R., & Pryce, J. (2001). Jury decision making: 45 years of empirical research on deliberating groups. *Psychology, Public Policy, and Law, 7*, 622–727.

Diamond, S. S., Casper, J. D., Heiert, C. L., & Marshall, A. (1996). Juror reactions to attorneys at trial. *The Journal of Criminal Law & Criminology, 87*, 17–47. http://dx.doi.org/10.2307/1143971

Diamond, S. S., Rose, M. R., Murphy, B., & Meixner, J. (2011). Damage anchors on real juries. *Journal of Empirical Legal Studies, 8*, 148–178. http://dx.doi.org/10.1111/j.1740-1461.2011.01232.x

Dolnik, L., Case, T. I., & Williams, K. D. (2003). Stealing thunder as a courtroom tactic revisited: Processes and boundaries. *Law and Human Behavior, 27*, 267–287. http://dx.doi.org/10.1023/A:1023431823661

Ellsworth, P. C. (1999). Jury reform at the end of the century: Real agreement, real changes. *University of Michigan Journal of Law Reform, 32*, 213–225.

Feigenson, N., & Park, J. (2006). Emotions and attributions of legal responsibility and blame: A research review. *Law and Human Behavior, 30*, 143–161. http://dx.doi.org/10.1007/s10979-006-9026-z

Hans, V. P., & Albertson, S. (2003). Empirical research and civil jury reform. *The Notre Dame Law Review, 78*, 1497–1523.

Hastie, R. (Ed.). (1993). *Inside the juror: The psychology of juror decision making.* http://dx.doi.org/10.1017/CBO9780511752896

Heuer, L., & Penrod, S. (1994). Juror note taking and question asking during trials: A national field experiment. *Law and Human Behavior, 18*, 121–150. http://dx.doi.org/10.1007/BF01499012

Honess, T. M., & Mathews, G. A. (2012). Admitting evidence of a defendant's previous conviction (PCE) and its impact on juror deliberation in relation to both juror-processing style and juror concerns over the fairness of introducing PCE. *Legal and Criminological Psychology, 17*, 360–379. http://dx.doi.org/10.1111/j.2044-8333.2011.02019.x

Hoolihan, J. W. (2014). What jurors think about attorneys. *Bench & Bar of Minnesota.* http://mnbenchbar.com/2014/02/what-jurors-think-about-attorneys/

Horowitz, I. A., & Bordens, K. S. (1990). An experimental investigation of procedural issues in complex tort trials. *Law and Human Behavior, 14*, 269–285. http://dx.doi.org/10.1007/BF01352753

Hunt, J. S., & Budesheim, T. L. (2004). How jurors use and misuse character evidence. *Journal of Applied Psychology, 89*, 347–361. http://dx.doi.org/10.1037/0021-9010.89.2.347

Kassin, S. M., Williams, L. N., & Saunders, C. L. (1990). Dirty tricks of cross-examination: The influence of conjectural evidence on the jury. *Law and Human Behavior, 14*, 373–384. http://dx.doi.org/10.1007/BF01068162

Kellerman, K. (2013). Trial advocacy: Truthiness, falsiness, and nothingness. *The Jury.* Retrieved from http://www.thejuryexpert.com/2013/11/trial-advocacy-truthiness-falseness-and-nothingness/

Kerr, N. (1993). Stochastic models of juror decision making. In R. Hastie (Ed.), *Inside the juror* (pp. 116–135). http://dx.doi.org/10.1017/CBO9780511752896.007

Kovera, M. B., Levy, R. J., Borgida, E., & Penrod, S. D. (1994). Expert witnesses in child sexual abuse cases: Effects of expert evidence type and cross-examination. *Law and Human Behavior, 18*, 653–674. http://dx.doi.org/10.1007/BF01499330

Krauss, D. A., & Sales, B. D. (2001). The effects of clinical and scientific expert testimony on juror decision making in capital sentencing. *Psychology, Public Policy, and Law, 7*, 267–310. http://dx.doi.org/10.1037/1076-8971.7.2.267

Lubet, S. (2004). *Modern trial advocacy: Analysis and practice* (3rd ed.). South Bend, IN: NITA.

Mazzella, R., & Feingold, A. (1994). The effects of physical attractiveness, race, socioeconomic status, and gender of defendants and victims on judgments of mock jurors: A meta-analysis. *Journal of Applied Social Psychology, 24*, 1315–1338. http://dx.doi.org/10.1111/j.1559-1816.1994.tb01552.x

McAuliff, B. D., & Bornstein, B. H. (2010). All anchors are not created equal: The effects of per diem versus lump sum requests on pain and suffering awards. *Law and Human Behavior, 34*, 164–174. http://dx.doi.org/10.1007/s10979-009-9178-8

Ostrom, T. M., Werner, C., & Saks, M. J. (1978). An integration theory analysis of jurors' presumptions of guilt or innocence. *Journal of Personality and Social Psychology, 36*, 436–450. http://dx.doi.org/10.1037/0022-3514.36.4.436

Pennington, N., & Hastie, R. (1986). Evidence evaluation in complex decision making. *Journal of Personality and Social Psychology, 51*, 242–258. http://dx.doi.org/10.1037/0022-3514.51.2.242

Pennington, N., & Hastie, R. (1988). Explanation-based decision making: Effects of memory structure on judgment. *Journal of Experimental Psychology: Learning, Memory, and Cognition, 14*, 521–533. http://dx.doi.org/10.1037/0278-7393.14.3.521

Pennington, N., & Hastie, R. (1991). A cognitive theory of juror decision making: The story model. *Cardozo Law Review, 13*, 519–558.

Pyszczynski, T. A., Greenberg, J., Mack, D., & Wrightsman, L. S. (1981). Opening statements in a jury trial: The effect of promising more than the evidence will show. *Journal of Applied Social Psychology, 11*, 434–444. http://dx.doi.org/10.1111/j.1559-1816.1981.tb00834.x

Schum, D. A., & Martin, A. W. (1982). Formal and empirical research on cascaded inference in jurisprudence. *Law & Society Review, 17*, 105–151. http://dx.doi.org/10.2307/3053534

Schwarz, N. (2004). Meta-cognitive experiences in consumer judgment and decision making. *Journal of Consumer Psychology, 14*, 332–348. http://dx.doi.org/10.1207/s15327663jcp1404_2

Semmler, C., & Brewer, N. (2002). Effects of mood and emotion on juror processing and judgments. *Behavioral Sciences & the Law, 20*, 423–436. http://dx.doi.org/10.1002/bsl.502

Smith, V. L. (1991). Impact of pretrial instruction on jurors' information processing and decision making. *Journal of Applied Psychology, 76*, 220–228. http://dx.doi.org/10.1037/0021-9010.76.2.220

Smith, V. L., & Studebaker, C. A. (1996). What do you expect? The influence of people's prior knowledge of crime categories on fact-finding. *Law and Human Behavior, 20*, 517–532. http://dx.doi.org/10.1007/BF01499039

Sommers, S. R., & Ellsworth, P. C. (2000). Race in the courtroom: Perceptions of guilt and dispositional attributions. *Personality and Social Psychology Bulletin, 26*, 1367–1379. http://dx.doi.org/10.1177/0146167200263005

Spiecker, S. C., & Worthington, D. L. (2003). The influence of opening statement/closing argument organizational strategy on juror verdict and damage awards. *Law and Human Behavior, 27*, 437–456. http://dx.doi.org/10.1023/A:1024041201605

Steblay, N. M., Besirevic, J., Fulero, S. M., & Jimenez-Lorente, B. (1999). The effects of pretrial publicity on juror verdicts: A meta-analytic review. *Law and Human Behavior, 23*, 219–235. http://dx.doi.org/10.1023/A:1022325019080

Studebaker, C. A., & Penrod, S. D. (1997). Pretrial publicity: The media, the law, and common sense. *Psychology, Public Policy, and Law, 3*, 428–460. http://dx.doi.org/10.1037/1076-8971.3.2-3.428

Visher, C. A. (1987). Juror decision making: The importance of evidence. *Law and Human Behavior, 11*, 1–17. http://dx.doi.org/10.1007/BF01044835

Weaver, K., Garcia, S. M., Schwarz, N., & Miller, D. T. (2007). Inferring the popularity of an opinion from its familiarity: A repetitive voice can sound like a chorus. *Journal of Personality and Social Psychology, 92*, 821–833. http://dx.doi.org/10.1037/0022-3514.92.5.821

Wiener, R. L., Krauss, D. A., & Lieberman, J. D. (2011). Mock jury research: Where do we go from here? *Behavioral Sciences & the Law, 29*, 467–479. http://dx.doi.org/10.1002/bsl.989

Williams, K. D., Bourgeois, M. J., & Croyle, R. T. (1993). The effects of stealing thunder in criminal and civil trials. *Law and Human Behavior, 17*, 597–609.

Wood, S. M., Sicafuse, L. L., Miller, M. K., & Chomos, J. C. (2011). The influence of jurors' perception of attorneys and their performance on verdict. *The Jury Expert*. Retrieved from http://www.thejuryexpert.com/wp-content/uploads/Woodetal.TJEJan2011Vol23Num1.pdf

4

STUDYING THE EFFECTS OF RACE, ETHNICITY, AND CULTURE ON JURY BEHAVIOR

JENNIFER S. HUNT

Equality before the law is considered a basic human right throughout much of the world. The 14th Amendment to the United States Constitution states that no person can be denied the equal protection of the law. Section 15 of the Canadian Charter of Rights and Freedoms (1982) dictates, "Every individual is equal before and under the law and has the right to the equal protection and equal benefit of the law without discrimination" (Government of Canada, 2016). Protocol No. 12 of the European Convention for the Protection of Human Rights and Fundamental Freedoms (2000; Council of Europe, 2016) asserts that equality before the law and equal protection of law are "fundamental principles," and freedom from discrimination in legal contexts is included in the United Nations (1948) Universal Declaration of Human Rights. Implicit in these assertions is that people deserve not only fairness in legal outcomes but also equal access to participation in legal contexts, such as jury service.

http://dx.doi.org/10.1037/0000026-005
The Psychology of Juries, M. B. Kovera (Editor)

Despite these protections, both individual cases and aggregate data suggest that race and ethnicity influence the administration of justice, including trial outcomes and access to participation in the legal system (see Hunt, 2015b, for a review). To illustrate the influence of race on jury decision making and trial outcomes, consider recent cases in Florida involving controversial stand your ground laws (Justifiable Use of Force, 2005). Stand your ground laws allow individuals to use force against others, including deadly force, instead of retreating if they believe their lives are in danger, providing a defense in a criminal trial or even immunity from prosecution. However, many argue that race plays a role in the way that prosecutors, jurors, and judges evaluate stand your ground claims. For example, a Black woman named Marissa Alexander was convicted of aggravated assault for firing a single warning shot into a wall in the direction of her husband, who she claimed was trying to strangle her. Although Alexander had an order for protection and did not injure anyone, a jury rejected her stand your ground claim after 12 minutes of deliberation. She received a 20-year sentence before accepting a plea deal during the appeals process (Frumin, 2014). In contrast, a jury acquitted George Zimmerman on the basis of a stand your ground argument in the shooting death of a Black teenager, which occurred under arguably less threatening circumstances. Zimmerman, a neighborhood watch volunteer, initiated contact with Trayvon Martin because he thought the teen looked "suspicious" as he walked through his neighborhood wearing a hoodie. During the ensuing altercation, he shot and killed the unarmed youth (Alvarez & Buckley, 2013). An analysis of 192 cases confirmed that race influences the effectiveness of stand your ground arguments, with fewer charges and higher rates of acquittal for individuals who kill Black rather than White victims (Martin, Hundley, & Humburg, 2012). Thus, prosecutors and jurors may place a higher value on the lives of White individuals or at least have more skepticism about whether their deaths were justified.

Race, ethnicity, and cultural background also may influence access to and experiences during jury service. Despite the prohibitions established by *Batson v. Kentucky* (1986) and subsequent cases (e.g., *Miller-El v. Dretke*, 2005; *Snyder v. Louisiana*, 2007), racial and ethnic minorities are more likely than Whites to be excused during the jury selection process (e.g., Baldus, Woodworth, Zuckerman, Weiner, & Broffitt, 2001; Equal Justice Initiative, 2010). Further, even when minorities are selected for juries, they may experience negative treatment or other barriers to full participation (e.g., Hunt, 2014b). For example, a jury of six women, five Whites and one Puerto Rican decided the George Zimmerman case. Following Zimmerman's acquittal, many commentators raised the question of whether the verdict would have been the same if the jury had included Black people. Further, in interviews following the trial, the Puerto Rican juror indicated that she was confused by the U.S. legal system and intimidated by the attorneys, and she felt belittled and excluded by the other jurors (Bloom, 2014).

Thus, equal protection of law may be more of an ideal than a reality for both defendants and jurors. Although there is a growing literature examining the influence of race on jury processes and decisions, an important goal for the future is to expand both the breadth and depth of this work. In this chapter, I review the existing literature on race and jurors. I then propose an agenda for future research on the ways in which (a) the race and ethnicity of the defendant and other trial parties influence jurors' judgments and (b) the race, ethnicity, and culture of jurors influence their judgments and behaviors during jury service. Key elements of this agenda include expanding the groups and cases studied, focusing more on underlying psychological processes, developing more comprehensive theoretical models, giving greater emphasis to the influence of culture, increasing attention to complex interactions between variables, and developing interventions to help promote equality in both trial process and outcomes.

A BRIEF REVIEW OF THE EXISTING LITERATURE

Several decades of research, consisting of both experimental and archival studies, have revealed numerous ways in which race influences jurors' judgments. Although there has been substantially less research on these issues, race also affects jury selection and the dynamics of jury deliberation. In this section, I briefly review the major findings from this body of research; for a more thorough review, see Hunt (2015b).

Effects of Race on Juror Judgments

Defendant race influences verdicts, sentencing decisions, and other trial judgments made by jurors. In experimental research, there is consistent support for a similarity–leniency effect, in which mock jurors render more favorable judgments for ingroup (same race) defendants or, conversely, make harsher judgments of outgroup (other race) defendants. Meta-analyses show that the overall similarity–leniency effect in verdicts tends to be small but can vary considerably across trial contexts (Devine & Caughlin, 2014; Mitchell, Haw, Pfeifer, & Meissner, 2005). For example, bias against outgroup defendants tends to be larger when White jurors make judgments about Latino defendants and Black jurors make judgments about White defendants than when White jurors make judgments about Black defendants. There are several potential reasons for these differences (Hunt, 2015a); White jurors may be more willing to express bias against Latino than Black defendants, and Black jurors may be trying to correct for the possibility of institutional bias in cases involving Black defendants (Sommers & Adekanmbi, 2008). Notably, patterns consistent with the similarity–leniency effect also are seen in deliberating juries, such that juries with higher proportions of White jurors are more likely to convict minority defendants (e.g., Perez, Hosch, Ponder, & Trejo, 1993).

Race may affect verdicts by influencing intermediate judgments about the defendant and evidence, such as the attributions or explanations that jurors make for a defendant's behaviors. Jurors are more likely to make internal attributions, inferring that criminal behavior is the result of stable personal characteristics (e.g., dispositions), when the defendant is an outgroup member; in contrast, they are more likely to make external attributions, explaining criminal behavior with reference to situational factors, when the defendant is an ingroup member (e.g., Sommers & Ellsworth, 2000). Jurors also may interpret trial evidence in a manner that makes them more likely to see minority defendants as guilty. For instance, White jurors are more likely to consider damaging inadmissible evidence when cases involve Black rather than White defendants (Hodson, Hooper, Dovidio, & Gaertner, 2005) and to judge defense witnesses to be less reliable than prosecution witnesses when the defendants are Black (Abshire & Bornstein, 2003).

However, the effects of race on jurors' judgments are complex and moderated by several factors. To give only a few examples, defendant race has a stronger effect on judgments when crimes are stereotypically associated with the defendant's racial group—for example, when Black defendants are accused of homicide or when White defendants are accused of embezzlement (e.g., Jones & Kaplan, 2003). Jurors also make harsher judgments about minority defendants when the victims of crimes are White (e.g., Mazzella & Feingold, 1994). Bias in juror judgments is stronger when judicial instructions are not provided (e.g., Mitchell et al., 2005) and when trials are racially charged (Sommers & Ellsworth, 2000, 2001).

Archival analyses of death penalty cases consistently demonstrate that jurors are more likely to give the death penalty in cases in which a Black or Latino defendant is convicted of killing a White victim (e.g., Baldus, Brain, Weiner, & Woodworth, 2009; S. L. Johnson, Blume, Eisenberg, Hans, & Wells, 2012). This pattern persists even after controlling for dozens of factors related to the crime, the defendant, and other relevant issues. As with verdicts, racial and ethnic minority defendants are more likely to receive the death penalty when juries have a higher proportion of White individuals. For example, Bowers, Steiner, and Sandys (2001) found that Black defendants in capital cases were 41% more likely to receive the death penalty when juries included five or more White men (*White male dominance* pattern), and they were 34% more likely to be sentenced to death when there were no Black men on their juries (*Black male presence* pattern). Disparities in capital sentences may reflect a number of processes, including racial prejudice, negative stereotypes about the criminality and dangerousness of minorities, and dispositional attributions about criminal behavior by minorities (for a review, see Lynch & Haney, 2011). Further, jurors may underutilize evidence about mitigating factors (i.e., factors that argue against the death penalty) in cases with Black defendants and White victims (Baldus, Broffitt, Weiner, Woodworth, & Zuckerman, 1998; Lynch & Haney, 2009).

Effects of Race on Jury Participation and Behavior

Race also has an impact on the experiences of jurors and potential jurors. Racial and ethnic minorities may be underrepresented in the jury pools of many communities (e.g., Fukurai & Krooth, 2003; Hannaford-Agor & Waters, 2011). Once called, minorities are less likely to be selected for juries, especially by prosecutors (Baldus et al., 2001; Equal Justice Initiative, 2010). In *Batson v. Kentucky* (1986), the U.S. Supreme Court held that attorneys may not use peremptory challenges to excuse venire members because of their race. *Batson* and subsequent cases (e.g., *Miller-El v. Dretke*, 2005; *Snyder v. Louisiana*, 2007) established a procedure for challenging potentially race-based peremptories and provided guidelines for trial judges to use in evaluating them. Yet attorneys continue to use peremptory challenges in a discriminatory manner (Baldus et al., 2001; Equal Justice Initiative, 2010) and easily generate race-neutral explanations for dismissing Black venire members (Sommers & Norton, 2007). Thus, legal challenges to the use of race-based peremptories rarely are successful (Gabbidon, Kowal, Jordan, Roberts, & Vincenzi, 2008).

There are several problems associated with racial bias in jury selection. Nonrepresentative jury pools and race-based peremptory challenges may deprive racial and ethnic minorities of the opportunity to participate in the legal system by serving on a jury. Also, when juries are nonrepresentative, the public has less confidence that court systems use fair procedures and generate just outcomes (Diamond & Ellis, 2003; Fukurai & Krooth, 2003). Finally, minority defendants are less likely to be convicted and given harsh sentences when juries are more diverse (Bowers et al., 2001; Perez et al., 1993); thus, empirical evidence supports the importance of having "a jury of one's peers."

In fact, racial diversity influences jury dynamics, improving the quality of deliberation and the fairness of verdicts. Sommers (2006) experimentally created mock juries that consisted of either six White jurors or four White and two Black jurors. The jurors deliberated after hearing a criminal trial involving a Black defendant. The diverse juries deliberated longer, discussed more evidence, and made fewer errors when discussing the evidence. In addition, the presence of Black jurors appeared to sensitize White jurors to the potential influence of race on the case, with diverse juries more likely than all-White juries to explicitly discuss race during deliberations. Thus, juror race can affect the content and process of jury deliberations, with beneficial outcomes associated with racially diverse juries.

A RESEARCH AGENDA

As seen in this brief review, researchers have established a solid foundation of knowledge about the effects of race on jury decision making and, to a much smaller extent, documented the interplay between race, ethnicity, and jury behavior. However, considerably more research is needed on both topics. Although race and ethnicity are, to a greater or lesser extent, relevant factors in every trial, those factors are examined in only a small percentage of jury research. A series of searches in the American Psychological Association's PsycNET conducted in May 2014 found that, out of 1,631 peer-reviewed journal articles, books, and chapters with the keyword *juries*, only 101 (6.19%) included the words *race* or *ethnicity* in the abstract or keywords. Similar searches on Academic Search Premier, which indexes a broader range of fields, found an even smaller proportion of jury scholarship focused on race or ethnicity (160 out of 4341 or 3.68%). Although these searches likely missed a few papers that address race or ethnicity in some way, they clearly illustrate the fact that only a small number of jury studies emphasize the role of race and ethnicity.

Thus, what we know about the effects of race and ethnicity on juries may be the proverbial tip of the iceberg. A deeper, more thorough, and more systematic examination of the interplay between race, juror decision making, and jury behavior is clearly an important goal. To this end, I propose a research agenda to build a more comprehensive empirical and theoretical understanding of the effects of race, ethnicity, and culture on juries.

This agenda borrows a framework that is commonly used in research on gender. Deaux (1984) identified three major approaches to the study of gender. One approach involves examining gender as a social category—that is, an organizing framework that affects the way people perceive, judge, evaluate, and behave toward others. These effects often are labeled *target* or *object* effects because a person is the target or recipient of certain treatment on the basis of his or her gender. A second approach involves gender as a subject variable—that is, a factor that influences people's traits, beliefs, and behaviors. These effects often are referred to as *subject* or *actor* effects because they examine gender as an internalized system that influences the characteristics of individuals and the ways in which they experience and act on the external environment. The third approach is similar to the second, except that it focuses on individual differences in masculinity, femininity, and/or androgyny rather than broad gender categories.

This framework provides a useful way to think about and organize a research agenda for work on race and juries. Research on *target effects*, which is the majority of current research, examines how judgments made by jurors and other legal actors vary on the basis of the race or ethnicity of defendants, victims, and other parties. Research on *subject effects* addresses the ways in which the race and ethnicity of jurors influence their beliefs, perspectives, and judgments, as well as their behaviors in legal contexts (e.g., deliberation behavior). The *individual differences* approach emphasizes the variability that occurs within broad race and ethnic groups, as well as the understanding of the psychological processes that drive those differences. This approach focuses on examining the influence of cultural variables (e.g., individualism and collectivism) and practices that may lead to differences between and within groups of jurors.

In the remainder of this chapter, I discuss important issues to study in future jury research related to both target and subject effects. Reflecting its conceptual similarity, as well as the limited research in the area, I discuss culture as part of the section on subject effects. I also address the importance of studying interactions between variables and the development of interventions as important directions for future jury research related to race.

Target Effects

Research on target effects investigates the influence of race and ethnicity on judgments made by jurors or other legal actors. These judgments can include important trial outcomes such as verdicts and sentencing decisions in capital cases. They also can include a range of psychological judgments (e.g., impressions, evidence assessments, culpability beliefs, predictions of future dangerousness) and emotional responses that influence ultimate trial decisions. Studies examining how race affects jury selection and the use of peremptory challenges also fall in this category because juror race is the target of attorney judgments. As noted earlier, most of the existing literature on race and juries has used the target approach, using simple manipulations involving the name or picture associated with a defendant. Although much has been learned, this body of research has several notable limitations in breadth and depth, and there still is considerable knowledge to be gained by taking the next steps.

Beyond the Black–White Binary

First, there is a strong need for research on judgments about defendants and other legal parties to extend beyond the traditional Black–White paradigm that has been used in the majority of research on race and juror decision making in the United States. Although I focus on the United States in this section, in other countries, there is a corresponding need to extend research beyond comparisons of the dominant group and most salient, historically oppressed minority group. In the field of psychology and law, as in many other domains, researchers often artificially reduce the study of race to Black versus White (or sometimes, White vs. non-White). Although the legacy of racial oppression makes it crucial to examine the ongoing treatment of African Americans in the legal system, it also is important for researchers to go beyond the simple Black–White binary and study the experiences of the many other sizable minority groups involved in the legal system. In addition, perceivers have different stereotypes of and emotional responses to members of different racial and ethnic groups (Fiske, Cuddy, Glick, & Xu, 2002), so it is unreasonable to expect that the biases jurors demonstrate against Black defendants will generalize to all minority defendants. A complete understanding of racial and ethnic bias in juror decision making can be obtained only by studying judgments made about defendants from a variety of racial and ethnic groups.

According to the U.S. Census Bureau (2013), although Black individuals constitute 13% of the U.S. population, the largest "minority" group has become Latinos, with 16% of U.S. residents reporting Hispanic or Latino origin. A growing body of research has suggested that Latinos experience discrimination in sentencing, including the death penalty, which is relatively similar to that experienced by Blacks (Demuth & Steffensmeier, 2004); however, there are relatively few juror decision-making studies examining judgments of this group. A recent meta-analysis by Devine and Caughlin (2014) identified seven studies on bias against Latino defendants. Overall, there was a significant but small effect in which White jurors gave higher guilt judgments for Latino versus White defendants, but not surprisingly, there was variability in the effect sizes. Clearly, much more research is needed to develop a better understanding of when and how bias against Latino defendants may be manifested.

Other racial groups are numerically smaller but have unique histories and stereotypically associated characteristics that may affect juror judgments. For example, despite a long history of discrimination and exclusion (Takaki, 2008), people currently see Asians as a "model minority" that is hardworking, intelligent, and successful (Chao, Chiu, Chan, Mendoza-Denton, & Kwok, 2013). Consistent with these views, Asian defendants are less likely to receive sentences involving incarceration than are White, Black, or Latino defendants (B. D. Johnson & Betsinger, 2009). Native Americans and Native Alaskans constitute only 1% of the U.S. population (Takaki, 2008), and the negative stereotypes associated with these groups include lack of education and substance abuse. There is little research examining how fairly Native Americans and Native Alaskans are treated in cases heard by nontribal courts.

In addition, jury researchers have to examine potential discrimination against groups defined by nationality, regional origin, and other categories that often are omitted from traditional race classifications. For example, although they currently constitute only 0.5% of the population, the number of individuals with Arab ancestry in the United States is increasing (Asi & Beaulieu, 2013). Since the 9/11 attacks, Arab individuals have been targets of considerable prejudice (e.g., Park, Felix, & Lee, 2007), and they are discriminated against in hiring judgments (e.g., Park, Malachi, Sternin, & Tevet, 2009). Thus, there may be potential for discrimination against Arab defendants by jurors, especially in cases involving violence that may be interpreted as being related to terrorism. To date, the only two studies that have investigated jurors' judgments of Arab or Middle Eastern defendants have not produced consistent evidence of bias, but the crimes used in these studies (physical and sexual assault) were not closely aligned with the terrorist stereotype (Adams, Bryden, & Griffith, 2011; Maeder, Dempsey, & Pozzulo, 2012).

The number of individuals who belong to two or more racial groups is growing rapidly, with 2.3% of the population currently identifying as multiracial (U.S. Census Bureau, 2013). Understanding how perceivers categorize, evaluate, and treat multiracial individuals is an important goal for many researchers, including jury researchers. Categorizing multiracial individuals is a cognitively challenging task (Chen & Hamilton, 2012), and multiracial individuals often are categorized in terms of their lower status groups (Ho, Sidanius, Levin, & Banaji, 2011). Given the tendency to emphasize minority status, it seems likely that jurors may make more negative judgments about multiracial defendants, but currently, there is no research on the issue. Conducting research on multiracial defendants is likely to present challenges, given the wide range of phenotypical presentations and the likely variability in reactions to particular combinations of racial groups (Ho et al., 2011); however, it is an important issue nonetheless.

Finally, it is critical for jury researchers to remember the concept of *intersectionality*: the effects of race depend on other social categories and identities, including gender, socioeconomic status (SES), sexual orientation, religion, and age. An intersectional analysis suggests that racial and ethnic bias in jury decision making is likely to be moderated by characteristics of the defendant that currently receive little research attention. For example, as discussed earlier, jurors may make negative judgments against Latino defendants from low SES backgrounds but not high SES backgrounds (e.g., Espinoza & Willis-Esqueda, 2008). Thus, paying more attention to defendant characteristics that often are treated as "background" is likely to provide a more sophisticated and accurate understanding of racial bias in jury decision making.

Beyond Criminal Defendants

A second direction for future research on race and juries involves extending the scope of our studies to include consideration of how the race and ethnicity of individuals other than the criminal defendant—for example, attorneys or expert witnesses—influence jurors' judgments. Stereotypes about Asians' lack of assertiveness and poor English skills are associated with negative judgments of Asian attorneys (Kang, Dasgupta, Yogeeswaran, & Blasi, 2010), and Mexican American attorneys who represent low SES Mexican American defendants are seen as less competent (Espinoza & Willis-Esqueda, 2008). The race of the jury foreperson also affects jury decision making; specifically, jurors may make more favorable judgments about a Black defendant when the foreperson is Black, perhaps in an attempt to appear unbiased (Foley & Pigott, 2002). In contrast, in the context of a medical malpractice case about birth defects, an ob–gyn testifying as an expert witness was considered most persuasive when depicted as a Black woman, but there is no research suggesting that this finding generalizes to other trial types or expertise.

Nearly all research on race and juries involves criminal trials, so there is a need for research on the effects of race in civil cases. Civil cases can involve a range of judgments (e.g., responsibility, negligence) and outcomes (e.g., damages) that may be affected by the race of the plaintiff and/or defendant. Negative stereotypes about Blacks, Latinos, and Native Americans may cause jurors to render more frequent judgments of negligence, and prejudice toward minorities might decrease the amount of damages juries award. Consistent with this analysis, college student and community mock jurors awarded lower damages when either the defendant or plaintiff in a sexual harassment trial was depicted as Black rather than White (Bothwell, Pigott, Foley, & McFatter, 2006). In a different vein, Schwartz and Hunt (2011) investigated whether jurors would be sensitive to cultural norms that might make Latina women less likely to respond assertively to and promptly report sexual harassment (e.g., Wasti & Cortina, 2002). Plaintiff ethnicity (Latina vs. European American) did not have an overall effect on verdicts, but the use of a cultural relativist argument explaining how the Latina plaintiff's culture influenced her behavior had a negative effect on jurors, making them less likely to return a favorable verdict. Further, consistent with the similarity–leniency effect, Latino/a jurors made more favorable judgments of the Latina plaintiff than did European American jurors. These studies illustrate the possibilities that a more systematic examination of civil cases presents for advancing our current understanding of the effects of race on juror decision making.

Focusing on Psychological Processes

Third, jury researchers should pay greater attention to the psychological mechanisms underlying racial bias. Although researchers have identified several important processes, such as biased attributions and processing of trial evidence, that can lead to negative judgments about minority defendants (Hodson et al., 2005; Sommers & Ellsworth, 2000), there has been a tendency for jury researchers to emphasize legally relevant situational variables over process variables (Kleider, Knuycky, & Cavrak, 2012). As a result, there is considerable potential to expand our understanding of juror bias by studying psychological processes that affect prejudice or stereotyping. For example, Kleider et al. (2012) demonstrated the importance of cognitive resources in juror bias; defendant race had a greater influence on high prejudice jurors when they had high cognitive loads and low working memory.

In particular, jury researchers should examine the role of implicit stereotyping and prejudice—biases that can occur without intent, awareness, and/or conscious control—on juror judgments (for a review, see Andersen, Moskowitz, Blair, & Nosek, 2007). Implicit biases reflect deeply ingrained, negative associations with minorities that may be developed through exposure to prejudiced statements, stereotypical representations, and other products of a society with deep racial inequalities. When people are exposed to cues related to a particular social group, these associations may automatically become cognitively active and thus have the potential to influence judgments and behaviors. Despite thoughtful analyses on the implications of implicit racism for several areas of the law (e.g., Kang et al., 2012; Levinson & Smith, 2012), there is still relatively little empirical research related to juror bias.

Implicit bias may influence the initial stages of juror decision making (e.g., impressions of the defendant, interpretations of trial evidence) as well as ultimate trial judgments. For example, both implicit stereotypes linking "Black" and "guilty" and implicit prejudice toward Black people predict beliefs about the strength of the evidence against a Black defendant (Levinson, Cai, & Young, 2010). Likewise, jurors who have implicit associations between race and the value of life are more likely to give the death penalty to a Black defendant in a capital case (Levinson, Smith, & Young, 2014). Black defendants are more likely to receive death sentences when their faces are more Afrocentric (i.e., have more stereotypically Black facial features; Eberhardt, Davies, Purdie-Vaughns, & Johnson, 2006) and when they are discussed in the media using dehumanizing "ape" imagery (Goff, Eberhardt, Williams, & Jackson, 2008). Although the latter two studies involved archival analyses, it is reasonable to posit an underlying process in which Afrocentric features or ape imagery may prime negative stereotypes or prejudice against Black people in jurors, leading to more negative trial judgments. These provocative findings illustrate the potential insights that may be gained from a more systematic examination of the role of implicit processes in juror bias. A stronger focus on psychological processes, implicit or otherwise, would greatly enhance our understanding of when and how jurors' judgments are influenced by race and also facilitate the development of interventions to reduce biases in trial outcomes.

Developing More Comprehensive Theoretical Models

Future research on juror bias should be more theoretically grounded, with an emphasis on the development of more comprehensive theoretical models to explain when, how, and why race influences jurors' judgments. When seemingly inconsistent or unexpected effects of race occur, they often are explained narrowly by referencing specific characteristics of the case or sample. Greater emphasis on theory and theory development would enable jury researchers to have a broader framework for predicting when race is and is not likely to influence jurors' judgments.

The most common theory used in research on racial bias in juror decision making is aversive racism theory (Gaertner & Dovidio, 1986; Pearson, Dovidio, & Gaertner, 2009). According to this theory, most people believe in racial equality and want to act fairly but still have at least some negative associations with racial minorities. As long as people are aware of race and the potential for bias, they can correct for their negative associations, making judgments that are nondiscriminatory or that potentially even favor minorities. However, if race is not salient, situations are ambiguous, or judgments can be explained by factors other than race, negative racial associations are likely to result in judgments that are biased against minorities, in spite of the egalitarian intentions of the decision maker. Consistent with aversive racism theory, jurors showed less bias against Black defendants when a case was racially charged, probably because the explicit focus on race sensitized jurors to the potential for biased trial judgments (Sommers & Ellsworth, 2000, 2001). Similarly, jury instructions may reduce bias by lessening ambiguity about the jurors' task (Mitchell et al., 2005), and jurors may be more influenced by inadmissible evidence in cases involving a Black defendant because that evidence can provide a justification for negative trial judgments (Hodson et al., 2005).

Aversive racism theory has greatly advanced our understanding of why there may be situations in which race is and is not likely to influence jurors' judgments. However, the theory is unlikely to provide a complete explanation of the influence of race on trial judgments, so it is important for jury researchers to expand their use of existing theories and develop new theories focused on the jury context. For example, the combination of the justification–suppression model (JSM; Crandall & Eshleman, 2003) and the flexible correction model (FCM; Wegener & Petty, 1997) may provide a useful framework for analyzing the effects of race on trial judgments (Hunt, 2014a). According to the JSM, the amount of prejudice that is expressed in a given context reflects the relative strength of justification and suppression factors. Justification factors facilitate biased judgments by making negative assessments of an individual seem valid or merited, whereas suppression factors reduce biased judgments by increasing internal or external motivations to avoid the expression of prejudice. The FCM addresses when and how perceivers attempt to correct their judgments for perceived bias. According to the FCM, the accuracy of correction attempts depends on whether people can recognize sources of bias and infer both the direction and magnitude of the influence. If people fail to identify a biasing agent, they will not engage in correction, and if they misperceive the direction or magnitude of the effect, they may under- or overcorrect their original judgment. Taken together, the JSM and FCM may provide a valuable framework for understanding and predicting juror bias. Cases can be analyzed to identify justification and suppression factors, as well as their relative strengths, leading to better predictions about the likelihood of bias (Hunt, 2014a).

Overall, more theory development has the potential to greatly benefit research on juror bias, helping researchers to predict when race is and is not likely to have a strong effect on juror judgments, when it is likely to be moderated by other factors, and even when "reverse racism" (more favorable judgments of minority defendants; e.g., Kerr, Hymes, Anderson, & Weathers, 1995) may occur. Understanding the larger picture of when and how the effects of race may vary as a function of psychological, social, and contextual variables has many important benefits, including the potential to make research on juror bias more compelling to legal professionals and policy makers, help researchers identify important new avenues of research, and provide insights into potentially effective interventions to facilitate equality before the law.

Subject Effects

The subject effect approach conceptualizes jurors as agentic forces—that is, as actors who form judgments, make choices, and engage in behaviors that affect themselves and others. In the current context, this approach involves examining how jurors' racial and ethnic background, cultural values and practices, and/or social identity may affect their beliefs, values, behaviors, and decisions. The subject effect approach may seem like an obvious way to conceptualize jurors, who in fact play an agentic role as the fact finder in a trial. However, there is little work in this area because jury researchers have usually conceptualized race as a passive target variable instead of considering racial and ethnic minorities as actors in their own right.

In particular, there has been almost no research examining the role of culture in jurors' judgments and behavior. Culture can be thought of as a shared set of knowledge, values, and practices among people from a common background. For the past 2 decades, a thriving theoretical and empirical literature on cultural psychology has repeatedly demonstrated that culture influences the ways that people make sense of their environment, interpret and evaluate the actions of others, and make decisions about appropriate behaviors and interactions (for a review, see Heine, 2010). Despite its clear relevance for understanding an increasingly diverse body of jurors, few connections have been made between cultural psychology and jury processes, so this is a critically important avenue for future jury research to pursue.

Effects of Race, Ethnicity, and Culture on Juror Judgments

Attitudes toward, expectations of, and experiences with the criminal justice and legal system vary substantially across racial and ethnic groups. Although Whites tend to believe that the police treat members of different racial and ethnic groups equally, Blacks and Latinos are more likely to believe that police officers are prejudiced, treat minorities more negatively than White individuals, and engage in negative behaviors such as racial profiling and excessive use of force (Reitzel, Rice, & Piquero, 2004; Weitzer & Tuch, 2005). Blacks and Latinos also are less likely than Whites to believe that courts have fair procedures and outcomes, and they often express concerns about the negative treatment and lack of representation of minorities in the legal system (Rottman, Hansen, Mott, & Grimes, 2003; Sun & Wu, 2006). Although Latinos may have more positive attitudes than Blacks toward the courts (de la Garza & DeSipio, 2001; cf. Sun & Wu, 2006), both groups express skepticism about participation in the jury system as jurors or defendants (Rose, 2009).

An important direction for jury research is to investigate the ways in which minority jurors' judgments, including verdicts, may be influenced by their attitudes toward the criminal justice and legal system and/or previous experiences. For example, as mentioned earlier, one explanation that has been offered for the stronger similarity–leniency effect in Black jurors is that they are trying to safeguard against potential institutional discrimination against minority defendants (Sommers & Adekanmbi, 2008). Some authors have suggested that distrust of the legal system may lead Black jurors to engage in *nullification*—that is, to acquit minority defendants, even if they actually believe they are guilty (Butler, 1995; Fukurai & Krooth, 2003). Fukurai and Krooth (2003) argued that even though Black jurors express greater support for nullification, racial differences in judgments about trials such as the O. J. Simpson case actually reflect the tendency for Black jurors to have higher standards for reasonable doubt and a stronger adherence to the presumption of innocence. This argument is consistent with research showing that minority jurors in capital cases are more likely to consider mitigating evidence (Lynch & Haney, 2009). However, despite these intriguing findings, our understanding of how views of the legal system may influence trial judgments made by minority jurors is limited.

In addition, cultural values and practices may affect the process and/or outcome of jurors' trial judgments. For example, when explaining the causes of behavior, people from individualist (generally Western) cultures tend to overemphasize personal factors (e.g., dispositions) relative to situational and environmental factors. As a result, they are likely to experience the fundamental attribution error, making internal attributions for behaviors even when significant situational pressures are involved. In contrast, people from collectivist (e.g., Asian) cultures are more attuned to situational influences on behavior and therefore tend to make more external attributions. Levinson and Peng (2004) argued that this pattern could lead to cultural differences in jurors' judgments in civil trials; for instance, in a torts case, European American jurors may ascribe more responsibility to the defendant compared with Asian jurors.

Another potential cultural influence involves judgments of morality. Several studies have documented cultural differences in views of morality, suggesting the possibility that culture may affect jurors' reactions to certain crimes, contexts, or defendant behaviors. Moral foundations theory posits that people consider five factors when evaluating the morality of a behavior: whether the behavior harms others, is fair, shows loyalty to an ingroup, shows respect for authority and society, and reflects standards of purity and decency (Haidt & Joseph, 2007). Although harm and fairness are consistent standards across cultures, people from more collectivist cultures place more emphasis on ingroups and purity when evaluating morality (Graham et al., 2011). These patterns suggest the possibility that jurors from collectivist cultures may make more negative judgments in cases involving behaviors that harm one's community (e.g., drug dealing) or that are seen as impure (e.g., sexual offenses; Levinson & Peng, 2004). Future research should explore these possibilities, as well as other potential influences of culture on juror judgments.

Effects of Race, Ethnicity, and Culture on Juror Behavior

Extending beyond judgments, it also is important to investigate how race, ethnicity, and culture affect jurors' behaviors during deliberation. As discussed earlier, research has demonstrated that racially diverse juries tend to perform better (e.g., deliberating longer, discussing more evidence) and show less bias against minority defendants (e.g., Bowers et al., 2001; Sommers, 2006). However, there has been little research directly examining the ways that minority jurors communicate and behave during deliberation. Notably, a few studies have suggested that racial and ethnic minorities may be less likely to participate actively in juries compared with majority members. For example, racial and ethnic minorities may speak less during deliberation. Preliminary results from an analysis of deliberations from 50 civil trials in the Arizona Jury Project revealed that racial and ethnic minorities spoke an average of 867 fewer words than White jurors (Rose & Diamond, 2008).

Hunt (2014b) argued that cultural factors may contribute to racial and ethnic differences in jury behavior. Jurors from individualist backgrounds (e.g., European Americans) are more likely to have independent self-construals, leading them to value personal expression and self-determination (Markus & Kitayama, 1991). As a result, they are more likely to use direct communication behaviors (Gudykunst et al., 1996) during deliberation, such as making clear statements about their views, even when they contradict the opinions of other jurors. In contrast, jurors from collectivist backgrounds (e.g., Asians) are more likely to have interdependent self-construals and emphasize harmonious interactions over the expression of personal views. Accordingly, these jurors may be more likely to rely on indirect communication strategies or remain silent during deliberation. A survey of former jurors provided support for this model. White and Black jurors reported higher levels of communication and participation during deliberation than did Asians and East Indians, and Whites also reported greater participation than did Latinos. Both independent self-construal and preference for direct communication mediated these group differences, and there was support for a serial mediation model in which race and ethnicity predict self-construal, which in turn predicts direct communication, which finally predicts jury communication and participation. One implication of this research is that cultural differences in communication strategies may lead jurors from certain cultural backgrounds to have a greater influence on deliberations and potentially even verdicts.

However, it is important to note that there are some inconsistencies in findings about race and ethnic differences in jury behavior. For example, an analysis of survey data from the National Center for State Courts indicated that self-reported participation in deliberation was higher for Black jurors than White and Latino jurors, although it did find that the lowest levels of participation occurred in Asian Americans, especially women (Cornwell & Hans, 2011). In contrast, another survey examining jurors' views of their peers found that social class predicted perceived participation and influence better than either race or gender (Cornwell & Cornwell, 2008). Thus, there is a strong need for additional research to examine the influence of race, ethnicity, and culture on jurors' behaviors during deliberation.

Interactions and Interventions

Finally, a research agenda for studying the effects of race, ethnicity, and culture on juries must acknowledge and even embrace the need to study interactions among variables. As seen throughout this chapter, the effects of race on juror judgments are complex and frequently moderated by other variables, such as type of crime, strength of evidence, and victim characteristics. Likewise, defendant race may interact with other social categories, such as SES. In addition, there are target × subject interactions, in which reactions to racial elements in a trial (target effects) depend on the race or ethnicity of the juror (subject effects). Thus, it is critical for jury researchers to avoid oversimplifying the potential effects of race, ethnicity, and culture when developing new research. We have to expand work on the moderators of both racial bias and jury participation, testing the potential effects of additional variables related to the case; characteristics of jurors besides race, ethnicity, and culture; and variables related to the judgment or deliberation context. More programmatic research that systematically examines and explains variability in the effects of race, ethnicity, and culture on juries is essential for the development of the overarching theoretical models discussed earlier.

Further, jury researchers should examine procedures that could be used by the legal system to minimize the effects of race on trial outcomes, as well as remove barriers related to race, ethnicity, and culture that may prevent citizens from fully participating in jury service. Borrowing a framework from the literature on eyewitness identification and testimony (e.g., Wells, Memon, & Penrod, 2006), the races of the parties in a trial generally would be considered *estimator effects*—factors that cannot be controlled by the legal system. However, there is considerable potential for jury researchers to identify variables that are under the control of the legal system and could be used in interventions to promote fair trial judgments and full participation among jurors.

Social psychological research has shown that racial and other forms of bias can be reduced through strategies such as egalitarian norms, clear guidelines for judgments, and positive, counterstereotypical images of minorities (for reviews, see Hunt, Girvan, Deason, & Borgida, 2013; Kang et al., 2012). These findings can be applied to the jury context; for instance, clear, understandable jury instructions can reduce racial bias in trial judgments (Lynch & Haney, 2009; Mitchell et al., 2005). In addition, researchers can develop new interventions that take advantage of the structure of a trial; for example, juror bias may be reduced by incorporating reflective questions about the potential influence of race into the jury selection process (Schuller, Kazoleas, & Kawakami, 2009) or by having the judge provide information about implicit bias (Kang et al., 2012). Finally, given the benefits of diverse juries (e.g., Bowers et al., 2001; Sommers, 2006), interventions that increase the diversity of jury pools and decrease race-based peremptory challenges may improve the quality and fairness of jury verdicts (Fukurai & Krooth, 2003; Sommers & Norton, 2007). Thus, a greater emphasis on system variables related to race, ethnicity, and culture can facilitate the development of interventions that may be able to reduce bias in trial judgments, decrease discrimination in jury selection, and promote positive interracial and cultural dynamics in jury deliberation.

CONCLUSION

In this chapter, I have argued for the importance of race, ethnicity, and culture in understanding jurors' judgments and behaviors. Race, ethnicity, and culture are complex factors that influence a range of jury processes and outcomes. They create target effects by affecting impressions of trial parties and interpretations of evidence in a way that often leads to bias against minority defendants in verdicts and sentencing judgments. They also can lead to subject effects in which the race, ethnicity, and/or culture of jurors influence their trial judgments and behavior during deliberation. All of these effects may be moderated by other factors, leading to variability in the effects of race across cases.

To advance our understanding of these effects, I have outlined a challenging agenda for future jury research. This agenda involves expanding current research to study a wider range of racial and ethnic groups as well as case types, expanding our understanding of the psychological processes involved in juror bias, developing more complete theoretical models, and increasing attention to interactions and factors that moderate the effects of race on juries. There also should be a substantial increase in research on the effects of race, ethnicity, and culture on jurors' judgments and behaviors because those issues have received fairly limited attention. Finally, as we expand our knowledge of the effects of race, ethnicity, and culture on juries, it is important to develop and test potential interventions that can reduce biases in the judgments of jurors and promote greater participation in jurors from all backgrounds.

Clearly, there are challenges associated with this ambitious agenda. For example, to better understand the effects of race, ethnicity, and culture on jury processes, researchers will have to analyze the behaviors (e.g., communication strategies) of diverse, deliberating juries. Such research presents the difficulties of recruiting or otherwise gaining access to large, diverse groups of jurors, as well as the challenges of coding and analyzing group interactions. In addition to logistic issues, some researchers may lack expertise in cultural psychology or behavioral coding, which are necessary for this work. Thus, effectively pursuing research in this area is likely to require both intradisciplinary and interdisciplinary collaborations.

Despite these challenges, the research questions outlined in this chapter are critical to address, from both psychological and legal perspectives. Ultimately, it boils down to this fact: Jury systems in the United States and throughout the world are becoming more diverse. Our current research only addresses a small slice of the way that race, ethnicity, and culture affect the judgments made in jury trials, as well as the behavior of jurors. If our work is going to remain relevant and help the legal system to protect the basic right to equality before the law, we need jury research that uses multiple approaches and examines a range of groups, behaviors, processes, and outcomes to develop a fuller understanding of the many complex ways in which race, ethnicity, and culture affect juries.

REFERENCES

Abshire, J., & Bornstein, B. H. (2003). Juror sensitivity to the cross-race effect. *Law and Human Behavior, 27*, 471–480. http://dx.doi.org/10.1023/A:1025481905861

Adams, L. T., Bryden, M. W., & Griffith, J. D. (2011). Middle Eastern racial bias and the impact of jury deliberation. *American Journal of Forensic Psychology, 29*, 41–59.

Alvarez, L., & Buckley, C. (2013, July 14). Zimmerman is acquitted in killing of Trayvon Martin. *The New York Times*. Retrieved from http://www.nytimes.com/2013/07/14/us/george-zimmerman-verdict-trayvon-martin.html

Andersen, S. M., Moskowitz, G. B., Blair, I. V., & Nosek, B. A. (2007). Automatic thought. In A. W. Kruglanski & E. T. Higgins (Eds.), *Social psychology: Handbook of basic principles* (2nd ed., pp. 138–175). New York, NY: Guilford Press.

Asi, M., & Beaulieu, D. (2013, May). *Arab households in the United States, 2006–2010*. Retrieved from http://www.census.gov/prod/2013pubs/acsbr10-20.pdf

Baldus, D. C., Brain, J., Weiner, N. A., & Woodworth, G. (2009). Evidence of racial discrimination in the use of the death penalty: A story from Southwest Arkansas (1990–2005) with special reference to the case of death row inmate Frank Williams, Jr., *Tennessee Law Review, 76*, 555–613.

Baldus, D. C., Broffitt, B., Weiner, N. A., Woodworth, G., & Zuckerman, D. (1998). Racial discrimination and the death penalty in the post-Furman era: An empirical and legal overview, with recent findings from Philadelphia. *Cornell Law Review, 83*, 1638–1770.

Baldus, D. C., Woodworth, G., Zuckerman, D., Weiner, N. A., & Broffitt, B. (2001). The use of peremptory challenges in capital murder trials: A legal and empirical analysis. *University of Pennsylvania Journal of Constitutional Law, 3*, 3–170.

Batson v. Kentucky, 476 U.S. 79 (1986).

Bloom, L. (2014). *Suspicion nation: The inside story of the Trayvon Martin injustice and why we continue to repeat it*. Berkeley, CA: Counterpoint.

Bothwell, R. K., Pigott, M. A., Foley, L. A., & McFatter, R. M. (2006). Racial bias in juridic judgment at private and public levels. *Journal of Applied Social Psychology, 36*, 2134–2149. http://dx.doi.org/10.1111/j.0021-9029.2006.00098.x

Bowers, W. J., Steiner, B. D., & Sandys, M. (2001). Death sentencing in Black and White: An empirical analysis of the role of jurors' race and jury racial composition. *University of Pennsylvania Journal of Constitutional Law, 3*, 171–274.

Butler, P. (1995). Racially based jury nullification: Black power in the criminal justice system. *The Yale Law Journal, 105*, 677–725. http://dx.doi.org/10.2307/797197

Chao, M. M., Chiu, C., Chan, W., Mendoza-Denton, R., & Kwok, C. (2013). The model minority as a shared reality and its implication for interracial perceptions. *Asian American Journal of Psychology, 4*, 84–92. http://dx.doi.org/10.1037/a0028769

Chen, J. M., & Hamilton, D. L. (2012). Natural ambiguities: Racial categorization of multiracial individuals. *Journal of Experimental Social Psychology, 48*, 152–164. http://dx.doi.org/10.1016/j.jesp.2011.10.005

Cornwell, E. Y., & Cornwell, B. (2008). Access to expertise as a form of social capital: An examination of race- and class-based disparities in network ties to experts. *Sociological Perspectives, 51*, 853–876. http://dx.doi.org/10.1525/sop.2008.51.4.853

Cornwell, E. Y., & Hans, V. P. (2011). Representation through participation: A multilevel analysis of jury deliberations. *Law & Society Review, 45*, 667–698.

Council of Europe. (2016). *Protocol no. 12 to the Convention for the Protection of Human Rights and Fundamental Freedoms*. Retrieved from http://www.conventions.coe.int/Treaty/en/Treaties/Html/177.htm

Crandall, C. S., & Eshleman, A. (2003). A justification–suppression model of the expression and experience of prejudice. *Psychological Bulletin, 129*, 414–446.

Deaux, K. (1984). From individual differences to social categories: Analysis of a decade's research on gender. *American Psychologist, 39*, 105–116. http://dx.doi.org/10.1037/0003-066X.39.2.105

de la Garza, R. O., & DeSipio, L. (2001). A satisfied clientele seeking more diverse services: Latinos and the courts. *Behavioral Sciences & the Law, 19*, 237–248. http://dx.doi.org/10.1002/bsl.436

Demuth, S., & Steffensmeier, D. (2004). Ethnicity effects on sentence outcomes in large urban courts: Comparisons among White, Black, and Hispanic defendants. *Social Science Quarterly, 85*, 994–1011. http://dx.doi.org/10.1111/j.0038-4941.2004.00255.x

Devine, D. J., & Caughlin, D. E. (2014). Do they matter? A meta-analytic investigation of individual characteristics and guilt judgments. *Psychology, Public Policy, and Law, 20*, 109–134. http://dx.doi.org/10.1037/law0000006

Diamond, S., & Ellis, L. (2003). Race, diversity, and jury composition: Battering and bolstering legitimacy. *Chicago-Kent Law Review, 78*, 1033–1058.

Eberhardt, J. L., Davies, P. G., Purdie-Vaughns, V. J., & Johnson, S. L. (2006). Looking deathworthy: Perceived stereotypicality of Black defendants predicts capital-sentencing outcomes. *Psychological Science, 17*, 383–386. http://dx.doi.org/10.1111/j.1467-9280.2006.01716.x

Equal Justice Initiative. (2010). *Illegal racial discrimination in jury selection: A continuing legacy*. Montgomery, AL: Equal Justice Initiative.

Espinoza, R. K. E., & Willis-Esqueda, C. (2008). Defendant and defense attorney characteristics and their effects on juror decision making and prejudice against Mexican Americans. *Cultural Diversity and Ethnic Minority Psychology, 14*, 364–371. http://dx.doi.org/10.1037/a0012767

Fiske, S. T., Cuddy, A. J. C., Glick, P., & Xu, J. (2002). A model of (often mixed) stereotype content: Competence and warmth respectively follow from perceived status and competition. *Journal of Personality and Social Psychology*, *82*, 878–902. http://dx.doi.org/10.1037/0022-3514.82.6.878

Foley, L. A., & Pigott, M. A. (2002). Race, self presentation and reverse discrimination in jury decisions. *American Journal of Forensic Psychology*, *20*, 37–52.

Frumin, A. (2014, Nov. 24). Marissa Alexander accepts plea deal. *MSNBC*. Retrieved from http://www.msnbc.com/msnbc/marissa-alexander-accepts-plea-deal

Fukurai, H., & Krooth, R. (2003). *Race in the jury box: Affirmative action in jury selection*. Albany: State University of New York Press.

Gabbidon, S. L., Kowal, L. K., Jordan, K. L., Roberts, J. L., & Vincenzi, N. (2008). Race-based peremptory challenges: An empirical analysis of litigation from the U.S. Court of Appeals, 2002–2006. *American Journal of Criminal Justice*, *33*, 59–68. http://dx.doi.org/10.1007/s12103-007-9027-6

Gaertner, S. L., & Dovidio, J. F. (1986). The aversive form of racism. In J. F. Dovidio & S. L. Gaertner (Eds.), *Prejudice, discrimination, and racism* (pp. 61–89). San Diego, CA: Academic Press.

Goff, P. A., Eberhardt, J. L., Williams, M. J., & Jackson, M. C. (2008). Not yet human: Implicit knowledge, historical dehumanization, and contemporary consequences. *Journal of Personality and Social Psychology*, *94*, 292–306. http://dx.doi.org/10.1037/0022-3514.94.2.292

Government of Canada. (2016). *Canadian charter of rights and freedoms*. Retrieved from http://www.laws-lois.justice.gc.ca/eng/const/page-15.html

Graham, J., Nosek, B. A., Haidt, J., Iyer, R., Koleva, S., & Ditto, P. H. (2011). Mapping the moral domain. *Journal of Personality and Social Psychology*, *101*, 366–385. http://dx.doi.org/10.1037/a0021847

Gudykunst, W. B., Matsumoto, Y., Ting-Toomey, S., Nishida, T., Kim, K., & Heyman, S. (1996). The influence of cultural individualism-collectivism, self construals, and individual values on communication styles across cultures. *Human Communication Research*, *22*, 510–543. http://dx.doi.org/10.1111/j.1468-2958.1996.tb00377.x

Haidt, J., & Joseph, C. (2007). The moral mind: How five sets of innate intuitions guide the development of many culture-specific virtues, and perhaps even modules. In P. Carruthers, S. Laurence, & S. Stich (Eds.), *The innate mind* (Vol. 3, pp. 367–391). New York, NY: Oxford University Press.

Hannaford-Agor, P., & Waters, N. L. (2011). Safe harbors from fair-cross-section challenges? The practical limitations of measuring representation in the jury pool. *Journal of Empirical Legal Studies*, *8*, 762–791. http://dx.doi.org/10.1111/j.1740-1461.2011.01240.x

Heine, S. J. (2010). Cultural psychology. In S. T. Fiske, D. T. Gilbert, & G. Lindzey (Eds.), *Handbook of social psychology* (5th ed., Vol. 2, pp. 1084–1121). http://dx.doi.org/10.1002/9780470561119.socpsy002037

Ho, A. K., Sidanius, J., Levin, D. T., & Banaji, M. R. (2011). Evidence for hypodescent and racial hierarchy in the categorization and perception of biracial individuals. *Journal of Personality and Social Psychology*, *100*, 492–506. http://dx.doi.org/10.1037/a0021562

Hodson, G., Hooper, H., Dovidio, J. F., & Gaertner, S. L. (2005). Aversive racism in Britain: The use of inadmissible evidence in legal decisions. *European Journal of Social Psychology*, *35*, 437–448. http://dx.doi.org/10.1002/ejsp.261

Hunt, J. S. (2014a, March). *The JuStiCe model: Integrating justification, suppression, and correction processes to understand the effects of race on juror decision making*. Paper presented at the meeting of the American Psychology-Law Society, New Orleans, LA.

Hunt, J. S. (2014b, May). *Understanding the effects of race and ethnicity on jury experiences and deliberation behavior: A cultural analysis*. Paper presented at the Law and Society Association conference, Minneapolis, MN.

Hunt, J. S. (2015a). Race, ethnicity, and culture in jury decision making. *Annual Review of Law and Social Science*, *11*, 269–288. http://dx.doi.org/10.1146/annurev-lawsocsci-120814-121723

Hunt, J. S. (2015b). Race in the justice system. In B. L. Cutler & P. A. Zapf (Eds.), *APA handbook of forensic psychology* (Vol. 2, pp. 125–161). Washington, DC: American Psychological Association.

Hunt, J. S., Girvan, E. J., Deason, G., & Borgida, E. (2013). Gender stereotyping. In J. Sanders, D. L. Faigman, E. Cheng, J. Mnookin, E. Murphy, & J. Blumenthal (Eds.), *Modern scientific evidence: The law and science of expert testimony* (pp. 707–775). St. Paul, MN: West.

Johnson, B. D., & Betsinger, S. (2009). Punishing the "model minority": Asian-American criminal sentencing outcomes in federal district courts. *Criminology: An Interdisciplinary Journal*, *47*, 1045–1090. http://dx.doi.org/10.1111/j.1745-9125.2009.00169.x

Johnson, S. L., Blume, J. H., Eisenberg, T., Hans, V. P., & Wells, M. T. (2012). The Delaware death penalty: An empirical study. *Iowa Law Review*, *97*, 1925–1964.

Jones, C. S., & Kaplan, M. F. (2003). The effects of racially stereotypical crimes on juror decision-making and information-processing strategies. *Basic and Applied Social Psychology*, *25*, 1–13. http://dx.doi.org/10.1207/S15324834BASP2501_1

Justifiable Use of Force, Fla. Stat. § 776.013 (2005).

Kang, J., Bennett, M., Carbado, D., Casey, P., Dasgupta, N., Faigman, D., . . . Mnookin, J. (2012). Implicit bias in the courtroom. *UCLA Law Review*, *59*, 1124–1186.

Kang, J., Dasgupta, N., Yogeeswaran, K., & Blasi, G. (2010). Are ideal litigators White? Measuring the myth of colorblindness. *Journal of Empirical Legal Studies*, *7*, 886–915. http://dx.doi.org/10.1111/j.1740-1461.2010.01199.x

Kerr, N. L., Hymes, R. W., Anderson, A. B., & Weathers, J. E. (1995). Defendant–juror similarity and mock juror judgments. *Law and Human Behavior*, *19*, 545–567. http://dx.doi.org/10.1007/BF01499374

Kleider, H. M., Knuycky, L. R., & Cavrak, S. E. (2012). Deciding the fate of others: The cognitive underpinnings of racially biased juror decision making. *Journal of General Psychology, 139*, 175–193. http://dx.doi.org/10.1080/00221309.2012.686462

Levinson, J. D., Cai, H., & Young, D. (2010). Guilty by implicit racial bias: The guilty/not guilty implicit association test. *Ohio State Journal of Criminal Law, 8*, 187–207.

Levinson, J. D., & Peng, K. (2004). Different torts for different cohorts: A cultural psychological critique of tort law's actual cause and foreseeability inquiries. *Southern California Interdisciplinary Law Journal, 13*, 195–226.

Levinson, J. D., & Smith, R. J. (Eds.). (2012). *Implicit racial bias across the law*. http://dx.doi.org/10.1017/CBO9780511820595

Levinson, J. D., Smith, R. J., & Young, D. M. (2014). Devaluing death: An empirical study of implicit racial bias on jury eligible citizens in six death penalty states. *NYU Law Review, 89*, 513–581.

Lynch, M., & Haney, C. (2009). Capital jury deliberation: Effects on death sentencing, comprehension, and discrimination. *Law and Human Behavior, 33*, 481–496. http://dx.doi.org/10.1007/s10979-008-9168-2

Lynch, M., & Haney, C. (2011). Mapping the racial bias of the White male capital juror: Jury composition and the "empathic divide." *Law & Society Review, 45*, 69–102. http://dx.doi.org/10.1111/j.1540-5893.2011.00428.x

Maeder, E., Dempsey, J., & Pozzulo, J. (2012). Behind the veil of juror decision making: Testing the effects of Muslim veils and defendant race in the courtroom. *Criminal Justice and Behavior, 39*, 666–678. http://dx.doi.org/10.1177/0093854812436478

Markus, H. R., & Kitayama, S. (1991). Culture and the self: Implications for cognition, emotion, and motivation. *Psychological Review, 98*, 224–253. http://dx.doi.org/10.1037/0033-295X.98.2.224

Martin, S. T., Hundley, K., & Humburg, C. (2012, June 2). Race plays complex role in Florida's 'stand your ground' law. *Tampa Bay Times*. Retrieved from http://www.tampabay.com/news/courts/criminal/race-plays-complex-role-in-floridas-stand-your-ground-law/1233152

Mazzella, R., & Feingold, A. (1994). The effects of physical attractiveness, race, socioeconomic status, and gender of defendants and victims on judgments of mock jurors: A meta-analysis. *Journal of Applied Social Psychology, 24*, 1315–1338. http://dx.doi.org/10.1111/j.1559-1816.1994.tb01552.x

Miller-El v. Dretke, 545 U.S. 231 (2005).

Mitchell, T. L., Haw, R. M., Pfeifer, J. E., & Meissner, C. A. (2005). Racial bias in mock juror decision-making: A meta-analytic review of defendant treatment. *Law and Human Behavior, 29*, 621–637. http://dx.doi.org/10.1007/s10979-005-8122-9

Park, J., Felix, K., & Lee, G. (2007). Implicit attitudes toward Arab-Muslims and the moderating effects of social information. *Basic and Applied Social Psychology, 29*, 35–45. http://dx.doi.org/10.1080/01973530701330942

Park, J., Malachi, E., Sternin, O., & Tevet, R. (2009). Subtle bias against Muslim job applicants in personnel decisions. *Journal of Applied Social Psychology, 39,* 2174–2190. http://dx.doi.org/10.1111/j.1559-1816.2009.00520.x

Pearson, A. R., Dovidio, J. F., & Gaertner, S. L. (2009). The nature of contemporary prejudice: Insights from aversive racism. *Social and Personality Psychology Compass, 3,* 314–338. http://dx.doi.org/10.1111/j.1751-9004.2009.00183.x

Perez, D. A., Hosch, H. M., Ponder, B., & Trejo, G. C. (1993). Ethnicity of defendants and jurors as influences on jury decisions. *Journal of Applied Social Psychology, 23,* 1249–1262. http://dx.doi.org/10.1111/j.1559-1816.1993.tb01031.x

Reitzel, J. D., Rice, S. K., & Piquero, A. R. (2004). Lines and shadows: Perceptions of racial profiling and the Hispanic experience. *Journal of Criminal Justice, 32,* 607–616. http://dx.doi.org/10.1016/j.jcrimjus.2004.08.011

Rose, M. R. (2009). Access to juries: Some puzzles regarding race and jury participation. *Sociology of Crime, Law, and Deviance, 12,* 119–144. http://dx.doi.org/10.1108/S1521-6136(2009)0000012009

Rose, M. R., & Diamond, S. S. (2008, November). *Tell it to the jury: Investigating who talks during real deliberations.* Invited talk at the University of California-Berkeley Law School/Jurisprudence and Social Policy Program.

Rottman, D. B., Hansen, R., Mott, N., & Grimes, L. (2003). *Perceptions of the courts in your community: The influence of experience, race, and ethnicity.* Williamsburg, VA: National Center for State Courts.

Schuller, R. A., Kazoleas, V., & Kawakami, K. (2009). The impact of prejudice screening procedures on racial bias in the courtroom. *Law and Human Behavior, 33,* 320–328. http://dx.doi.org/10.1007/s10979-008-9153-9

Schwartz, S. L., & Hunt, J. S. (2011). Sexual harassment trials involving Latina plaintiffs: Effects of a cultural relativist argument and juror background. *Behavioral Sciences & the Law, 29,* 418–439.

Snyder v. Louisiana, 552 U.S. 472 (2007).

Sommers, S. R. (2006). On racial diversity and group decision making: Identifying multiple effects of racial composition on jury deliberations. *Journal of Personality and Social Psychology, 90,* 597–612. http://dx.doi.org/10.1037/0022-3514.90.4.597

Sommers, S. R., & Adekanmbi, O. O. (2008). Race and juries: An experimental psychology perspective. In G. S. Parks, S. Jones, & W. J. Cardi (Eds.), *Critical race realism: Intersections of psychology, race, and law* (pp. 78–93). New York, NY: New Press.

Sommers, S. R., & Ellsworth, P. C. (2000). Race in the courtroom: Perceptions of guilt and dispositional attributions. *Personality and Social Psychology Bulletin, 26,* 1367–1379. http://dx.doi.org/10.1177/0146167200263005

Sommers, S. R., & Ellsworth, P. C. (2001). White juror bias: An investigation of prejudice against Black defendants in the American courtroom. *Psychology, Public Policy, and Law, 7,* 201–229. http://dx.doi.org/10.1037/1076-8971.7.1.201

Sommers, S. R., & Norton, M. I. (2007). Race-based judgments, race-neutral justifications: Experimental examination of peremptory use and the Batson challenge procedure. *Law and Human Behavior, 31*, 261–273. http://dx.doi.org/10.1007/s10979-006-9048-6

Sun, I. Y., & Wu, Y. (2006). Citizens' perceptions of the courts: The impact of race, gender, and recent experience. *Journal of Criminal Justice, 34*, 457–467. http://dx.doi.org/10.1016/j.jcrimjus.2006.09.001

Takaki, R. (2008). *A different mirror: A history of multicultural America.* New York, NY: Back Bay Books/Little, Brown & Company.

United Nations. (1948). *The universal declaration of human rights.* Retrieved from http://www.un.org/en/universal-declaration-human-rights/index.html

U.S. Census Bureau. (2013). *Annual estimates of the resident population by sex, race, and Hispanic origin for the United States, states, and counties: April 1, 2010 to July 1, 2012.* Retrieved from https://factfinder.census.gov/faces/tableservices/jsf/pages/productview.xhtml?src=bkmk

Wasti, S. A., & Cortina, L. M. (2002). Coping in context: Sociocultural determinants of responses to sexual harassment. *Journal of Personality and Social Psychology, 83*, 394–405. http://dx.doi.org/10.1037/0022-3514.83.2.394

Wegener, D. T., & Petty, R. E. (1997). The flexible correction model: The role of naive theories of bias in bias correction. In M. P. Zanna (Ed.), *Advances in experimental social psychology* (Vol. 29, pp. 141–208). Mahwah, NJ: Erlbaum.

Weitzer, R., & Tuch, S. A. (2005). Racially biased policing: Determinants of citizen perceptions. *Social Forces, 83*, 1009–1030. http://dx.doi.org/10.1353/sof.2005.0050

Wells, G. L., Memon, A., & Penrod, S. D. (2006). Eyewitness evidence: Improving its probative value. *Psychological Science in the Public Interest, 7*, 45–75.

5

JURIES COMPARED WITH WHAT? THE NEED FOR A BASELINE AND ATTENTION TO REAL-WORLD COMPLEXITY

JENNIFER K. ROBBENNOLT AND THEODORE EISENBERG

Juries draw criticism from a variety of quarters. Juries are variously described as arbitrary, pro-plaintiff, not able to effectively handle complex evidence (including statistical and scientific evidence), and both overgenerous and overly stingy (Daniels & Martin, 2000; Hans & Eisenberg, 2011). But these concerns about jury decision making are often put forward and discussed in a relative empirical vacuum. First, the data from empirical studies of jury decision making belie many of these concerns. Indeed, reviewers of the empirical research exploring juror and jury decision making identify some areas of difficulty, but find jurors to be careful and competent decision makers who make decisions in accordance with the evidence presented (Devine, 2012; Hans & Eisenberg, 2011; Vidmar & Hans, 2007). Second, and more important for this chapter, discussion of jury competence gives

Excellent research assistance was provided by Lucas Rael.

http://dx.doi.org/10.1037/0000026-006
The Psychology of Juries, M. B. Kovera (Editor)

little consideration to the benchmark against which juries should be appropriately compared.

Even with high rates of settlement, plea bargaining, and other nontrial dispositions (e.g., Galanter, 2004), adjudicatory decision making will always be necessary in some subset of cases. Given that adjudicators must resolve some disputes, the central question is not how jurors or juries perform in the abstract. A more useful question is how juries perform compared with an alternative set of decision makers. The natural alternative decision maker is a judge sitting in a bench trial or, perhaps, an arbitrator. Indeed, criticism of juries is sometimes linked to calls to limit the role of juries, substituting judges as the appropriate decision maker (e.g., Conn. Gen. Stat. Ann. § 52-340b; Sunstein, Hastie, Payne, Schkade, & Viscusi, 2002).

In contrast to the vast attention that has been given to juror decision making, there has been relatively little exploration of how trial court judges make similar decisions and relatively little attention paid to how jury decision making compares with judicial decision making (see Robbennolt, 2005). Although researchers' attention to judges has increased in recent years, research on judicial decision making and comparisons of jurors and judges is still relatively sparse. For jury researchers, and students of the courts more generally, such comparisons are crucial. Without research that compares the relative abilities of jurors and judges, reforms are unlikely to be appropriately designed and targeted (Ellsworth, 1999).

It is also important for jury researchers to think about the extent to which judicial decision making is a useful benchmark for jury decision making. Indeed, some degree of disagreement between judges and juries might be expected and even desirable. For example, divergence between judicial and jury decision making might, in some cases, be the result of differences in "value judgments that are properly made by the jury in close cases" (Lempert, 1981, p. 104) or result from the advantages conferred on the jury by the processes of group decision making. Thus, it is also important for jury researchers to attend carefully to the nuances of defining benchmarks against which to compare juror or jury decision making.

In this chapter, we review research that has explored the connections between jury decision making and the decision making of judges. First, we examine research conducted using a variety of methods that allows for a comparison between judges and juries. Second, we consider the ways in which the judge–jury comparison is useful and the limits of this comparison as a benchmark for evaluating jury decision making. Considering how judges and jurors compare in how they make legal decisions, their comparative advantages and disadvantages, and appropriate benchmarks suggests a variety of questions still to be explored by jury researchers.

JURORS COMPARED WITH JUDGES

Researchers have used a number of different approaches to studying the similarities and differences between jurors and judges, including studies of judge–jury agreement in particular cases, comparisons of broad patterns of outcomes in bench and jury trials, and experimental simulations. Approaching this comparison using a variety of methods is important because, as we will see, each of these approaches has advantages as well as disadvantages.

Judge–Jury Agreement

In what is the most famous study of judge–jury agreement, Harry Kalven and Hans Zeisel (1966) assessed rates of agreement between juries and the judges who presided over the trials in which the juries sat. They found that judges reported that they would have reached the same verdict as did the jury in 78% of the cases. This rate of agreement was the same for criminal guilt decisions and civil liability determinations. When there was disagreement in criminal cases, juries tended to acquit more often than did judges; when judges and juries disagreed in civil cases, the type of decision maker did not predict which side was favored. When the judges disagreed with the juries' verdicts, they did not attribute the difference to any misunderstanding on the part of the juries. And, indeed, rates of judge–jury disagreement in cases that judges assessed as difficult to understand were comparable to cases that the judges assessed as being relatively easy. In contrast, judges and juries were more likely to disagree when there was more room for disagreement—that is, in cases that the judges assessed as being "close" cases compared with those that they described as being "clear."

Other studies have found substantially similar results (see Table 5.1). Most recently, Eisenberg and colleagues (2005) set out to partially replicate Kalven and Zeisel's (1966) classic study using data collected in criminal cases from four counties in 2000 and 2001. They found a rate of judge–jury agreement (75%) that was strikingly similar to that found in the original study. And a recent study examining judge–jury agreement during the first 3 years of the use of juries in Korea also found high levels of agreement (91%; Kim, Park, Park, & Eom, 2013).

Judges' own self-reported rates of agreement with juries across the mass of cases over which they have presided parallel these findings, with large majorities of judges reporting that they agree with the jury all or most of the time (e.g., Attanasio, 2001; Lyon, Toben, Underwood, Underwood, & Wren, 2007). More generally, judges tend to have positive views of juries (see Bermant, Cecil, Chaset, Lind, & Lombard, 1981; Hannaford, 1998; Kalven & Zeisel, 1966; Louis Harris & Associates, 1989; Sentell, 1991, 1992).

TABLE 5.1
Rates of Judge–Jury Agreement

Study	Jurisdiction	Agreement	N
	Criminal cases[a]		
Kalven & Zeisel (1966)	United States	78%	3,576
Eisenberg et al. (2005)	Four counties	75%	290
Hartshorne (1949)[b]	New Jersey	89%	270
Heuer & Penrod (1994)	33 states	75%	77
Kim, Park, Park, & Eom (2013)	Korea	91%	323
	Civil cases		
Kalven & Zeisel (1966)	United States	78%	~ 4,000
Diamond, Vidmar, Rose, Ellis, & Murphy (2003)	Arizona	84%	32
Hartshorne (1949)[b]	New Jersey	85%	253
Heuer & Penrod (1994)	33 states	62%	67
McCook (1928)[c]	New York	72%	114
Ullman (1933)	Maryland	64%	42

Note. [a]Hung juries excluded. [b]Reporting the judge–jury agreement within a single judge's court. [c]Described in Wheery, 1931.

Rates of interjudge agreement have been less frequently studied. One recent study, however, suggested that rates of judge–judge agreement are similar to the rates of judge–jury agreement found across these studies. Wallace and Kassin (2012) experimentally explored judges' reactions to a hypothetical criminal case. For their control scenario, they found that 83% of the judges agreed on a verdict of guilty when the evidence was strong and that 83% of the judges agreed on a verdict of not guilty when the evidence against the defendant was weak. This rate of agreement is strikingly similar to the judge–jury rates of agreement described earlier. It is also consistent with other research exploring rates of agreement among judges' responses to hypothetical cases. Exploring trial court judges' responses to five different criminal scenarios, Austin and Williams (1977) found rates of agreement on verdict ranging from 62% to 100%. Rates of agreement for preferences for a particular sentencing mode were lower, ranging from 29% to 84%. Viscusi (2001) found rates of interjudge agreement on decisions about whether a repair should be undertaken and liability for punitive damages ranging from 52% to 100%. And in a study of English lay magistrate judges asked to make bail decisions, Dhami (2005) found agreement rates between 41% and 92%, depending on the case assessed.

Diamond and Zeisel (1975) examined rates of agreement among judges who participated in sentencing councils in which each judge was provided with a presentencing report and asked to make a recommendation about the proper sentence. Judges agreed about whether the defendant should receive a prison sentence approximately 70% of the time. Again, this rate of agreement is similar to the rates of agreement that have been found between juries and judges.

Rates of judge–jury agreement are also comparable to rates of agreement between other professional decision makers. Diamond (1983) reviewed studies reporting rates of agreement across a variety of professionals and a range of decision tasks, finding that judge–jury agreement rates of 78% were comparable to the agreement rates of scientific peer reviewers (75%), employment interviewers (70%), psychiatrists diagnosing psychiatric illness (70%), and physicians diagnosing physical illnesses (67%–77%). Recent studies of determinations of competence to stand trial by psychologists and psychiatrists found similar rates of interrater agreement (Gowensmith, Murrie, & Boccaccini, 2012: 71%; Robinson & Acklin, 2010: 70%; Skeem, Golding, Cohn, & Berge, 1998: 82%).

Thus, juries and judges tend to agree at rates that are similar to the levels of agreement that we observe among judges themselves, among professionals making other sorts of decisions, and among professionals making legally relevant decisions. As Saks (1992) noted, judge–jury agreement rates "are particularly impressive given [the jury's] unique situation of having to deal with a body of cases from which the easiest 80–95% have been removed" (p. 1236).

Archival Comparisons

The advantage of exploring judge–jury agreement rates is that this approach compares the decisions of juries and judges for the same real cases. At the same time, however, the judges in these studies (with the exception of the studies examining decisions in the Korean system) were not making binding decisions and their role in the cases was that of presiding judge rather than fact finder. Asking a jury and a judge to make binding decisions in the same cases is logistically prohibitive. That judges in these studies are not making binding decisions echoes a common criticism of mock jury research—that participants' decisions lack consequentiality. The limited research on this question has resulted in mixed evidence as to whether consequentiality affects the decision making of mock jurors and, if so, in what ways (see the review in Bornstein & McCabe, 2005). Nevertheless, it is plausible that differences in the consequences of the decision may affect attention or motivation in ways that have consequences for decision-making processes and verdicts. Jury researchers should, therefore, continue to work to understand the implications of asking research participants—whether they are judges or jurors—to make nonbinding decisions.

Other approaches to comparing the decisions of jurors or juries and those of judges equate the two groups on whether their decisions have binding consequences. In particular, researchers have compared the decisions of juries and judges across large groups of cases actually decided by the two groups of adjudicators. In addition, researchers using experimental methods have asked groups of laypeople and judges to assess identical, but simulated, cases.

Using the first of these approaches, researchers have found many similarities between judges and juries but have also identified areas of divergence. Clermont and Eisenberg (1992) compared the outcomes of federal civil cases tried by judges and juries from 1979 through 1989. In most types of cases, they found that plaintiffs were equally successful in jury trials and bench trials—that is, for most types of cases there were no differences in plaintiff win rates. In addition, plaintiff win rates in jury and bench trials across different types of cases were correlated, suggesting that "plaintiffs tend to do well before judges in the same case categories in which they tend to do well before juries" (Clermont & Eisenberg, 1992, p. 1138). However, for some types of cases—for example, medical malpractice, products liability, and motor vehicle cases—plaintiffs had higher win rates in bench trials than they did in jury trials.

A number of studies have explored the punitive damage award decisions of juries and judges in civil cases (e.g., Eisenberg et al., 2006; Eisenberg & Heise, 2011; Eisenberg, Heise, Waters, & Wells, 2010; Eisenberg, LaFountain, Ostrom, Rottman, & Wells, 2002; Hersch & Viscusi, 2004). For example, Eisenberg and colleagues (2010) found evidence that punitive damages are more likely to be awarded in jury trials compared with bench trials. They found, however, that rates of awarding punitive damages by judges and juries depended on the type of case. In nonpersonal injury cases, juries tended to award punitive damages at higher rates than did judges. In personal injury cases, however, the pattern was reversed—judges tended to make more frequent punitive damage awards in such cases than did juries (see Figure 5.1). Eisenberg and Heise (2011) examined state trial court data for 1991 to 1992, 1996, 2001, and 2005. They found that in cases in which punitive damages are awarded the ratio between the punitive damage award and the compensatory damages awarded to the plaintiff showed similar patterns for judges and juries (see Figure 5.2). But they also found that beginning in 2005, there was evidence that jury awards of punitive damages were higher than the awards made by judges.

The outcomes of cases tried by judges and juries have also been examined in the context of criminal cases. Leipold (2005) compared the outcomes of federal criminal cases tried to judges and juries. He found that conviction rates for judges and juries across the years 1946 to 2002 were strikingly similar—75% for juries and 73% for judges. But during the later years of this

A. Personal injury cases				
	Jury trials		Judge trials	
Compensatory award level	Punitive award rate	N	Punitive award rate	N
$0 to $9,999	32.1% (11.2%)	28 (228)	0.0% (0 .0%)	2 (15)
$10,000 to $49,999	21.1% (17.8%)	19 (100)	0.0% (0 .0%)	3 (16)
$50,000 to $99,999	44.4% (15.2%)	9 (37)	100.0% (100%)	2 (27)
$100,000 to $199,999	62.5% (40.2%)	8 (48)	100.0% (100%)	1 (1)
$200,000 to $999,999	22.2% (7.6%)	9 (37)	100.0% (100%)	1 (1)
$1 million to $9,999,999	50.0% (15.8%)	4 (18)	33.3% (33.3%)	3 (4)
$10 million or more	100.0% (100%)	1 (1)	100.0% (100%)	1 (1)
Total	34.6% (16.1%)	78 (462)	46.2% (49.0%)	13 (67)

B. Nonpersonal injury cases				
	Jury trials		Judge trials	
$0 to $9,999	23.8% (24.7%)	21 (127)	5.9% (1.3%)	17 (109)
$10,000 to $49,999	40.0% (51.2%)	30 (152)	20.8% (18.7%)	48 (141)
$50,000 to $99,999	28.0% (20.4%)	25 (108)	21.4% (29.2%)	14 (56)
$100,000 to $199,999	64.0% (70.4%)	25 (84)	26.7% (8.1%)	15 (70)
$200,000 to $999,999	54.5% (30 .6%)	22 (55)	30.0% (30.0%)	10 (14)
$1 million to $9,999,999	60.0% (76.3%)	25 (59)	50.0% (50.0%)	2 (3)
$10 million or more	100.0% (100%)	4 (18)		0
Total	46.7% (44.8%)	152 (603)	20.8% (14.1%)	106 (392)

Figure 5.1. Punitive damage award rates by compensation level, adjudicator, and case type. From "The Decision to Award Punitive Damages: An Empirical Study," by T. Eisenberg, M. Heise, N. L. Waters, and M. T. Wells, 2010, *Journal of Legal Analysis*, *2*, p. 604. Copyright 2010 by Oxford University Press.
Reprinted with permission.

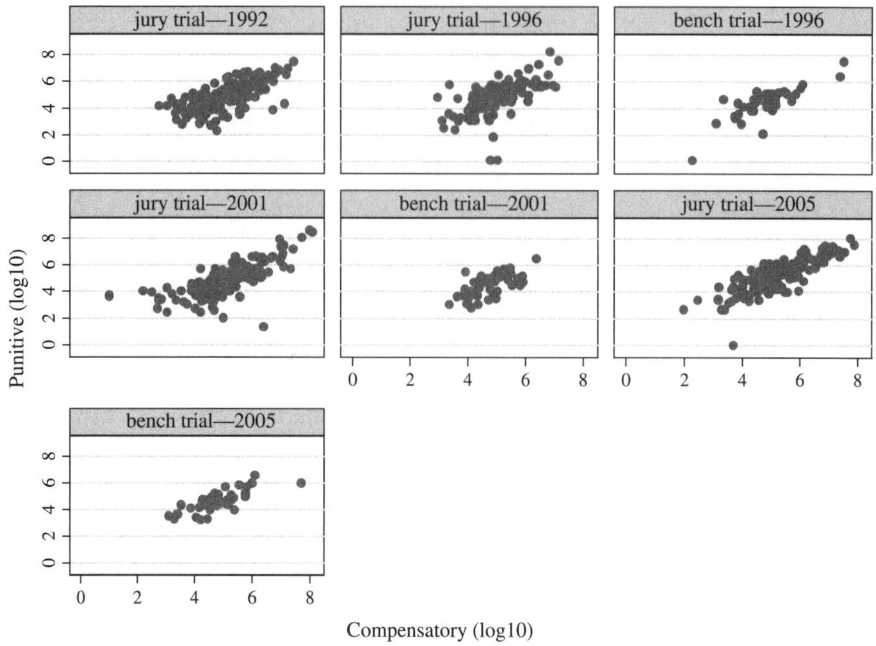

Figure 5.2. Punitive–compensatory awards by adjudicator and year. From "Judge–Jury Difference in Punitive Damages Awards: Who Listens to the Supreme Court?" by T. Eisenberg and M. Heise, 2011, *Journal of Empirical Legal Studies, 8*, p. 337. Copyright 2011 by John Wiley & Sons. Reprinted with permission.

period—1989 to 2002—juries were more likely to convict (84%) than were judges (55%). The size of the conviction gap varied by case type—conviction rates in immigration cases were the most similar (87% for juries and 80% for judges), whereas conviction rates in public order cases were much more disparate (83% for juries and 47% for judges; Leipold, 2005).

Some of the differences found between judges and juries in these cases might be due to differences in decision making between the two types of decision maker. Leipold (2005) explored the possibility that judges are influenced by their particular knowledge of and reactions to the federal sentencing guidelines. But each of the authors of these archival studies also noted that some of the differences found might be explained by differences in the mix of cases heard by judges and juries. For example, Eisenberg and Heise (2011) noted that civil cases with high stakes were more likely to be heard by juries than by judges. Similarly, Leipold noted that public order criminal cases are much more likely to be heard by judges. These sorts of selection effects influence the ways in which the findings of these types of archival studies can be interpreted. The possibility that differences between judges and juries may result from different streams of cases being tried to judges and juries, the nuances of those differences, and the decision making that results in the routing of cases to judges or juries deserves much greater attention (Eisenberg et al., 2010; Leipold, 2005).

Fewer studies have compared judge and jury decision making in more specialized types of cases. In one study, juries were more likely to find for the patent holder (68% of the time) than were judges (51%) and juries awarded more in damages than did judges (Moore, 2000). Judges and juries made large awards (those over $5 million) in similar proportions of cases, and overall affirmance rates on appeal were the same for cases decided by judges and juries. Similar comparisons of outcomes in bench and jury trials in other areas would be quite useful in helping to identify areas in which outcomes are more likely to diverge or converge and factors that may account for patterns of agreement and disagreement.

Experimental Comparisons

The previously described studies of outcomes in real cases are valuable, but their interpretation is limited by the real possibility that different cases are routed to judges and jurors. One way of dealing with this selection problem is to ask judges and jurors to evaluate the same case using simulation methodologies. By definition, these studies involve some degree of simulation (even when case descriptions or materials are based on real cases) but ensure that judges and jurors are responding to the same underlying stimulus.

Experimental comparisons of judge and jury damage awards have been relatively common. Wissler, Hart, and Saks (1999), for example, asked judges and jury-eligible laypeople (as well as attorneys) to evaluate hypothetical cases and make decisions about the appropriate amounts to award to compensate the plaintiffs for pain and suffering. They found that the awards given by the laypeople were higher and more variable than the awards made by the judges, perhaps because laypeople tended to see the plaintiff's injuries as being more severe. Judges and laypeople showed striking similarities, however, in the ways in which attributes of the injuries influenced the level of their awards. Both groups' dollar awards were less predictable than their injury severity ratings. And judges and laypeople ordered cases similarly—cases that tended to receive more from laypeople also tended to receive more from judges.

Vidmar and Rice (1993) compared the reactions of arbitrators and laypeople with a description of a medical malpractice case in which the plaintiff's injuries included permanent scarring. Arbitrators and laypeople awarded the same level of pain and suffering damages. Like Wissler and colleagues (1999), however, they found that laypeople's awards were more variable than were those made by judges and that the amounts given by arbitrators and by laypeople were correlated with their assessments of the attributes of the injuries—for example, how disfiguring the scarring was, the extent to which the scarring affected the plaintiff's quality of life, the degree of the plaintiff's embarrassment about the scarring, and the degree to which the effects of the scar were worse because the plaintiff was female.

Experimental comparisons of how laypeople and judges award punitive damages have had somewhat mixed results. Studies by Viscusi (2001) and Hastie and Viscusi (1998) found that judges were less likely to award punitive damages than were laypeople. Robbennolt (2002) found that the awards of trial court judges and laypeople were similar in size and variability and that judges and laypeople considered similar factors—the severity of the injury to the plaintiff, the degree of harm risked by the defendant's conduct, and the wealth of the defendant—in making their punitive damage awards. Additional research that explores factors that might influence judges and jurors differently would be useful.

Decision making in criminal cases has also been explored experimentally. Howe (1991) and Howe and Loftus (1992) obtained similar results for blame attributions in response to criminal scenarios. Though laypeople attributed more blame to defendants overall than did judges, judges and laypeople were similarly influenced in their judgments of blame by a defendant's level of intent, the possibility of justification, and the seriousness of the harm caused. In another study, laypeople assigned either similar or more lenient sentences to hypothetical defendants compared with judges, but judges and laypeople assessed offense seriousness, sentencing goals, and the potential for recidivism in similar ways (Diamond & Stalans, 1989).

Researchers have also compared how judges and jurors react to various types of evidence. Wells (1992), for example, found that judges and laypeople made similar probability estimates and liability decisions in response to "naked statistical evidence" (p. 739). In a study comparing judge and jury assessments of scientific evidence (mitochondrial DNA), Hans (2007) found that judges and jury pool participants had similar backgrounds in math and science and made similar assessments of the reliability of the evidence. Overall, judges were somewhat more likely to report that the testimony was easy to follow, but similar proportions of judges and jurors reported having difficulty following the evidence, and judge and jury comprehension of the evidence (as assessed by a series of true–false questions) was similar, with differences emerging on only a few individual questions.

McQuiston-Surrett and Saks (2009) compared judges and jury pool members' reactions to an expert in microscopic hair examination. Overall, jurors were more likely than judges to believe that the defendant was the source of the hair. But judges' and jurors' judgments of the probability that the defendant was the source were influenced in similar ways by the form in which the evidence was presented. The form of the testimony, however, influenced juror, but not judicial, judgments of the degree to which the evidence would contribute to a finding of guilt and judicial, but not juror, assessments of how well they understood the evidence. Whether the expert opined on the ultimate question of identity did not influence either judges or jurors. In addition, judges and jurors performed similarly on an objective measure of understanding.

Recent studies (Benton, Ross, Bradshaw, Thomas, & Bradshaw, 2006; Magnussen, Melinder, Stridbeck, & Raja, 2010; Wise & Safer, 2004) have found that both jurors' and judges' knowledge about eyewitness memory is imperfect. The beliefs of both groups diverge from the state of the research, although the divergence is larger in some areas for jurors than for judges.

Finally, Landsman and Rakos (1994) compared the ability of judges and prospective jurors to ignore inadmissible evidence, making decisions in a hypothetical case. Some participants were told that a particular piece of evidence was proffered by the plaintiff and admitted by the judge. Other participants were told that the plaintiff proffered the evidence, but the judge had ruled it to be inadmissible. A third group of control participants were not told about that evidence. Both judges and prospective jurors were more likely to find the defendant liable when they heard the piece of evidence than when they were not aware of it. This finding held irrespective of whether they were told it was admissible or inadmissible. The jurors seemed to be more aware of their inability to ignore the inadmissible evidence than were the judges.

Like the judge–jury agreement studies and the archival studies of outcomes in actual cases, experimental studies have also shown a great deal of similarity in the decision making of judges and jurors across a range of different decision tasks. In particular, the studies show that judges and jurors tend to be influenced in similar ways by various aspects of the evidence presented and by their assessments of the case facts. The experimental studies also showed some areas in which judges and jurors may differ. Future research might usefully focus on developing a better understanding of these areas of divergence, their degree, their sources, and appropriate responses.

STUDIES OF JUDGES' DECISION MAKING

Other studies have not directly compared the decisions of judges and juries but have separately explored the decision making of judges. These studies have often explored judicial decision making in areas that have also been explored by jury researchers. Because these studies were not designed to compare explicitly the decisions of judges and jurors, there may be methodological differences—such as differences in the stimulus materials used—across studies. Nonetheless, examination of judges and jurors in similar domains provides an additional opportunity to make useful comparisons.

For example, there is evidence that jurors have difficulty ignoring inadmissible evidence (Steblay, Hosch, Culhane, & McWethy, 2006). As a comparison, Wistrich, Guthrie, and Rachlinski (2005) explored the conditions under which judges have difficulties in ignoring inadmissible evidence. They found that even when judges ruled settlement demands, admissions that were protected by attorney–client privilege, prior sexual history, and prior criminal convictions as inadmissible, they were unable to ignore the evidence when making their decisions (see also Guthrie, Rachlinski, & Wistrich, 2009; Rachlinski, Wistrich, & Guthrie, 2013). Similarly, just as there is evidence that jurors have some difficulty with scientific, expert, and statistical evidence (see, e.g., Faigman & Baglioni, 1988; Koehler, Chia, & Lindsey, 1995; McAuliff, Kovera, & Nunez, 2009; Thompson & Schumann, 1987), judges also have difficulty with this type of evidence (see Gatowski et al., 2001; Guthrie, Rachlinski, & Wistrich, 2001; Kovera & McAuliff, 2000; Redding & Reppucci, 1999; Wells, 1992).

Importantly, there is a significant body of work demonstrating the ways in which various cognitive heuristics can affect lay decision making (see Gilovich, Griffin, & Kahneman, 2002). Recent work, however, has explored the degree to which the cognitive heuristics that can influence human decision making more generally can also influence decision making by judges. Not surprisingly—given that judges are human beings—judicial decisions are influenced by anchoring (Englich & Mussweiler, 2001; Englich, Mussweiler, & Strack, 2006; Guthrie et al., 2001; Rachlinski, Wistrich, & Guthrie, 2015), framing (Guthrie et al., 2001, 2009; Rachlinski, Guthrie, & Wistrich, 2006), hindsight bias (Guthrie et al., 2001, 2009; but see Rachlinski, Guthrie, & Wistrich, 2011), representativeness (Guthrie et al., 2001), egocentric bias (Eisenberg, 1994; Guthrie et al., 2001, 2009), contrast effects (Rachlinski, Guthrie, & Wistrich, 2013), the lure of intuitive reasoning (Guthrie, Rachlinski, & Wistrich, 2007; Guthrie et al., 2009), whether data are presented in probabilistic or frequentist formats (Rachlinski, Wistrich, & Guthrie, 2013), and the salience of particular information (Rachlinski, Wistrich, & Guthrie, 2013). Political scientists have found that judges' decisions are influenced by their backgrounds, experience, and policy preferences (see Braman, 2009; Epstein, Landes, & Posner, 2013, for a review). And research is beginning to emerge that explores the effects of procedural justice (Heuer, Penrod, & Kattan, 2007) and apologies (Rachlinski, Guthrie, & Wistrich, 2013; Robbennolt & Lawless, 2013) on judges.

Like the judge–jury agreement studies and the studies that compare judges and juries more directly, these studies have also suggested a great deal of similarity in the decision-making processes of judges and jurors. In particular, these studies have suggested that judges' education and legal expertise does not insulate them from many of the same influences experienced by laypeople. Work in this area might be expanded to explore whether there are ways in which legal expertise or targeted training might mitigate some of these effects or whether certain aspects of legal experience might exacerbate them. Given that the research so far suggests many similarities, the development of aids for both judges and jurors would be useful, as would careful thinking about the relative structural advantages of the different decision makers.

TRIANGULATING AND BENCHMARKING

As we have noted, studies comparing judges and juries and studies exploring the decision making of judges or juries have used a variety of methodologies. Judge–jury agreement studies capitalize on the ability to compare judge and jury reactions to the same real cases but suffer from the fact that the judges are not actually sitting as fact finders in the cases. Comparisons of outcomes in jury trials and bench trials examine binding decisions in real cases, but selection effects complicate the comparison. And experimental studies enjoy the benefit of placing the two groups of decision makings in the same role assessing the same cases, but rely on simulations in which decisions are not binding. Across methods, researchers and consumers of the research should pay attention to the real-world context within which judges and jurors decide cases, their respective roles, the institutional constraints they face, the questions they are asked to decide, and more (see Vidmar, 1999, 2011). Studies using varied methods should be read in conjunction with each other, with each providing insight that can be used the help interpret the findings of the others. And, indeed, triangulating across methods, the findings of studies using each of these methods point in a similar direction. On balance, the existing studies reveal some areas of divergence but many similarities between the decision making of judges and juries.

How much agreement or similarity between judges and juries is desirable? It is not at all clear that we should expect or even aspire to perfect symmetry of decision making between judges and jurors. As Harry Kalven (1958) once noted:

> We are by no means clear on how much like the judge and how different from him we wish the jury to be. If it is too much like the judge, the jury may lose all claim to a distinctive function. If it is too little like him we are disturbed by how easily jury equity elides into jury anarchy. (p. 178)

When there is disagreement, there is often no clear benchmark for determining whether judge or jury has it right (Lempert, 1981; MacCoun, 1999).

Moreover, judge and jury each bring different things to the table. Judges, of course, bring legal knowledge and experience across many cases. Juries, in contrast, bring a fresh perspective and the ability to make decisions in groups. Both judges and jurors are influenced by their experiences and perspectives, but juries—though not a perfect representation of the community—likely provide a broader and more diverse perspective to their task than do judges, bringing a more complete range of community values to their decision-making tasks (Feigenson, 2003; Hans, 2014; MacCoun, 1999).

In sum, simple comparisons between judges and juries are likely to be insufficient. Hastie and Rasinski (1988) proposed four different approaches to making comparisons and judging accuracy that can guide analysis in this area. First, one might examine agreement rates, with disagreement signaling error. Judge–jury agreement comparisons fall into this category and have been helpful in demonstrating relatively high agreement. But agreement does not necessarily mean that a decision is accurate. Similarly, disagreement does not necessarily indicate that one decision maker or the other has erred—particularly in the sorts of close cases that are likely to go to trial and in cases that are determined, in part, by community values.

Second, one might compare a decision to a demonstrably correct answer (see also Feigenson, 2003; Park, 2011). In some cases, it might be possible to define a correct answer and compare judge or jury decision making to that standard. Consistency with legal rules in clear cases or clear cases of factual error (e.g., DNA exoneration cases) might be instances of this sort of comparison. But often the cases that must be decided at trial do not have clear answers.

A third approach involves looking to see whether a decision maker is effectively using good cues in making decisions. And a fourth approach looks to see whether the decision making is inappropriately allowing bad cues to influence decision making. In each case, we are concerned whether either judges or juries are appropriately using legally relevant information or whether they are inappropriately influenced by extralegal factors. Much of the experimental research reviewed here has explored the ways judges and jurors use such cues—that is, whether judges or jurors are influenced by legally appropriate facts, can appropriately use scientific evidence, are able to ignore inadmissible evidence, are subject to cognitive heuristics, and so on.

CONCLUSION

In reviewing the emerging research that explores the decision making of trial court judges and the research that more directly compares the decision making of judges and juries, we see consistent evidence across methodologies that judges and juries tend to agree at fairly high rates and make decisions in ways that are often quite similar. Although there are areas of disagreement or divergence, the degree of convergence is striking. Judges and jurors appear to be largely influenced by similar factors when making decisions, struggle with similar kinds of evidence, and are susceptible to cognitive heuristics. "Judges, it seems, are human" (Guthrie et al., 2001, pp. 778). There is little evidence that judges and juries systematically differ any more than other pairs of decision makers—whether the decision makers be judges or other professionals.

Although the attention that has been paid to studying judicial decision making has increased in recent years, there is still much to be done. Researchers who study trial decision making ought to focus their attention on both judges and juries and on the comparison between them, striving to provide comparable information about both sets of decision makers. Attention should also be given to the ways in which judges influence jury trials through their decisions about jurisdiction and venue, discovery plans, trial scheduling, the admissibility of evidence, jury selection, jury instructions, and post-trial motions (Rowland, Traficanti, & Vernon, 2010; see also Vidmar, 2011).

Finally, future research ought to focus on the varied and interrelated roles of bench trial judges, judges presiding over jury trials, and jurors, the ways in which trial processes might be structured to improve decision making, and how such adjustments to the process might moderate any differences between judges and juries. Recognizing the relatively high rate of agreement between judges and juries, understanding the nuances of the similarities and differences in jury and judge decision making, and thinking about both in light of the real-world context of trials are necessary if we are to be able to focus on appropriate mechanisms for improving the process.

REFERENCES

Attanasio, J. B. (2001). Foreword: Juries rule. *Southern Methodist University Law Review, 54*, 1681–1689.

Austin, W., & Williams, T. A. (1977). A survey of judges' responses to simulated legal cases: Research note on sentencing disparity. *The Journal of Criminal Law & Criminology*, 68, 306–310. http://dx.doi.org/10.2307/1142852

Benton, T. R., Ross, D. F., Bradshaw, E., Thomas, W. N., & Bradshaw, G. S. (2006). Eyewitness memory is still not common sense: Comparing jurors, judges, and law enforcement to eyewitness experts. *Applied Cognitive Psychology, 20*, 115–129. http://dx.doi.org/10.1002/acp.1171

Bermant, G., Cecil, J. S., Chaset, A. J., Lind, E. A., & Lombard, P. A. (1981). *Protracted civil trials: Views from the bench and the bar*. Washington, DC: Federal Judicial Center.

Bornstein, B. H., & McCabe, S. G. (2005). Jurors of the absurd? The role of consequentiality in jury simulation research. *Florida State University Law Review, 32*, 443–467.

Braman, E. (2009). *Law, politics, and perception: How policy preferences influence legal reasoning*. Charlottesville: University of Virginia Press.

Clermont, K. M., & Eisenberg, T. (1992). Trial by jury or judge: Transcending empiricism. *Cornell Law Review, 77*, 1124–1177.

Daniels, S., & Martin, J. (2000). "The impact it has had is between people's ears": Tort reform, mass culture and plaintiffs' lawyers. *De Paul Law Review, 50*, 453–496.

Devine, D. J. (2012). *Jury decision making: The state of the science*. New York: New York University Press.

Dhami, M. K. (2005). From discretion to disagreement: Explaining disparities in judges' pretrial decisions. *Behavioral Sciences & the Law, 23*, 367–386. http://dx.doi.org/10.1002/bsl.619

Diamond, S. S. (1983). Order in the court: Consistency in criminal-court decisions. In C. J. Scheirer & B. L. Hammonds (Eds.), *The Master lecture series: Psychology and the law* (pp. 123–146). http://dx.doi.org/10.1037/10085-004

Diamond, S. S., & Stalans, L. J. (1989). The myth of judicial leniency in sentencing. *Behavioral Sciences & the Law, 7*, 73–89. http://dx.doi.org/10.1002/bsl.2370070106

Diamond, S. S., Vidmar, N., Rose, M., Ellis, L., & Murphy, B. (2003). Juror discussions during civil trials: Studying an Arizona innovation. *Arizona Law Review, 45*, 1–81.

Diamond, S. S., & Zeisel, H. (1975). Sentencing councils: A study of sentence disparity and its reduction. *The University of Chicago Law Review, 43*, 109–149. http://dx.doi.org/10.2307/1599193

Eisenberg, T. (1994). Differing perceptions of attorney fees in bankruptcy cases. *Washington University Law Quarterly, 72*, 979–995.

Eisenberg, T., Hannaford-Agor, P. L., Hans, V. P., Waters, N. L., Munsterman, G. T., Schwab, S. J., & Wells, M. T. (2005). Judge–jury agreement in criminal cases: A partial replication of Kalven and Zeisel's *The American jury*. *Journal of Empirical Legal Studies, 2*, 171–207. http://dx.doi.org/10.1111/j.1740-1461.2005.00035.x

Eisenberg, T., Hannaford-Agor, P. L., Heise, M., LaFountain, N., Munsterman, G. T., Ostrom, B., & Wells, M. T. (2006). Juries, judges, and punitive damages: Empirical analyses using the Civil Justice Survey of State Courts 1992, 1996, and 2001 data. *Journal of Empirical Legal Studies, 3*, 263–295. http://dx.doi.org/10.1111/j.1740-1461.2006.00070.x

Eisenberg, T., & Heise, M. (2011). Judge–jury difference in punitive damages awards: Who listens to the Supreme Court? *Journal of Empirical Legal Studies, 8*, 325–357. http://dx.doi.org/10.1111/j.1740-1461.2011.01211.x

Eisenberg, T., Heise, M., Waters, N. L., & Wells, M. T. (2010). The decision to award punitive damages: An empirical study. *Journal of Legal Analysis, 2*, 577–620. http://dx.doi.org/10.1093/jla/2.2.577

Eisenberg, T., LaFountain, N., Ostrom, B., Rottman, D., & Wells, M. T. (2002). Juries, judges, and punitive damages: An empirical study. *Cornell Law Review, 87*, 743–782.

Ellsworth, P. (1999). Jury reform at the end of the century: Real agreement, real changes. *University of Michigan Journal of Law Reform, 32*, 213–225.

Englich, B., & Mussweiler, T. (2001). Sentencing under uncertainty. *Journal of Applied Social Psychology, 31*, 1535–1551. http://dx.doi.org/10.1111/j.1559-1816.2001.tb02687.x

Englich, B., Mussweiler, T., & Strack, F. (2006). Playing dice with criminal sentences: The influence of irrelevant anchors on experts' judicial decision making. *Personality and Social Psychology Bulletin, 32*, 188–200. http://dx.doi.org/10.1177/0146167205282152

Epstein, L., Landes, W. M., & Posner, R. A. (2013). *The behavior of federal judges: A theoretical and empirical study of rational choice*. Boston, MA: Harvard University Press.

Faigman, D., & Baglioni, A. J. (1988). Bayes' theorem in the trial process: Instructing jurors on the value of statistical evidence. *Law and Human Behavior, 12*, 1–17. http://dx.doi.org/10.1007/BF01064271

Feigenson, N. (2003). Can tort juries punish competently? *Chicago-Kent Law Review, 78*, 239–288.

Galanter, M. (2004). The vanishing trial: An examination of trials and related matters in federal and state courts. *Journal of Empirical Legal Studies, 1*, 459–570. http://dx.doi.org/10.1111/j.1740-1461.2004.00014.x

Gatowski, S. I., Dobbin, S. A., Richardson, J. T., Ginsburg, G. P., Merlino, M. L., & Dahir, V. (2001). Asking the gatekeepers: A national survey of judges on judging expert evidence in a post-Daubert world. *Law and Human Behavior, 25*, 433–458. http://dx.doi.org/10.1023/A:1012899030937

Gilovich, T., Griffin, D., & Kahneman, D. (Eds.). (2002). *Heuristics and biases: The psychology of intuitive judgment*. http://dx.doi.org/10.1017/CBO9780511808098

Gowensmith, W. N., Murrie, D. C., & Boccaccini, M. T. (2012). Field reliability of competency to stand trial evaluations: How often do evaluators agree, and what do judges decide when evaluators disagree? *Law and Human Behavior, 36*, 130–139. http://dx.doi.org/10.1037/h0093958

Guthrie, C., Rachlinski, J. J., & Wistrich, A. J. (2001). Inside the judicial mind. *Cornell Law Review, 86*, 777–830.

Guthrie, C., Rachlinski, J. J., & Wistrich, A. J. (2007). Blinking on the bench: How judges decide cases. *Cornell Law Review, 93*, 1–43.

Guthrie, C., Rachlinski, J. J., & Wistrich, A. J. (2009). The "hidden judiciary": An empirical examination of executive branch justice. *Duke Law Journal, 58*, 1477–1530.

Hannaford, P. L. (1998). How judges view civil juries. *De Paul Law Review, 48*, 247–263.

Hans, V. P. (2007). Judges, juries, and scientific evidence. *Journal of Law and Policy, 16*, 19–46.

Hans, V. P. (2014). What's it worth? Jury damage awards as community judgments. *William and Mary Law Review, 55*, 935–969.

Hans, V. P., & Eisenberg, T. (2011). The predictability of juries. *De Paul Law Review, 60*, 375–396.

Hartshorne, R. (1949). Jury verdicts: A study of their characteristics and trends. *ABA Journal, 35*, 113–117.

Hastie, R., & Rasinski, K. A. (1988). The concept of accuracy in social judgment. In D. Bar-Tal & A. W. Kruglanski (Eds.), *The social psychology of knowledge* (pp. 193–208). Cambridge, England: Cambridge University Press.

Hastie, R., & Viscusi, W. K. (1998). What juries can't do well: The jury's performance as risk manager. *Arizona Law Review, 40*, 901–922.

Hersch, J., & Viscusi, W. K. (2004). Punitive damages: How judges and juries perform. *The Journal of Legal Studies, 33*, 1–36. http://dx.doi.org/10.1086/380412

Heuer, L., & Penrod, S. (1994). Trial complexity: A field investigation of its meaning and its effects. *Law and Human Behavior, 18*, 29–51. http://dx.doi.org/10.1007/BF01499142

Heuer, L., Penrod, S., & Kattan, A. (2007). The role of societal benefits and fairness concerns among decision makers and decision recipients. *Law and Human Behavior, 31*, 573–610. http://dx.doi.org/10.1007/s10979-006-9084-2

Howe, E. S. (1991). Integration of mitigation, intention, and outcome damage information by students and circuit court judges. *Journal of Applied Social Psychology, 21*, 875–895. http://dx.doi.org/10.1111/j.1559-1816.1991.tb00448.x

Howe, E. S., & Loftus, T. C. (1992). Integration of intention and outcome information by students and circuit court judges: Design economy and individual differences. *Journal of Applied Social Psychology, 22*, 102–116. http://dx.doi.org/10.1111/j.1559-1816.1992.tb01524.x

Kalven, H. (1958). The jury, the law, and the personal injury damage award. *Ohio State University Law Journal, 19*, 158–178.

Kalven, H., & Zeisel, H. (1966). *The American jury*. Chicago, IL: University of Chicago Press.

Kim, S., Park, J., Park, K., & Eom, J. (2013). Judge–jury agreement in criminal cases: The first three years of the Korean jury system. *Journal of Empirical Legal Studies, 10*, 35–53. http://dx.doi.org/10.1111/jels.12001

Koehler, J. J., Chia, A., & Lindsey, S. (1995). The random match probability (RMP) in DNA evidence: Irrelevant and prejudicial? *Jurimetrics, 35*, 201–219.

Kovera, M. B., & McAuliff, B. D. (2000). The effects of peer review and evidence quality on judge evaluations of psychological science: Are judges effective gatekeepers? *Journal of Applied Psychology, 85*, 574–586. http://dx.doi.org/10.1037/0021-9010.85.4.574

Landsman, S., & Rakos, R. F. (1994). A preliminary inquiry into the effects of potentially biasing information on judges and jurors in civil litigation. *Behavioral Sciences & the Law, 12*, 113–126. http://dx.doi.org/10.1002/bsl.2370120203

Leipold, A. D. (2005). Why are federal judges so acquittal prone? *Washington University Law Quarterly, 83*, 151–227.

Lempert, R. O. (1981). Civil juries and complex cases: Let's not rush to judgment. *Michigan Law Review, 80*, 68–132. http://dx.doi.org/10.2307/1288085

Louis Harris & Associates. (1989). Judges' opinions on procedural issues: A survey of state and federal trial judges who spend at least half of their time on general civil cases. *Boston University Law Review, 69*, 731–763.

Lyon, L., Toben, B. J. B., Underwood, J. M., Underwood, W. D., & Wren, J. (2007). Straight from the horse's mouth: Judicial observations of jury behavior and the need for tort reform. *Baylor Law Review, 59*, 419–434.

MacCoun, R. J. (1999). Epistemological dilemmas in the assessment of legal decision making. *Law and Human Behavior, 23*, 723–730. http://dx.doi.org/10.1023/A:1022353825440

Magnussen, S., Melinder, A., Stridbeck, U., & Raja, A. Q. (2010). Beliefs about factors affecting the reliability of eyewitness testimony: A comparison of judges, jurors, and the general public. *Applied Cognitive Psychology, 24*, 122–133. http://dx.doi.org/10.1002/acp.1550

McAuliff, B. D., Kovera, M. B., & Nunez, G. (2009). Can jurors recognize missing control groups, confounds, and experimenter bias in psychological science? *Law and Human Behavior, 33*, 247–257. http://dx.doi.org/10.1007/s10979-008-9133-0

McQuiston-Surrett, D., & Saks, M. J. (2009). The testimony of forensic identification science: What expert witnesses say and what factfinders hear. *Law and Human Behavior, 33*, 436–453. http://dx.doi.org/10.1007/s10979-008-9169-1

Moore, K. A. (2000). Judges, juries, and patent cases—An empirical peek inside the black box. *Michigan Law Review, 99*, 365–409. http://dx.doi.org/10.2307/1290297

Park, K. (2011). Estimating juror accuracy, juror ability, and the relationship between them. *Law and Human Behavior, 35*, 288–305. http://dx.doi.org/10.1007/s10979-010-9240-6

Rachlinski, J. J., Guthrie, C., & Wistrich, A. J. (2006). Inside the bankruptcy judge's mind. *Boston University Law Review, 86*, 1227–1265.

Rachlinski, J. J., Guthrie, C., & Wistrich, A. J. (2011). Probable cause, probability, and hindsight. *Journal of Empirical Legal Studies, 8*, 72–98. http://dx.doi.org/10.1111/j.1740-1461.2011.01230.x

Rachlinski, J. J., Guthrie, C., & Wistrich, A. J. (2013). Contrition in the courtroom: Do apologies affect adjudication? *Cornell Law Review, 98*, 1189–1243.

Rachlinski, J. J., Wistrich, A. J., & Guthrie, C. (2013). Altering attention in adjudication. *UCLA Law Review, 60*, 1586–1618.

Rachlinski, J. J., Wistrich, A. J., & Guthrie, C. (2015). Can judges make reliable numeric judgments? Distorted damages and skewed sentences. *Indiana Law Journal, 90*, 695–739.

Redding, R. E., & Reppucci, N. D. (1999). Effects of lawyers' sociopolitical attitudes on their judgments of social science in legal decision making. *Law and Human Behavior, 23*, 31–54. http://dx.doi.org/10.1023/A:1022322706533

Robbennolt, J. K. (2002). Punitive damage decision making: The decisions of citizens and trial court judges. *Law and Human Behavior, 26*, 315–341. http://dx.doi.org/10.1023/A:1015376421813

Robbennolt, J. K. (2005). Evaluating juries by comparison to judges: A benchmark for judging? *Florida State University Law Review, 32*, 469–509.

Robbennolt, J. K., & Lawless, R. M. (2013). Bankrupt apologies. *Journal of Empirical Legal Studies, 10*, 771–796. http://dx.doi.org/10.1111/jels.12027

Robinson, R., & Acklin, M. W. (2010). Fitness in paradise: Quality of forensic reports submitted to the Hawaii judiciary. *International Journal of Law and Psychiatry, 33*, 131–137. http://dx.doi.org/10.1016/j.ijlp.2010.03.001

Rowland, C. K., Traficanti, T., & Vernon, E. (2010). Every jury trial is a bench trial: Judicial engineering of jury disputes. In D. Klein & G. Mitchell (Eds.), *The psychology of judicial decision making* (pp. 183–202). http://dx.doi.org/10.1093/acprof:oso/9780195367584.003.0012

Saks, M. J. (1992). Do we really know anything about the behavior of the tort litigation system—and why not? *University of Pennsylvania Law Review, 140*, 1147–1292. http://dx.doi.org/10.2307/3312403

Sentell, R. P. (1991). The Georgia jury and negligence: The view from the bench. *Georgia Law Review, 26*, 85–178.

Sentell, R. P. (1992). The Georgia jury and negligence: The view from the (federal) bench. *Georgia Law Review, 27*, 59–120.

Skeem, J. L., Golding, S. L., Cohn, N. B., & Berge, G. (1998). Logic and reliability of evaluations of competence to stand trial. *Law and Human Behavior, 22*, 519–547. http://dx.doi.org/10.1023/A:1025787429972

Steblay, N., Hosch, H. M., Culhane, S. E., & McWethy, A. (2006). The impact on juror verdicts of judicial instruction to disregard inadmissible evidence: A meta-analysis. *Law and Human Behavior, 30*, 469–492. http://dx.doi.org/10.1007/s10979-006-9039-7

Sunstein, C. R., Hastie, R., Payne, J. W., Schkade, D. A., & Viscusi, W. K. (2002). *Punitive damages: How juries decide.* http://dx.doi.org/10.7208/chicago/9780226780160.001.0001

Thompson, W. C., & Schumann, E. L. (1987). Interpretation of statistical evidence in criminal trials: The prosecutor's fallacy and the defense attorney's fallacy. *Law and Human Behavior, 11*, 167–187. http://dx.doi.org/10.1007/BF01044641

Ullman, J. N. (1933). *A judge takes the stand.* New York, NY: Alfred A. Knopf.

Vidmar, N. (1999). Juries don't make legal decisions! And other problems: A critique of Hastie et al. on punitive damages. *Law and Human Behavior, 23*, 705–714. http://dx.doi.org/10.1023/A:1022397607693

Vidmar, N. (2011). The psychology of trial judging. *Current Directions in Psychological Science, 20*, 58–62. http://dx.doi.org/10.1177/0963721410397283

Vidmar, N., & Hans, V. P. (2007). *American juries: The verdict*. Amherst, NY: Prometheus Books.

Vidmar, N., & Rice, J. J. (1993). Assessments of noneconomic damage awards in medical negligence: A comparison of jurors with legal professionals. *Iowa Law Review, 78*, 883–903.

Viscusi, W. K. (2001). Jurors, judges, and the mistreatment of risk by the courts. *The Journal of Legal Studies, 30*, 107–142. http://dx.doi.org/10.1086/468113

Wallace, D. B., & Kassin, S. M. (2012). Harmless error analysis: How do judges respond to confession errors? *Law and Human Behavior, 36*, 151–157. http://dx.doi.org/10.1037/h0093975

Wells, G. L. (1992). Naked statistical evidence of liability: Is subjective probability enough? *Journal of Personality and Social Psychology, 62*, 739–752. http://dx.doi.org/10.1037/0022-3514.62.5.739

Wheery, W. M. (1931). A study of the organization of litigation and of the jury trial in the Supreme Court of New York County, *The Law Quarterly Review, 8*, 396–427, 640–673.

Wise, R. A., & Safer, M. A. (2004). What U.S. judges know and believe about eyewitness testimony. *Applied Cognitive Psychology, 18*, 427–443. http://dx.doi.org/10.1002/acp.993

Wissler, R. L., Hart, A. J., & Saks, M. J. (1999). Decisionmaking about general damages: A comparison of jurors, judges, and lawyers. *Michigan Law Review, 98*, 751–826. http://dx.doi.org/10.2307/1290315

Wistrich, A. J., Guthrie, C., & Rachlinski, J. J. (2005). Can judges ignore inadmissible information? The difficulty of deliberately disregarding. *University of Pennsylvania Law Review, 153*, 1251–1345. http://dx.doi.org/10.2307/4150614

6

GLOBAL JURIES: A PLAN FOR RESEARCH

VALERIE P. HANS, HIROSHI FUKURAI, SANJA KUTNJAK IVKOVIĆ, AND JAIHYUN PARK

In April 2014, the first all-citizen jury trial was held in the province of Neuquén in Argentina (Lorenzo, 2014). Some citizens who were chosen from the community were initially reluctant to serve. Nonetheless, they went to great lengths to attend and participate in the trial. Over 2 days, jurors observed witness testimony in a contested murder trial, listened to prosecutor and defense attorney arguments, and heard judicial instructions. After deliberating for 90 minutes, they reached a unanimous verdict that the defendant was guilty. Jurors described it as a moving *experiencia de vida* (life experience). They reported that it was not easy to sit in judgment on another individual but that this method of resolving a dispute was a huge step forward for justice.

In contemporary times, when expertise has come to dominate many domains of government, the province of Neuquén joins a number of other countries and jurisdictions that have taken the bold step of asking lay citizens to serve as legal decision makers. In the 1990s, Russia and Spain both launched jury systems. Following the breakup of the Soviet Union, Russia commenced

http://dx.doi.org/10.1037/0000026-007
The Psychology of Juries, M. B. Kovera (Editor)

jury trials, returning to a traditional form of fact finding that had been suppressed under Soviet rule (Thaman, 1995). Likewise, after Franco's oppressive and decades-long regime ended, Spain adopted a number of democratic reforms, including trial by jury (Jimeno-Bulnes, 2004; Thaman, 1998). Efforts to make government and law more responsive to the citizenry have included the introduction of varying forms of lay participation in Asian justice systems as well.

In this chapter, we provide an overview of different forms of lay participation in law, followed by several case studies illustrating the renaissance in the use of lay participation. These political developments offer significant scientific opportunities to assess the multiple effects and functioning of lay legal decision making. These opportunities, however, are accompanied by major methodological challenges. We discuss approaches that jury scholars might take to studying lay participation in a comparative way. We illustrate these suggestions with a close look at some of the recent research on lay participation systems in three Asian countries. We conclude the chapter by proposing research questions and strategies that take advantage of these valuable opportunities to understand the effects of incorporating lay voices into legal systems.

FORMS OF LAY PARTICIPATION

Countries searching for greater transparency and legitimacy have inaugurated a variety of forms of lay legal fact finding, including traditional juries, advisory juries, lay judges, and mixed tribunals that combine both professional judges and lay citizens (Dolidze & Hans, 2013; Fukurai, 2007; Malsch, 2009). Unlike professional judges, laypeople participating in trials usually have no formal education in law nor are they typically paid for their services, although they may receive a moderate fee to cover their transportation costs and food. Four major forms of lay participation are used by countries worldwide: jury, lay magistrates, lay courts, and mixed tribunals (Kutnjak Ivković, 1999).

Juries

Juries are a form of lay participation in which a professional judge conducts the trial and gives legal instructions to the jury; the jury makes the decision in the case. Around the world, juries have different functions. As grand juries (e.g., in the United States), they issue the bill (the indictment) and authorize the prosecutor to bring the prosecution forward. As trial juries (e.g., in the United States, United Kingdom), they make decisions about the guilt of the defendant in criminal cases. As advisory juries (e.g., in Korea), they make advisory decisions, leaving binding decisions to the professional judges (Kim, Park, Park, & Eom, 2013). Worldwide, most juries decide criminal, not civil, cases, with the United States being a notable exception (Hans, 2007, 2012).

Punishment decisions are typically left to the professional judge to resolve during subsequent proceedings. Only a few U.S. states permit jury sentencing (King, 2000). One major exception is the U.S. practice of death penalty sentencing, which is usually undertaken by juries. Advisory juries in Korea recommend a sentence in conjunction with professional judges.

Juries are typically found in common-law countries in which the adversarial procedure provides defendants incentives to plead guilty and resolve the case without a jury trial. In fact, there are estimates that the overwhelming majority of the criminal cases, close to 90% in the United States (Hans & Vidmar, 1986), are resolved through plea bargaining. More than 50 countries, including the United States (e.g., King, 2000; Vidmar, 2000), the United Kingdom (e.g., Lloyd-Bostock & Thomas, 2000), Australia (Chesterman, 2000), Canada (Vidmar, 2000), Ireland (Jackson, Quinn, & O'Malley, 2000), New Zealand (Cameron, Potter, & Young, 2000), Scotland (Duff, 2000), and many former Commonwealth colonies (Vidmar, 2000), use jury systems (Vidmar, 2000). Outside the common-law countries, juries are not frequent; they are used in Austria, Belgium, Norway, Denmark, Greece, Spain, and Russia (Jackson & Kovalev, 2006), as well as in South Korea (Park, 2010), with the newest jury systems emerging in Argentine provinces (Lorenzo, 2014) and the country of Georgia (Dolidze & Hans, 2013).

Lay Magistrates or Justices of the Peace

Lay magistrates or justices of the peace participate in a form of lay participation in which lay judges perform their judicial tasks either individually or in small groups. Magistrates are typically found in common-law countries such as the United Kingdom and the United States.

A comparison of lay magistrates and professionally trained judges shows both overlap and divergence. In England, lay magistrates have essentially the same rights and duties and may preside over the same types of cases as professionally trained district judges (Court and Tribunals Judiciary, 2014). There are about 28,000 magistrates in the United Kingdom today; they far outnumber district judges (e.g., Diamond, 1990; Parker, Sumner, & Jarvis, 1989). Indeed, magistrates' courts process over 95% of criminal cases in the United Kingdom (Court and Tribunals Judiciary, 2014).

Magistrates and district judges in the United Kingdom differ in terms of education, frequency of service, compensation, and whether they work independently or in tribunals. Since 1966, magistrates have been required to take a mandatory short legal training course, which includes legal education in substantive and procedural issues. They also must observe the courtroom behavior of their more experienced colleagues. Similarly, magistrates or justices of the peace in the United States may be required to take a mandatory training course in the basic principles of law. There are other differences. English magistrates are employed part-time and are limited to 26 half-day court sessions per year, whereas district judges are employed full-time (Court and Tribunals Judiciary, 2014). District judges earn a salary; lay magistrates are volunteers who receive only recompense for their expenses and a modest travel allowance. District judges preside over cases alone, whereas lay magistrates must sit in panels of two or three (Diamond, 1990).

Lay Courts

Lay courts are a form of lay participation in which lay judges try and decide simple civil cases and less serious criminal cases. Unlike magistrates, who try cases in regular state courts and follow the procedural rules prescribed by the state, lay judges in lay courts typically are not part of the regular state court system and procedural rules are relaxed. The methods tend to be nonlegalistic and nonformalistic and include discussions and mediation.

A form of popular justice, lay courts are found in socialist law countries (e.g., China: Reichel, 2008), Western democracies (e.g., United States: Merry & Milner, 1993), and African countries (e.g., Rwanda: Jones, 2010; South Africa: Grant & Schwikkard, 1991). Whereas the state systems in socialist law countries introduced lay courts in pursuit of official ideology and the planned replacement of laws by socialist morality, as was the case in the former Soviet Union (Smith, 1974), lay courts in African countries typically developed as a response to the inadequacies of formal courts or the continuation of the traditional role they played, as was the case in South Africa (Grant & Schwikkard, 1991) and Rwanda (Jones, 2010). Therefore, lay courts in socialist law countries are more uniform in their organization, nature, and scope than lay courts in African countries are.

Lay courts in socialist law countries started as "comrades' courts" in the former Soviet Union (Ramundo, 1965; see also Sperlich, 2007, for a discussion of comrades' courts in East Germany). They were initially established with the purpose of improving workers' discipline and productivity but subsequently were used to resolve a whole range of delinquent activities and petty crimes. In 1938, there were 45,000 comrades' courts in the Soviet Union (Ramundo, 1965). The numbers kept growing and, by 1963, there were 197,000 comrades' courts with half a million people serving on them (Ramundo, 1965). Comrades' courts appeared in other socialist law countries, such as Poland, Czechoslovakia, and the German Democratic Republic (Butler, 1972). In the former Yugoslavia, reconciliation boards were introduced (Felstiner & Drew, 1978). In the 1960s, Cuba introduced popular courts to serve a similar purpose (Berman, 1969) but abolished them in the 1970s.

The most prominent example of lay courts in a socialist law country today is Chinese peoples' mediation committees (PMCs). In accordance with Confucianism and the tradition of socialist legality, the PMCs mediate and resolve everyday disputes and, at the same time, educate the people about socialist laws and moral norms (Reichel, 2008). There are about 800,000 PMCs in China, with about 4.9 million mediators who decide close to 8 million disputes annually (Yan, 2010). Finally, some American cities have experimented with community mediation centers designed to handle local disputes (Merry & Milner, 1993).

Mixed Tribunals

Mixed tribunals are a form of lay participation in which lay judges (sometimes called *lay assessors*) hear, try, and decide criminal cases jointly with professional judges (Kutnjak Ivković, 1999, 2007; Vidmar, 2000). Lay and professional judges sit together during trials, hear and examine the evidence, deliberate, and jointly decide factual and legal issues in the case. They also routinely decide on the defendant's punishment.

Mixed tribunals are a unique form of lay participation. Professional judges have an opportunity to "correct" the views of lay judges and to explain the law. At the same time, lay judges have the opportunity to "correct" the professional judges' views by introducing the fresh approach of average citizens. The size of the tribunal varies across countries and across the severity of the cases, with larger tribunals assigned to hear more serious cases.

Mixed tribunals are used in Central, Eastern, and Northern Europe, in countries whose legal systems are based on the civil-law tradition (e.g., Croatia: Kutnjak Ivković, 1999; Denmark: Anderson, 1990; Finland and Sweden: Klami & Hämäläinen, 1992; France: Hans & Germain, 2011; Germany: Casper & Zeisel, 1972; Machura, 2011; Hungary: Jackson & Kovalev, 2006). Mixed tribunals are also found in socialist law countries (e.g., China: Yue, 2001; the former Czechoslovakia: Krystufek, 1976; Poland: Kubicki & Zawadzki, 1970; the former Yugoslavia: Ljubanovic, 1989). Finally, some countries with combined legal traditions have adopted mixed tribunals (e.g., Japan: Fukurai, 2010; South Africa: Seekings & Murray, 1998).

CASE STUDIES ILLUSTRATING THE RENAISSANCE OF LAY PARTICIPATION

To illustrate the context and motivation for new jury-like systems, we provide an overview of recently adopted systems of lay participation in three Asian countries: Japan, China, and Korea. China and Japan have each incorporated two forms of lay participation, one relating to prosecution decisions and the other to trial decision making. For trial decision making, Japan's adoption of mixed tribunals and China's embrace of people's courts offer useful contrasts to the new advisory jury system in Korea.

Japan's Mixed Tribunal System: *Saiban-in Seido*

Japan once had an all-citizen, 12-member jury system. The use of jury trials in Japan began in 1928 but was not frequently used, in part because litigants had to cover the costs of jury trial. In 1943, in the midst of World War II, the Japanese military government decided to suspend them (Fukurai, 2007; Maruta, 1990). After a break of nearly 70 years, in 2004, Japan adopted a new system, *Saiban-in Seido* (Fukurai, 2010), which began after a 5-year period of preparation. Instead of resurrecting Japan's suspended jury system, the government elected to institute a mixed panel of three professional and six lay judges to adjudicate criminal cases. The mixed tribunal was created as a compromise between conservative members of the Justice System Reform Council and strong public demands for the reinstitution of Japan's jury trials (Fukurai, 2010). However, there was substantial concern that professional judges would dominate the decision making of lay judges in the mixed tribunal.

On August 4, 2009, the first *Saiban-in* trial took place at the Tokyo District Courthouse. By 2011, more than a quarter million citizens (271,748) had participated as lay judges (Japanese Supreme Court, 2012b). However, the introduction of the new system did not lower the near-perfect conviction rate, which remained at 99.9% and was even higher than that of the bench trials before the introduction of the *Saiban-in* system (Japanese Supreme Court, 2012a; Japan Federation of Bar Associations, 2010).

Despite the mixed tribunals' strong proclivity toward conviction, many commentators have concluded that the new lay participation system has had a number of benefits. First, it helped to alter the way new trials were conducted. By necessity, legal officials had to change their presentations of evidence and legal arguments so that they were more understandable to the lay members of the mixed tribunal, which in turn made the court proceedings more accessible to the public at large. As we explore in more detail next, nearly all lay members of the mixed courts have reported a positive experience with *Saiban-in* trials (Japanese Supreme Court, 2012c).

Japan's Grand Jury System: Prosecutorial Review Commissions

Although the *Saiban-in* trial reform has had much greater visibility around the world, Japan also has used lay citizen fact finders for prosecutorial oversight. The Supreme Commander for the Allied Powers (SCAP) that occupied post-war Japan introduced Japan's grand jury system in 1948 (Fukurai, 2007). The U.S.-led SCAP proposed the establishment of the American-style grand jury system as an important democratic institution for engaging the broader Japanese public and guaranteeing international legitimacy to Japan's legal system. Prosecution Review Commissions (*Kensatsu Shinsakai* or PRCs) were established to review prosecutorial decisions. In total, 207 PRCs were created in each of Japan's 50 district court jurisdictions (Fukurai, 2011). Each commission consisted of 11 citizens randomly chosen from local electoral rolls. Given the fact that nearly all indictments by the prosecution resulted in conviction, the commissions' ex post facto examination of nonprosecution decisions had the potential to serve a critical oversight function on prosecutorial power. The prosecutor's nearly unfettered ability to charge (or to refrain from charging) made it all the more important to ensure there was no abuse of prosecutorial power. However, PRC decisions were regarded as merely advisory; prosecutors consistently failed to follow PRC recommendations for prosecution.

In 2004, the Japanese Diet revised the PRC by enacting the Act to Revise the Code of Criminal Procedure (PRC Act, 2004). The revision gave the PRC legally binding authority, and it led to a series of high-profile prosecutions of previously untouchable groups of individuals. A prominent politician, Ichiro Ozawa, was prosecuted for political fundraising violations in 2009. Three past presidents of a large corporation were charged with professional negligence in causing the death of more than 100 passengers in a train accident. Also charged was a member of the U.S. military who killed a Japanese youth in a drunk-driving accident in Okinawa and who was initially punished by the U.S. military with a 5-year suspension of driving privileges (Fukurai & Park, 2012). In these high-profile cases, the PRC was able to inject public perspectives about the need to bring these individuals to the courts. Citizens used their newly discovered ability to adjudicate crimes committed by groups of privileged individuals who had previously evaded prosecution (Fukurai, 2007). Scholars have argued that by reversing prosecutors' unpopular nonindictment decisions, the PRC was thus able to increase public confidence in law.

More than a half million Japanese citizens have participated in the PRC (Fukurai, 2011). The 2005 PRC survey found that the majority of PRC members were male (66.3%) and served during their 40s and 50s. The majority of them were employed when they served and supported the conservative

Liberal Democratic Party (53.6%). Nearly half of them said that they were conservative in their political views (48.9%). Almost all PRC participants reported that their experience was quite positive (98.6%; Fukurai, 2007).

China's Mixed Tribunal System: Reforming the "Ears of the Deaf"

The Chinese Constitution introduced the use of a lay assessor system in civil and criminal cases in 1954. However, that lay participation system was rarely used because China's leader Mao Zedong believed that these court institutions represented "a bastion of bourgeois justice" (Keyuan, 2002, p. 1062). After Mao's death, Deng Xiaoping began to rebuild China's legal system by reopening law schools and reforming criminal law (Lo & Snape, 2005). In 1998, the Supreme Court drafted laws to improve the system of mixed tribunals (Jiang, 2000).

Basic people's courts hear minor criminal cases; intermediate people's courts decide more serious cases (Reichel, 2008). Criminal cases are tried by either professional judges alone or mixed tribunals composed of one to three professional judges and two to four lay judges (Jiang, 2000), "depending on the law and the discretion of the court" (Yue, 2001, p. 51). Lay judges are citizens who are at least 23 years of age and who have the right to vote and stand for election (Jiang, 2000). They have the same rights as professional judges, including the right to examine documents in the case file and to question parties and witnesses. They collaborate with the professional judge to determine the court judgment and sentence (Jiang, 2000).

Despite the formal existence of mixed tribunals, China did not use them extensively to resolve cases (e.g., Jiang, 2000). It primarily relied on the use of highly educated lay judges in cases that required expertise (Jiang, 2000; Yue, 2001). Western observers noted infrequent usage, lay judges' passivity and incompetence, and insufficient funding and institutional support, all of which contributed to a lack of institutional effectiveness (Landsman & Zhang, 2008). In 2004, the Standing Committee of the National People's Congress promulgated a special directive to correct the shortcomings of the mixed tribunal system. Since that time, the system has become more frequently used and more efficient. In 2006, mixed tribunals processed more than a quarter million cases (339,965), making up nearly one fifth of all cases (19.7%; Chinese Government, 2012). In 2011, mixed tribunal panels processed over one million cases, making up nearly half of all cases in China (46.5%; Chinese Government, 2012).

China's Grand Jury System: People's Supervisor System

Like Japan, China has also included a lay element in criminal prosecution. In 2003, China introduced an experimental grand jury system called the People's Supervisor System (PSS) in 10 provinces and other autonomous regions. The PSS was proposed to promote democratic politics, partly in response to intense international criticisms about the closed nature of the Chinese judiciary (Fukurai & Wang, 2014). By 2010, the PSS was established throughout China, allowing a select group of Chinese citizens to make advisory recommendations and comments on procurators' (akin to prosecutors) investigations of criminal cases (Castellucci, 2007). People's supervisors are selected at the recommendation of various organizations, citizen groups, and local institutions. Their duties are to conduct independent assessments and submit supervisory comments on cases in which local procurators have withdrawn or halted the prosecution of criminal suspects (Chinese Government, 2005). By invitation of the procurator, people's supervisors also participate in the investigation of crimes committed by civil servants and weigh in on prosecution decisions.

People's supervisors are also allowed to raise objections to the procurators' handling of criminal cases, including (a) failure to file cases or inappropriate filing of cases; (b) extended detention of suspects; (c) illegal searches or withholding and freezing of property; (d) failure to pay criminal compensation; and (e) fraudulent practices for personal gain, taking bribes to bend the law, extorting confessions through torture, extracting evidence by violence, and other illegal or undisciplined practices (United Nations, 2006). People's supervisors disagree with the procurators' decisions at low rates: 5% or less in 2006 to 2008. In contrast, the rates at which the procurators have adopted the supervisors' pro-prosecution suggestions have been comparatively high, with nationwide rates between 58% and 74% in 2006 to 2008 (Wang & Fukurai, 2015).

In 2006, 20,848 individuals served as people's supervisors; the majority (60.1%) were members of the National People's Congress or the Upper House or the Chinese People's Political Consultative Conference or the Lower House (Zhi, 2008). Another survey in Yunan Province found similar results: 73% were Chinese Communist Party members (Zhi, 2008). People's supervisors have reportedly helped reduce public complaints against arbitrary handling of criminal cases by procurators (Chinese Government, 2008).

South Korea's Jury System: Advisory Jury

In 2008, South Korea implemented one of the most significant judicial reforms in its history by introducing jury trials to its criminal justice system (Act for Civil Participation in Criminal Trials, 2007). The notion of citizen participation in law was first raised in the late 1990s as part of judicial reform efforts, but it did not receive much support from legislators and law professionals at the time. In 2004, the Judicial Reform Committee officially included the introduction of a jury system in its agenda. The Judicial Reform Committee argued that an all-citizen jury system would be more suitable to Korean social and cultural contexts than the system of mixed tribunals because the all-citizen jury system would enhance the legitimacy and transparency of legal procedures. After intense discussions and political debate, the judicial reform bill was finally approved on April 30, 2007 (Han, 2010).

Although the legislature had given its imprimatur to the jury trial, the government decided to proceed cautiously. The overall operation of the jury system was to be closely monitored during the first 5 years to ensure the validity and accuracy of the legal judgments that ordinary citizens rendered. In January 2013, the Committee for Citizen Participation in Law of the Supreme Court of South Korea, having performed an extensive review, recommended that jury trials be maintained, albeit with some procedural modifications (Committee for Citizen Participation in Law, 2013).

The Korean jury trial was largely modeled after the American jury system (Park, 2010). A panel of randomly selected citizens serves as triers of fact, and jurors deliberate and render a verdict independently of the judge. Korean jury trials, however, have several distinct features. Jury trials can be held only in felony cases. Each jury is composed of five, seven, or nine jurors in proportion to the severity of the crime. A unanimous verdict is required in principle, but if unanimity is unlikely, jurors can reach a verdict by a simple majority vote after consulting the presiding judge. If the defendant is found guilty, jurors also make a sentencing recommendation.

One unusual aspect of the Korean jury system is the fact that the jury's verdict is only advisory to the judge (Hans, 2014). Several justifications have been offered for the advisory nature of the jury's verdict. Some legal commentators argued that if jury verdicts were legally binding, that might violate the Constitution (Ahn & Han, 2005). The current Constitution (Daehanminkuk Hunbeob, 1987) states that "all citizens have the right to a trial by a judge as stipulated by the Constitution and the law" (Article 27). Heated debate ensued among legal professionals and researchers over the interpretation of "a judge" in Article 27 (Lee, 2003). To avoid an anticipated charge of unconstitutionality, the Judicial Reform Committee resolved the issue by making jury verdicts advisory to the judges (Ahn & Han, 2005). Another rationale for the advisory jury was linked to concerns over jury competence. With no history of jury trials in South Korea, some considered it risky to make jury verdicts legally binding without confirming the reliability and accuracy of juries' legal decision making (Ahn & Han, 2005).

Under the current Korean law (Act for Civil Participation in Criminal Trials, 2007), jurors must unanimously agree on the verdict if at all possible. If they cannot reach unanimity, they must consult the presiding judge. After these discussions with the presiding judge, the advisory jury may render a majority verdict. Initially, only a simple majority was required. However, as Korean advisory juries have come to play a more significant role in legal decision making, the Committee for Citizen Participation in Law (2013) recommended the replacement of the simple majority rule with a supermajority rule (three quarters). Even if judges have the power to make official decisions at odds with the juries', the juries' verdicts will serve as references. If judicial decisions are inconsistent with the juries', judges must submit to the court statements to explain why they arrived at different decisions.

COMPARATIVE EXPLORATION OF LAY PARTICIPATION

The recent renaissance of lay participation across the world, including the examples just discussed from Argentina, China, Japan, and Korea, raises fascinating questions about the functioning and effects of lay participation. What legal procedures and frameworks encourage strong and well-functioning systems of lay participation? Do lay citizens have a more active voice in the more independent fact finding of jury systems, as opposed to mixed tribunals in which they may have less influence than the professional judges? Do legal systems with lay decision makers gain greater public support and legitimacy? Do they function competently and fairly, compared with alternative approaches?

Addressing these questions about the influence and operation of diverse lay participation systems raises major methodological challenges for the jury research community. Questions about societal influence and legitimacy may be difficult to study using traditional jury research methodologies such as mock jury experiments. Jury verdict analyses, questionnaire studies of real jurors, and surveys of the public may hold more promise. Systematic case studies such as those used by comparative scholars might also be informative. Yet, comparative research approaches are typically not in the toolbox of most jury scholars (Samuel, 2013).

The comparative approach has a long lineage. During his talk at the Royal Anthropological Institute of Great Britain in 1889, the anthropologist E. B. Taylor called for comparative studies and identified the advantages of engaging in comparative research (Bennett, 2004). Although there were occasional comparative studies of justice systems, including lay participation in legal decision making, such projects increased notably in the 1970s (Bennett, 2004). The recent renaissance in lay participation across the world ignites our interest in exploring the potential value of, and strategies for, a comparative approach to lay participation.

Our goals in this section are to provide a brief overview of the types of existing comparative studies of lay participation and propose suggestions for further research. The reality is that existing studies of lay participation vary on a multitude of dimensions, ranging from qualitative to quantitative, single country to multicountry, and cross-sectional to longitudinal. These studies of lay participation can be classified using a certain number of dimensions. For example, if the chosen dimension focuses on the number of countries included in the study, a literature search might yield studies exploring lay participation in one country; studies exploring lay participation in two, three, or several countries; and studies exploring lay participation in a large number of countries. All these studies, including those devoted to single countries, could be viewed as comparative studies. To better highlight potential avenues of comparative research in a systematic way, we use an organizational scheme developed by Bennett (2004).

Bennett (2004) proposed a typology of comparative studies in criminal justice, which has been extensively cited in the field of criminal justice ever since. Participation of laypeople as decision makers in criminal trials fits well within the larger umbrella of criminal justice. At the same time, because the nature of the field of lay participation is inherently interdisciplinary, studies of lay participation are conducted by scholars from a broad range of disciplines outside of criminal justice, such as psychology, sociology, political science, economics, and law.

Bennett's (2004) typology assumes that cross-country comparisons focus on the same part of the criminal justice system (e.g., organizational features of the police in the United States, Australia, and England) or the criminal justice system as a whole. In that sense, comparative studies of lay participation focus on the same part of the criminal justice system—the court system's decision makers. As we discussed earlier, participation of laypeople in legal decision making can take several different forms. Wherever possible, we draw comparisons and make suggestions for comparative research across different forms of lay participation.

Bennett's typology of comparative studies (2004) is based on four dimensions: approach, scope, data, and design. Any empirical study could be classified according to each of these dimensions. We first briefly describe each dimension and provide examples of lay participation studies. Then, we offer a critical analysis of the open topics for research within each dimension.

Approach of the Research

The first dimension along which comparative studies could be classified includes the approach of the research (Bennett, 2004). On the basis of the approach to the research, studies could be classified as either descriptive or analytical. If the purpose of the research is to "increase understanding of the structure, nature, or scope of one or more nations' criminal justice systems or crime problems" (Bennett, 2004, p. 4), the approach is descriptive. Such a description, however basic, may be critical for subsequent analyses and reform recommendations (Reichel, 2008). As such, a simple description of the systems of lay participation should be the first step in comparing across countries.

Having answers to the descriptive questions is an important first step. Although lay participation in some countries has been extensively studied (e.g., the United States, the United Kingdom, Germany), the literature about lay participation in many other countries across the world is quite scarce. We can ask some specific questions about a lay participation system in one country (e.g., What does the jury system in the United States look like?), compare across the same form of lay participation (e.g., What is a typical jury size across the world? Are juries more likely to be found in criminal cases than in civil cases?), or compare across forms and/or countries (e.g., What does the lay participation map of the world indicate about the geographical patterns of lay legal decision making? Which forms of lay participation are most common? What social and political milieus are associated with lay participation? What is the proportion of countries using more than one form of lay participation? Is there a relation between the legal tradition and lay participation?).

Another possibility in the realm of comparative studies is reliance on the analytical approach, in which the focus of the research is on understanding how systems work and what factors cause them to operate as they do (Bennett, 2004). A study following this approach would contain not only the basic description of how the system should operate (i.e., the descriptive approach) but also incorporate a critical analysis of how the system actually operates (i.e., the analytical approach). This analytical approach allows a researcher to move beyond descriptions of systems in place toward more challenging analyses and assessments. Depending on the goal of research, the researchers may use a historical approach (studying the mistakes and successes that have already occurred in the country or countries that use such a system) or a political economy approach (studying the interplay between economics, law, and politics in understanding the societal role of lay participation; Reichel, 2008). Analytical questions allow an exploration of deeper questions about the independence and sovereignty of lay voices in legal decision making, both within a country and across countries and forms of lay participation.

Within a country, we can obtain a more comprehensive understanding of how the system actually operates. How has the United States Supreme Court shaped the American jury system? What is the role of race, gender, and social class in the work of American juries? What effect would proposed changes in judicial instructions have on juries' understanding of legal issues?

For the same form of lay participation, but across different countries, we can analyze similarities and differences in legal, social, political, and cultural contexts and their influence on the performance of a particular form of lay participation. To what extent are social, political, legal, and cultural contexts significant factors to consider in global jury developments? To what degree is judicial independence related to the effectiveness of the mixed tribunal?

We also can ask challenging analytical questions simultaneously spanning both different countries and diverse forms of lay participation. What legal procedures and frameworks encourage strong and well-functioning systems of lay participation? Do lay citizens have a more active voice in the more independent fact finding of jury systems, as opposed to mixed tribunals, in which they may have less influence than the professional judges? What are the effects of media coverage, juror bias, instructions, or group decision making on the quality of decisions made by lay participants? What are the similarities and differences between the decision making of lay participants and professional judges? What are the effects of different types of crimes (for example, street crimes versus white collar crimes where suspects are corporate elites or politicians) on the quality of deliberation and jury verdicts?

Scope of Research

The second dimension along which comparative studies could be classified in Bennett's (2004) typology is the *scope* or the number of countries included in the study. On the basis of the scope of research, lay participation studies can be classified as national or multinational. The majority of existing research on the topic of lay participation involves exploration of a specific form of lay participation in one country (e.g., the United States, the United Kingdom, Australia, Germany). Such studies could be classified as national or single-country studies. An important next step would be to expand the inquiry about the same form of lay participation to other countries. Examples of such studies include projects comparing juries in England and Russia (Ziyadov, 2013) or comparing mixed tribunals in China and Japan (Landsman & Zhang, 2008). These types of studies allow us to explore both differences and similarities within the specific form of lay participation, but across multiple countries.

Adding even more complexity, we can imagine truly multinational comparative studies of a specific form of lay participation (regardless of whether the underlying methodology in the project is primarily coming from psychology, sociology, criminal justice, political science, or law) that would include a still larger number of countries. We can explore questions that focus on the success of the specific form of lay participation or even lay participation in general. What characteristics make lay participation flourish or founder? What legal, political, social, or economic environments are most supportive of lay participation? Can changes in political leadership account for the success and failure of lay participation?

We can focus on the purposes that countries seek to achieve with the introduction of lay participation, be it at the level of a specific form of lay participation or lay participation in general. Which purposes of lay participation are countries most likely to emphasize? What are the typical criticisms or reasons against the introduction of lay participation? How different are the purposes in theory and practice? Are all forms of lay participation equally successful in achieving the goals of lay participation? If the goal of introducing lay participation reform is to enhance the legitimacy of the system, which forms of lay participation are more appropriate? Other important questions address the effect of a lay-participation element on other parts of a legal system and whether the public and legal and political elites support lay participation. Studies of public and elite support might address whether lay participation enhances legitimacy, as it is presumed to do.

Although it is challenging to do so, we can study the broader relation between lay participation and democratization (Gastil, Deess, Weiser, & Simmons, 2010). Is lay participation related to the perceived legitimacy of the government? Are lay participants more confident in their government? Are lay participants more likely to obey the law? Are democracies more likely to use lay participation? Are some forms of lay participation more suitable for different kinds of democracy (i.e., representative democracy vs. direct participatory democracy)? What is the relation between lay participation and legal tradition or religion?

Past research on these questions has yielded a mixed review on the performance of mixed tribunals in Europe. Studies exploring mixed tribunals in Europe typically show that lay participants view their participation as important (e.g., Casper & Zeisel, 1972; Kamhi & Čalija, 1974; Kulcsàr, 1982; Kutnjak Ivković, 1999; Machura, 2001). Although professional judges tend to support lay participation in abstract, they are more critical of the lay participants' actual contributions (e.g., Kamhi & Čalija, 1974; Kulcsàr, 1982; Kutnjak Ivković, 1999, 2007). Professional judges typically argue that lay participants are not active during trials and deliberations, that lay judges make a relatively minor contribution to the resolution of the case, and that lay judges disagree with the professional judges infrequently (e.g., Kutnjak Ivković, 1999, 2002; Lapaine, 1986; Perron, 2001). In Germany, for example, lay judges were called puppets with strings in the hands of judicial authority, and in Croatia lay judges were called "two heads of cabbage behind . . . the professional judge" (Kutnjak Ivković, 2007, p. 430).

Asia's recent experience with mixed tribunals has produced more positive reports. Both the general public and lay participants have evaluated Japan's mixed tribunal favorably. In post-trial surveys, most lay participants indicated that their experiences were positive, the quality of deliberation was excellent, and the trial was easy to understand (Japanese Supreme Court,

2012b). Nearly all of the Japanese public reported being familiar with *Saiban-in* trials, and the majority felt that people's collective sentiments were reflected in *Saiban-in* verdicts (Japanese Supreme Court, 2014). Many Japanese district courts have published reports of professional judges who participated in mixed tribunals. According to the reports, professional judges were impressed with the "extraordinarily high percentage of summoned candidates who appear at the courthouse" (Japanese Supreme Court, 2014, p. 170) and with lay judges' "commitment to high standards of justice" (Japanese Supreme Court, 2014, p. 181). They also stated that lay judges were "less likely than expected to be swayed by emotion" (Japanese Supreme Court, 2014, p. 199).

In contrast to Japan, the critics of the Chinese system of mixed tribunals provided less positive assessments (Landsman & Zhang, 2008; Yue, 2001). They argued that professional judges dominated the system:

> Lay assessors are influenced by the professional judges and are passive during the trial. Normally, the presiding judge decides in advance which lay assessor should read which testimony. Even if lay assessors have a different opinion about the case, professional judges may try to convince them with their own knowledge. This happens even when lay assessors are a majority on the panel. There is a saying in China to describe the role of lay assessors. They are the ears of the deaf—like furniture or decoration. (Yue, 2001, p. 57)

More recent surveys have indicated more positive views: A 2007 survey revealed that Chinese professional judges are also appreciative of lay participants' contributions and support the lay assessors' participation in trials (Wang & Fukurai, 2015). A 2007 survey of Chinese lay assessors showed that the large majority were quite confident in their fact-finding abilities and reported that they participated effectively in decision making (Wang & Fukurai, 2015). In-depth interviews of professional and lay judges in 2013 also revealed lay participants' significant contribution to deliberation and mediation, especially in civil trials (Wang & Fukurai, 2015).

Why are mixed tribunals in Asian countries, which traditionally embrace Confucianism and respect for authority, receiving more positive reviews than mixed tribunals in Europe? In Asia, lay participation in legal decision making has been a relatively recent phenomenon. Is the enthusiasm for a new system of lay participation likely to fade over time? A comparative analysis of mixed tribunals in East Asia and Europe would allow researchers to elucidate the causes of differing experiences among lay judges and find ways to effectively use lay participation in the equitable disposition of criminal and/or civil cases.

To date, only a few studies of lay participation have adopted a broad scope and are true multinational or multicountry studies. Jackson and Kovalev's study

(2006) explored the relation between lay participation and the 46 Council of Europe countries' state of human rights. On the basis of a survey of experts in the field of lay participation, the authors found that 12 countries (26%) do not use any form of lay participation (Jackson & Kovalev, 2006). Among the countries that use lay participation, there is substantial variation, including traditional juries, mixed tribunals, and magistrates/justices of the peace. In the end, Jackson and Kovalev (2006) concluded,

> Both the collaborative and jury models are capable of fulfilling basic human rights norms, but there is also a considerable variation in the ways in which these models operate; some practices vary considerably in the degree to which they may be said to enhance human rights. What is missing from many of the debates on lay adjudication is a human rights focus on how human rights might be enhanced, both in terms of maximizing the political right of citizens to participate meaningfully in their judicial systems and in terms of enhancing the civil right to a fair trial, within the particular model chosen. (p. 121)

The second study with a broad comparative sweep is Vidmar's (2000) study of juries across the world. Vidmar's research strategy was twofold. First, experts from several countries (Australia, Canada, England, Japan, New Zealand, the Republic of Ireland, Northern Ireland, Russia, Scotland, Spain, and the United States) furnished an in-depth analysis of the jury system in their respective countries, examining the way in which the jury system in each country actually operated. Second, Vidmar surveyed 46 Commonwealth members from several continents (e.g., Ghana, Hong Kong, Jamaica, the Marshall Islands). On the basis of the results of the survey, Vidmar drew conclusions regarding the composition, competence, and impartiality of the jury system in each country. Despite the complexity of his project, Vidmar was clear that this extensive work was only "a partial picture but an important start" (p. 52).

There are also a handful of high-quality comparative studies using mixed methodological approaches to make comparisons across smaller numbers of countries. For example, Kovalev (2010) contrasted lay participation in Russia, Ukraine, and the former republics of the Soviet Union, offering a compelling picture of the political, social, and legal factors that led to criminal justice reform and using case studies and survey techniques to examine the functioning of lay participation systems. Malsch (2009) used interviews and courtroom observations to compare the use of lay participation in five European countries, concluding that judges and other legal officials could do much more in all five countries to encourage more vigorous and effective lay participation.

Types of Data or Forms of Empirical Evidence

The third dimension along which comparative studies could be classified in Bennett's (2004) typology includes the types of data or the forms of empirical evidence collected in the research. Bennett proposed that research studies use either qualitative (e.g., interviews, observations, case studies) or quantitative data (e.g., surveys). However, jury scholars may use both qualitative and quantitative methods in conducting juror interviews, mock jury experiments, jury verdict comparisons, deliberation analyses, questionnaire studies of real jurors, and surveys of the public. Therefore, empirical studies can be classified into qualitative studies, quantitative studies, and studies using both qualitative and quantitative data.

One direction for comparative research is reliance on the same methodology in different countries. For example, Kim et al. (2013) explored the issue of jury competence among Korean jurors using the methodology of U.S. judge–jury disagreements developed by Kalven and Zeisel (1966). They examined all jury trials conducted during the first 3 years of the new jury system's operation; Korean judges and advisory juries agreed on verdicts in 91.4% of cases. In the remaining cases in which judges and juries disagreed, juries made judgments that were more lenient toward the defendant. A more recent governmental report, covering trials from 2008 to 2011, yielded similar findings (Committee for Citizen Participation in Law, 2013).

The high level of agreement rates and the asymmetric pattern of disagreement parallel the findings reported in previous studies conducted in common-law countries (e.g., Eisenberg et al., 2005; Hans, Hannaford-Agor, Mott, & Munsterman, 2003; Kalven & Zeisel, 1966). The high level of agreement should ease concerns about jury competence raised by Korean legal elites and researchers. What is more, from a global perspective, it is remarkable that the Korean judge–jury agreement patterns are largely consistent with patterns of judge–jury agreement in other countries that have dissimilar historical, social, and legal contexts. The robustness of these findings may have important implications for comparative research and theory on lay decision making.

Design of the Data Collection Activity

The fourth dimension along which comparative studies could be classified in Bennett's (2004) typology includes the design of the data collection activity. On the basis of the design of the data collection activity, studies can be classified as either longitudinal or cross-sectional. Whereas longitudinal data are collected in several sweeps, cross-sectional data refer to data collected at one point in time. Both types of studies could be national or multinational.

Longitudinal studies follow the same respondents over a period and obtain repeated measures of the same concepts. Compared with cross-sectional surveys, longitudinal surveys tend to be more complex and more expensive to carry out. If the unit of analysis is an individual citizen, we can repeatedly ask questions of the same citizens and see whether their attitudes change over time (e.g., Does the experience of being called to participate in legal decision making enhance confidence in the government? Is the effect long term or short term?). If the unit of analysis is a country, we can repeatedly survey the citizens and see whether there is a change in the participants' confidence in the government as time passes (e.g., Did the 1994 legal reform of the jury system in a specific country influence the participants' confidence in the courts? Was the 2004 reform more successful in enhancing the confidence in the government?).

Two studies of jury verdicts over time, although each was limited to a single country, show the possibilities of longitudinal research. Donovan (2010) examined historical court records of jury trials in France. He found significant changes over time, the most substantial change coming when France shifted from an all-citizen jury to a mixed court of citizens and law-trained judges during the Vichy regime. In another longitudinal analysis of 40 years of civil jury verdicts in two U.S. counties, changes in damage awards were largely explained by the shifting mix of cases presented to juries over the period (Seabury, Pace, & Reville, 2004).

Combining two dimensions of Bennett's (2004) typology creates more complex combinations. For example, the cross-sectional approach can use either a descriptive approach or an analytical approach. Specifically, if the study is using the descriptive approach, we can ask basic operational questions. What role do lay citizens play in the newly proposed lay participation system in Taiwan? What is the most dominant form of lay participation today? If the study uses the analytical approach, we can ask more in-depth questions. How is the representativeness of groups of lay participants related to their ability to understand legal issues in the case? What are the causes of the renaissance of lay participation today?

The two multinational studies on lay participation that we described both relied on a cross-sectional approach in their study designs (Jackson & Kovalev, 2006; Vidmar, 2000). They surveyed experts (Jackson & Kovalev, 2006) or country representatives (Vidmar, 2000) at a specific time to obtain information about lay participation in a large number of countries. As historical changes in virtually all the countries demonstrate, the institute of lay participation is a living organism, shaped by larger political, social, and legal forces. We can anticipate that in 10 or 20 years, the information obtained in these studies may well become obsolete. Juries might be introduced or abolished, or mixed tribunals could replace juries. The quest for up-to-date information may be in order. A new sweep of the survey can potentially provide current information. However, unlike longitudinal surveys of individuals in which the individuals' views over multiple time periods are analyzed, surveys of experts on lay participation may not depend critically on whether the experts remain the same in all sweeps of the survey. Although rare to date, longitudinal studies of lay participation could produce valuable insights about the political, social, and legal factors that shape the success or failure of lay participation in law.

CONCLUSION

The diversity in forms of lay participation in legal decision making presents unparalleled scientific opportunities to study the effects of their introduction. Many of the world's jury systems are generations or even centuries old. They have already been well integrated into the legal systems of their jurisdictions. They are highly familiar to the countries' citizens. In contrast, with newly introduced systems, we can study their immediate and longer term effects, observing what occurs when a novel and unfamiliar form of citizen participation is introduced to the citizens, the legal professionals, and the machinery of justice. Lay participation has been regarded as a vehicle for enhancing the transparency and the legitimacy of the legal system and for bringing the outcomes of the legal system more in line with the values and perspectives of the community. We believe a critical issue that jury researchers should address is the extent to which the legitimacy of the legal system changes when lay participation is introduced.

For both practical and scientific reasons, it is important to understand the distinctive contributions of lay participation and to analyze what works best. Empirical research on existing and new systems of lay participation can educate the public as well as legal elites and policymakers about their operation. Nonetheless, addressing these significant questions about the effect and operation of diverse jury systems raises major methodological challenges for the jury research community. As we noted earlier, although traditional jury research approaches like mock jury experiments might be able to address some important jury issues, questions about societal impact and legitimacy may be difficult to study using such traditional jury research methodologies. Jury verdict analyses, questionnaire studies of real jurors, and surveys of the public may hold more promise (Diamond & Rose, 2005; see also Chapter 5, this volume). Systematic analysis of juries in different countries may require research strategies such as case studies and comparative approaches that are unfamiliar to many jury researchers. Perhaps, then, it is not surprising that empirical research (especially research reported in English) about the development, operation, and effects of diverse and new systems of lay participation is modest.

Nonetheless, many of the questions implicated by global jury developments overlap substantially with issues covered in other chapters. For example, Hunt (Chapter 4, this volume) argues that the role of race, ethnicity, and culture in jury decision making is not well understood. The social, political, legal, and cultural contexts for lay participation are significant factors to consider in global jury developments. We agree that such factors influence both the approach that decision makers take in their task and the judgments they make about the parties to a legal dispute.

Legislators, court officials, and policymakers face a host of questions about the most efficacious designs of new jury systems. There is a substantial connection between these efforts and the work done by jury task forces and state commissions in the United States in recent years to attempt to modernize the American jury system. These efforts can benefit from a thorough understanding of the strengths and limitations of individual and group decision making (Devine, 2012; see also Chapter 1, this volume). The American Bar Association created a Commission on the American Jury, for example. Its reports and recommendations have drawn heavily on jury research (American Jury Project, 2005). Nonetheless, in light of the importance of cultural context noted earlier, jurors' perspectives and group engagement might differ because of distinctive political and social factors in different countries. Thus, it is imperative that we take a global approach in our research, rather than simply make inferences from jury experiences and jury research in a single or small number of countries. Bennett's (2004) analysis described earlier offers a fruitful way to characterize the types of research projects we may conduct. It can encourage us to explore a range of comparative research strategies as well.

We urge jury researchers to work together toward developing a common set of research questions and methodological approaches that take advantage of these scientifically valuable opportunities to understand the diverse effects of incorporating lay citizens into legal systems as decision makers. To have the biggest scientific payoff, we believe it is important to coordinate research efforts across countries, studying overlapping sets of topics and using similar questions.

REFERENCES

Act for Civil Participation in Criminal Trials, Korean Government Code 8495 (2007).

Ahn, K., & Han, I. (2005). *Jury system and civil participation in law.* Seoul, Korea: Jip-Mun Dang.

American Jury Project. (2005). *Principles for juries and jury trials*. Chicago, IL: American Bar Association.

Anderson, S. (1990). Lay judges and jurors in Denmark. *The American Journal of Comparative Law*, *38*, 839–864. http://dx.doi.org/10.2307/840614

Bennett, R. R. (2004). Comparative criminology and criminal justice research: The state of our knowledge. *Justice Quarterly*, *21*, 1–21. http://dx.doi.org/10.1080/07418820400095721

Berman, J. (1969). The Cuban popular tribunals. *Columbia Law Review*, *69*, 1317–1354. http://dx.doi.org/10.2307/1121395

Butler, W. E. (1972). Comradely justice in Eastern Europe. *Current Legal Problems*, *25*, 200–218.

Cameron, N., Potter, S., & Young, W. (2000). The New Zealand jury: Towards reform. In N. Vidmar (Ed.), *World jury systems* (pp. 167–210). http://dx.doi.org/10.1093/acprof:oso/9780198298564.003.0005

Casper, G., & Zeisel, H. (1972). Lay judges in German criminal courts. *The Journal of Legal Studies*, *1*, 135–191. http://dx.doi.org/10.1086/467481

Castellucci, I. (2007). Rule of law with Chinese characteristics. *Annual Survey of International and Comparative Law*, *13*, 35–58.

Chesterman, M. (2000). Criminal trial juries in Australia: From penal colonies to a federal democracy. In N. Vidmar (Ed.), *World jury systems* (pp. 125–166). http://dx.doi.org/10.1093/acprof:oso/9780198298564.003.0004

Chinese Government. (2005). *White paper on political democracy published.* Retrieved from http://www.china.org.cn/english/2005/Oct/145718.htm

Chinese Government. (2008). *PRC state council white paper: China's efforts and achievements in promoting the rule of law*. Beijing, China: Author.

Chinese Government. (2012). *China improves systems of people's jurors, people's supervisors: White paper, People's Daily Online*. Beijing, China: Author.

Committee for Citizen Participation in Law. (2013). *Outcome report of hearings for determining the final form of civil participation trial.* Seoul, Korea: The Korean Supreme Court.

Court and Tribunals Judiciary. (2014). Magistrates. Retrieved from http://www.judiciary.gov.uk/about-the-judiciary/the-judiciary-in-detail/judicial+roles/magistrates

Daehanminkuk Hunbeob [Constitution] (1987) (S. Kor.).

Devine, D. J. (2012). *Jury decision making: The state of the science*. New York: New York University Press.

Diamond, S. S. (1990). Revising images of public punitiveness: Sentencing by lay and professional English magistrates. *Law & Social Inquiry*, *15*, 191–221. http://dx.doi.org/10.1111/j.1747-4469.1990.tb00586.x

Diamond, S. S., & Rose, M. (2005). Real juries. *Annual Review of Law and Social Science*, *1*, 255–284. http://dx.doi.org/10.1146/annurev.lawsocsci.1.041604.120002

Dolidze, A., & Hans, V. P. (2013, May). *Jury trial as legal translation: The case of the Republic of Georgia.* Paper presented at the meeting of the Law & Society Association, Boston, MA.

Donovan, J. M. (2010). *Juries and the transformation of criminal justice in France in the nineteenth and twentieth centuries.* http://dx.doi.org/10.5149/9780807895771_donovan

Duff, P. (2000). The Scottish criminal jury: A very peculiar institution. In N. Vidmar (Ed.), *World jury systems* (pp. 249–282). http://dx.doi.org/10.1093/acprof:oso/9780198298564.003.0007

Eisenberg, T., Hannaford-Agor, P. L., Hans, V. P., Waters, N. L., Munsterman, G. T., Schwab, S. J., & Wells, M. T. (2005). Judge–jury agreement in criminal cases: A partial replication of Kalven and Zeisel's *The American Jury*. *Journal of Empirical Legal Studies, 2*, 171–207. http://dx.doi.org/10.1111/j.1740-1461.2005.00035.x

Felstiner, W. L. F., & Drew, A. B. (1978). *European alternatives to criminal trials and their applicability in the United States.* Washington, DC: National Institute of Law Enforcement and Criminal Justice.

Fukurai, H. (2007). The rebirth of Japan's petit quasi-jury and grand jury systems: A cross-national analysis of legal consciousness and the lay participatory experience in Japan and the U.S. *Asian-Pacific Law & Policy Journal, 12*, 95–142.

Fukurai, H. (2010). People's panels vs. imperial hegemony: Japan's twin lay justice systems and the future of American military bases in Japan. *Cornell International Law Journal, 40*, 314–354.

Fukurai, H. (2011). Japan's prosecutorial review commissions: Lay oversight of the government's discretion of prosecution. *East Asia Law Review*, 6, 1–34.

Fukurai, H., & Park, S. (2012). Korea's two key legal reforms of lay adjudication: The possible introduction of the grand jury (Japan's Prosecutorial Review Commission) system and the elimination of consent requirement to allow lay adjudication of American military felons in South Korea. *Yonsei Law Journal, 3*, 68–93.

Fukurai, H., & Wang, Z. (2014). People's grand jury panels and the state's inquisitorial institutions: Prosecution Review Commissions in Japan and People's Supervisors in China. *Fordham International Law Journal, 37*, 929–971.

Gastil, J. E., Deess, P., Weiser, P., & Simmons, C. (2010). *The jury and democracy: How jury deliberation promotes civic engagement and political participation.* New York, NY: Oxford University Press.

Grant, B., & Schwikkard, P. (1991). People's courts? *South African Journal on Human Rights, 7*, 304–316.

Han, I. (2010). The process of judicial democratization and the birth of trial by citizens: The historical meanings. In I. Han & S. Han (Eds.), *Citizen participation in law* (pp. 37–45). Seoul, Korea: Kyungin.

Hans, V. P. (2007). Introduction: Citizens as legal decision makers: An international perspective. *Cornell International Law Journal, 40*, 303–314.

Hans, V. P. (2012). What difference does a jury make? *Yonsei Law Journal, 3*, 36–54.

Hans, V. P. (2014). Reflections on the Korean jury trial. *Journal of Korean Law, 14*, 81–115.

Hans, V. P., & Germain, C. (2011). The French jury at a crossroads. *Chicago-Kent Law Review, 86*, 737–768.

Hans, V. P., Hannaford-Agor, P. L., Mott, N. L., & Munsterman, G. T. (2003). The hung jury: *The American Jury*'s insights and contemporary understanding. *Criminal Law Bulletin, 39*, 33–50.

Hans, V. P., & Vidmar, N. (1986). *Judging the jury*. http://dx.doi.org/10.1007/978-1-4899-6463-2

Jackson, J., & Kovalev, N. (2006). Lay adjudication and human rights in Europe. *Columbia Journal of European Law, 13*, 83–123.

Jackson, J. D., Quinn, K., & O'Malley, T. (2000). The jury system in contemporary Ireland: In the shadow of a troubled past. In N. Vidmar (Ed.), *World jury systems* (pp. 283–318). http://dx.doi.org/10.1093/acprof:oso/9780198298564.003.0008

Japan Federation of Bar Associations. (2010). *Proposal for the criminal justice meeting people's expectation*. Tokyo, Japan: Author.

Japanese Supreme Court. (2012a). *Heisei 23-nen ni Okeru Saiban-in Saiban no Jishijokyo-to ni Kansuru Shiryo* [Report on the implementation of *Saiban-in* trials in 2011]. Retrieved from http://www.saibanin.courts.go.jp/vcms_lf/h23_siryo1.pdf

Japanese Supreme Court. (2012b). *Saiban-in Saiban Jisshi Jokyo no Kensho Hokokusho* [Investigative report on the implementation of *Saiban-in* trials]. Retrieved from http://www.moj.go.jp/content/000096892.pdf

Japanese Supreme Court. (2012c). *Saiban-in to Keikensha ni Taisuru Anketo* [Survey of the *Saiban-in* participants]. Retrieved from http://www.saibanin.courts.go.jp/vcms_lf/h24_keikensya.pdf

Japanese Supreme Court. (2014). *Saiban-in Seido no Unyo ni Kansuru Ishiki Chosa* [Opinion survey on the utilization of *Saiban-in Seido*]. Retrieved from http://www.saibanin.courts.go.jp/vcms_lf/H25_survey_2.pdf

Jiang, D. (2000). Judicial reform in China: New regulations for the lay assessor system. *Pacific Rim Law & Policy Journal, 9*, 569–590.

Jimeno-Bulnes, M. (2004). Lay participation in Spain: The jury system. *International Criminal Justice Review, 14*, 164–185. http://dx.doi.org/10.1177/105756770401400107

Jones, N. A. (2010). *The courts of genocide*. New York, NY: Routledge.

Kalven, H., & Zeisel, H. (1966). *The American jury*. Boston, MA: Little, Brown.

Kamhi, S., & Čalija, B. (1974). *Sistem porote u našoj zemlji i problemi vezani za učešce gradjana u vršenju pravosudja* [The jury system in our country and the problems of lay participation in the administration of justice]. Sarajevo, Bosnia and Herzegovina: Svjetlost.

Keyuan, Z. (2002). Judicial reform in China: Recent developments and future prospects. *International Lawyer*, *36*, 1039–1062.

Kim, S., Park, J., Park, K., & Eom, J.-S. (2013). Judge–jury agreement in criminal cases: The first three years of the Korean jury system. *Journal of Empirical Legal Studies*, *10*, 35–53. http://dx.doi.org/10.1111/jels.12001

King, N. J. (2000). The American criminal jury. In N. Vidmar (Ed.), *World jury systems* (pp. 93–124). http://dx.doi.org/10.1093/acprof:oso/9780198298564.003.0003

Klami, H. T., & Hämäläinen, M. (1992). *Lawyers and laymen on the bench*. Helsinki, Finland: Suomalainen Tiedeakatemia.

Kovalev, N. (2010). *Criminal justice reform in Russia, Ukraine and the Former Republics of the Soviet Union: Trial by jury and mixed courts*. Lewiston, NY: The Edwin Mellen Press.

Krystufek, Z. (1976). The function of the lay judge in Czechoslovakia. In L. Friedman & M. Rehbinder (Eds.), *Zur soziologie des gerichtsverfahrens* [Sociology of the judicial process] (pp. 301–306). http://dx.doi.org/10.1007/978-3-322-96982-8_17

Kubicki, L., & Zawadzki, S. (1970). Lay assessor judges in penal proceedings in the light of empirical research. In S. Zawadzki & L. Kubicki (Eds.), *Udzial Lawników W Postepowaniu Karnym* [Lay participation in criminal procedure] (pp. 97–111). Warsaw, Poland: Wydawnictwo Prawnicze.

Kulcsàr, K. (1982). *People's assessors in the courts*. Budapest, Hungary: Akadémiai Kiadó.

Kutnjak Ivković, S. (1999). *Lay participation in criminal trials: The case of Croatia*. Lanham, MD: Winfield.

Kutnjak Ivković, S. (2002). Croatia—Mixed tribunals in Croatia. *International Review of Penal Law*, *72*, 57–85.

Kutnjak Ivković, S. (2007). Exploring lay participation in legal decision-making: Lessons from mixed tribunals. *Cornell International Law Journal*, *40*, 429–453.

Landsman, S., & Zhang, J. (2008). A tale of two jurors: Lay participation comes to Japanese and Chinese courts. *UCLA Pacific Basin Law Journal*, *25*, 179–227.

Lapaine, M. (1986). Neka razmisljanja o sudjelovanju sudaca porotnika u nasem krivicnom postupku [Some thoughts on participation of lay judges in our criminal procedure]. *Nasa zakonitost*, *40*, 605–612.

Lee, J. (2003). An examination of the Constitution about civil participation in law. *Law and Society*, *25*, 27–35.

Ljubanovic, V. (1989). *Demokratizacija krivicnog pravosudja* [Democratization of criminal procedure]. Osijek, Croatia: Pravni fakultet Sveucilista u Osijeku.

Lloyd-Bostock, S., & Thomas, C. (2000). The continuing decline of the English jury. In N. Vidmar (Ed.), *World jury systems* (pp. 53–92). http://dx.doi.org/10.1093/acprof:oso/9780198298564.003.0002

Lo, W. H., & Snape, E. (2005). Lawyers in the People's Republic of China: A study of commitment and professionalization. *The American Journal of Comparative Law*, *53*, 433–455.

Lorenzo, L. (2014, Apr. 11). Las enseñanzas del primer juicio por jurados [Lessons from the first jury trial]. Retrieved from http://www.jusneuquen.gov.ar/index.php?option=com_content&view=article&id=3515

Machura, S. (2001). Interaction between lay assessors and professional judges in German mixed courts. *International Review of Penal Law, 72*, 451–479.

Machura, S. (2011). Silent lay judges—Why their influence in the community falls short of expectations. *Chicago-Kent Law Review, 86*, 769–788.

Malsch, M. (2009). *Democracy in the courts: Lay participation in European criminal justice systems*. Surrey, England: Ashgate.

Maruta, T. (1990). *Baishin saiban o kangaeru: Hotei ni miru nichibei bunka hikaku* [Research on jury trials: Intercultural comparison between the Japanese and U.S. courts]. Tokyo, Japan: Chuko Shinsha.

Merry, S. E., & Milner, N. (Eds.). (1993). *The possibility of popular justice: A case study of community mediation in the United States*. Ann Arbor: University of Michigan Press.

Park, J. (2010). *The jury system and legal psychology*. Seoul, Korea: Ore.

Parker, H., Sumner, M., & Jarvis, G. (1989). *Unmasking the magistrates*. Milton Keynes, England: Open University Press.

Perron, W. (2001). Germany—Lay participation in Germany. *International Review of Penal Law, 72*, 181–195.

PRC Act. (2004). *Keiji Soshohoto no Ichibu o Kaiseisuru Horitsu* [Act to Revise the Code of Criminal Procedure], Law No. 62 of 2004.

Ramundo, B. A. (1965). The comrades' court: Molder and keeper of socialist morality. *The George Washington Law Review, 33*, 693–727.

Reichel, P. L. (2008). *Comparative criminal justice systems: A topical approach*. Upper Saddle River, NJ: Prentice Hall.

Samuel, G. (2013). Comparative law and its methodology. In D. Watkins & M. Burton (Eds.), *Research methods in law* (pp. 100–118). New York, NY: Routledge.

Seabury, S. A., Pace, N. M., & Reville, R. T. (2004). Forty years of civil jury verdicts. *Journal of Empirical Legal Studies, 1*, 1–25. http://dx.doi.org/10.1111/j.1740-1461.2004.00001.x

Seekings, J., & Murray, C. (1998). *Lay assessors in South Africa's Magistrates' Courts*. Retrieved from http://www.cls.uct.ac.za/usr/lrg/publications/LayAssessors.pdf

Smith, G. (1974). Popular participation in the administration of justice in the Soviet Union: Comrades' courts and the Brezhnev regime. *Indiana Law Journal, 49*, 238–252.

Sperlich, P. W. (2007). *The East German social courts: Law and popular justice in a Marxist-Leninist society*. Westport, CT: Praeger.

Thaman, S. C. (1995). The resurrection of trial by jury in Russia. *Stanford Journal of International Law, 31*, 61–274.

Thaman, S. C. (1998). Spain returns to trial by jury. *Hastings International & Comparative Law Review, 21*, 241–537.

United Nations. (2006). *Consideration of reports submitted by states parties under Article 19 of the Convention*. Retrieved from http://www.univie.ac.at/bimtor/dateien/china_cat_2007_report.pdf

Vidmar, N. (Ed.). (2000). *World jury systems*. http://dx.doi.org/10.1093/acprof:oso/9780198298564.001.0001

Wang, Z., & Fukurai, H. (2015). China's lay participation in the justice system: Surveys and interviews of contemporary lay assessors in Chinese courts. In S. Miyazawa, J. Weidong, H. Fukurai, & K. W. Chan (Eds.), *East Asia's renewed respect for the rule of law in the 21st century: The future of legal and judicial landscape in East Asia* (pp. 111–136). http://dx.doi.org/10.1163/9789004274204_008

Yan. (2010). *Chinese legislature passes People's Mediation Law*. Retrieved from http://news.xinhuanet.com/english2010/china/2010-08/29/c_13467472.htm

Yue, L. (2001). The lay assessor system in China. *Revue internationale de droit penal, 72*, 51–56. http://dx.doi.org/10.3917/ridp.721.0051

Zhi, Y. (2008). *The investigation report of the people's supervisors system: Sampling the procuratorates in the autonomous region of Hong He Hani and Yi Ethnic Minorities* (Unpublished LL.M. degree dissertation). Lanzhou University, Gansu, China.

Ziyadov, N. (2013). *Choosing for juries: Application and development of juries in old and new jury trial countries*. Antwerp, Belgium: Maklu.

II

VALIDITY AND TRIAL SIMULATION METHODOLOGY

7

JURY SIMULATION GOALS

JONATHAN J. KOEHLER AND JOHN B. MEIXNER, JR.

Juries have long been of special interest to psychologists who study the way individuals and groups make decisions. Juries are charged with making some of the most important decisions in our society (including, in some cases, whether a criminal defendant lives or dies), and the secrecy of their deliberations adds to their mystique. For decades, psychologists interested in legal decision making have conducted a type of controlled experiment, known as a *jury simulation* or mock trial. Jury simulations are experimental studies in which the researcher attempts to construct a setting that mirrors, to some extent, a jury decision-making environment. Jury simulations vary widely in terms of participants, materials, physical settings, realism, methods, independent variables, dependent measures, and other experimental features.

What are the goals that researchers who conduct jury simulations have or should have? Drawing on Pennington and Hastie (1981), we identify three

This research was supported, in part, by the Northwestern University School of Law Faculty Research Program. We thank Margaret Bull Kovera for helpful comments on an earlier draft.

http://dx.doi.org/10.1037/0000026-008
The Psychology of Juries, M. B. Kovera (Editor)

primary goals: (a) to develop theory, (b) to describe how juries perform, and (c) to improve the jury process. These goals are not exhaustive (other goals are possible), nor are the goals themselves mutually exclusive. For example, many jury researchers seek to provide insight into basic human cognition by describing a systematic influence on the behavior of participants in a jury simulation (Goal 1). Once the experimental demonstration is established, the researchers may then argue that real juries will behave similarly (Goal 2) and that this result points the way toward improving some aspect of the legal system (Goal 3). Having multiple goals is not itself a problem. But researchers should be aware that the validity concerns associated with each goal are different and may even tug in opposite directions.

The purpose of this chapter is to explore the three goals of jury simulation research and to suggest that the validity concerns associated with each goal have important implications for the design of these simulations. We also suggest that because much of this research appears to be more focused on affecting legal policy than on advancing basic psychological theory, researchers should attend more closely to matters of ecological and external validity when designing their studies.

The remainder of this chapter is organized as follows. First, we identify and discuss three validity matters that jury simulation researchers must consider in their research designs: internal validity, external validity, and ecological validity. Next, we discuss the three central goals of jury simulation research: advancing psychological theory, modeling jury behavior, and affecting legal policy. We conclude by suggesting that jury simulation researchers who wish to influence legal policy should design more ecologically valid studies and otherwise focus on the goals and concerns of the legal policymakers they seek to persuade.

VALIDITY CONCERNS

Cook and Campbell (1979) famously identified various threats to the validity of many types of experimental research. These include threats to *internal validity* (the causal connection between independent and dependent variables), *external validity* (the generalizability of results to other samples and settings), and *statistical conclusion validity* (the relationship between variables). *Construct validity* (how well the operationalized variables capture the underlying constructs that they are supposed to represent) and *ecological validity* (how well the experimental setting mimics real-world settings of interest) may also be of more or less concern depending on how a simulation is designed. For our purposes here, internal, external, and ecological validity are most relevant.

Internal Validity

Researchers who conduct jury simulations largely to advance basic theory (Goal 1) are interested in using research methods that maximize internal validity. Most people agree that properly conducted randomized experiments (including jury simulations) have relatively strong internal validity. In these studies, significant changes in the dependent variables of interest (e.g., damages awarded, subjective probabilities of guilt, or verdict) may be traced directly to the causal influence of one or more manipulated independent variables (e.g., use of emotional arguments, specific judicial instruction). As a general matter, internal validity is of concern in experimental designs because without strong internal validity researchers cannot draw valid conclusions about the result of their manipulations and thus cannot proceed to the second question of whether those results are generalizable.

External Validity

External validity is concerned with how well the results of a study generalize across various people, times, settings, and other specific elements in the study. Studies that find consistent results across different types of participants and experimental contexts and stimuli have higher external validity than those that do not. Jury simulations commonly focus more on matters of internal than external validity. Researchers are usually more concerned with gaining the control needed to identify causal relationships among variables; they are relatively less concerned with demonstrating that those relationships hold across an array of real-life situations or a variety of populations. Of course, as Anderson and Bushman (1997) noted, a focus on internal validity does not necessarily come at the expense of external validity. It is an empirical question as to whether the relations among variables identified in laboratory settings generalize, and Anderson and Bushman (1997) provided evidence that some do indeed generalize.

Ecological Validity

Ecological validity is related to external validity but is more directly concerned with how well the experimental setting mimics the real-world setting or settings of interest.[1] Field studies—in which the behaviors of jurors in various actual cases are observed—have a certain claim to ecological validity

[1]This working definition of *ecological validity* is widely used and accepted (see e.g., Penrod, Kovera, & Groscup, 2011; Robbennolt, 2002–2003). However, the term originally had a different meaning that some have argued should be retained (Hammond, 1998).

by virtue of the fact that the examined setting and people are real. Whether the relations observed in a field study generalize to other settings and populations (i.e., have external validity) is an empirical question. Jury simulations that include many key features of actual jury trials (e.g., live opening arguments from attorneys, cross-examination of witnesses, jury deliberation) have higher ecological validity than short, paper-and-pencil studies (Breau & Brook, 2007). Whereas there is general agreement that much jury research suffers from low ecological validity, there is less agreement about the extent to which this shortcoming matters (cf. Vidmar, 1979, 2008; Penrod, Kovera, & Groscup, 2011; Weiten & Diamond, 1979). Our view is that the negative impact of low ecological validity on a study depends largely on the investigators' goals and claims. Researchers interested primarily in Goal 1—advancing basic psychological theory—need not worry as much about this issue. However, researchers interested in Goals 2 and 3—describing jury behavior and affecting legal policy—should be more concerned. In a sense, this point is self-evident: An investigator's goals must play a large role in the design of his or her studies. At the same time, our view is that many, if not most, jury simulations would likely be conducted differently if investigators took this recommendation to heart at the earliest stages of their research programs.

GOAL 1: THEORY DEVELOPMENT

As indicated earlier, theory development (Goal 1) is a goal that many jury researchers have and should have. Psychologists and others who are interested in addressing basic questions about cognition, decision making, and social dynamics will find that the jury simulation paradigm—in which participants act as mock jurors in a civil or criminal case—often offers an appropriate method for studying these questions.

Consider, for example, a study that was designed to test a general theory of how people think about low probability events (exemplar cueing theory). Koehler and Macchi (2004) presented the results from two controlled, highly simplified simulations that included statistical evidence from a hypothetical criminal case. From an ecological validity standpoint, the study was lacking. Jurors did not receive judicial instructions, watch witnesses undergo cross-examination, hear objections, receive comprehensive judicial instructions, or deliberate. Although the participants were selected from two countries (Italy and the United States), the external validity of the study remains unknown both for the reasons described earlier and because the study used a rather narrow range of stimulus materials. In light of these ecological limitations, one might legitimately question the authors' claim that the results could have implications for how lawyers may wish to present statistical evidence at trial. But the central purpose of the study was theory testing. The legal context was simply a convenient one in which to explore the notion that people may give more and less weight to low-frequency statistical information as a function of the ease with which they are able to generate relevant exemplars.

Similar comments could be made about other legal decision-making studies. For example, James Davis's work on social decision scheme (SDS) theory (see, e.g., Davis, 1973; Stasser & Davis, 1981) was motivated by a desire to understand the way small groups aggregate the individual judgments and decisions of its individual members. Jury simulations that included deliberation provided an obvious context for Davis's work in this area. Davis and other SDS researchers did not go to great lengths to create a realistic jury atmosphere, but this shortcoming did not interfere with the primary goals of the research program.

In some cases, psychologists might conduct their studies in a jury setting simply to show how a group (including a jury) could be induced to behave, rather than to show how they often do behave. In these situations, neither the study's ecological validity nor its external validity would be of great concern. Suppose, for example, a researcher is interested in demonstrating that groups can be bullied by a single member into doing something all its members know to be illegal, inappropriate, or unethical. A jury simulation might be conducted in which the bully is introduced into a mock jury to convince the jury to find the defendant guilty of charges that are obviously false. Such a study, which may be quite artificial and may not have direct applicability to actual jury deliberations, might be informative simply as a way to test the null hypothesis that groups of laypeople would not behave in that manner (cf. Mook, 1983).

These points are not new. Both critics and defenders of the jury simulation paradigm have long noted that theory testing is a legitimate purpose and that the reduced ecological and potentially external validities that commonly accompany such research do not themselves undermine the value of these studies (Kerr & Bray, 2005; Weiten & Diamond, 1979). But theory testers commonly suggest that their research has significant implications for how real juries behave and what types of reforms should be implemented on the basis of their results (Vidmar, 1979).

In many cases, the practical implications claimed for jury simulations reach well beyond anything that is justified by the research. Indeed, Thompson (1993) concluded that "the credibility of the field as a whole has been damaged by researchers who have made sweeping and misleading generalizations about the real legal system based on" brief, unrealistic jury simulations (p. 205). Others counter that failure to seek insights from these studies for actual juries would undersell our own research efforts (Kerr & Bray, 2005).

Reasonable people may agree with one view or the other. Our view is that those who wish to draw implications from jury simulations to real-life jury trials should and could do more at the design stage to support their speculations regarding Goal 2 (describing jury behavior) and Goal 3 (affecting legal policy) matters. The fact that short, unrealistic simulations may have value beyond theory development and testing should not be used to justify failures to introduce study design features that increase the validity of Goal 2 and Goal 3 inferences. There is no question that introducing design features that enhance the ecological validity of jury simulations is a time-consuming and costly endeavor, but it will often be time and money well spent. If the effects that our brief studies identify persist in more realistic legal environments, our confidence in the importance of those effects for jury decision making increases. Of course, many effects identified in Goal 1 studies will not affect relevant legal measures (e.g., verdicts) when realism is increased to make those studies more appropriate for Goals 2 and 3. That is, some genuine effects may simply wash out in the more complex environment of a full-length trial (Dillehay & Nietzel, 1980). Other effects may interact in complex ways with various trial features.

GOAL 2: MODELING JURIES

As previously noted, jury simulations are often a legitimate methodological option for researchers seeking to advance basic psychological theory. But we also noted that, in these types of studies, the jury context might be of secondary importance. Researchers conducting studies that focus on basic theory are often more interested in demonstrating or testing a particular phenomenon, leaving it to subsequent studies to identify whether that phenomenon is broadly applicable or whether it persists in a particular applied setting (e.g., real jury trials).

Some studies, however, focus primarily on what might be called *jury modeling*. Researchers conducting jury modeling studies are expressly interested in borrowing from the theoretical frameworks and phenomena identified by past work and using them to learn about juries' decision processes. Jury modeling is fundamentally different from theory development and thus is best achieved by attending to a different set of considerations. By its nature, jury modeling is an applied goal that can be met only through applied means: If jury modelers want their studies to persuade scientists and policymakers about how real juries operate, they must model the aspects of the trial that are relevant to the decision making of real jurors. In our view, the central purpose of such studies is to allow extrapolation from the lab to the real jury context.

Although these separate goals and corresponding separate considerations might seem obvious, we think they are worth considering carefully when planning experiments because jury modelers are faced with unique challenges not present in some other contexts. The jury and trial context are exceptionally difficult to model (Pennington & Hastie, 1981). A number of unique factors are present: The voir dire process winnows the jury-eligible population in case-specific (and perhaps attorney-specific) ways, jury trials are notoriously lengthy and complex, and the stakes of the jury's decisions are high. The difficulties of simulating a jury trial in a controlled laboratory setting have been discussed in various reviews (e.g., Bornstein, 1999; Bray & Kerr, 1979; Diamond, 1997; Weiten & Diamond, 1979; Wiener, Krauss, & Lieberman, 2011). Next, we provide a brief overview of what we regard to be some of the most significant aspects of the jury decision-making context that are commonly not accounted for in jury simulations.

Stakes and Duration

Several aspects of the jury's role are likely almost impossible to simulate in the lab. First, real trials are typically high-stakes affairs. The decisions juries make can implicate large amounts of money in civil cases and determine the freedom of defendants in criminal trials. Mock jurors in simulations know that no real consequences will result from the choices they make. Whereas jurors in real cases may agonize for hours or even days over their decisions, mock jurors contemplating their hypothetical decisions will likely not do the same.

Even putting aside concerns about effort, there may be something about the sheer enormity of the stakes that influences real jurors' decisions but cannot be modeled in the lab. In 2013, a jury found in favor of the plaintiffs in a class-action price-fixing case against Dow Chemical for $400 million. In accordance with federal antitrust law, this verdict was then trebled, yielding a $1.2 billion final verdict (*In re Urethane Antitrust Litigation*, 2013). In 2005, a jury acquitted actor Robert Blake of murder after deliberating for nearly 9 days (Associated Press, 2005). The stakes and intensity associated with such decisions surely played a role in the minds of jurors. Yet neither can be recreated with any degree of confidence in the laboratory.

Occasionally, researchers attempt to simulate the high stakes of a real-world trial (Bornstein & McCabe, 2005; Diamond & Zeisel, 1974). However, such efforts are rare and may raise ethical concerns. In one study, Breau and Brook (2007) used deception to make half of their participants in a mock law school honor code hearing think they were participating in an actual hearing. Students who thought the hearing was real spent more time deliberating and reached more lenient outcomes than students who knew the hearing was staged. This result, though not dispositive, suggests that our inability to replicate the stakes associated with real trials may point to an important limitation to our ability to predict real jury behavior. Likewise, recently accumulated data that point to the importance of hard-to-replicate emotion on jurors' judgments and decisions (see, e.g., Salerno & Bottoms, 2009) suggested that jury simulations not accounting for this element may miss an important aspect of jury decision making.

The duration and volume of information presented to jurors at trial is a second set of considerations that is also difficult, if not impossible, to model in the lab. More than half of all civil trials last at least 2 days, and many cases last for weeks (Galanter, 2004). Most jury decision-making studies take much less than an hour from start to finish; yet the average jury in simple misdemeanor federal cases deliberates for more than 3 hours (Mize, Hannaford-Agor, & Waters, 2007). Not only does this create a potentially important disparity between jury studies and jury experiences in terms of detail and complexity but also it means that mock jurors are unlikely to experience the slow pace and potential boredom that may come with a long trial. This problem may not be trivial, particularly if the process of culling the most relevant evidence from the sea of information presented in actual trials requires a type of heuristic processing that is not required in shorter studies (e.g., Pennington & Hastie, 1986).

Other Trial Features

Although the stakes, duration, and information volume of trials are nearly impossible to simulate, other potentially important trial features may be modeled in the labs of researchers who have sufficient time, resources, and motivation. These features include (a) juror demographics, (b) the evidence presentation modality, (c) the judge–jury interaction, (d) group deliberation, and (e) the questions answered by the jury. Many of these characteristics and the difficulty of modeling them have been written about elsewhere (e.g., Dillehay & Nietzel, 1980; Vidmar, 1979, 2008; Weiten & Diamond, 1979). Here, we review the topic briefly and focus on what we see as the most pressing issues facing jury-modeling researchers.

Jurors

Perhaps the most visible difference between real-world juries and mock juries in a typical jury-modeling experiment is the sample of jurors themselves. Whereas real-world juries are at least theoretically constructed of a random sample of jury-eligible citizens, the majority of jury-modeling studies use a more readily available population: students. This problem is well known (for an early review, see Weiten & Diamond, 1979), though there is no consensus as to its significance. One review concluded that there is rarely a main effect of sample when comparing the verdicts of student and nonstudent mock juror participants (e.g., Bornstein, 1999; see also Chapter 9, this volume). However, other recent studies have suggested that the mock jury population may interact with other experimental variables (for a review, see Wiener et al., 2011). For example, several studies published in a special issue of *Behavioral Sciences and the Law* demonstrated that when damage awards were a dependent variable, the jury sample (student vs. nonstudent) interacted with such variables as the type of damages in a medical malpractice case (punitive vs. compensatory; Fox, Wingrove, & Pfeifer, 2011) and ethnicity in a Title VII discrimination case (Schwartz & Hunt, 2011). More significantly, there are few available data about how juror type interacts with a variety of other variables, including an important but commonly neglected variable: jury deliberation (Nuñez, McCrea, & Culhane, 2011). The conclusion, then, is an uncertain one. Whereas the makeup of a mock jury may not matter in certain situations or with regard to certain dependent measures, it may matter strongly in others, making it difficult for jury modelers to know whether drawing mock jurors from a student population is a reasonable way to learn about real jury behavior.

Evidence Presentation Modality

An area that has received less attention in the literature is the modality in which mock trial testimony is presented to participants in jury-modeling studies. In real trials, jurors are presented with stimuli almost entirely through visual and auditory methods—they listen to witnesses' testimony and watch witnesses as they testify, assessing both the content and the demeanor of the witnesses. And there are visual and auditory cues at trial beyond the witness box; jurors also listen to the questions of attorneys and observe their demeanor. And there are visual and auditory "offstage" events occurring at trial as well: Jurors may visually observe the parties seated with their counsel (including, notably, criminal defendants)[2] and other individuals in the courtroom, such as audience members (Rose, Diamond, & Baker, 2010). Despite the nearly exclusive visual and auditory stimulus presentation method at trial and the increasing ease of conducting jury simulations that include visual and audio components, about half the jury simulation research published in the field's top journal (*Law and Human Behavior*) is still conducted instead using entirely written stimulus materials. Bornstein (Chapter 9, this volume) reports that nine of 13 jury simulation studies published in *Law and Human*

[2]Indeed, the U.S. Supreme Court has recognized that requiring criminal defendants to be tried while wearing identifiable prison clothes violates the prisoners' due process guarantees (*Estelle v. Williams*, 1976).

Behavior in 2005 to 2006 used written materials, as did three of seven studies in 2011 to 2012.

Is such a difference important? The data are not clear. Bornstein (1999) surveyed 11 studies that presented both written trial materials and more realistic materials, such as videotaped mock trials or live testimony. He noted that the presentation medium only affected the mock jurors' verdicts in three of the 11 studies, and among those in which main effects were found, the direction of the effects was inconsistent. Furthermore, Bornstein did not find that presentation medium interacted with other variables (e.g., type of testimony presented), and recent data from Pezdek, Avila-Mora, and Sperry (2010) are consistent with this conclusion.

Nevertheless, the data collected to date are not sufficient to justify a conclusion that presentation mode is irrelevant to jury modeling efforts. First, presentation modality (written vs. video stimuli) has not yet been tested in a variety of situations where there is reason to suspect that modality may matter. Visual cues often affect judgments, including those made in a legal context. For example, the confidence of mock expert witnesses (manipulated by tone of voice, postural awkwardness, or eye contact) affects the perceived credibility of those witnesses as well as the verdicts that mock jurors render, even when the experts use identical words (Cramer, Brodsky, & DeCoster, 2009). Such an influence could not be captured in studies that use written stimuli. Similarly, the perceived likability of witnesses, as influenced by demeanor and appearance, could affect their perceived credibility (Brodsky, Neal, Cramer, & Ziemke, 2009). Because demeanor is difficult to capture in written materials, modality seems to matter in at least some contexts. Also, real jurors discuss the offstage behavior of parties and other individuals in deliberations, though it is not clear whether those behaviors affect trial outcomes (Rose et al., 2010). Finally, a few studies have detected presentation modality effects in limited contexts. Presentation modality interacts with the perceived honesty and emotionality of witnesses (Heath, Grannemann, & Peacock, 2004) and can affect verdicts by interacting with jurors' attitudes (Nietzel, McCarthy, & Kern, 1999). Of course, these effects of stimulus modality will not always affect the variable of interest in a particular study. But given the relatively sparse data regarding the effect of stimulus modality on jury decision making, we think it would be premature to accept the convenient conclusion that presentation modality is unimportant to jury modeling, and we caution against extrapolating results across modalities without data supporting such a conclusion.

The Judge–Jury Interaction

Another relatively unexamined aspect of jury decision making at trial is the judge–jury relationship. Unlike the parties and their representatives, judges are widely viewed as disinterested, fair minded, and authoritative. As such, judicial words and behaviors may have a significant impact on jurors. For example, judges who frequently overrule one party's objections while sustaining the other's may inadvertently provide a signal to jurors about the relative credibility of the arguments offered by the two parties. Although empirical data on judge–jury interactions are sparse, Blanck, Rosenthal, and Cordell (1985) showed that judges' expectations about trial outcomes affected their verbal and nonverbal behavior, and these behaviors, in turn, influenced jurors' decisions. Other research has indicated that jurors may not always respond to the judge's instructions and interventions as intended. For example, mock jurors had difficulty disregarding inadmissible evidence following an instruction from the judge to do so (Steblay, Hosch, Culhane, & McWethy, 2006). There is also some evidence that mock jurors may not heed a judge's instruction to use evidence for one purpose but not another (Wissler & Saks, 1985). Although these types of effects do not tell us whether omission of the judge from jury simulations harms the external validity of the research, they do hint that the judge–jury relationship is a multifaceted one and that judicial actions and inactions may affect juries in complex ways. For example, failing to model the judge–jury relationship might reduce the depth of processing of evidence or jury instructions among mock jurors because of the lack of an authoritative judge explaining evidentiary burdens and decisions or reading and explaining jury instructions, as commonly occurs in real jury trials.

Group Deliberation

A more well-explored and frequently simulated aspect of the jury is its group nature, especially at the deliberative stage. Numerous studies have examined the effects of deliberation on jury decision making (for reviews, see Devine, 2012; Diamond, 1997; Nuñez et al., 2011), and it appears that deliberation affects some of the decisions jurors make. Here we touch on a few ways in which deliberation likely matters, particularly with respect to the potential for group deliberation to mitigate or exacerbate errors in jurors' understanding.

Although intuition might suggest that groups should be better than individuals at avoiding factual errors (e.g., mathematical computation errors, use of an improper evidentiary standard), the data do not clearly support this view. Indeed, groups often make more errors, and make more extreme errors, than individuals. For example, Tindale (1993) demonstrated that groups might make more *conjunction errors*—probability errors in which decision makers improperly assume that more specific conditions are more probable than a single general condition—than individuals. Drawing on a larger set of findings, Kerr and Tindale (2004) concluded that individual-level decision biases that promote suboptimal decision strategies are exacerbated in groups and lead to even worse decisions.

Relatedly, some studies have found that group deliberation increases jurors' confidence in their verdicts without any corresponding increase in their understanding of the relevant facts. For example, Kaye, Hans, Dann, Farley, and Albertson (2007) asked mock jurors to watch a videotaped trial involving mitochondrial DNA evidence, after which they made a series of judgments about the evidence and the case before and after deliberating in groups. Group deliberation increased jurors' confidence in their own judgments. Postdeliberation, the proportion of jurors who reported a very high degree of uncertainty about the defendant's guilt (i.e., P[Guilt] = 50%) dropped from 16% to 10%. Correspondingly, the proportion of jurors who were highly certain about the defendant's guilt (i.e., P[Guilt] = 100%) increased from 8% to 17% following deliberation. Despite this increase in confidence, deliberating jurors did not appear to have a better grasp of the evidence than they had before deliberating. Their overall scores on a DNA evidence comprehension test increased by just 3% following deliberation (from 70% to 73%). More strikingly, a whopping 40% of jurors—both before and after group deliberation—mistakenly believed that the DNA evidence was irrelevant because it was possible that people other than the defendant contributed the hairs in question. When most jurors are confused, "deliberation may simply reinforce the inaccuracies of the majority" (Diamond, 1997, p. 565).

Deliberation may exert different types of influence, some positive, in other contexts. For example, there is evidence that deliberation may reduce mock jurors' willingness to endorse extreme verdicts (McCoy, Nuñez, & Dammeyer, 1999), reduce the biasing effects of inadmissible evidence (London & Nuñez, 2000; Wheatman & Shaffer, 2001), and may induce jurors to give larger damage awards to plaintiffs than they otherwise would give (Diamond & Casper, 1992; Schkade, Sunstein, & Kahneman, 2000). Deliberation may affect legal judgments in many other ways as well (for a review, see Salerno & Diamond, 2010). Our point here is a fairly modest one: In some contexts that jury-modeling researchers likely care about, deliberation may affect the judgments and decisions juries make. Deliberation may also interact with other aspects of the trial. If this is the case, it would seem unwise for jury modelers to ignore deliberation when planning their studies, except perhaps in those limited situations in which there is good reason to believe that deliberation will not affect the independent or dependent variables of interest. For example, deliberation may not matter much in simple, dry cases, but may matter a great deal in cases that are complex and potentially emotional. In the latter types of cases, one or more jurors may be in a better position to offer expertise, an anecdote, or an emotional argument that may influence the judgments of other jurors.

Questions Answered

Finally, we note that many of the questions that mock jurors and juries answer in jury modeling research are different from those answered by real juries. Researchers commonly ask individual mock jurors to provide a variety of judgments pertaining to such matters as witness credibility, evidentiary strength, probability of guilt, and confidence regarding various decisions. Although real jurors and juries do not make such judgments (at least not explicitly), these continuous measures often provide a more statistically powerful way to detect small effects than a binary verdict offered by a group entity. But one danger associated with asking for such judgments is that researchers may inadvertently direct jurors' attention to matters they might otherwise have ignored. By manipulating attention in this way, researchers may be generating results that have limited external validity. We are not aware of data that address the issue, but we merely raise the point that researchers' efforts to obtain more data may itself distort the data they receive.[3]

The discussion to this point may seem to paint a gloomy picture of Goal 2 (jury modeling) research. However, we do not mean to suggest that jury simulations that do not incorporate every feature of real jury trials are worthless for Goal 2 purposes. Studies that lack ecological validity may well still yield results that generalize across a range of actual trials if those aspects of actual trials that are not modeled in the simulation are not relevant to the question being studied. For example, if the stakes of a trial do not affect the way in which jurors interpret DNA random match probabilities (RMPs), then a failure to model the high-stakes nature of the trial is not a shortcoming of a study that sets out to examine the limited question of whether some other variable—such as the way in which RMPs are presented to jurors—affects the impact of this evidence. The problem, however, is that it is difficult to know which aspects of the trial are relevant in a given context. Research may provide some clues over time, though answers will be slow in coming given the many potential interactions among trial variables and the current lack of theory as to why certain trial variables may not influence decision making or may only influence it in certain contexts (Diamond, 1997). Consequently, we think researchers should err on the side of caution rather than convenience when conducting jury simulations for purposes of modeling jury decision making. Although we recognize that improving the ecological validity of our studies will take a toll on resources—and may ultimately limit the quantity of

[3]We also note that researchers can minimize this problem by ensuring that such questions are asked after questions that are analogous to decisions that real juries make (e.g., binary liability decisions). The problem remains, however, that more complex questions may influence others that follow, potentially limiting their usefulness.

studies we conduct—our view is the field would do well to push more in this direction, particularly when we wish to make claims about real jury behavior.

At the very least, we suggest that jury researchers who have Goal 2 in mind should generally be extremely cautious when making claims based on data from individual jurors who did not deliberate in groups and who based their judgments entirely on short written materials. There may be cases in which an exception is justified, such as when there are affirmative reasons to believe that visual evidence and group deliberation would have no influence on the results. But we reject that the high cost involved in designing and conducting more ecologically valid studies justifies the traditional approach to Goal 2 research. The cost of doing unpersuasive research is even higher. For those interested in Goal 3 research (i.e., persuading policymakers to make reforms), it is even more imperative to conduct ecologically valid studies. As we discuss next, policymakers want to see research that they can trust and that is broadly applicable.

GOAL 3: JURY IMPROVEMENT AND POLICY CHANGES

This third goal among jury researchers—improving the jury process—is different from the other two goals in that the intended audience is not other jury researchers. Instead, the focal audience is policymakers—a group including judges, legislators, attorneys general, prosecutors, rules committees, and the like. These are the people who have the power to decide, for example, whether a procedural rule or judicial instruction should be modified. Policymakers likewise may be empowered to permit jurors to ask questions in open court, allow jurors to engage in informal deliberations prior to the end of a case, or recommend that deliberating jurors refrain from conducting straw polls on the ultimate issue until all jurors have expressed their initial views. Though policy decisions should be grounded in methodologically sound empirical facts, few policymakers are trained in such methodological concepts as construct validity, internal validity, or experimental design. Indeed, these decision makers may not have any background in scientific and methodological matters. Moreover, it is not clear that even those policymakers who have technical backgrounds would be persuaded to take corrective actions on the basis of the results of the typical jury simulation.

Judiciary's Response to Jury Simulations

Scholars who have looked at the judiciary's response to social science evidence, including evidence from jury simulations, have reported that the courts are not impressed (Bornstein & McCabe, 2005; Caprathe, 2011;

Fradella, 2003). One famous Seventh Circuit case illustrates what can happen when a brilliant social scientist meets a brilliant legal scholar. In *Free v. Peters* (1993), Judge Richard Posner lambasted a jury simulation conducted by social science luminary Professor Hans Zeisel.

In the case, defendant Free appealed his death penalty conviction on grounds that the instructions the jurors received were confusing and misleading. In support, Free produced a study by Professor Zeisel showing that mock jurors who heard the same instructions that Free's jurors received misinterpreted much of what they were told. On the basis of their answers to 18 true–false questions, Zeisel concluded that nearly half the mock jurors misunderstood key questions, and a significant proportion of these individuals thought that the instructions actually conveyed points that were opposite to what they were intended to convey.

A district court concluded that Zeisel's study "should be taken seriously" and ordered a new sentencing hearing for Free (*Free v. Peters*, 1991). But the Seventh Circuit Court of Appeals reversed on grounds that Zeisel's study was "deficient" and could not be "taken seriously in light of the extraordinary vulnerability of his method" (*Free v. Peters*, 1993, p. 706). Writing for the majority, Judge Posner dismissed Zeisel's study as fatally flawed, in part, because there was a "lack of comparability between the test setting and the setting of the sentencing hearing" (*Free v. Peters*, 1993, p. 705). The majority reasoned as follows:

> There is little a priori reason to think that the results of such an examination offer insight into the ability of a real jury, which has spent days or weeks becoming familiar with the case and has had the benefit of oral presentations by witnesses, lawyers, and the judge, and which renders a verdict after discussion rather than in the isolation of an examination setting. (*Free v. Peters*, 1993, pp. 705–706)

In other words, the majority felt that a simulation that did not map onto a target case in terms of length, oral presentation, and deliberation was unlikely to provide insight into what a real jury did. A concurring opinion also noted that the lack of voir dire reduced the value of simulation results because voir dire excuses jurors who are "easily confused or easily swayed by non-significant matters" (Bauer, J., concurring, as cited in *Free v. Peters*, 1993, p. 707). As we noted previously, whether variables such as length, oral presentation, jury deliberation, and voir dire actually matter in jury decisions are empirical questions.

Whether the criticism is empirically justified or not, many judges will likely take the position that empirical studies that contain obvious ecological imperfections should not be given much weight. Consider, for example, *State v. Deck* (1999). Like *Free v. Peters* (1993), *State v. Deck* involved a criminal defendant's introduction of an empirical study calling into question how well jurors understood judicial instructions. Similar to *Free v. Peters*, in *Deck* the Supreme Court of Missouri rejected the study "because the people interviewed for the study . . . were given hypothetical facts that were different than the facts in this case, and they did not hear the testimony of witnesses, observe physical evidence or deliberate with eleven other jurors" (p. 542). Although not all judges will reach the same conclusions, the point is that even in the absence of data indicating that poor ecological validity results in poor external validity in jury simulations, judges may not be willing to assume that ecologically invalid simulations can be trusted to describe the behavior (or likely behavior) of real jurors.

Greater Attention to Ecological Validity

The larger point of these admittedly selective cases is that if jury simulation research is to have an impact on the judiciary and other legal policymakers, researchers will have to pay close attention to matters of ecological validity. They should do so for at least two reasons. One reason is simply because policymakers care about how well the laboratory setting captures various potentially influential factors in real trials. Many policymakers will likely view with caution studies that use students (as opposed to "real" jurors) or short written stimuli (as opposed to detailed trial videos) or that lack group deliberation. Even when jury simulation studies have high degrees of internal validity, policymakers may have a hard time getting past their artificiality. A second and related reason jury researchers should place more attention on ecological validity is that doing so will enhance what Dillehay and Nietzel (1980) referred to as the "applied explanatory power" of the effects their studies uncover. Effects that are identified from internally valid studies—including those that appear to generalize across a variety of settings and populations—may not tell us much about whether those effects explain a meaningful proportion of variance in the more complex, applied setting of interest—namely, jury trials. For example, suppose that a series of well-controlled studies finds that the precise language that a forensic science expert uses to describe a match affects jury verdicts (compared with the use of slightly different language conveying the same general concept). If the ecological validity of those studies is low, we may not assume that this language effect captures a meaningful proportion of verdict variance in complex real cases in which the forensic experts may be examined and cross-examined for hours and in which jurors hear testimony from other witness, arguments from attorneys, and instructions from a judge.

Some jury researchers will reject this perspective. For example, Kerr and Bray (2005) suggested that social scientists should pay relatively little attention to the wishes of policymakers and matters of ecological validity and instead focus on conducting high quality, internally valid studies. They argued that rather than simply giving policymakers the kind of studies that they want, jury researchers should try to educate policymakers (e.g., as expert witnesses and through amicus curiae briefs) about the value of highly controlled, albeit highly artificial, jury simulations. Relatedly, one might also argue that social scientists should inform policymakers that some scholars (e.g., Bornstein, 1999; Camerer & Hogarth, 1999; Desmarais & Read, 2011) have suggested that their intuitions about the importance of running high ecological validity studies, including those that have high stakes are wrong. In other words, according to this argument, we should try to persuade policymakers that practical implications for real juries and ideas for reform can be extracted from highly artificial simulations.

We agree that social scientists should never stop trying to educate policymakers, many of whom are lawyers, about matters of science and inference. For this reason, we support recent efforts to increase social science training in law schools by offering courses in empirical research methods, science and law, jury decision making, statistics, quantitative reasoning, and the like. At the same time we think it is unrealistic to expect that policymakers will ignore ecological validity shortcomings, nor do we think they should do so until a body of research specifically designed to address these issues emerges that shows such concerns to be misguided.

Practical Considerations

Introducing greater realism into jury simulations is often difficult and costly (Penrod et al., 2011), providing simulation researchers with some incentive to dig in and challenge the wisdom of what we are suggesting here. But here is where the investigators' goals should be consulted. If jury researchers wish to advance basic scientific theory, then traditional, unrealistic, randomized, controlled laboratory studies that place a premium on internal validity are fine. But researchers seeking to have an impact on trial policy cannot assume that the legitimate explanations they provide for not producing realistic simulations will persuade judges, policymakers, and advisory groups to give greater weight to their studies.

Those who are interested in conducting Goal 3 research also should take greater care in matters of problem selection. Jury researchers too often address questions that "lawyers consider obvious, trivial, unimportant or uninteresting" (Thompson, 1993, p. 204; see also Vidmar, 1979). Similarly, jury researchers often study questions that have already been decided by the courts and therefore have little practical impact (Lempert, 1991). This gulf between the questions that social scientists ask and the questions that policymakers want answered may also widen when social scientists, who are really most interested in Goal 3 research, identify and design studies with Goal 1 in mind. We therefore recommend that jury simulation researchers who wish to affect policy try putting themselves in the shoes of policymakers when selecting research questions. What are the problems that the system is currently grappling with, and how might an empirical study point the way toward a cost-effective and reliable solution? Researchers who think along these lines may ultimately find themselves in the best position to affect legal policy.

CONCLUSION

There are at least three goals that drive jury simulation research: (a) theory development, (b) jury modeling, and (c) jury reform. Researchers should think hard about which goals are of primary interest before locking into a research question and design. When basic theory (Goal 1) matters most, internal validity should be stressed. When describing the behaviors of real juries (Goal 2) or persuading policymakers about changes that should be made (Goal 3), external and ecological validity must be stressed as well.

We pushed this idea a bit further by offering the (admittedly untested) empirical claim that most jury researchers are more interested in describing actual jury behavior and affecting legal policy than they are in advancing basic psychological theory. This is not to say that jury researchers are uninterested in identifying general psychological phenomena. But we suspect that the jury setting is of special interest to most of those who conduct jury simulations, as opposed to being just a handy setting in which to test psychological theory.

If our suspicions are correct, jury researchers should focus more energy on matters related to ecological and external validity in their experimental designs. Such focus will likely increase the amount of time and money needed to conduct jury research and may even lead to fewer published studies (Penrod et al., 2011). Kerr and Bray (2005) rejected this strategy as too costly, and Penrod et al. (2011) noted that the impact of low ecological validity on the external validity of jury simulation studies remains an unanswered empirical question. Still, we throw our lot in with critics who have suggested that the poor ecological validity of jury simulations is a major problem for the field and one that requires corrective action (Diamond, 1997; Dillehay & Nietzel, 1980, Vidmar, 2008). We also agree with Wells (2005), who suggested that jury researchers should think more about how to communicate effectively with legal policymakers who are unlikely to be satisfied by evidence of internal validity. If psychologists want to have a meaningful impact on the legal system, they will have to maintain a sharp focus on the goals and concerns of the legal policymakers they seek to persuade: "Policymakers are not going to find useful a body of research that undermines their current policies and practices, unless there are clear demonstrations of better policies and practices to take their place" (Wells, 2005, p. 497).

This conclusion may not be a popular one among jury researchers. Many will continue to believe that a well-designed study can simultaneously achieve all three goals (i.e., advance basic theory, describe real jury behavior, and reform legal policy). Indeed, it can (for a sample of such studies, see reviews by Bornstein, 1999; Diamond, 1997; Wiener et al., 2011). At the same time, however, with the rise of Mechanical Turk, Qualtrics, and various related Internet-based survey research platforms, the temptation to conduct short, cheap, highly artificial legal studies is greater than ever. So long as we, as a field, fail to take ecological validity seriously, we must be prepared to accept that our impact on the courts and other policymakers will be small.

REFERENCES

Anderson, C. A., & Bushman, B. J. (1997). External validity of "trivial" experiments: The case of laboratory aggression. *Review of General Psychology, 1*, 19–41. http://dx.doi.org/10.1037/1089-2680.1.1.19

Associated Press. (2005, March 16). *Blake found not guilty*. Retrieved from http://www.today.com/id/7211376/ns/today-today_entertainment/t/blake-found-not-guilty/#.U5nkLy-vy3k

Blanck, P. D., Rosenthal, R., & Cordell, L. D. H. (1985). The appearance of justice: Judges' verbal and nonverbal behavior in criminal jury trials. *Stanford Law Review, 38*, 89–164. http://dx.doi.org/10.2307/1228603

Bornstein, B. H. (1999). The ecological validity of jury simulations: Is the jury still out? *Law and Human Behavior, 23*, 75–91. http://dx.doi.org/10.1023/A:1022326807441

Bornstein, B. H., & McCabe, S. G. (2005). Jurors of the absurd? The role of consequentiality in jury simulation research. *Florida State University Law Review, 32*, 443–467.

Bray, R. M., & Kerr, N. L. (1979). Use of the simulation method in the study of jury behavior: Some methodological considerations. *Law and Human Behavior, 3*, 107–119. http://dx.doi.org/10.1007/BF01039151

Brodsky, S. L., Neal, T. M., Cramer, R. J., & Ziemke, M. H. (2009). Credibility in the courtroom: How likeable should an expert witness be? *Journal of the American Academy of Psychiatry and the Law, 37*, 525–532.

Breau, D. L., & Brook, B. (2007). "Mock" mock juries: A field experiment on the ecological validity of jury simulations. *Law & Psychology Review, 31*, 77–92.

Camerer, C. F., & Hogarth, R. M. (1999). The effects of financial incentives in experiments: A review and capital–labor–production framework. *Journal of Risk and Uncertainty, 19*, 7–42. http://dx.doi.org/10.1023/A:1007850605129

Caprathe, W. J. (2011). Commentary: Participant differences and validity of jury studies. *Behavioral Sciences & the Law*, *29*, 328–330. http://dx.doi.org/10.1002/bsl.988

Cook, T. D., & Campbell, D. T. (1979). *Quasi-experimentation: Design and analysis issues for field settings*. Boston, MA: Houghton Mifflin.

Cramer, R. J., Brodsky, S. L., & DeCoster, J. (2009). Expert witness confidence and juror personality: Their impact on credibility and persuasion in the courtroom. *Journal of the American Academy of Psychiatry and the Law*, *37*, 63–74.

Davis, J. H. (1973). Group decision and social interaction: A theory of social decision schemes. *Psychological Review*, *80*, 97–125. http://dx.doi.org/10.1037/h0033951

Desmarais, S. L., & Read, J. D. (2011). After 30 years, what do we know about what jurors know? A meta-analytic review of lay knowledge regarding eyewitness factors. *Law and Human Behavior*, *35*, 200–210. http://dx.doi.org/10.1007/s10979-010-9232-6

Devine, D. J. (2012). *Jury decision making: The state of the science*. New York: New York University Press.

Diamond, S. S. (1997). Illuminations and shadows from jury simulations. *Law and Human Behavior*, *21*, 561–571. http://dx.doi.org/10.1023/A:1024831908377

Diamond, S. S., & Casper, J. D. (1992). Blindfolding the jury to verdict consequences: Damages, experts, and the civil jury. *Law & Society Review*, *26*, 513–563. http://dx.doi.org/10.2307/3053737

Diamond, S. S., & Zeisel, H. (1974). A courtroom experiment on juror selection and decision-making. *Personality and Social Psychology Bulletin*, *1*, 276–277. http://dx.doi.org/10.1177/014616727400100193

Dillehay, R. C., & Nietzel, M. T. (1980). Constructing a science of jury behavior. In L. Wheeler (Ed.), *Review of Personality and Social Psychology* (Vol. 1, pp. 246–264). Beverly Hills, CA: Sage.

Estelle v. Williams, 425 U.S. 501 (1976).

Fox, P., Wingrove, T., & Pfeifer, C. (2011). A comparison of students' and jury panelists' decision-making in split recovery cases. *Behavioral Sciences & the Law*, *29*, 358–375. http://dx.doi.org/10.1002/bsl.968

Fradella, H. F. (2003). A content analysis of federal judicial views of the social science "researcher's black arts." *Rutgers Law Journal*, *35*, 103–170.

Free v. Peters, 778 F. Supp. 431 (N.D. Ill. 1991).

Free v. Peters, 12 F.3d 700 (7th Cir. 1993).

Galanter, M. (2004). The vanishing trial: An examination of trials and related matters in federal and state courts. *Journal of Empirical Legal Studies*, *1*, 459–570. http://dx.doi.org/10.1111/j.1740-1461.2004.00014.x

Hammond, K. R. (1998). *Ecological validity: Then and now*. Retrieved from http://www.brunswik.org/notes/essay2.html#Now

Heath, W. P., Grannemann, B. D., & Peacock, M. A. (2004). How the defendant's emotion level affects mock jurors' decisions when presentation mode and evidence strength are varied. *Journal of Applied Social Psychology*, *34*, 624–664. http://dx.doi.org/10.1111/j.1559-1816.2004.tb02563.x

In re Urethane Antitrust Litigation, MDL No. 1616, Case No. 04-1616-JWL., 08-2617-JWL, 09-2026-JWL (M.D. Kan 2013).

Kaye, D. H., Hans, V. P., Dann, B. M., Farley, E. J., & Albertson, S. (2007). Statistics in the jury box: How jurors respond to mitochondrial DNA probabilities. *Journal of Empirical Legal Studies*, *4*, 797–834. http://dx.doi.org/10.1111/j.1740-1461.2007.00107.x

Kerr, N. L., & Bray, R. M. (2005). Simulation, realism, and the study of the jury. In N. Brewer & K. D. Williams (Eds.), *Psychology and law: An empirical perspective* (pp. 322–364). New York, NY: Guilford Press.

Kerr, N. L., & Tindale, R. S. (2004). Group performance and decision making. *Annual Review of Psychology*, *55*, 623–655. http://dx.doi.org/10.1146/annurev.psych.55.090902.142009

Koehler, J. J., & Macchi, L. (2004). Thinking about low-probability events: An exemplar-cuing theory. *Psychological Science*, *15*, 540–546. http://dx.doi.org/10.1111/j.0956-7976.2004.00716.x

Lempert, R. O. (1991). Why do jury research? In R. Hastie (Ed.), *Inside the juror* (pp. 242–254). Cambridge, England: Cambridge University Press.

London, K., & Nuñez, N. (2000). The effect of jury deliberations on jurors' propensity to disregard inadmissible evidence. *Journal of Applied Psychology*, *85*, 932–939. http://dx.doi.org/10.1037/0021-9010.85.6.932

McCoy, M. L., Nuñez, N., & Dammeyer, M. D. (1999). The effect of jury deliberations on jurors' reasoning skills. *Law and Human Behavior*, *23*, 557–575. http://dx.doi.org/10.1023/A:1022348229558

Mize, G. E., Hannaford-Agor, P., & Waters, N. L. (2007). *The state-of-the-states survey of jury improvement efforts: A compendium report*. Williamsburg, VA: National Center for State Courts. Retrieved from http://www.ncsc-jurystudies.org/~/media/Microsites/Files/CJS/SOS/SOSCompendiumFinal.ashx

Mook, D. G. (1983). In defense of external invalidity. *American Psychologist*, *38*, 379–387. http://dx.doi.org/10.1037/0003-066X.38.4.379

Nietzel, M. T., McCarthy, D. M., & Kern, M. J. (1999). Juries: The current state of the empirical literature. In R. Roesch, S. D. Hart, & J. R. P. Ogloff (Eds.), *Psychology and law: The state of the discipline* (pp. 23–52). http://dx.doi.org/10.1007/978-1-4615-4891-1_2

Nuñez, N., McCrea, S. M., & Culhane, S. E. (2011). Jury decision making research: Are researchers focusing on the mouse and not the elephant in the room? *Behavioral Sciences & the Law*, *29*, 439–451. http://dx.doi.org/10.1002/bsl.967

Pennington, N., & Hastie, R. (1981). Juror decision making models: The generalization gap. *Psychological Bulletin*, *89*, 246–287. http://dx.doi.org/10.1037/0033-2909.89.2.246

Pennington, N., & Hastie, R. (1986). Evidence evaluation in complex decision making. *Journal of Personality and Social Psychology, 51*, 242–672. http://dx.doi.org/10.1037/0022-3514.51.2.242

Penrod, S. D., Kovera, M. B., & Groscup, J. (2011). Jury research methods. In B. Rosenfeld & S. D. Penrod (Eds.), *Research methods in forensic psychology* (pp. 191–214). Hoboken, NJ: Wiley.

Pezdek, K., Avila-Mora, E., & Sperry, K. (2010). Does trial presentation medium matter in jury simulation research? Evaluating the effectiveness of eyewitness expert testimony. *Applied Cognitive Psychology, 24*, 673–690. http://dx.doi.org/10.1002/acp.1578

Robbennolt, J. (2002–2003). Evaluating empirical research methods: Using empirical research in law and policy. *Nebraska Law Review, 81*, 777–804.

Rose, M. R., Diamond, S. S., & Baker, K. M. (2010). Goffman on the jury: Real jurors' attention to the "offstage" of trials. *Law and Human Behavior, 34*, 310–323. http://dx.doi.org/10.1007/s10979-009-9195-7

Salerno, J. M., & Bottoms, B. L. (2009). Emotional evidence and jurors' judgments: The promise of neuroscience for informing psychology and law. *Behavioral Sciences & the Law, 27*, 273–296. http://dx.doi.org/10.1002/bsl.861

Salerno, J. M., & Diamond, S. S. (2010). The promise of a cognitive perspective on jury deliberation. *Psychonomic Bulletin & Review, 17*, 174–179. http://dx.doi.org/10.3758/PBR.17.2.174

Schkade, D., Sunstein, C. R., & Kahneman, D. (2000). Deliberating about dollars: The severity shift. *Columbia Law Review, 100*, 1139–1176. http://dx.doi.org/10.2307/1123539

Schwartz, S. L., & Hunt, J. S. (2011). Considering her circumstances: How ethnicity and cultural relativist arguments affect sexual harassment judgments by undergraduate and community mock jurors. *Behavioral Sciences & the Law, 29*, 419–438. http://dx.doi.org/10.1002/bsl.972

Stasser, G., & Davis, J. H. (1981). Group decision making and social influence: A social interaction sequence model. *Psychological Review, 88*, 523–551. http://dx.doi.org/10.1037/0033-295X.88.6.523

State v. Deck, 994 S.W.2d 527 (Mo. 1999).

Steblay, N., Hosch, H. M., Culhane, S. E., & McWethy, A. (2006). The impact on juror verdicts of judicial instruction to disregard inadmissible evidence: A meta-analysis. *Law and Human Behavior, 30*, 469–492. http://dx.doi.org/10.1007/s10979-006-9039-7

Thompson, W. C. (1993). Research on jury decision-making: The state of the science. In N. J. Castellan (Ed.), *Individual and group decision making* (pp. 203–218). Hillsdale, NJ: Erlbaum.

Tindale, R. S. (1993). Decision errors made by individuals and groups. In N. J. Castellan (Ed.), *Individual and group decision making* (pp. 109–124). Hillsdale, NJ: Erlbaum.

Vidmar, N. (1979). The other issues in jury simulation research: A commentary with particular reference to defendant character studies. *Law and Human Behavior*, *3*, 95–106. http://dx.doi.org/10.1007/BF01039150

Vidmar, N. (2008). Civil juries in ecological context: Methodological implications for research. In B. H. Bornstein, R. L. Wiener, R. Schopp, & S. L. Willborn (Eds.), *Civil juries and civil justice: Psychological and legal perspectives* (pp. 35–65). http://dx.doi.org/10.1007/978-0-387-74490-2_3

Weiten, W., & Diamond, S. S. (1979). A critical review of the jury simulation paradigm: The case of defendant characteristics. *Law and Human Behavior*, *3*, 71–93. http://dx.doi.org/10.1007/BF01039149

Wells, G. L. (2005). Helping experimental psychology affect legal policy. In N. Brewer & K. D. Williams (Eds.), *Psychology and law: An empirical perspective* (pp. 483–500). New York, NY: Guilford Press.

Wheatman, S. R., & Shaffer, D. R. (2001). On finding for defendants who plead insanity: The crucial impact of dispositional instructions and opportunity to deliberate. *Law and Human Behavior*, *25*, 167–183. http://dx.doi.org/10.1023/A:1005645414992

Wiener, R. L., Krauss, D. A., & Lieberman, J. D. (2011). Mock jury research: Where do we go from here? *Behavioral Sciences & the Law*, *29*, 467–479. http://dx.doi.org/10.1002/bsl.989

Wissler, R. L., & Saks, M. J. (1985). On the inefficacy of limiting instructions: When jurors use prior conviction evidence to decide on guilt. *Law and Human Behavior*, *9*, 37–48. http://dx.doi.org/10.1007/BF01044288

8

MANAGING DIFFERENT ASPECTS OF VALIDITY IN TRIAL SIMULATION RESEARCH

DANIEL A. KRAUSS AND JOEL D. LIEBERMAN

Since the early development of psychology as a field in the early 20th century, jury decision making has been a central research area for those interested in the intersection of law and psychology. As Hugo Munsterberg (1908) stated in his book, *On the Witness Stand*, "the mental life—perception and memory, attention and thought, feelings and will—plays too important a role in court procedure to reject the advice of those who devote their work to the study of these functions" (p. 525). His focus on the application of psychological research to real-world problems, however, was criticized by many of his experimental colleagues; his ideas also received a scathing reception from legal commentators for his overreaching extrapolation of laboratory-based research findings to the complexities of legal processes. In fact, in the year following publication of Munsterberg's book a leading evidence scholar, Charles Wigmore, published a satirical trial in which Munsterberg's pronouncements were prosecuted as fraudulent misrepresentations, and a fictionalized

http://dx.doi.org/10.1037/0000026-009
The Psychology of Juries, M. B. Kovera (Editor)

jury found him liable for overstepping the actual benefits psychology could provide to law (Fulero & Wrightsman, 2009).

It would not be until the second half of the 20th century, when psychology and law had developed more formally as a field, that systematic study of juries and jury decision making would occur. Yet, despite this reawakened interest, the field continued to be plagued by what Greene et al. (2002) characterized as an identity crisis. For psychologists, it was fundamentally unclear (a) where jury decision-making research fit into the disciplines of psychology (e.g., social, cognitive, or a distinct area), (b) what training is necessary for its study, (c) whether empirical work should be primarily laboratory or field based, (d) whether basic psychological theory should drive research questions or whether research questions should simply aid the functioning of the court system, and (e) who should be the primary audience for the dissemination of the empirical findings—psychologists or members of the legal field (Greene et al., 2002).

In the past 40 years, these tensions have not abated for psychological researchers, nor has the legal field's skepticism of the relevance and applicability of experimental psychological jury research to legal practice dissipated, even as a sizable and significant body of social science research has emerged relevant to juries. In addition, the alarming decrease in jury trials in the United States, with some estimates suggesting that less than 2% of criminal and civil trials in state and federal courts now end in resolutions by a jury (Galanter & Frozena, 2011), has led some to question the importance of studying the vanishing jury. Yet, even with the use of juries in precipitous decline, the National Center for State Courts reported that in a recent year well over 1.5 million jurors were empanelled and over 150,000 trials occurred (Mize, Hannaford-Agor, & Waters, 2007). Moreover, as trial by jury has decreased in the United States, more and more countries and international courts (e.g., Argentina, Japan, Russia, Spain, Venezuela; Hans, 2008; see also Chapter 6, this volume) have adopted juries or hybrid systems that use legal determinations made by combinations of laypeople jurors and professional legal actors (Devine, 2012; Vidmar, 2000). Thus, juries are a fundamental component of legal systems throughout the world, and jury research remains a robust area of psychological study with potential to inform law, psychology, and society.

In this chapter, we examine jury research methods, with a special emphasis on the different validity concerns raised by trial simulation methodology. We argue that the field's identity crisis should not be viewed as a crisis at all, but rather as a reminder to choose research methods that emphasize different validity concerns. In particular, both researchers' ultimate goal regarding what they hope to accomplish by conducting a study and the targeted audience for dissemination of results should drive the balancing of validity concerns in experimental design. In addition, we discuss results from a recent survey that assessed how psychology and law scholars believe various validity concerns should be balanced. Finally, we offer a series of suggestions for improving jury research, its acceptance by the legal field, and the generalizability of its findings. Before turning to these issues, however, it is important to understand how jury research developed as a prominent area in psychology and law scholarship, as well as the key weaknesses of the most common research methodologies used by scholars in the field.

DEVELOPMENT OF JURY RESEARCH

Psychologists were not the first to complete large-scale, systematic empirical studies of juries. In the 1950s and 1960s, the Chicago Jury Project, headed by Harry Kalven, a law professor, and Hans Zeisel, a sociologist, investigated juries using all the primary research methodologies that are still used today: archival records reviews, posttrial interviews of jurors, surveys of legal practitioners, naturalistic observation or field studies, and mock trial simulations (Kalven & Zeisel, 1966). Each of the methodologies poses problems for the inferences that can be drawn from the research. First, reviewing archival records involves coding previously recorded data by the court to discern trends or relationships between variables (DeMatteo & Anumba, 2009). As such, this approach requires adequate and accurate records of the variables of interest to researchers, which are often not recorded by court personnel. This methodology also does not allow the researcher to manipulate variables of interest to determine how they directly cause changes in other important variables (Schuller & Yarmey, 2001). In the Chicago Jury Project, this method was used to investigate the number of annual trials in the United States, the number of hung juries, the amount of jury verdict awards, and the rate at which defendants waived their right to trial (Devine, 2012). Thus, this type of methodology is useful for descriptive research but is problematic for establishing why particular results occurred because the lack of experimental manipulation makes discerning causal relationships among variables (i.e., how change in one variable causes change in another variable) difficult, if not impossible.

Second, the Chicago Project's posttrial interviews allowed researchers to ask pertinent questions of juries and attorneys after they have completed their jury service, including querying juries about their views about their service. Unfortunately, interview responses are subject to the frailties of the jury members' memories, impression management by participants, selection bias in those who participate, and participants' lack of awareness of their actual, rather than stated, reasons for their beliefs or decisions (Devine, Clayton, Dunford, Seying, & Pryce, 2001).

Third, the Chicago Project surveyed over 3,500 trial judges who had presided over jury trials and compared their verdicts with those of the actual jury (archival records) to calculate rates of agreement between judges and juries (Devine, 2012). In general, surveys are subject to even greater selection bias than are interviews, in that many participants fail to complete the survey and those that do may fundamentally differ from those that respond. To increase the likelihood that respondents will complete the entire questionnaire, many surveys are relatively brief. Moreover, item wording and participants' attitudes may affect the veracity and reliability of responses. Although survey brevity was not relevant when Kalven and Zeisel (1966) measured only judicial verdict preference, it may present problems in other jury research contexts. Further, the other biases mentioned earlier (e.g., participant selection bias, impression management) likely affected what decisions judges endorsed when indicating verdict preferences.

Natural observation and field studies of jury behavior were also used in the Chicago Jury Project because the researchers taped a number of trials. In this paradigm, researchers code and analyze the behavior of legal participants while engaged in a specific activity, such as jury decision making. This type of research is infrequently performed in the legal arena because of ethical, legal, cost, and small sample issues (DeMatteo & Anumba, 2009). For example, courts are loath to allow recording and eventual coding of actual jury deliberations because the mere presence of recording might affect the outcome of trials; the recording process might also indicate that different juries decided factually similar cases differently or that jurors relied on inappropriate evidence in their decisions (e.g., inadmissible evidence); and/or interpretable results would require coordination, recording, and coding of a large number of jury deliberations to achieve the requisite sample size—to name just a few of the problems with this methodology.

In addition, researchers are limited to observing preexisting processes rather than being able to directly compare experimental manipulations of different legal procedures in the same context. As a result of this constraint, it is difficult to draw causal relationships among variables (cf. Hans, Hannaford, & Munsterman, 1999). In fact, the Chicago Project researchers' recording of juror deliberations may have unwittingly reduced the likelihood that future researchers could observe deliberations for research purposes because it was discovered that the jurors were not informed that they were being recorded (the judges had consented to the procedure). As a result of the furor following this surreptitious recording, legislation was adopted in 30 states and the federal system prohibited the taping of jury deliberations (Zimring, 2003).

The Chicago Project also used the most common method that psycholegal researchers use to study jury behavior, the mock trial simulation. In this methodology, researchers create trial vignettes in which they experimentally manipulate evidence and/or procedures in an attempt to discern cause-and-effect relationships between specific variables of interest. This staple method of jury research has often been criticized for inadequate participant sampling, impoverished trial simulations, lack of jury deliberations, and perhaps most important, the fact that participants must usually be informed that there are no real-world consequences to their actions (Diamond, 1997; see also Chapter 9, this volume). Although these threats to validity are not necessarily inherent to this methodology (i.e., trial simulation research has been completed that is not subject to any of these problems), the vast majority of published simulation research evidences one or more of these methodological limitations.

What set the Chicago Jury Project apart from previous and subsequent jury research was its use of divergent research methodologies in a series of systematic studies, the collaboration of researchers from a wide variety of social and behavior sciences, and the courts' willingness to allow this research to be performed. The hallmark of the best jury research science remains the convergence of findings from a variety of different research paradigms in examining a single research question, a so-called triangulation of results. This occurs when field, experimental, survey, and interview studies all produce consistent findings when used to examine a specific research question. The combination of methodological approaches collectively overcomes deficiencies associated with any single approach used, in that the limitations associated with any one approach are not reintroduced in the other methodologies, thus eliminating the possibility that a particular weakness unfairly biased a study's results (Devine et al., 2001).

Following the success of the Chicago Jury Project, psycholegal scholars began more intensely investigating jury decisions and processes, with some of their findings affecting important U.S. Supreme Court decisions, particularly during the era of the Warren and Burger Courts (Monahan & Walker, 2014). In a series of cases during this period, the Court clearly recognized the importance of jury research in reaching decisions on the constitutionally acceptable size of juries (e.g., *Ballew v. Georgia*, 1978; *Colgrove v. Battin*, 1973; *Williams v. Florida*, 1970) and asked for additional research on the effects of death qualification on guilt decisions in capital sentencing (e.g., *Witherspoon v. Illinois*, 1968). The ultimate decisions in some of these cases indicate the Court did not always adequately understand the complexities and nuances of the research conducted by social scientists; however, the Court, at the very least, began acknowledging the empirical research that had been completed and that it was relevant to their decisions. For example in the *Williams* decision, examining the constitutionally acceptable size of juries, the Court cited in Footnote 49 of the decision a series of empirical studies examining the effects of six-person versus 12-person juries on eventual decisions. Unfortunately, the Court misrepresented some of the findings and suggested there were few important differences between 12- and six-person juries (Monahan & Walker, 2014).

During the same period, both the recognition of the American Psychology and Law Society by the American Psychological Association as a division and the creation of the first law and psychology focused journal, *Law and Human Behavior*, contributed to a proliferation of jury research (DeMatteo & Anumba, 2009). The majority of jury studies published in this era and subsequent decades used trial simulation designs (Greene et al., 2002). Most researchers empirically exploring jury issues were experimental psychologists, and their training emphasized experimental designs and internal validity. *Internal validity* refers to the extent to which causal relationships can be inferred between key variables by ruling out all other possible explanations. Internal validity is most easily maximized in laboratory-based mock juror research because the experimenter can manipulate the variables of interest while controlling all other aspects of the simulation. These often-unrealistic simulations, however, often have little relationship to the complex legal process being studied and, therefore, might not generalize to real-world practices, which is central to *external validity*. Yet, for academic researchers interested in publication, external validity concerns are often less important because psychology journals place a premium on internal validity (see Chapter 9, this volume, as well as our empirical research in a later section of this chapter). Jury researchers may also emphasize internal validity as a function of their backgrounds and training. Many psychological researchers in this area do not receive formal training in the law and, as a result, may not fully appreciate the complexities and nuances of the legal system and its processes (Sales & Krauss, 2015). Further, they may not have access to legal collaborators to aid them in creating more realistic simulations.

Several conclusions can be drawn from this historical review of the development of jury research. First, for over half a century, dating back to the Chicago Jury Project, researchers have had a multitude of methodological techniques to draw on and have been aware of the strength of using a triangulation approach to investigate research questions. Second, rather than using triangulation, the field has typically gravitated toward an emphasis on internal validity, due at least in part to the typical training of individuals working in the area. Third, despite this limitation, courts have sometimes been receptive to considering social science findings.

However, many in the legal community have criticized psycholegal research on the basis of the realism of studies. Underlying this criticism is an inherent tension between the fields of psychology and law. On one hand, psychological researchers are often primarily interested in psychological processes that underlie human decision making. The legal context is ultimately used as an arena to empirically evaluate and apply psychological theories. On the other hand, individuals in the legal field are typically primarily concerned with the functioning of the jury system and whether it is achieving its goals in the vagaries of actual legal practice. The difference in focus between underlying psychological processes and effective jury system processes has led to a differential emphasis on the importance of various aspects of validity.

BALANCING VALIDITY CONCERNS

As trial simulation research became even more prevalent, growing from fewer than 300 published studies in the 1970s to over 1,500 by the close of the century (Greene et al., 2002), scholars within and outside psychology, including legal community members, continued to criticize important aspects of research validity. In particular, critics highlighted the fact that jury researchers were failing to adequately address real-world practice issues while making broad pronouncements about the generalizability of simulations that often included unrepresentative samples (e.g., college students), inadequate trial stimuli (e.g., brief written transcripts), limited legal procedures (e.g., no voir dire, opening and closing statements, jury instructions, and deliberations), and unrealistic outcome measures (e.g., sentencing decision in situations in which juries do not sentence; Bray & Kerr, 1979; Diamond, 1997; Weiten & Diamond, 1979).

This lack of realism in trial simulations is commonly characterized as an *ecological validity* concern and has been the central criticism of jury research from the legal community. For example, in the majority opinion in *Lockhart v.* McCree (1986), soon-to-be Chief Justice Rehnquist dismissed 15 jury studies that suggested a relationship between death penalty attitudes and juror decisions during the guilt phase of a capital trial because, in his view, the proffered studies lacked methodological rigor. His critique of the research was based largely on the fact that the research studies lacked elements of ecological validity (i.e., deliberations, empanelled juror samples). In addition, many reported studies focused on attitudes toward the death penalty, rather than verdict decisions capital cases, and responses obtained from laypeople, rather than from actual jurors or those summoned for jury duty. More recently, Vidmar (2008) articulated the more general concern that "if research is to have its best chance of having an impact on a judge and other policy-makers more ecologically valid research is needed" (p. 36).

Unfortunately, within the fields of law and psychology, ecological and external validity have often been used interchangeably when describing the inadequacies of trial simulation research when in fact they are related, but not identical, concepts (Sales & Krauss, 2015). To be clear, the external validity or generalizability of jury research may be improved as simulation elements more accurately resemble the working of the trial, but the external validity can also decrease as the ecological validity of a trial simulation increases. For example, a video of an actual trial may increase ecological validity by using a more complete version of a real case than would be feasible in a written transcript format, using paid actors to play the role of legal personnel and defendants, administering pattern jury instructions from a particular jurisdiction, and allowing jurors to deliberate. Yet, as the case facts become more specific and the legal procedures become more unique to a jurisdiction, the ability to generalize the results to other types of cases, legal contexts, jurisdictions, and legal actors becomes more difficult. So, increasing ecological validity can increase external validity, but it can decrease it as well.

Wiener, Krauss, and Lieberman (2011) argued that what psychology and legal scholars should be most concerned with in trial simulation research is the notion of construct validity (Cook & Campbell, 1979), rather than the related concepts of external or ecological validity. *Construct validity* in this context refers to whether the experimenter was sufficiently successful in translating reality into an experimental design that allows the researcher to interpret the findings in an appropriate manner to make a meaningful statement about the original reality that generated the research question (Wiener et al., 2011). Put more simply, it asks whether "once an experimentalist disassembles the gestalt of the courtroom in the laboratory for purposes of analysis" (Wiener et al., 2011, p. 470), will they ever be able to generalize back to the courtroom? Returning to the ecological validity problems of most trial simulation research, it is clear why this is an issue because

> there is lingering concern that research studies involving college students pretending to be jurors in a trial that consists entirely of a brief written summary do not yield information that is relevant to and predictive of the behavior of actual jurors in an actual trial. (Kerr & Bray, 2005, p. 32)

Similar to the relationship between ecological and external validity, increasing ecological validity in a trial simulation usually increases construct validity but can also weaken it as the facts and legal processes become more idiosyncratic.

The construct validity concerns, along with other related external validity questions, can only be answered by empirical testing (Wiener et al., 2011). It is impossible for experimenters to know whether their procedures and materials accurately mimic the real-world characteristic of jury trials unless they continually test each potentially relevant aspect of the simulation. A successful trial simulation researcher must balance internal validity against ecological, construct, and external validity. This balancing of validity may be of less importance if the variables of interest, processes being studied, legal contexts examined, and participant samples being used do not interact with each other in determining the relevant outcomes. For example, the concern of using college students as mock jurors may be of little significance if college students make legally relevant decisions similar to real jurors across all types of cases and factors, such as definitions of key legal terms, legal procedures, trial complexities, evidence strength of cases, verdict outcomes, type of trial stimuli, and demographic characteristics of litigants and jury members. Further, it is even more important that none of the listed factors significantly interact with each other in affecting the outcome of interest.

It is hard to imagine that some significant interactions between different trial elements would not occur. However, initial meta-analytic and qualitative reviews have suggested that perhaps the most repeatedly criticized aspect of juror simulation validity, participant sample (college student vs. a more representative sample), has little effect on the case outcome and rarely significantly interacts with other important legal variables or processes. Several meta-analyses demonstrated little or no main or interaction effect of participant sample (student vs. community members) on one of the most central outcome variables, verdicts (e.g., Nietzel, McCarthy, & Kern, 1999; Steblay, Besirevic, Fulero, & Jimenez-Lorente, 1999). This null finding may explain why according to several large-scale reviews, the use of college student samples has remained relatively constant over time, historically amounting to approximately two thirds of all published jury research, and student sample use was reported as increasing rather than decreasing (Bornstein, 1999). Although more recent analyses have suggested that this trend may be changing, college student samples are still used in a sizable portion of published jury research (Chapter 9, this volume). As in participant samples, the existing, albeit limited, meta-analyses that examine the interplay of various variables and legal procedures have found few significant main and interaction effects that affect other important legal outcomes (e.g., Devine et al., 2001).

Several recent jury studies, however, have indicated that factors such as case type, strength of evidence, and participant sample moderate the effects of juror characteristics (e.g., age, gender, race, education, socioeconomic status) and juror attitudes toward the legal system. These variables exert a significant influence on juror decisions (Devine & Caughlin, 2014; Wiener et al., 2011). For example, in a meta-analysis of trial simulation studies, the type of case studied and outcome measure used (e.g., predeliberation verdicts, dichotomous vs. continuous guilty verdicts) moderated the effects of 10 of 11 juror characteristics (Devine & Caughlin, 2014). Early trial simulation research indicated that juror characteristics had limited effects on most legally relevant outcome variables. For instance, in previous jury selection research, female jurors were slightly more likely to convict than male jurors (Lieberman & Sales, 2007). The weak overall gender effect may be an artifact of case type studied (Schutte & Hosch, 1997). In fact, there was a strong relationship between juror gender and conviction of offenders in sexual crime cases, whereas there was no relationship between gender and verdict when sexual crime cases were removed. In addition, dichotomous outcome measures of verdict produced stronger overall effects than continuous measures even though the existing literature assumed the opposite was true (Devine & Caughlin, 2014). Taken together, this recent research highlights the importance of considering multiple elements of trial simulations, such as the type of outcome measures and type of case, to fully understand the relationship between the variables of interest. It further indicates that psycholegal researchers must be cognizant of the complex interactions that might exist between various aspects of the simulation and manipulated variables.

Furthermore, although jury research has not found differences between participant samples studied and legal outcomes of interest (Bornstein, 1999), several recent studies have suggested that these sampling differences may matter for several specific types of cases (Wiener et al., 2011). For instance, Keller and Wiener (2011) investigated whether college student mock jurors and a community sample differed in their explicit attitudes toward homicide and sexual assault as well as their culpability decisions in a series of sexual assault and homicides cases. They found that the two groups differed significantly in their explicit attitude measures and these differences affected their guilt judgments across both sets of cases. Overall, the college student sample was more lenient in both homicide and sexual assault cases than was the community sample. In addition, they determined that both participant samples and attitudes interacted with the specific charges in the sexual assault cases to produce culpability judgments. Taken together, this research demonstrates that subtle and not so subtle differences in sample characteristics may affect the ways in which mock jurors' attitudes can affect guilt judgments.

Clearly, differences in participant sampling and/or aspects of a trial simulation can affect the conclusions drawn from jury research, and these nuanced differences are often ignored by researchers because the complexities of the trial process and different case types are not frequently tested. It is imperative that jury researchers are aware of these various validity concerns and attempt to balance them in their research.

Empirical Study of Reviewers' and Researchers' Balancing of Validity Concerns

Given the complexity and competing tensions of the validity concerns in trial simulation research, how then should internal, external, construct, and ecological validity be balanced in generating future trial simulation research? Individuals who are actively producing and reviewing jury research report placing greater emphasis on internal validity than ecological validity. A recent survey assessed scholars' perceptions of the importance of different types of validity and methods in jury research (Lieberman, Krauss, Heen, & Sakiyama, 2014). Their sample was obtained from the population of corresponding authors, editorial board members, associate editors, and editors of *Law and Human Behavior*, *Psychology, Public Policy, and Law*, and *Behavioral Sciences and the Law* for a 5-year period (2008–2012). Respondents (overall response rate was 41%) indicated where they felt the appropriate balance point was between internal and ecological validity. Although one third of the sample reported that ecological validity was equally as important as internal validity, a majority (59%) indicated that internal validity was more important. Only 8% reported that emphasis should be placed on ecological validity at the expense of internal validity. Further, when asked about the features that should be included for a trial simulation study to be minimally acceptable for publication, only 16% of participants indicated that representative jurors were necessary, with the vast majority willing to publish studies using college students. The scholars' emphasis on internal over external validity was also apparent on several questions asking whether it was necessary to include various trial elements and procedures in a trial simulation. For example, 90% of respondents reported that jury deliberation was not a necessary component for a study to merit publication. Only 14% reported that studies that used college students were too artificial to merit publication, and less than 10% indicated that the use of written transcripts should prohibit publication.

Respondents also ranked the importance of a number of components to a jury decision-making study. Using theory to guide a research study was the highest ranked item, with close to half of respondents ranking it the most important component. Jury instructions were ranked second, followed by sample (college students vs. representative participants), trial format, (written vs. video presentation), verdict (type of verdict rendered—dichotomous guilty/not guilty vs. continuous measure), including case evidence (supplemental evidence presented), and finally deliberations. Over half the sample (52%) ranked deliberations either last or second to last. The pattern of findings indicates that respondents believe that aside from manipulated factors, the key components that influence a simulated trial's results are the types of participants selected and the way the law is explained to them; however, the process of rendering a verdict (through deliberations and dependent measure choice) is not of great importance (Lieberman et al., 2014). Given the tensions between various forms of validity and psychology and law journal reviewers' and researchers' apparent preference for internal validity over other forms, what should then be the appropriate framework for researchers to balance these sometimes disparate interests?

A Framework for Balancing Validity Concerns

An initial suggestion for balancing internal and ecological validity was proposed by Diamond (1997). In her critical review of the trial simulation literature, she proposed to a two-stage model for future research in the field. In the first stage of research on a topic, psycholegal researchers should initially maximize internal validity and should be less concerned about the ecological validity of the sample, trial, and outcome measures. Once Stage 1 research had been conducted, researchers were urged by Diamond to complete a second stage of research that would be designed to produce empirical conclusions that would be more useful and applicable to the legal profession. In this second wave of research, researchers should place greater weight on ecological validity by using more realistic juror samples, trial simulations, and outcome measures, as well as increasing the use of field studies (Diamond, 1997).

With regard to both participant sample and type of trial simulation, there is some limited evidence to indicate that Diamond's (1997) suggestions are now being heeded. A recent review of *Law and Human Behavior*'s trial simulation research articles from 2005 to 2006 and 2011 to 2012 demonstrated that the use of college student jurors had fallen below 50%, and the use of non-written trial stimuli had risen over 50% (see Chapter 9, this volume). There is, however, still reason to believe that the majority of Diamond's advice has not been followed, because it is still common for researchers to simply cite Bornstein's (1999) qualitative review of jury research methods as justification for not using more realistic samples, measures, procedures, and stimuli in trial simulations (Wiener et al., 2011). In addition, academic psychology's reluctance to publish replications or studies that simply test whether a variable interacts with a methodological feature such as participant sample or deliberations has likely contributed to the reluctance of psycholegal researchers to perform Stage 2 research. However, it is worth noting that the *Journal of Personality and Social Psychology* recently announced a new policy that encourages submissions that are replication attempts of previously published social and personality psychology studies. Given that this policy change is being implemented by a premier journal in the field of psychology, it may inspire other primary outlets to be receptive to publishing replication studies. Similarly, *Current Perspectives in Psychological Science* has begun publishing large-scale replications of previous work (e.g., Alogna et al., 2014). It remains to be seen, however, whether this newfound interest in replications will translate to publication of empirical jury research that investigates incremental changes in ecological validity, including but not limited to more complex trial vignettes and presentations, more complete trial procedures (e.g., voir dire, opening and closing statements, judicial instructions, deliberations), and participant samples.

Although Diamond's (1997) framework is informative and has led to some modest improvements in the validity of recent trial simulation research, a more nuanced relationship between internal, ecological, external, and construct validity concerns may be in order for future experimental research on juries, especially given recent research demonstrating some of the complex interactions of variables commonly ignored in psycholegal experimental studies (e.g., Wiener et al., 2011) and the legal field's continued reluctance to accept the conclusions of less ecologically valid trial simulation studies (Caprathe, 2011).

The balancing of validity tensions in trial simulations might be better accomplished by answering a series of questions related to the extent to which psychological theory has been developed and is being tested in the design and whether the research is intended to answer more directly a legal or a psychological question. In other words, the most central concerns for the psycholegal researcher in designing a trial simulation study may be two of Greene et al.'s (2002) identity crisis issues: (a) whether basic psychological theory should drive research questions or whether research questions should simply aid the functioning of the court system and (b) who should be the primary audience for dissemination of the empirical findings—psychologists or legal professionals? As psycholegal research attempts to aid the functioning of the court system and serve the functions of the legal community, the ecological validity of trial simulation should increase. However, the nature of the research question and the existence of psychological theory appropriate to address it should determine the degree to which internal validity is balanced with, and sometimes outweighed by, the verisimilitude of participant sample, legal procedures, trial stimuli, and outcome measures chosen.

Potential Aids for Improving Ecological, External, and Construct Validity

Although the field of jury decision-making research has grown considerably over the last 4 decades, the process of conducting studies has not changed much over that time. Researchers work independently to develop sample materials that often consist of written transcripts, which include no exhibits and minimal or no jury instructions. These materials are often shown to college students, who typically render an individual verdict without the benefit of deliberation with fellow mock jurors. Case materials vary dramatically from study to study in terms of the length of materials and the charges against the defendant. However, researchers can implement a number of methods that may improve jury decision-making research by improving ecological, external, and construct validity while maintaining internal validity.

More Realistic Participant Samples

College students historically have been the most convenient sample of participants for mock jury researchers because they can often be recruited easily and inexpensively. Not surprisingly, they remain the most frequently used group (Lieberman et al., 2014). However, in the past few years, there has been an increasing trend to use samples that can be obtained online. These online samples typically show greater age, ethnicity, and occupational diversity than college student samples, creating a demographic distribution closer to actual jury samples.

The most widely used online participant recruitment option may currently be Mechanical Turk. Mechanical Turk (see http://www.mturk.com) was created in 2005 and serves as an online source for data collection and conducting experimental research. The site, run by Amazon.com, is an "online labor market where employees (called *workers*) are recruited by employers (called *requesters*) for the execution of tasks (called *HITs*, acronym for Human Intelligence Tasks) in exchange for a wage (called a *reward*)" (Paolacci, Chandler, & Ipeirotis, 2010, pp. 411–412). Rewards range from low as low as $0.01 to more than $10.00 depending on what type of task is required (Goodman, Cryder, & Cheema, 2013; Paolacci et al., 2010).

Despite the low financial incentive paid to Mechanical Turk workers, participants do complete typical jury decision-making studies and appear to pay relatively close attention to the materials. For example, in a recent study examining juror perceptions of forensic evidence analyzed by different types of crime labs, Heen (2014) was able to recruit several hundred participants in a single day, paying each person only $0.75. Participants were presented with three sets of personality questionnaires, 10 pages of case summary and trial transcript, several visual exhibits, two pages of jury instructions, and 26 questions measuring their verdict, perceptions of case evidence, manipulation checks, and questions assessing their attention to trial facts (which indicated that they did indeed pay close attention to the stimulus materials).

An alternative method of conveniently gathering research participants is to use the respondent gathering services of major online survey firms. For example, both Survey Monkey (http://www.surveymonkey.com) and Qualtrics (http://www.qualtrics.com) offer online survey tools that researchers can use as a platform for running online experiments. Researchers can independently direct individuals to these websites (e.g., from a direct e-mail solicitation or by using a service such as Mechanical Turk) or can pay the websites to generate a pool. These companies use different approaches to recruit respondents. Survey Monkey currently recruits samples by contacting individuals who have previously completed electronic surveys on Survey Monkey. Qualtrics outsources the sampling process to one of a number of sample paneling firms with which they have contracts. Sample paneling firms are professional organizations that specialize in recruiting samples for market research and other purposes. By contrast, Mechanical Turk relies on individuals who are looking for projects to work on. The costs for using Survey Monkey's or Qualtrics's respondent gathering service are considerably higher than that of Mechanical Turk, with a minimum of $5.00 per respondent.

Heen, Miethe, and Lieberman (2014) recently compared the demographic characteristics of samples constructed with Mechanical Turk, Survey Monkey, and Qualtrics with U.S. Census estimates. They examined differences between the samples on a variety of demographic factors including gender, age, race, education, marital status, housing type (i.e., single-unit dwelling, duplex, and multiunit dwelling), and political affiliation. They found that none of the approaches produced a sample that matched U.S. population characteristics and that significant differences emerged among the samples on almost all the demographic characteristics. For example, only 43% of the Mechanical Turk sample was male, compared with 51% and 52% in the Survey Monkey and Qualtrics samples, respectively. In the Qualtrics sample, 57% of respondents were over 50 years old, compared with 49% of the Survey Monkey sample and 14% of the Mechanical Turk sample, which was much younger. Indeed, 43% of the Mechanical Turk sample fell in the 20- to 29-year-old age range. Further, the education level of the Survey Monkey sample was quite high (26.2% reported having postgraduate degrees compared with 11% and 9% in the Qualtrics and Mechanical Turk Samples, respectively). However, Survey Monkey produced a sample that more closely matched the U.S. population on self-reported political affiliation, with 22% identifying themselves as Republicans, compared with 17.5% in the Qualtrics sample and only 12% of Mechanical Turk respondents. Finally, 33% of the Survey Monkey sample had incomes of $100,000 or more, compared with 10% and 9% in the Qualtrics and Mechanical Turk samples, respectively. This finding is particularly concerning given the fact that numerous jury decision-making studies have found socioeconomic status to be correlated with verdicts (Hastie, Penrod, & Pennington, 1983; Visher, 1987).

Given that sampling bias is present in the Mechanical Turk, Survey Monkey, and Qualtrics samples, the best approach may be to use a quota sampling approach and attempt to construct a sample that matches prespecified population characteristics. Both Survey Monkey and Qualtrics offer this option at an additional cost. Alternatively, poststratification weighting can be used to adjust sample characteristics to a known population distribution. This type of sample adjustment is a widely accepted practice among survey researchers (Loosveldt & Sonck, 2008). Researchers have not concerned themselves with these types of sampling issues because they have worked with convenience samples of college students and relied on random assignment to experimental conditions to control for the influence of individual differences (or used statistical analysis control techniques). However, using a national sample that matches the population of interest (e.g., jury-eligible adults in the United States or those that actually participate in trials) would increase both the ecological and external validity of studies.

More Standardized and Realistic Stimuli

The development of a set of standards for mock trial stimuli may create an opportunity to more easily studies that are methodologically sound and that have greater ecological validity. As previously noted, mock jurors are presented with trial information in a variety of formats (i.e., brief case summary form or a written, audio, or video simulation). Regardless of format, there is little consistency in the inclusion of specific types of stimulus materials used in a given study. For example, there are often variations in the inclusion or exclusion of accompanying evidence, expert testimony, cross-examinations, and substantive and/or procedural jury instructions. The result is a set of materials that is highly idiosyncratic. Because researchers often develop materials independently, there is little consistency, making it extremely difficult to interpret any studies that fail to replicate previous research. The development of a set of standards regarding what features should be included in trial stimuli would serve to reduce methodological variability within the field, potentially making it easier to compare across studies and reduce discrepancies between the expectation of different manuscript reviewers and/or between authors and reviewers.

Increased Stimuli Sampling

It would be useful for greater stimulus sampling to occur within jury research studies—that is, comparing whether reported psychological and legal effects are consistent across a variety of case types, fact patterns, and other characteristics. Stimulus sampling would increase the generalizability of results and, in particular, investigate whether idiosyncratic facts of a particular case or other factors are driving results. As mentioned earlier, increasing the ecological validity of stimuli often decreases external validity or generalizability; empirical testing is necessary to further investigate this issue. Unlike trial consultants and litigators, scholars in both the legal and psychological fields are more interested in inferring conclusions about the psychological aspects of decision making from a particular trial simulation than making fact-specific predictions about particular jury decisions. Of course, the need to sample other case types or fact patterns depends on the specific research question being investigated, but rarely if ever is scholarly psycholegal research primarily concerned with one set of facts in one particular trial simulation context.

For instance, researchers should want to examine whether female jurors' proclivity to convict in sexual abuse cases holds true when the perpetrator of the crime is female and the victim is male or if statutory rape cases demonstrate the same bias depending on the ages of the victim. Similarly, the influence of expert testimony on jurors' assessment of risk could be compared across death penalty, sexual predator, and parole proceedings using a similar fact pattern to determine whether the type of cases used affects jurors' perception of, and reliance on, the manipulated expert testimony.

Improved Collaboration With the Legal Field

Trial simulation research could also benefit from greater collaboration among psychological researchers and legal scholars, legal practitioners, and other social scientists who study the law. Unfortunately, the multidisciplinary nature of jury research has decreased rather than increased since the Chicago Jury Project, and juror simulation research has become more and more the exclusive province of experimental psychologists. Going forward, the insights and unique knowledge attorneys and legal actors have about the intricate workings of the courts and how law is actually practiced (in contrast to what is taught in law school or books) could serve as invaluable resources to psycholegal researchers in fashioning more realistic and, even more important, relevant simulation research (Sales & Krauss, 2015). Without this knowledge, it may not be possible for psycholegal researchers to produce conditions that effectively mimic the legal conditions and reflect the legal world to which they wish to generalize their research findings.

Likewise, these collaborations could be broadened beyond the realm of trial simulation research to the other types of jury research previously mentioned (i.e., archival research, surveys and posttrial interviews, and field studies) so that other social science researchers, as well as legal scholars, could benefit from the experimental perspective and the internal validity focus that psychologists bring to these research methodologies. For example, in a series of field studies in the Arizona courts, a multidisciplinary team of law professors, social psychologists, and sociologists videotaped jury deliberations in a number of different types of cases (e.g., Diamond & Rose, 2005). These studies offered real-world convergence for some trial simulation research findings (i.e., nonunanimous verdicts lead to the marginalization of minority viewpoints) while contradicting others (i.e., jurors often do not pay attention to legal instructions).

CONCLUSION

In the end, trial simulation methodology will and should continue to be a mainstay of jury research. The nature of the research question, the level of development of psychological theory, and the intended audience for the research should all help researchers balance the inherent tensions between various validity concerns. Further, the import, generalizability, and ecological validity of much trial simulation research could be improved through the use of more realistic participant samples, more standardized and realistic stimuli, and increased stimuli sampling while maintaining the internal validity of manipulated variables that is the most central concern to peer reviewers. In addition, collaborative efforts among trial simulation researchers and the use of more multidisciplinary approaches across all jury research paradigms (i.e., triangulation) should be where psycholegal researchers can have their greatest impact on the legal field and produce the most scientifically valid research results. Jury research completed using archival data collection, posttrial interviews and questionnaires, and field studies should lead to further development and a more nuanced interpretation of trial simulation results and suggest further areas for additional study. Last, the recent Arizona Jury Project studies offer a hopeful note that courts may once again recognize the value that psychological jury research has for the legal system and that the legal community will exhibit a renewed interest in psycholegal research, leading to a willingness to open the courtroom doors to researchers in this field.

REFERENCES

Alogna, V. K., Attaya, M. K., Aucoin, P., Bahník, Š., Birch, S., Birt, A. R., . . . Zwaan, R. A. (2014). Registered replication report: Schooler and Engstler-Schooler (1990). *Perspectives on Psychological Science*, 9, 556–578. http://dx.doi.org/10.1177/1745691614545653

Ballew v. Georgia, 435 U.S. 223 (1978).

Bornstein, B. H. (1999). The ecological validity of jury simulations: Is the jury still out? *Law and Human Behavior*, *23*, 75–91. http://dx.doi.org/10.1023/A:1022326807441

Bray, R. M., & Kerr, N. L. (1979). Use of the simulation method in the study of jury behavior: Some methodological considerations. *Law and Human Behavior*, *3*, 107–119. http://dx.doi.org/10.1007/BF01039151

Caprathe, W. J. (2011). Commentary: Participant differences and validity of jury studies. *Behavioral Sciences & the Law*, *29*, 328–330. http://dx.doi.org/10.1002/bsl.988

Colgrove v. Battin, 413 U.S. 149 (1973).

Cook, T. D., & Campbell, D. T. (1979). *Quasi-experimentation: Design and analysis issues for field settings*. Boston, MA: Houghton Mifflin.

DeMatteo, D., & Anumba, N. (2009). The validity of jury decision-making research. In J. D. Lieberman & D. A. Krauss (Eds.), *Jury psychology: Social aspects of trial processes* (Vol. 1, pp. 1–23). Surrey, England: Ashgate.

Devine, D. (2012). *Jury decision making: The state of the science*. New York: New York University Press.

Devine, D., & Caughlin, D. (2014). Do they matter? A meta-analytic investigation of individual characteristics and guilt judgments. *Psychology, Public Policy, and Law, 20*, 109–134. http://dx.doi.org/10.1037/law0000006

Devine, D. J., Clayton, L. D., Dunford, B. B., Seying, R., & Pryce, J. (2001). Jury decision making: 45 years of empirical research on deliberating groups. *Psychology, Public Policy, and Law, 7*, 622–727. http://dx.doi.org/10.1037/1076-8971.7.3.622

Diamond, S. S. (1997). Illuminations and shadows from jury simulations. *Law and Human Behavior, 21*, 561–571. http://dx.doi.org/10.1023/A:1024831908377

Diamond, S. S., & Rose, M. R. (2005). Real juries. *Annual Review of Law and Social Science, 1*, 255–284. http://dx.doi.org/10.1146/annurev.lawsocsci.1.041604.120002

Fulero, S., & Wrightsman, L. S. (2009). *Forensic psychology* (3rd ed.). Belmont, CA: Wadsworth/Thomson Learning.

Galanter, M., & Frozena, A. (2011). *The continuing decline of civil trials in American courts*. Retrieved from the Pound Civil Justice Institute website: http://www.poundinstitute.org/sites/default/files/docs/2011%20judges%20forum/2011%20Forum%20Galanter-Frozena%20Paper.pdf

Goodman, J. K., Cryder, C. E., & Cheema, A. (2013). Data collection in a flat world: The strengths and weaknesses of Mechanical Turk samples. *Journal of Behavioral Decision Making, 26*, 213–224. http://dx.doi.org/10.1002/bdm.1753

Greene, E., Chopra, S. R., Kovera, M. B., Penrod, S. D., Rose, V. G., Schuller, R., & Studebaker, C. (2002). Jurors and juries: A review of the field. In J. R. P. Ogloff (Ed.), *Taking psychology and law into the twenty-first century* (pp. 225–284). New York, NY: Kluwer.

Hans, V. P. (2008). Jury systems around the world. *Annual Review of Law and Social Science, 4*, 275–297. http://dx.doi.org/10.1146/annurev.lawsocsci.4.110707.172319

Hans, V. P., Hannaford, P. L., & Munsterman, G. T. (1999). The Arizona jury reform permitting civil jury trial discussions: The views of trial participants, judges, and jurors. *University of Michigan Journal of Law Reform, 32*, 349–377.

Hastie, R., Penrod, S., & Pennington, N. (1983). *Inside the jury*. http://dx.doi.org/10.4159/harvard.9780674865945

Heen, M. (2014). *Putting the microscope on crime labs: The effects of evidence complexity and laboratory type on jurors' perceptions of forensic evidence*. Manuscript in preparation.

Heen, M., Miethe, T., & Lieberman, J. D. (2014). *A comparison of different on-line sampling approaches for generating national samples* [state data brief]. Las Vegas, NV: Center for Crime and Justice Policy.

Kalven, H., Jr., & Zeisel, H. (1966). *The American jury*. Boston, MA: Little, Brown.

Keller, S. R., & Wiener, R. L. (2011). What are we studying? Student jurors, community jurors, and construct validity. *Behavioral Sciences & the Law, 29*, 376–394. http://dx.doi.org/10.1002/bsl.971

Kerr, N. L., & Bray, R. M. (2005). Simulation, realism, and the study of the jury. In N. Brewer & K. D. Williams (Eds.), *Psychology and law: An empirical perspective* (pp. 322–364). New York, NY: Guilford Press.

Lieberman, J. D., Krauss, D., Heen, M., & Sakiyama, M. (2014). The good, the bad, and the ugly: Professional perceptions of jury decision-making research practices. *Behavioral Sciences & the Law, 34*, 495–514. http://dx.doi.org/10.1002/bsl.2246

Lieberman, J. D., & Sales, B. D. (2007). *Scientific jury selection.* http://dx.doi.org/10.1037/11498-000

Lockhart v. McCree, 476 U.S. 162 (1986).

Loosveldt, G., & Sonck, N. (2008). An evaluation of the weighting procedures for an online access panel survey. *Survey Research Methods, 2*, 93–105.

Mize, G. E., Hannaford-Agor, P., & Waters, N. L. (2007). *The state-of-the-states survey of jury improvement efforts: A compendium report.* Retrieved from http://www.ncsc-jurystudies.org/~/media/Microsites/Files/CJS/SOS/SOSCompendiumFinal.ashx

Monahan, J., & Walker, L. (2014). *Social science in law* (8th ed.). New York, NY: The Foundation Press.

Munsterberg, H. (1908). *On the witness stand.* New York, NY: Doubleday.

Nietzel, M. T., McCarthy, D., & Kern, M. J. (1999). Juries: The current state of the empirical literature. In R. Roesch, S. D. Hart, & J. R. P. Ogloff (Eds.), *Psychology and law: The state of the discipline* (pp. 23–52). http://dx.doi.org/10.1007/978-1-4615-4891-1_2

Paolacci, G., Chandler, J., & Ipeirotis, P. G. (2010). Running experiments on Amazon Mechanical Turk. *Judgment and Decision Making, 5*, 411–419.

Sales, B., & Krauss, D. (2015). *The psychology of law: Human behavior, legal institutions, and law.* http://dx.doi.org/10.1037/14593-000

Schuller, R. A., & Yarmey, M. (2001). The jury: Deciding guilty and innocence. In R. A. Schuller & J. R. P. Ogloff (Eds.), *Introduction to psychology and law: Canadian perspectives* (pp. 3–28). Toronto, Ontario, Canada: University of Toronto Press.

Schutte, J., & Hosch, H. (1997). Gender differences in sexual assault verdicts: A meta-analysis. *Journal of Social Behavior & Personality, 12*, 759–772.

Steblay, N. M., Besirevic, J., Fulero, S., & Jimenez-Lorente, B. (1999). The effects of pre-trial publicity on juror verdicts: A meta-analytic review. *Law and Human Behavior, 23*, 219–235. http://dx.doi.org/10.1023/A:1022325019080

Vidmar, N. (Ed.). (2000). *World jury systems.* http://dx.doi.org/10.1093/acprof:oso/9780198298564.001.0001

Vidmar, N. (2008). Civil juries in ecological context: Methodological implications for research. In B. H. Bornstein, R. L. Wiener, R. Schopp, & S. Willborn (Eds.), *Civil juries and civil justice: Empirical perspectives* (pp. 35–65). http://dx.doi.org/10.1007/978-0-387-74490-2_3

Visher, C. A. (1987). Juror decision making; The importance of evidence. *Law and Human Behavior, 11*, 1–17.

Weiten, W., & Diamond, S. S. (1979). A critical review of the trial simulation paradigm: The case of defendant characteristics. *Law and Human Behavior, 3*, 71–93. http://dx.doi.org/10.1007/BF01039149

Wiener, R. L., Krauss, D. A., & Lieberman, J. D. (2011). Mock jury research: Where do we go from here? *Behavioral Sciences & the Law, 29*, 467–479. http://dx.doi.org/10.1002/bsl.989

Williams v. Florida, 399 U.S. 78 (1970).

Witherspoon v. Illinois, 391 U.S. 510 (1968).

Zimring, F. (2003). *The American Jury Project and the Chicago Law School* (Fulton Lectures). Retrieved from http://chicagounbound.uchicago.edu/cgi/viewcontent.cgi?article=1016&context=fulton_lectures

9

JURY SIMULATION RESEARCH: PROS, CONS, TRENDS, AND ALTERNATIVES

BRIAN H. BORNSTEIN

Jury trials have a hold on the popular imagination like few other public phenomena and arguably like no other component of the American legal system. John Peter Zenger, Sacco and Vanzetti, John Scopes, Alger Hiss, the Harrisburg Seven, the Ford Pinto, O. J. Simpson, McDonald's coffee, George Zimmerman: These names are synonymous with famous trials, and the cases are noteworthy not only for the historical import associated with the notoriety of the defendants and the particular crimes or torts of which they were accused but also for the jury's role in determining their fate. The jury's importance in these and countless other cases is one of the major factors motivating research on how juries make their decisions.

As the title of this chapter implies, I address here some of the challenges and benefits to conducting jury research, with an emphasis on experimental simulations, or mock juries. I begin by offering a short defense of studying juries in the first place. Next, I identify some pros and cons of conducting

http://dx.doi.org/10.1037/0000026-010
The Psychology of Juries, M. B. Kovera (Editor)

simulation research in general and jury simulations in particular. I present data on jury simulation research trends and consider the simulated nature of the research itself, an intractable problem for jury simulation research. Finally, I conclude the chapter with a brief discussion of alternatives to simulations and offer some recommendations.

WHY STUDY JURIES?

Jury trials have always been rare, resolving a small fraction (probably less than 1%) of all legal disputes (Vidmar & Hans, 2007). Moreover, they are becoming rarer all the time. For example, the portion of federal civil cases disposed of by trial dropped from 11.5% in 1962 to 1.8% in 2002, and approximately one third of those were bench trials (Galanter, 2004). Galanter (2004) found comparable declines in federal criminal courts, as well as in state civil and criminal courts. In addition, and as the remainder of this chapter shows, juries are hard to study systematically. Finally, courts and policymakers do not always take social science research seriously (Monahan & Walker, 2010). These factors might seem to suggest that we need not bother to study juries in the first place.

Fortunately, there are more compelling arguments for why we should study juries, as many of the chapters in this volume illustrate (see also Devine, 2012; Greene & Bornstein, 2003; Vidmar & Hans, 2007). Juries are one of the defining features of the American justice system, which one could, without sounding too grandiose, refer to as one of the bastions of democracy. The recent adoption or expansion of the jury system by other countries (see, e.g., Vidmar, 2000, as well as Chapter 6, this volume) suggests that juries do, indeed, have something to offer; as such, it is that much more important to understand how they work and how they could potentially be improved. Less philosophically and more practically, jury decisions matter not only for the parties directly involved but also for others, an effect sometimes referred to as the *jury's shadow* (e.g., Galanter, 1987). Jury decisions, actual and anticipated, influence settlement negotiations as well as individual and corporate behavior. In rare cases, they can have a major impact, as in those mentioned at the start of this chapter and many others (e.g., the death penalty, class actions).

Researchers can also study juries as a means of gauging community sentiment toward certain behaviors (Reed & Bornstein, 2015). Some trials, such as those involving obscenity, explicitly invoke community standards, whereas in other trials, the jury may rely on its notions of commonsense justice (Finkel, 1995) to trump the law, a process known as *jury nullification* (Hamm, Bornstein, & Perkins, 2013; Horowitz, Kerr, & Niedermeier, 2001). Nullification has been used to explain jury verdicts that are seemingly contrary to the law and the evidence in a number of different cases, such as those involving civil rights, the military draft, euthanasia, or drug legalization. Even when the jury does not explicitly nullify the law, jury members' attitudes toward certain litigants or offenses could nonetheless color their decisions. This "generic prejudice" can make them treat some classes of defendants unusually harshly, such as those accused of child sexual abuse (Vidmar, 1997). Thus, studying juries allows us to understand juries qua juries and also informs us about social attitudes writ on a grander scale.

PROS AND CONS OF JURY SIMULATIONS

An Overview of Jury Research Methods

As this volume illustrates, there are several techniques for conducting research on juries. The five most common methods are (a) direct observation of juries; (b) case studies and/or posttrial interviews with jurors; (c) archival analyses of (usually large) data sets of jury verdicts; (d) experimental simulations, or mock juror/jury studies; and (e) field studies. Importantly, all of these methods except for simulations use real jurors who are reaching or have already reached real verdicts. Jury simulations, however, use mock jurors who are role playing and making hypothetical decisions without actual consequences.

Directly observing juries is, with rare exceptions, impermissible. Jurors who know they are being watched might behave differently from jurors who know that what happens in the jury room stays in the jury room;[1] moreover, surreptitiously recording juries without their knowledge or consent would be unethical. A recent notable exception to the rule of not observing juries—conducted with the court's involvement and consent—is the Arizona Jury Project, which included videotaping and analysis of civil jury deliberations (e.g., Diamond, Vidmar, Rose, Ellis, & Murphy, 2003; Vidmar, 2008). In the main, however, this methodology is relatively impractical because it is hard to obtain the approval that is required from judges and/or legislators.

Case studies of individual juries, which often include posttrial interviews with jurors, are somewhat more practical because they may not require judicial approval; but they are still logistically complicated (e.g., locating jurors, compensating them, and persuading them to participate) and present problems

[1]Whether "differently" would be better, worse, or neither is, of course, an open question. On the one hand, observation might make some jurors reluctant to share their opinions, especially controversial ones, but on the other hand, it might make them feel more accountable, thereby improving the quality of their reasoning (e.g., Tetlock, 1983).

of biased and incomplete memory. Nonetheless, several excellent examples of this methodology exist (e.g., Hans, 2000; Mott, Hans, & Simpson, 2000; Vidmar, 1995). For example, Mott and colleagues (2000) interviewed jurors about the strategies they used and the factors they believed they considered when deciding damage awards. Jurors reported mainly considering appropriate evidence, such as aspects of the plaintiff's injury, but they also discussed several inappropriate factors (e.g., attorney fees, the litigant's insurance). Despite the limitations of self-report data (e.g., memory and self-presentation biases) and small, potentially unrepresentative sample sizes, data from posttrial interviews can provide a wealth of information about how jurors make their decisions (Vidmar, 2008)—at least, how jurors think they make their decisions, which is not necessarily the same thing, although it is interesting in its own right.

Archival analyses have become increasingly popular in the last 20 or so years and are a key component of the empirical legal studies toolbox (Eisenberg, 2011; Suchman & Mertz, 2010). They allow for inferences from large volumes of real-world data, although they can lead to disparate conclusions depending on the particular data set and statistical assumptions used. For example, the strength of the relationship between juries' compensatory and punitive damage awards—an important question in determining the constitutionality of large punitive damage awards—varies somewhat depending on which cases are in the sample and the regression models that are applied to the data (e.g., Eisenberg, Hans, & Wells, 2008; Eisenberg & Wells, 2006). The major drawback to this approach is that the analyses are limited to whatever variables happen to be coded for in the data sets. In addition, unknown confounds could accompany distinctions that the data sets do contain, leading to a lack of comparability, or what Vidmar (1994) referred to as an "apples and oranges" problem (e.g., differences in bench vs. jury trials might merely reflect differences in the kinds of cases that are routed to the two different kinds of decision makers).

As the name suggests, experimental simulations simulate the jury task by having a group of individuals, who are not actual jurors, make decisions "as if" they were hearing an actual case. In some studies they make decisions as a group, but in most studies they do so merely as individuals; hence, it is more accurate to say that they express their verdict preferences than that they reach a verdict because individual jurors in a real trial, acting alone, could not actually determine a final and binding verdict. Although it is hard to date when the use of jury simulations started, the method has been a prominent investigative tool for the past 40 years or so (e.g., Diamond, 1979; Gerbasi, Zuckerman, & Reis, 1977; Kerr & Bray, 1982).

In field studies, judges (or the researchers working with them) randomly assign juries to one of multiple experimental conditions. In some respects, field studies are the best of both worlds: They use random assignment with a fair degree of experimental control, which permits causal inferences, and they involve real juries making real decisions. Consequently, their results are persuasive, as in field studies investigating the effects of allowing jurors to take notes or ask questions (for review, see Mott, 2003; Penrod & Heuer, 1997). However, like observational studies, they require the cooperation of the courts and are therefore difficult, costly, and rare. In addition, even if judges are willing to participate, random assignment can sometimes break down, and some variables of interest might simply be logistically difficult, illegal, or unethical to manipulate (e.g., severity of charges, jury size).

In choosing among these diverse methodologies, one has to consider many questions, foremost among them the question of what it is one wants to know. Studies of jury behavior can be categorized in a number of different ways, but one useful classification scheme considers studies that examine outcomes and studies that examine processes. *Outcome studies* investigate the effects of certain variables on verdicts, which can include judgments of guilt, liability, sentencing, damages, and so forth. *Process studies*, however, assess the effects of certain variables on jurors' reasoning processes in reaching a verdict. This approach is highly amenable to an application, within the jury context, of fundamental decision-making processes such as heuristics and biases, story construction, persuasion, computation, comprehension, and so forth. Some research methods, such as archival studies, are geared primarily toward looking at outcomes simply because they lack any data on what jurors were thinking in the course of reaching a verdict, whereas other methods, such as case studies, are geared primarily toward looking at processes, because they contain only one or a small number of outcomes. An advantage of simulations is that they are useful for looking at both outcomes and processes.

A Closer Look at Simulations

A sizeable literature has debated the pros and cons of jury simulations (e.g., Bornstein, 1999; Diamond, 1997; Kerr & Bray, 2005; Wiener, Krauss, & Lieberman, 2011; see also Chapters 7, 8, and 11, this volume). The major drawbacks of experimental simulations are that they often lack verisimilitude—that is, a resemblance to the behavior of real jurors in the real world; they sometimes ask the wrong questions, and they often have limited impact on public policy. With respect to verisimilitude, many simulations use nonrepresentative (i.e., student) mock jurors who make individual judgments, without deliberation, about hypothetical cases based on relatively impoverished trial materials. Many studies also ask questions that are interesting from a theoretical psychological perspective but irrelevant or inappropriate from a legal, practical perspective. For example, an interest in attitudes toward punishment might lead to a study in which mock jurors make sentencing recommendations in a noncapital case, despite the fact that jurors almost never determine sentencing outside the death penalty context. Alternatively, studies might ask mock jurors to make a legally appropriate judgment, such as guilt or witness credibility, but measure it in a nonlegal manner, such as asking them to assign a number on a scale. Largely because of these features of much simulation research, courts, on the whole, have been skeptical about conclusions that the research generates, with correspondingly limited impact on public policy (Monahan & Walker, 2010); but there is some evidence that that situation is changing (Monahan & Walker, 2011; see also Chapter 10, this volume).

Importantly, this skepticism persists despite a paucity of research showing that the characteristics of jury simulations often cited as limitations, such as those related to verisimilitude, matter much in the sense of affecting the studies' results and the conclusions that can be drawn from them (e.g., Bornstein, 1999; Bornstein & McCabe, 2005). Whether verisimilitude matters is important not only in terms of influencing policy but also potentially for the generalizability to real-world contexts of the research results themselves (Chapter 7, this volume). Hence it is a positive sign for the field that more research is beginning to address these methodological concerns (e.g., Wiener et al., 2011).

There is no denying that the concerns about jury simulations expressed by courts, legislators, and jury researchers themselves are legitimate ones. Nonetheless, jury simulations do offer a number of advantages. As noted earlier, they can address both the processes involved in jury decision making and the outcomes of jury decision making. In addition, they allow for a high degree of experimental control, which confers high internal validity (i.e., whether the observed effects are due solely to the experimental manipulations) and permits causal inferences; they have both scientific and practical implications; they are, compared with other jury research methods, relatively economical to conduct; and they are consistent with a large body of psychological research using simulation methods as "stand-ins" for real-world behavior (Bornstein & McCabe, 2005).

Experimental simulations, along with field studies, are the only methods discussed previously that allow for causal inferences. Although the other methods are informative, to be sure, they do not permit the testing of causal hypotheses. In instances in which one wants to know whether A causes B—for example, whether increasing the ad damnum, or amount requested by a civil plaintiff, leads to larger damage awards (Bornstein & Greene, 2011)—only an experiment can provide a definitive answer. As with any psychological research, the experimental measures have to be reliable (measuring consistently), valid (measuring what they purport to measure), and sensitive (discriminating among respondents). When using established legal judgments such as verdicts, reliability is rarely much of an issue. However, the various aspects of validity—but especially external validity, or the extent to which the experimental results generalize to the relevant real-world behaviors—can raise a host of problems (Chapters 7 and 8, this volume). In addition, sensitivity can require careful attention so that the simulated trial is not too one-sided (Reed & Bornstein, 2015).

Experiments are, therefore, arguably the best way to advance the science by testing applicable theories. This is precisely why psychological researchers interested in the legal domain tend to rely on experiments—experiments are, by and large, what we know and do best.[2] The tradeoff is that a high degree of experimental control often (but not always) requires a sacrifice in ecological validity, which can limit the work's acceptability to policymakers.

Jury simulations can be relatively cheap and easy to run for many reasons, primarily because mock trials are usually considerably shorter than real trials, and researchers often have easy access to a large pool of undergraduate research participants. The ease of conducting research is not, of course, a sufficient reason for choosing one methodology over another; but it cannot be ignored, especially in an era when extramural funding—the sort needed to compensate nonstudent participants and create realistic mock trials—is becoming increasingly competitive.

In part because of these financial concerns, many kinds of behaviors are studied, or practiced, in simulated or analog conditions where real-world study or practice would be impractical (Bornstein & McCabe, 2005). Pilots train in flight simulators, medical students train on cadavers and dummies, and an abundance of social scientific research asks participants to imagine they are in a certain situation and then examines what they say they would, but do not actually, do. In other words, simulations are ubiquitous. In addition to being safer and more cost-effective, simulations minimize ethical concerns. Using flight simulators and cadavers instead of real planes and patients to train and to study the behavior of aspiring pilots and physicians saves money and lives. It avoids needless risks to both participants and innocent bystanders. Necessarily, it assumes that the simulation is sufficiently realistic that the results will generalize to more naturalistic contexts, something we cannot know for certain until we examine that real-world situation—that is, put the pilot in a plane, present the physician with a patient, or observe an actual jury.

Some research has examined whether people behave the same in real and hypothetical situations, and it shows that, by and large, their behavior is the same (e.g., Kühberger, Schulte-Mecklenbeck, & Perner, 2002). On the

[2]I do not mean to imply that psychologists are the only ones using experiments to study juries, in particular, or the legal system as a whole. Other social scientists and legal scholars do so as well. As a psychologist, I necessarily write (and think) from a psychological perspective; the majority of researchers conducting jury simulations also have a psychological background.

one hand, the few studies of decision making in jury (or jury-like) contexts similarly have shown no consistent differences as a function of whether individuals are making decisions with real or only hypothetical consequences (Diamond & Zeisel, 1974; Kaplan & Krupa, 1986; Kerr, Nerenz, & Herrick, 1979; Suggs & Berman, 1979; Wilson & Donnerstein, 1977; see Bornstein & McCabe, 2005). On the other hand, research on the "attitude–behavior gap" has shown that people's attitudes or behavioral intentions are often not good predictors of their actual behavior (e.g., Ajzen & Fishbein, 2005). Thus, whether the decisions of real jurors making consequential decisions differ from those of mock jurors making nonconsequential decisions is a bit of an open question, but no research to date has shown that they differ systematically.

JURY SIMULATION RESEARCH TRENDS

To provide a snapshot of jury simulation research, some years ago I conducted an analysis of simulation research trends (Bornstein, 1999). The study had two main purposes: first, to provide an overview of simulation studies over time and some of the methodological choices contained in those studies (for an independent review of a related and somewhat larger body of work, see Nietzel, McCarthy, & Kerr, 1999) and, second, to assess whether the methodological choices mattered in the sense of affecting the experimental findings.

Simulation Methods: A Snapshot at Three Time Points

To examine the number and type of simulations conducted, I coded all of the jury simulations published in *Law and Human Behavior* (*LHB*) from 1977 to 1996 (Bornstein, 1999; see Figure 9.1).[3] Jury simulations were operationalized as studies in which participants were asked, individually or as a group, to adopt the role of jurors. The mock jurors' task had to include processing trial evidence and making a legally relevant judgment (e.g., guilt; see Bornstein, 1999; Weiten & Diamond, 1979).

As Figure 9.1 shows, there were three main findings: First, the number of published jury simulations increased throughout the study period, a trend

[3]Including articles from a single journal for this portion of the analysis is a limitation of the study. I used *Law and Human Behavior* (*LHB*) as a representative source because (a) it is the official journal of the American Psychology–Law Society (Division 41 of the American Psychological Association); (b) it is a highly competitive journal with a consistently high rejection rate, publishing only the best work in the field; (c) a comparison with other relevant journals indicated that *LHB* published substantially more jury simulations than any other single outlet (Bornstein, 1999); and (d) I submitted the article for inclusion in a special 20th anniversary issue of the journal. Jury simulations published elsewhere may differ systematically from those published in *LHB*, but it seems unlikely.

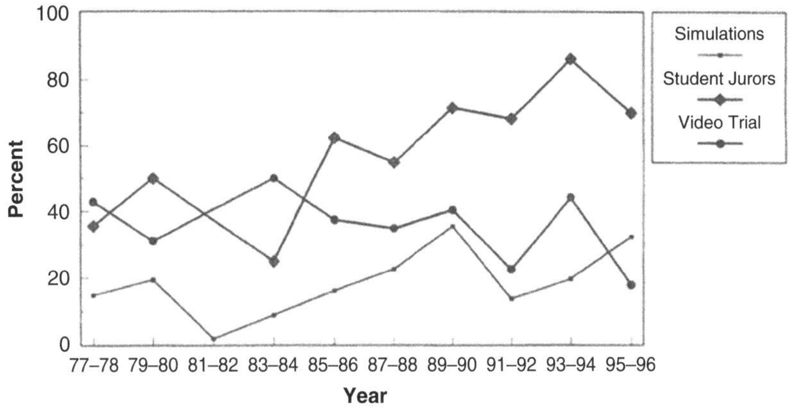

Figure 9.1. Jury simulation research trends in 20 years of *Law and Human Behavior.* Percentage of jury simulations (of total articles), percentage of simulations using student-jurors, and percentage of simulations using videotape trials, by 2-year intervals. Reprinted from "The Ecological Validity of Jury Simulations: Is the Jury Still Out?" by B. H. Bornstein, 1999, *Law and Human Behavior, 23*, p. 87. Copyright 1999 by the American Psychological Association.

mirrored in the field as a whole (Nietzel et al., 1999); second, the proportion of studies using a relatively naturalistic videotaped simulation decreased slightly; and third, the proportion of studies using students as the mock juror participants increased significantly over time, exceeding 50% for every period from 1985 to 1986 onward. My conclusion at the time was that simulation methodology as a technique for studying jury behavior was robust and well accepted but that any increasing methodological sophistication "has not been accompanied by increasing verisimilitude in terms of who the mock jurors are and how the simulated trial is presented to them" (Bornstein, 1999, p. 87).

Because the most recent data from that study are now nearly 20 years old, I thought it would be interesting to see how things have changed. I have updated the analysis twice, first for *LHB* articles published in 2005 to 2006 (13 studies in 11 articles) and more recently for articles published in 2011 to 2012 (seven studies in six articles). Again, these are convenience samples that can only provide a snapshot of what is going on in a single journal, albeit a prominent one that arguably sets the standards for the field. The results are presented in Figure 9.2, which for the sake of comparison also includes data for 1995 to 1996, the last time interval contained in the 1999 study. I coded the studies on the same methodological characteristics as the earlier study, with two modifications: First, the newer data were more likely to include audiotaped trials and even one live trial (Goodman et al., 2006),

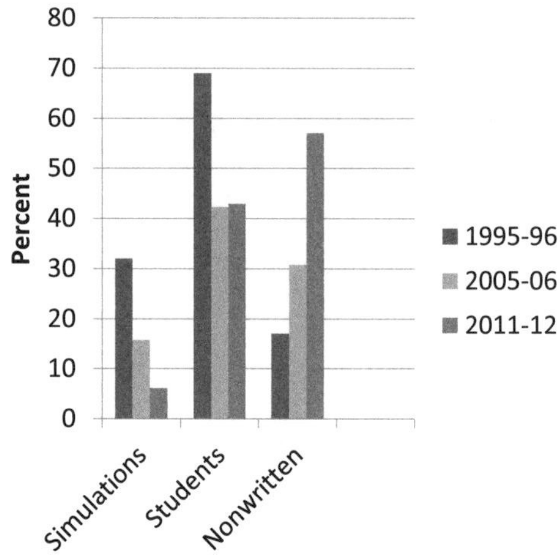

Figure 9.2. Jury simulation research trends in *Law and Human Behavior* articles at three points in time: 1995–1996, 2005–2006, and 2011–2012.

so the newer trial medium data (the bars on the right) indicate the proportion of simulations using any nonwritten format (i.e., audio, audio + static images, video, or live).[4] The second change was that I also coded studies in terms of whether they included group deliberation and consequentiality (i.e., whether mock jurors believed their decisions would have real consequences for anyone involved).

The results are somewhat surprising and essentially the opposite of those I obtained in 1999. Specifically, the number of jury simulations published in *LHB* appears to be going down; the proportion of articles containing jury simulations decreased from over 30% in 1995 to 1996 to 16% in 2005 to 2006, to only 6% in 2011 to 2012. Remarkably, 2012 saw not a single simulation study out of 56 published articles. It seems unlikely that this decrease reflects a diminution in the amount of jury simulation research being conducted, although it is certainly possible.[5] More likely, the expectations and standards for what constitutes publishable simulation research—at least in this one journal—have evolved over time. In support of this interpretation, despite their diminishing frequency, jury simulations' verisimilitude appears to be on the rise. Roughly 42% of studies in 2005 to

[4]For 1995 to 1996, the bar indicates the proportion of videotaped trials, so the comparable "nonwritten" figure would likely be slightly higher.

[5]Consider, for example, that there is an abundance of simulation research presented every year at conferences, such as at the annual meetings of the American Psychology–Law Society.

2006 and 2011 to 2012 used student mock jurors, a considerable decrease from 1995 to 1996. The number of trials presented in a nonwritten format (usually video) increased steadily, accounting for more than half of all studies in 2011 to 2012.

The deliberation data suggested that studies are fairly realistic in this sense as well. Nearly one quarter (23.1%) of studies in 2005 to 2006 included a deliberation component, as did 14.3% of studies in 2011 to 2012 (because of the small number of simulations overall, this was only a single study, by Hans, Kaye, Dann, Farley, & Albertson, 2011). Although most studies involved only individual mock jurors, without deliberation, the substantial minority that did include deliberation is impressive, considering the additional resources (e.g., greater time) and loss of statistical power such studies entail (see Devine, Clayton, Dunford, Seying, & Pryce, 2001, as well as the chapters in Part II of this volume). No study, across all three data sets, had real consequences (apart from the customary participant compensation) for either the participants or the litigants; that is, all mock jurors knew that they were role playing.

As in so many things in life, the conclusions from this analysis of chronological trends seem to fall into the "bad news/good news" category. The bad news—at least for researchers seeking to publish their simulations in *LHB* and, assuming *LHB* is representative, other journals—is that publication opportunities are fewer than they used to be. The good news—at least for courts and policymakers and, arguably, for the field as a whole—is that jury simulation research is becoming more realistic in terms of who the mock jurors are and how they process trial evidence. Although the 1999 study did not code studies for deliberation, precluding a full chronological analysis, there is also suggestive evidence that deliberation is, if not the norm, not uncommon. Nonetheless, the "mock" aspect of mock jury research is still present, with participants making decisions without any real consequences.

Methodological Comparisons

The second purpose of my 1999 paper was to review the results of studies that had directly (via experimental or quasi-experimental comparison) or indirectly (via cross-experiment replication) compared different mock juror samples or trial presentation media. Concerns with these variables arise if they produce main or interactive effects, but the latter are more problematic. Take, for example, a study that investigated the effect of expert testimony on eyewitness reliability on mock juror verdicts and that also compared the decisions of student mock jurors with those of a community sample. One possible main effect would be that community participants convicted the defendant more often than did student participants. Would that complicate the conclusions that can be drawn from the study? No more so than finding that men convicted more often than women, that Whites convicted more often than Blacks, or that other conceivable demographic variables were associated with participants' verdicts. The investigation of the role of demographic variables in jury decision making has a lengthy history, due primarily to its implications for jury selection (e.g., Devine, 2012; Kovera & Cutler, 2013). It would be useful for attorneys to know that jurors who are students are more or less likely to convict than nonstudents, but it is neither psychologically nor legally interesting and hardly invalidates the research as a whole.

It would be problematic, however, if this hypothetical study found an interaction, such as that student participants were influenced by the presence (or format or content) of expert testimony but community participants were not. Apart from the possible psychological implications related to how different individuals process the sort of information contained in expert testimony, it would call into question a conclusion that people in general are (or are not) influenced by eyewitness expert testimony, which bears on the debate over the admissibility of such testimony.

My previous review (Bornstein, 1999) found that relatively little research had directly compared different participant samples or trial presentation media, most of it was dated, and the results were inconclusive. In 26 comparisons of mock juror samples, there were only five main effects, which evinced a tendency for students to be more lenient than nonstudents, and only two interactions. I concluded that there was not much cause for concern. Since 1999 there has been a decent, though hardly voluminous, amount of research on the topic, especially with respect to the mock juror sample (for a review, see Wiener et al., 2011). It is not my purpose in this chapter to summarize that entire body of literature. My impression is that it shows that it does sometimes matter who the mock jurors are, we still lack much in the way of reliable patterns, and the effects are subtle and complex. They often reflect an effect of factors correlated with student status, rather than student status per se. For example, my colleagues and I compared the decisions of students and community members in a medical malpractice jury simulation (Reichert, Miller, Bornstein, & Shelton, 2011). One of two studies obtained a main effect of mock juror sample, with students more likely to find the defendant liable—an effect mediated by differential perceptions of the plaintiff's injury (e.g., students found the injury more severe) and the risk of the surgery. Neither study found interactions between the manipulated variables (surgery type, reason for surgery, patient weight) and the participant sample on verdict. There were a few additional effects on other measures (e.g., perceptions of the litigants), but in terms of the legally relevant decision of verdict, the only effect of mock juror sample was a main effect that reflected varying perceptions of students and community members, more than student status per se.

THE CONSEQUENTIALITY CONUNDRUM

No matter how realistic a simulation is, it is still just that—a simulation. Researchers can do a pretty good job of matching samples, trial presentation, complexity, and deliberation, but they still cannot effectively match the decision's consequences, which is the essence of a simulation as opposed to "real" behavior. The consequences affect more people than we might at first think. They are primarily for the litigants: Criminal defendants incur punishment (e.g., financial penalties, probation, incarceration, even death), and civil litigants experience a loss or gain of money, enhanced or damaged reputation, and personal satisfaction. In criminal cases, the state experiences consequences, at both the individual (e.g., prosecutors' job security and reelection chances) and societal level (e.g., public trust, society's safety). There are also consequences to the jurors, in terms of stress, the disruption to their lives caused by jury service, public scrutiny in highly publicized cases, and the "burden of justice" associated with the responsibility of making decisions that affect real people (Miller & Bornstein, 2013). The issue is complicated further by the fact that in most research on consequentiality, the consequences are present or absent for the decision maker him- or herself (Kühberger et al., 2002), whereas in the jury context, although there are some consequences for the decision makers (i.e., jurors), the major consequences are for others, namely, the litigants and aggrieved parties (e.g., victims). For these reasons, in an earlier paper I asked, "Is the enterprise of studying juries through experiments absurd?" (Bornstein & McCabe, 2005, p. 465).

Consequentiality has been alluded to in most critiques of jury research (e.g., Diamond, 1979, 1997) and cited in many court opinions dismissing jury simulation research (Bornstein & McCabe, 2005), but it has been largely overlooked in favor of more researchable problems, such as those discussed earlier in the previous section. The primary reason for this neglect is the sheer difficulty of conducting research on consequentiality (Bornstein & McCabe, 2005). There are essentially three options: First, researchers could lead (some) mock jurors to believe their decisions have consequences in situations when they actually do not; second, researchers could lead (some) real jurors to believe their decisions do not have consequences in situations where they really do; or third, researchers could randomly (or quasi-randomly) assign participants to conditions that differ solely in terms of their consequences—really real versus really hypothetical.

The first option raises ethical questions related to deception, but it is feasible and has been done, as in studies asking participants to make decisions as members of a judicial board in a student cheating scenario (e.g., Wilson & Donnerstein, 1977). To have any credibility, such a study would probably have to present participants with a live trial, as opposed to using a videotaped trial or written summary. Live presentation, though feasible, would be expensive and complicated (e.g., ensuring that the presentation was identical for each group of participants). The second option—leading some real jurors to believe their decisions have no consequences, whereas in actuality they do—is utterly unethical and impractical, not to mention potentially illegal. The third option is feasible and has been attempted on a handful of occasions in both jury research (e.g., by comparing shadow juries with real ones; see Diamond & Zeisel, 1974) and the larger decision-making literature (e.g., Kühberger et al., 2002). Such comparisons are time consuming and expensive, and they arguably still could not match participants' experiences in the consequential and nonconsequential conditions completely (e.g., interactions among jurors and with various courtroom personnel in the real vs. simulated groups might differ both qualitatively and quantitatively). Nonetheless, they are about as close as we are likely to get, and their findings are instructive. For example, Diamond and Zeisel (1974) found that conviction was more likely when the consequences were hypothetical (i.e., for shadow juries) than when the juries' decisions carried actual consequences. However, this literature as a whole—small though it is—has shown no consistent effects of consequentiality (Bornstein & McCabe, 2005).

ALTERNATIVES AND RECOMMENDATIONS

Where Do We Go From Here?

As the brief overview at the beginning of this chapter indicates, there are several alternatives to experimental simulations for studying juries, such as direct observation, case studies, archival analyses, and field studies. In addition, it is quite possible that there are other alternative methodologies that I have inadvertently overlooked or that researchers have not yet devised. Although it is difficult to quantify the prevalence of these various research methods, reviews of the literature (e.g., Devine, 2012; Nietzel et al., 1999) have suggested that simulations most likely constitute a "preponderance of the evidence," exceeding all the other methods combined.[6]

The question of whether this is a desirable state of affairs is a difficult one to answer. As discussed earlier, and as several other chapters in this volume explicate further, every research method—in jury research as in any other

[6]I borrow the "preponderance of the evidence" standard of proof used in civil cases, which is typically operationalized as "more likely than not," or greater than 50%. For the present assessment—that is, estimating the prevalence of different jury research methods—it is a purely subjective estimate based on my familiarity with the literature and not an objective tally.

research endeavor—has pros and cons. There are numerous advantages to using multiple methods to study a research question (see, e.g., Chapters 7 and 8, this volume). Most notably, multiple methods appeal to the principle of convergence. If the findings from diverse methodological approaches are consistent, they heighten confidence in both the underlying truth of the results and the generalization of the results to other contexts. Alternatively, if the findings are inconsistent or contradictory, they circumscribe the results' implications while also affording new research directions (e.g., to investigate why a certain variable exerts an effect in Research Approach A but not in Research Approach B). Insofar as the relative paucity of nonexperimental jury research limits opportunities to demonstrate convergence, it is fair to say that the field needs more of that type of research. This does not necessarily mean, however, that we need less simulation research, just that we need more of the other kinds.

One technique that would be especially beneficial is more field studies using real juries. Field studies raise a host of legal, ethical, and practical complications, which is probably why they are relatively rare in the jury research taxonomy. Nonetheless, they are an ideal approach in many respects because they maintain a fair degree of the experimental control that simulations possess but avoid the "consequentiality conundrum" and related shortcomings associated with low verisimilitude. Most jury researchers would probably be delighted to conduct field studies if the obstacles to doing so could be removed, or at least reduced. A number of different entities have the power to address these obstacles: funding agencies, which could encourage and appropriate more funding for field studies; courts (especially judges), which could be more welcoming to researchers and facilitate access to real jurors; journal editors, who could appreciate the value of field studies despite the fact that they are often somewhat "messy" in the sense of having less control and more procedural irregularities than the standard laboratory experiment; researchers' institutions, which could make allowances for the greater time and difficulty involved in conducting field work when evaluating researchers for promotion and tenure; and of course the researchers themselves, who have to be willing to undertake a more risky and challenging research approach in exchange for a potentially bigger payoff.

With respect to jury simulations themselves, there is some evidence that they are becoming more naturalistic. For example, over the last 15 years, simulations published in *LHB* have become less likely to use student mock jurors and written trial materials, and a sizeable minority of studies now include deliberation. These trends are, by and large, all to the good because they improve the chance that the research will be taken seriously by policymakers and the courts, and they also raise interesting and important psychological questions (e.g., the group dynamics involved in jury deliberation). It is natural for the tools used in any research to evolve over time. Nonetheless, it is important not to sacrifice internal validity and theoretical relevance in blind pursuit of verisimilitude (see, e.g., Chapter 11, this volume), especially in the absence of strong evidence indicating that the methodological choices made in simulation research matter in terms of yielding different results. To date, relatively few studies have directly addressed these concerns, and the results are largely inconclusive. This volume shows that although jury research has come a long way in the past few decades, the field still faces a lot of unanswered questions, especially with respect to methodology. The field is vibrant, but much work remains to be done.

Coda: Of Mock Jurors and Mock Turtles

Mock jury is something of an unusual term. About the only other times I encounter the word *mock* are with regard to a mock turtleneck or mock turtle soup. Can we learn anything about mock juries from mock turtles? In Lewis Carroll's *Alice in Wonderland*, the mock turtle has the head, tail, and hind hooves of a calf and the body, shell, and front flippers of a turtle. He is a forlorn character who longs for the days when he was a real turtle, although Carroll never explains how he went from a real turtle to a mock one. Alas, he does not even get to serve on the jury—whose members are, interestingly, allowed to take notes and ask questions—in the trial of the Knave of Hearts for stealing the Queen's tarts, which immediately follows the mock turtle's appearance in the story.

There is no evidence to suggest that mock jurors lament the fact that they are not real jurors, but there are similarities between them and Carroll's creation. Like the mock turtle, the mock juror is a combination of creatures—part essential cog in the justice system, deciding another's fate, part research participant in a noncourtroom setting answering hypothetical questions about a bare-bones case (unlike the mock turtle, both creatures are members of the same species). The mock juror is a confusing and at times confused hybrid about whom we know less than we might like.

What we do know about mock jurors is that they are important devices in the jury research tool kit. Although there are a number of legitimate concerns about generalizing from mock juries to real juries, and researchers should make efforts to enhance the validity of jury simulation research, there is as yet little evidence that mock jurors differ systematically from real jurors. Jury simulations in particular, and jury research as a whole, have made significant strides in the last half century or so, but there is clearly much more to be done. The 150th anniversary of *Alice's Adventures in Wonderland* occurred in 2015. If mock jury research is as highly regarded 150 years after its origin as Carroll's mock turtle, then simulation researchers will have nothing about which to complain.

REFERENCES

Ajzen, I., & Fishbein, M. (2005). The influence of attitudes on behavior. In D. Albarracín, B. T. Johnson, & M. P. Zanna (Eds.), *The handbook of attitudes* (pp. 173–221). Mahwah, NJ: Erlbaum.

Bornstein, B. H. (1999). The ecological validity of jury simulations: Is the jury still out? *Law and Human Behavior, 23*, 75–91. http://dx.doi.org/10.1023/A:1022326807441

Bornstein, B. H., & Greene, E. (2011). Consulting on damage awards. In R. L. Wiener & B. H. Bornstein (Eds.), *Handbook of trial consulting* (pp. 281–295). http://dx.doi.org/10.1007/978-1-4419-7569-0_13

Bornstein, B. H., & McCabe, S. G. (2005). Jurors of the absurd? The role of consequentiality in jury simulation research. *Florida State University Law Review, 32*, 443–467.

Devine, D. J. (2012). *Jury decision making: The state of the science*. New York: New York University Press.

Devine, D. J., Clayton, L. D., Dunford, B. B., Seying, R., & Pryce, J. (2001). Jury decision making: 45 years of empirical research on deliberating groups. *Psychology, Public Policy, and Law, 7*, 622–727. http://dx.doi.org/10.1037/1076-8971.7.3.622

Diamond, S. S. (Ed.). (1979). Simulation research and the law [Special issue]. *Law and Human Behavior, 3*(1–2).

Diamond, S. S. (1997). Illuminations and shadows from jury simulations. *Law and Human Behavior, 21*, 561–571. http://dx.doi.org/10.1023/A:1024831908377

Diamond, S. S., Vidmar, N., Rose, M., Ellis, L., & Murphy, B. (2003). Juror discussions during civil trials: Studying an Arizona innovation. *Arizona Law Review, 45*, 1–81.

Diamond, S. S., & Zeisel, H. (1974). A courtroom experiment on juror selection and decision-making. *Personality and Social Psychology Bulletin, 1*, 276–277. http://dx.doi.org/10.1177/014616727400100193

Eisenberg, T. E. (2011). The origins, nature, and promise of empirical legal studies and a response to concerns. *University of Illinois Law Review, 2011*, 1713–1738.

Eisenberg, T. E., Hans, V. P., & Wells, M. T. (2008). The relation between punitive and compensatory awards: Combining extreme data with the mass of awards. In B. H. Bornstein & R. L. Wiener (Eds.), *Civil juries and civil justice: Psychological and legal perspectives* (pp. 105–115). http://dx.doi.org/10.1007/978-0-387-74490-2_6

Eisenberg, T. E., & Wells, M. T. (2006). The significant association between punitive and compensatory damages in blockbuster cases: A methodological primer. *Journal of Empirical Legal Studies, 3*, 175–195. http://dx.doi.org/10.1111/j.1740-1461.2006.00067.x

Finkel, N. J. (1995). *Commonsense justice: Jurors' notions of the law*. Cambridge, MA: Harvard University Press.

Galanter, M. (1987). Jury shadows: Reflections on the civil jury and the "litigation explosion." In D. S. Shrager (Ed.), *The American civil jury* (pp. 15–42). Washington, DC: Roscoe Pound–American Trial Lawyers Foundation.

Galanter, M. (2004). The vanishing trial: An examination of trials and related matters in federal and state courts. *Journal of Empirical Legal Studies, 1*, 459–570. http://dx.doi.org/10.1111/j.1740-1461.2004.00014.x

Gerbasi, K. C., Zuckerman, M., & Reis, H. T. (1977). Justice needs a new blindfold: A review of mock jury research. *Psychological Bulletin, 84*, 323–345. http://dx.doi.org/10.1037/0033-2909.84.2.323

Goodman, G. S., Myers, J. E. B., Qin, J., Quas, J. A., Castelli, P., Redlich, A. D., & Rogers, L. (2006). Hearsay versus children's testimony: Effects of truthful and deceptive statements on jurors' decisions. *Law and Human Behavior, 30*, 363–401. http://dx.doi.org/10.1007/s10979-006-9009-0

Greene, E., & Bornstein, B. H. (2003). *Determining damages: The psychology of jury awards*. http://dx.doi.org/10.1037/10464-000

Hamm, J. A., Bornstein, B. H., & Perkins, J. (2013). Jury nullification: The myth revisited. In D. Fung (Ed.), *Psychology of policy-making* (pp. 49–71). Hauppauge, NY: Nova.

Hans, V. P. (2000). *Business on trial: The civil jury and corporate responsibility*. New Haven, CT: Yale University Press.

Hans, V. P., Kaye, D. H., Dann, B. M., Farley, E. J., & Albertson, S. (2011). Science in the jury box: Jurors' comprehension of mitochondrial DNA evidence. *Law and Human Behavior, 35*, 60–71. http://dx.doi.org/10.1007/s10979-010-9222-8

Horowitz, I. A., Kerr, N. L., & Niedermeier, K. E. (2001). Jury nullification: Legal and psychological perspectives. *Brooklyn Law Review, 66*, 1207–1249.

Kaplan, M. F., & Krupa, S. (1986). Severe penalties under the control of others can reduce guilt verdicts. *Law & Psychology Review, 10*, 1–18.

Kerr, N. L., & Bray, R. M. (1982). *The psychology of the courtroom*. New York, NY: Academic Press.

Kerr, N. L., & Bray, R. M. (2005). Simulation, realism, and the study of the jury. In N. Brewer & K. D. Williams (Eds.), *Psychology and law* (pp. 322–364). New York, NY: Guilford Press.

Kerr, N. L., Nerenz, D. R., & Herrick, D. (1979). Role playing and the study of jury behavior. *Sociological Methods & Research, 7*, 337–355. http://dx.doi.org/10.1177/004912417900700305

Kovera, M. B., & Cutler, B. L. (2013). *Jury selection*. New York, NY: Oxford University Press.

Kühberger, A., Schulte-Mecklenbeck, M., & Perner, J. (2002). Framing decisions: Hypothetical and real. *Organizational Behavior and Human Decision Processes, 89*, 1162–1175. http://dx.doi.org/10.1016/S0749-5978(02)00021-3

Miller, M. K., & Bornstein, B. H. (2013). The experience of jurors: Reducing stress and enhancing satisfaction. In M. K. Miller & B. H. Bornstein (Eds.), *Stress, trauma, and wellbeing in the legal system* (pp. 247–267). New York, NY: Oxford University Press.

Monahan, J., & Walker, L. (2010). *Social science in law: Cases and materials* (7th ed.). New York, NY: Foundation Press.

Monahan, J., & Walker, L. (2011). Twenty-five years of *Social Science in Law*. *Law and Human Behavior, 35*, 72–82. http://dx.doi.org/10.1007/s10979-009-9214-8

Mott, N. L. (2003). The current debate on juror questions: "To ask or not to ask, that is the question." *Chicago-Kent Law Review, 78*, 1099–1125.

Mott, N. L., Hans, V. P., & Simpson, L. (2000). What's half a lung worth? Civil jurors' accounts of their award decision making. *Law and Human Behavior, 24*, 401–419. http://dx.doi.org/10.1023/A:1005540229224

Nietzel, M. T., McCarthy, D. M., & Kerr, M. J. (1999). Juries: The current state of the empirical literature. In R. Roesch, S. D. Hart, & J. R. P. Ogloff (Eds.), *Psychology and law: The state of the discipline* (pp. 23–52). http://dx.doi.org/10.1007/978-1-4615-4891-1_2

Penrod, S. D., & Heuer, L. B. (1997). Tweaking commonsense: Assessing aids to jury decision making. *Psychology, Public Policy, and Law, 3*, 259–284. http://dx.doi.org/10.1037/1076-8971.3.2-3.259

Reed, K., & Bornstein, B. H. (2015). Using mock jury research to measure community sentiment toward child sexual abusers. In M. K. Miller, J. A. Blumenthal, & J. Chamberlain (Eds.), *Handbook of community sentiment* (pp. 57–68). New York, NY: Springer.

Reichert, J., Miller, M. K., Bornstein, B. H., & Shelton, H. D. (2011). How reason for surgery and patient weight affect verdicts and perceptions in medical malpractice trials: A comparison of students and jurors. *Behavioral Sciences & the Law, 29*, 395–418. http://dx.doi.org/10.1002/bsl.969

Suchman, M. C., & Mertz, E. (2010). Toward a new legal empiricism: Empirical legal studies and new legal realism. *Annual Review of Law and Social Science*, 6, 555–579. http://dx.doi.org/10.1146/annurev.lawsocsci.093008.131617

Suggs, D., & Berman, J. J. (1979). Factors affecting testimony about mitigating circumstances and the fixing of punishment. *Law and Human Behavior, 3*, 251–260. http://dx.doi.org/10.1007/BF01039805

Tetlock, P. E. (1983). Accountability and complexity of thought. *Journal of Personality and Social Psychology, 45*, 74–83. http://dx.doi.org/10.1037/0022-3514.45.1.74

Vidmar, N. (1994). Making inferences about jury behavior from jury verdict statistics: Cautions about the Lorelei's Lied. *Law and Human Behavior, 18*, 599–617. http://dx.doi.org/10.1007/BF01499327

Vidmar, N. (1995). *Medical malpractice and the American jury: Confronting the myths about jury incompetence, deep pockets, and outrageous damage awards*. Ann Arbor: University of Michigan Press.

Vidmar, N. (1997). Generic prejudice and the presumption of guilt in sex abuse trials. *Law and Human Behavior, 21*, 5–25. http://dx.doi.org/10.1023/A:1024861925699

Vidmar, N. (Ed.). (2000). *World jury systems*. http://dx.doi.org/10.1093/acprof:oso/9780198298564.001.0001

Vidmar, N. (2008). Civil juries in ecological context: Methodological implications for research. In B. H. Bornstein & R. L. Wiener (Eds.), *Civil juries and civil justice: Psychological and legal perspectives* (pp. 35–65). http://dx.doi.org/10.1007/978-0-387-74490-2_3

Vidmar, N., & Hans, V. P. (2007). *American juries: The verdict*. New York, NY: Prometheus.

Weiten, W., & Diamond, S. S. (1979). A critical review of the jury simulation paradigm: The case of defendant characteristics. *Law and Human Behavior, 3*, 71–93. http://dx.doi.org/10.1007/BF01039149

Wiener, R. L., Krauss, D. A., & Lieberman, J. D. (2011). Mock jury research: Where do we go from here? *Behavioral Sciences & the Law, 29*, 467–479. http://dx.doi.org/10.1002/bsl.989

Wilson, D. W., & Donnerstein, E. (1977). Guilty or not guilty? A look at the "simulated" jury paradigm. *Journal of Applied Social Psychology, 7*, 175–190. http://dx.doi.org/10.1111/j.1559-1816.1977.tb01338.x

10

HOW TYPICAL IS *LOCKHART* V. McCREE? ECOLOGICAL VALIDITY CONCERNS IN COURT OPINIONS

MARY R. ROSE

In 1986, the U.S. Supreme Court handed down its decision in *Lockhart v. McCree*, which rejected claims that Ardia McCree's jury was biased in favor of conviction because it had been selected to be "death qualified." In other words, those whose opposition to the death penalty was incompatible with their ability to serve impartially during sentencing had been removed. The majority rejected the implications of multiple survey and experimental studies showing that death-qualified individuals held attitudes that tended to favor the state and that death qualification procedures were likely to produce "conviction-prone" juries (for one review of this research, see Thompson, 1989). Before rejecting the claims as a matter of law, Chief Justice Rehnquist, writing for the majority, stated that he was "constrained to point out several serious flaws in the evidence" (p. 168) and went on to dismiss whole fields of inquiry by citing one or more problems with methodology. In his view, these limitations meant that the studies failed to support the defendant's

http://dx.doi.org/10.1037/0000026-011
The Psychology of Juries, M. B. Kovera (Editor)

argument that his jury violated his Sixth Amendment rights. Such flaws included whether the studies "even purported to measure the potential effects on the guilt–innocence determination" of removing jurors opposed to the death penalty, failure to use "actual jurors sworn under oath to apply the law to the facts of an actual case," and failure to remove so-called nullifiers (those whose anti–death penalty beliefs might lead them to refuse to convict at all; *Lockhart v.* McCree, 1986, pp. 169–172).

The decision was heavily criticized (see, e.g., Thompson, 1989), but even some who disagreed with the Court took the decision as a signal to psychologists that realistic methods matter. Reflecting on the case, Bersoff (1987) wrote that if social scientists "wish to contribute to constitutional adjudication, they must do so in the most methodologically rigorous and situation-specific way possible" (p. 58). Situation-specific is another way of saying that the most influential research—that is, work that shapes high court opinions—must have high ecological validity, mimicking the conditions under which actual jurors make decisions (see Brewer, 2000). In defending the need for ecological validity, jury scholars have specifically referenced the treatment of research in *McCree* (e.g., Diamond, 1997).

The need for ecological validity remains an area of controversy among jury scholars, with some suggesting that a more realistic mock trial simulation is but one of "several viable methods for the study of jury behavior" (Bray & Kerr, 1979, p. 117) and others arguing that a study that claims to be about juries should include as many features of the jury experience as possible (Diamond, 1997; Weiten & Diamond, 1979). Some work has found that key methodological features, such as use of students versus community members and type of trial stimulus (video vs. written summary) do not largely affect results (see Bornstein, 1999; Pezdek, Avila-Mora, & Sperry, 2010; see also Chapter 9, this volume), whereas other work has pointed to subject effects (McCabe, Krauss, and Lieberman, 2010), and some case-study data have suggested that a sense of decision responsibility leads to different outcomes and a more careful deliberation (Breau & Brook, 2007).

Despite important questions about how much jury researchers have to prioritize ecological validity, we know little about whether mock jury research typically suffers the fate of the work presented to the Court in *Lockhart v. McCree* (1986). Diamond (1997) pointed to other case outcomes to suggest that although some courts are "skeptical" about simulations, there is "enormous variation in response" (p. 569). Bersoff (1986) suggested that courts are fickle, citing "psychological research when they believe it will enhance the elegance of their opinions" while "discarding" data when more traditional or legally acceptable bases for decision making are available (p. 156). To date, case examples remain the primary way in which jury scholars discuss the extent to which courts make use of mock jury research (e.g., Chapter 7, this volume).

The purpose of this chapter is to examine a broader swath of state and federal appellate opinions for citations to work published in *Law and Human Behavior* (*LHB*), with particular focus on citations to jury-relevant research. I examine to what extent courts comment critically on the research, particularly with respect to issues of ecological validity, analyzing when concerns arise and what implications this has for a jury research agenda.

A REVIEW OF COURT OPINIONS

To examine how often and in what ways reviewing courts use psychological research on the jury, I conducted a search in Lexis for any citation to either "Law and Human Behavior" or its Bluebook form "Law and Hum. Behav." (I searched only on "Hum. Behav" in case some opinions used "L." for "law"), limiting the search to cases from the U.S. Supreme Court, U.S. Courts of Appeals, or state supreme courts through mid-2014. I focused on federal appellate and state high courts because their presentations of research are most likely to be used as precedents by lower courts and fellow high courts. Although this chapter focuses on a single journal, *LHB* has the strengths of being the oldest, and a premiere specialty journal on law and psychology, and is a highly sought-after outlet for mock jury research, precisely the work that raises questions about ecological validity. Further, by being peer reviewed, *LHB* avoids some of the pitfalls of research reported in law review sources (see Epstein & King, 2002). (A search on other peer-reviewed outlets, such as *Psychology, Public Policy, and the Law* and a few social psychology journals, yielded few jury-relevant citations and nothing that changed this chapter's conclusions.)

My search yielded 172 opinions, only six of which were not usable for this review; three of these unusable opinions used the phrase "law and human behavior" in sentences, not as citations. In two other cases, *LHB* was mentioned in saying something about an expert in a case (e.g., Professor Roy Malpass was on the *LHB* editorial board), but no specific *LHB* research was cited. Finally, one case from the search on "hum. behav" turned up a different journal. Over half of the 166 usable citations ($n = 94$) were deemed jury relevant. For example, opinions considering the need for expert testimony in an eyewitness case may make a claim about the jury (e.g., jurors find even inaccurate eyewitness testimony persuasive) but cite an article that was not a report on jury behavior (e.g., Wells et al., 1998). If the same article was used only to support a claim about common eyewitness mistakes or police practices—for example, to assert that the trial court erred in accepting the evidence—then I did not count the ruling as jury relevant.

Another definitional issue concerns the term *mock jury*. I counted any study that looked at legally relevant judgments using an experimental approach. Such work could include judgments of even nonlaypersons (e.g., attorneys) so long as a legally relevant decision was being simulated. Because *Lockhart v. McCree* (1986) criticized survey research as a means to gauge jurors' likely attitudes, I also counted nonexperimental evidence from surveys of citizens (e.g., Brigham & Bothwell, 1983; Fitzgerald & Ellsworth, 1984) as one form of mock jury research, although such studies clearly are not jury simulations.

I went through each citation to see what article was cited, by whom (i.e., in the majority, concurring, or dissenting opinion), and for what purpose in the opinion (e.g., to reject a party's claim, to argue for the need for a new approach). I did not attempt a detailed coding of whether the study received positive or negative treatment or whether the party presenting the research won the claim or the case. My review of the cases was quite narrow, designed to answer the question, "When appellate courts discuss jury-relevant research, how much do concerns about the use of mock jurors and/or ecological validity more generally enter into their discussions?"

U.S. Supreme Court Cases

A total of 12 U.S. Supreme Court cases have cited *LHB* research, with jury-related work constituting the bulk of the citations (seven of 12). Of the seven jury citations, four came from either the dissent (*Perry v. New Hampshire*, 2012: citing Brigham & Bothwell, 1983; *Shannon v. U.S.*, 1994: citing Silver, Cirincione, & Steadman, 1994; *Wainwright v. Witt*, 1985: citing Gross, 1984) or concurrence (*Miller-El v. Dretke*, 2005: citing Rose, 1999); of the remaining three jury-relevant citations in majority opinions, none were cited with approval (*Exxon Shipping Co. v. Baker*, 2008: citing Hastie, Schkade, & Payne, 1998; *Holbrook v. Flynn*, 1986: citing Fontaine & Kiger, 1978; *Lockhart v. McCree*, 1986: citing multiple studies from the 1984 symposium on death qualification [Haney, 1984a]).

Ecological validity concerns played little role in the citations to these studies. One reason is that, of jury-related citations, two were not to mock jury work (Gross, 1984; Rose, 1999). Yet even for mock jury studies, discussion of methodology was mostly absent. In *Perry*, Justice Sotomayor straightforwardly cited Brigham and Bothwell's (1983) survey in a footnote to the claim "that jurors routinely overestimate the accuracy of eyewitness identifications" (*Perry v. New Hampshire*, 2012, p. 739), and Justice Stevens in *Shannon* likewise quoted Silver et al. (1994) to assert that the public has inaccurate perceptions about the insanity defense (p. 590). Other studies were discussed in somewhat dismissive terms but for reasons other than a clear statement about ecological validity. In *Holbrook v. Flynn* (1986), the defendant contended that the presence of four uniformed state troopers sitting in the first row of the spectators' section prejudiced the jury against him. A unanimous court disagreed, finding no "unacceptable risk of prejudice" (*Holbrook v. Flynn*, 1986, p. 571) and footnoting that the defendant had proffered only a single study in support. Justice Marshall seemed more troubled by the mixed results than the design:

> [The study's] tentative conclusion is that defendants clad in prison garb or accompanied by guards are more likely to be found guilty than unsupervised defendants wearing their own clothes. However, the study also found that favored treatment was accorded defendants who had both supervision and prison clothing. . . . In view of these curious and concededly tentative results, we will, at least for now, rely on our own experience and common sense. (*Holbrook v. Flynn*, 1986, p. 571, citation omitted)

Perhaps the most remarkable thing about such a footnote is its inclusion. The Court unanimously rejected the defendant's claim of prejudice, and the justices could have dismissed the study with fewer sentences. Although the precise reasons are unclear, the qualifier "at least for now" suggests that perhaps Justice Marshall wished to signal openness to later considering new data.

The opinion in *Exxon Shipping Co. v. Baker* (2008) possibly raised ecological validity concerns, but if so, such concerns were oblique. The Court cited Hastie and colleagues (1998), a study of punitive damages. The citation appeared in a footnote to a sentence asserting that no studies show that such awards are not variable. The footnote made use of quotation marks:

> The Court is aware of a body of literature running parallel to anecdotal reports, examining the predictability of punitive awards by conducting numerous "mock juries," where different "jurors" are confronted with the same hypothetical case [*multiple citations given*]. Because this research was funded in part by Exxon, we decline to rely on it. (p. 501, Footnote 17)

As commentators have noted, perhaps the "scare quotes mock experiments for their failure to capture the experience of serving on a real jury" (Epstein & Clarke, 2010, p. 34). Further, the opinion made liberal (and generally favorable) use of data from studies of actual verdict outcomes (e.g., a full paragraph on Eisenberg, LaFountain, Ostrom, Rottman, & Wells, 2002), which could signal a preference for data from actual verdicts. But at least explicitly, the Court stated that it would not rely on the *LHB* work because one of the parties had funded the studies.

Thus, *Lockhart v. McCree* (1986), the seemingly paradigmatic case about the Court's demanding standards for ecological validity, turns out to be an outlier. The chief justice dismissed studies because the mock jurors "were not actual jurors sworn under oath to apply the law to the facts of an actual case involving the fate of an actual capital defendant" (1986, p. 171) and faulted other studies (but not Cowan, Thompson, & Ellsworth, 1984) for failing to eliminate "nullifiers." By no means do the set of jury-relevant citations, particularly those in the majority opinions, indicate a clear acceptance of mock jury research; however, apart from *McCree*, *LHB* research did not generate much discussion of ecological validity.

U.S. Courts of Appeals

My search yielded 41 cases in which a U.S. Court of Appeals cited *LHB* research. Table 10.1 reports the 21 cases that gave a citation in relation to a claim about jury behavior.

Patterns in Citations

Citations to jury-relevant work came from nearly all the circuits, save the Third and the Fifth (and also the Federal Circuit, whose unusual caseload, which includes patent and trademark claims, would likely make less use of the crime-oriented jury research appearing in *LHB*). Some circuits cited *LHB* more than others. The Seventh Circuit produced *LHB* citations in four cases, two of which were authored by Judge Richard Posner, who is an outlier in terms of his fluency with social science research (e.g., Posner, 2014); the other two came from Judge David Hamilton.

According to Table 10.1, citations to jury work in *LHB* were not a yearly event—there were, for example, none between the years 1997 and 1999—however, citations continued into the present, with eight cases occurring within the last 5 years. The work cited was somewhat more dated; just four of the citations were to studies conducted since 1998. There have been fewer *LHB* articles on the jury in recent years (see Chapter 9, this volume), but it also appears that some work, once cited, has a certain staying power. For example, work on prior record effects (Wissler & Saks, 1985) or the claim that jurors overestimate eyewitness accuracy (Brigham & Bothwell, 1983), although decades old, remains a part of even fairly recent U.S. appellate opinions (e.g., *U.S. v. Hardy*, 2011; *Young v. Conway*, 2012), although these pieces were often discussed alongside citations to other social science or law review sources.

Interestingly, up through 2000, it was more common for *LHB* jury research to appear in the majority opinion, rather in the dissent or concurrence. By contrast, after 2000, seven of the 11 citations were offered by a dissenter or in a concurring opinion. Thus, over time, use of *LHB* in U.S. appellate cases has come to better resemble the concurrence and dissent-heavy pattern observed in U.S. Supreme Court opinions, in which jury research rebuts particular points made on the other side. There are many possible explanations for this result, including random noise, but it could also reflect changes in laws, case composition, or composition of the judiciary (see Catterson, 2006, for an analysis of changes in federal dockets).

TABLE 10.1
Jury-Related *Law and Human Behavior* Citations in U.S. Courts of Appeals Opinions

Case	Author(s)	Cited for
Keeten v. Garrison (1984) 4th Cir.	Cowan, Thompson, & Ellsworth (1984); Fitzgerald & Ellsworth (1984)	Reviewed results of surveys and mock jury studies submitted to the district court; agreed with state's argument that lower court's habeas grant should be overturned.
Grigsby v. Mabry (1985) 8th Cir.	Cowan et al. (1984); Fitzgerald & Ellsworth (1984); Gross (1984); Haney (1984b); Thompson, Cowan, Ellsworth, & Harrington (1984)	Reviewed, with favorable commentary, results of surveys, mock jury studies, and legal reviews about death qualification.
U.S. v. Lewis (1986) 9th Cir.	Bordens & Horowitz (1985); Tanford, Penrod, & Collins (1985)	Studies have shown that joinder tends to prejudice jurors' perceptions of the defendant and the strength of evidence on both sides.
Trujillo v. Sullivan (1987) 10th Cir.	Haney (1984b)	Defendant is "incongruous" in requesting more extensive questioning regarding death qualification while also discussing Haney study on how the death qualification process can increase the tendency to find guilt.
U.S. v. Johnson (1989) 8th Cir., concurrence (to oppose juror questioning)	Heuer & Penrod (1988)	There are no data on the effect of juror questioning on jury neutrality; the Heuer and Penrod study was unable to test this hypothesis.
U.S. v. Johnson (1992) D.C. Cir.	Wissler & Saks (1985)	In a "generic claim of prejudicial effect" (p. 913), defendant offered social science data about futility of limiting instructions. "This does not get defendant very far" (p. 913).
U.S. v. Chischilly (1994) 9th Cir.	Thompson & Schumann (1987)	There is a "defense fallacy" that corresponds to, but is distinct from, the "prosecutor's fallacy."
Weekley v. Jones (1996) 8th Cir.	Boehnert (1989)	Example of "considerable empirical evidence that insanity pleas . . . are not received favorably by jurors." (p. 1463)
U.S. v. Richardson (2000) 11th Cir.	Heuer & Penrod (1988)	Juror questioning leads to more attentive jurors and thereby a more informed verdict.
U.S. v. Smithers (2000) 6th Cir.	Loftus (1986; source of citation to a dissertation study)	Jurors' assumptions about memories can be wrong; one study estimates that half of all wrongful convictions result from false identifications.[a]

(*continues*)

TABLE 10.1
Jury-Related *Law and Human Behavior* Citations in U.S. Courts of Appeals Opinions (*Continued*)

Case	Author(s)	Cited for
U.S. v. Amaya-Manzanares (2004) 1st Cir., dissent; recited in *U.S. v. Hardy* (2011), 6th Cir., dissent	Wissler & Saks (1985)	Juries treat prior bad acts as highly probative of the charged crime.[a]
Brown v. Farwell (2008) 9th Cir.	Thompson & Schumann (1987)	The so-called "prosecutor's fallacy" can lead to serious error in verdicts, particularly where the other evidence in the case is weak.
Bell v. Bell (2008) 6th Cir., dissent	Kassin & McNall (1991)	Tacit agreements should be disclosed by prosecution; both implicit and explicit promises can skew a witness's testimony.
Stephenson v. Wilson (2010) 7th Cir.	Neuschatz, Lawson, Swanner, Meissner, & Neuschatz (2008)	Empirical study of the effect of visible restraints on jurors does not exist but would be helpful to the court; "rigorous empirical studies of jury behavior" (p. 673) do exist that challenge many premises of the jury system.[a]
U.S. v. Blagojevich (2010) 7th Cir., dissent	Hazelwood & Brigham (1998)	"Some psychologists have speculated that jury anonymity increases the probability of conviction" (p. 292), but the procedure tested differs from that used in this trial.
U.S. v. Owens (2012) 11th Cir., dissent	Wells et al. (1998)	Eyewitness misidentification is a leading cause of false convictions; despite its low reliability, such evidence is persuasive to juries.[a]
Harris v. Thompson (2012) 7th Cir.	Kassin et al. (2010)	The jury had reasons to question the reliability of a videotaped confession, reasons in line with leading research.[a]
Young v. Conway (2012) 2nd Cir.	Brigham & Bothwell (1983)	Jurors tend to overestimate the accuracy of eyewitness evidence.[a]
U.S. v. Gomez (2013) 7th Cir., dissent	Greene & Dodge (1995); Pickel (1995); Wissler & Saks (1985)	Experiments using mock jurors find jurors are more likely to convict, limiting instructions are ineffective, and jurors are especially influenced when a prior bad act resembles that charged.[a]
Littlejohn v. Trammel (2013) 10th Cir., dissent	McAuliff, Kovera, & Nunez (2009)	Some jurors will be persuaded by testimony that sounds more technical and scientific; others will not. Jurors may not be able to evaluate methodological issues.[a]

Note. [a]Denotes instances in which *LHB* study was one of multiple citations in that section or footnote.

Ecological Validity

Before discussing the circuits' attention to ecological validity, it bears mentioning that Table 10.1 reveals quite a number of citations to mock jury studies—citations to jury-relevant work that was not based on a survey or mock jury approach were in fact rare (Heuer & Penrod, 1988; Loftus, 1986; Wells et al., 1998). Yet, of all the cases in Table 10.1, there were only four in which a judge made any comment suggesting that the study cited had limited applicability to the current case. In only two of these did the reviewing court explicitly state that a study was questionably relevant because of limits in generalizability to the trial setting. The first to discuss ecological validity was a pre-*McCree* death qualification case out of the Fourth Circuit, *Keeten v. Garrison* (1984). The court reviewed a district court's habeas petition grant and described the results of different studies that had been presented to the judge, including the mock jury and survey research that appeared in the 1984 *LHB* symposium (Haney, 1984a). The court also recapped the State's argument in the case, asserting that the studies were flawed:

> According to these [State] witnesses, the most serious flaws were the lack of random samples in most of the studies, poor test design, and failure to check for consistency in a person's responses to related survey questions. The State's experts also expressed the view that the attitudes asked about in the surveys were too general to predict behaviors, and that past behaviors caused attitudes rather than vice versa. These conclusions were supported by the research of Dr. Steven Penrod, a psychologist specializing in jury research. Dr. Penrod found almost no correlation between attitudes about the criminal justice system and verdicts in mock trials which he conducted, between the verdicts themselves, or between the several attitudes about which he inquired. Finally, the State relied on statistics from petitioners' own studies, which established that the impact of conviction-prone differences between groups, to the extent it exists, is minimal, except in one respect: opposition to the death penalty strongly increases the likelihood of juror nullification. (1984, p. 132)

In other words, the flaws the State laid out were not about the limits of mock jury research, per se—indeed, the State relied on Steve Penrod's mock jury research, in part, to make its arguments about the limited relationship between attitudes and behaviors. Explicit concern about generalizability instead appeared in a footnote to a section in which the court temporarily conceded the quality of the science to reject the death qualification argument on other grounds (the approach Justice Rehnquist adopted later in McCree's case):

> Although we are willing to decide the case upon this assumption [that the social science evidence is persuasive], we do not necessarily agree

> with petitioners' viewpoint that attitudinal surveys imply a relationship between attitudes toward the criminal justice system and behavior as jurors. Both law and trial practice evidence a belief that attitudes can often be put aside by prospective jurors. Examples of this include permitting jurors to serve despite exposure to prejudicial pretrial publicity, and permitting jurors to serve despite employment affiliation with or affinity to the prosecution. Moreover, the Supreme Court stated that a juror is not impartial in an unconstitutional sense just because a general attitude "affects" his decision-making process. (1984, p. 133, legal citations omitted)

Of course, modern jury scholars would strongly question whether jurors actually do put aside prejudicial pretrial publicity (see Otto, Penrod, & Dexter, 1994) and whether affiliations with parties to the case are unproblematic (see Rose & Diamond, 2008). The footnote clearly reflects an uncritical judicial philosophy that presumes impartiality whenever jurors claim it.

Explicit ecological validity concerns also emerged in *U.S. v. Johnson* (1992). Here, the D.C. Circuit considered a defendant's claim that his prior acts (involving wire fraud) should not have been admitted because they were more prejudicial than probative. The unanimous court disagreed, arguing that "Johnson points to nothing special" (*U.S. v. Johnson*, 1992, p. 912), citing only the Wissler and Saks (1985) study about the weaknesses of limiting instructions and concluding,

> This does not get defendant very far. . . . At most the data might alter our conception of how to weigh the elements in the balance, raising the weight given to the risk of prejudice. . . . The authors themselves, however, acknowledge the hazards of transposing this kind of sampling to the deliberations of actual juries, noting especially that in a real trial any prior conviction evidence will constitute a far lower proportion of the total evidence received by the jurors. [*Citations to other authorities on the problems with such extrapolation.*] Accordingly, we defer to another day the issue of what sort of evidence (if any) should induce a court to re-assess the way in which it implements the Rule 403 balance. (*U.S. v. Johnson*, 1992, p. 913)

"Another day" apparently never came, at least with respect to engagement with social science studies on the effect of prior acts. I found no further use of the Wissler and Saks study, or other *LHB* research on this topic, in the D.C. Circuit. The study nonetheless appeared in the dissenting opinions of three other cases (see Table 10.1), cited along with other studies that questioned the ability of jurors not to use defendants' prior acts as evidence of their current guilt, including two *LHB* studies (see Greene & Dodge, 1995; Pickel, 1995, in *U.S. v. Gomez*, 2013).

The remaining two cases that mentioned the limited applicability of an *LHB* jury study pointed to conceptual issues rather than ecological validity. In *U.S. v. Johnson* (1989), a concurring opinion noted that a study by Heuer and Penrod (1988), which was not a mock jury study, did not test any hypothesis about the relationship between juror questioning and juror neutrality. Another case concerned an appeal of a decision to allow jurors' identities to be withheld until the end of the trial (*U.S. v. Blagojevich*, 2010). Judge Posner distinguished this situation from the one examined in an *LHB* study of the effects of allowing jurors to remain anonymous throughout their decision-making process (Hazelwood & Brigham, 1998). Apart from a curious assertion that the authors have "speculated" (p. 292) about the effects of juror anonymity—when, in fact, Hazelwood and Brigham studied such effects—there was little indication that Posner was troubled by the mock nature of the research; indeed, he summarized the study results to suggest that anonymity might sometimes improve decision making. In *Stephenson v. Wilson* (2010), Judge Posner also included one mock jury study (Neuschatz, Lawson, Swanner, Meissner, & Neuschatz, 2008) in a string citation of "rigorous empirical studies of jury behavior" (p. 673) when he lamented the absence of data in the extant case.

State Supreme Courts

The final data source came from appeals to state high courts. My search uncovered a total of 113 cases that cited an *LHB* study, 58% of which were jury-relevant cites ($n = 66$). This large number of results prohibits a detailed presentation of each case and how the research was used, but the following summary of the citations outlines the patterns observed. (A lengthy table detailing which state cases used which studies is available from the author on request.)

Patterns in Citations

Unlike the pattern in federal appellate courts, *LHB* was more often cited in the majority opinion ($n = 46$) than strictly in the dissent or concurrence ($n = 20$), although a few of the 46 majority opinions also contained commentary about a cited study in the dissent or concurrence. The most *LHB* citations emerged in areas of death penalty decision making ($n = 19$, nine of which were in concurring or dissenting opinions). Citations were to death qualification research, including the symposium studies (Haney, 1984a), as well as subsequent work in the area (Allen, Mabry, & McKelton, 1998; Luginbuhl & Middendorf, 1988) and critiques (Elliott, 1991; Elliott & Robinson, 1991). Death penalty cites also included challenges to capital instructions (Haney & Lynch, 1994, 1997), the lack of a deterrent effect (Bailey, 1977), and former capital jurors' views about future dangerousness (Costanzo & Costanzo, 1994).

LHB research on jurors' understanding of factors affecting eyewitness memory (e.g., Deffenbacher & Loftus, 1982) or their need for either expert testimony or a special instruction (e.g., Cutler, Penrod, & Dexter, 1990) occurred in 16 different cases, six of these in the concurrence or dissent. Citations to one or more studies on the effects of joinder or prior record (Greene & Dodge, 1995; Greene & Loftus, 1985; Wissler & Saks, 1985) emerged in five cases (two dissenting). One or more studies of the peremptory challenge (Rose, 1999; Sommers & Norton, 2007), public impressions of the insanity defense (Silver et al., 1994; Skeem, Louden, & Evans, 2004), and jurors being permitted to ask questions (Heuer & Penrod, 1988, 1994) were cited in three cases each. Two different states each offered at least one *LHB* study in discussion of the need for expert witness assistance in cases involving confessions (Kassin et al., 2010; Kassin & Neumann, 1997; Kassin & Sukel, 1997), reactions to DNA evidence (Schklar & Diamond, 1999; Thompson & Schumann, 1987), views of reasonable doubt (Connolly, 1987; Kagehiro & Stanton, 1985), and expert testimony about violence prediction (Cooper, Bennett, & Sukel, 1996; Klassen & O'Connor, 1988; Steadman & Morrissey, 1981) and battered women's syndrome (Schuller & Vidmar, 1992). The remaining jury-relevant topics, covered by just one state high court, were reactions to polygraph evidence (Cavoukian & Heslegrave, 1980; Honts & Perry, 1992), rape trauma syndrome (Frazier & Borgida, 1988), views about hypnosis (Coleman, Stevens, & Reeder, 2001), jurors' self-assessments of bias (Carroll et al., 1986), judge versus attorney-conducted voir dire (Jones, 1987), the effect of knowing the insurance status of parties (Hans & Ermann, 1989), and reactions to strong imagery in trials (Douglas, Lyon, & Ogloff, 1997).

In state high courts, a few states, particularly those in the Northeast (Connecticut and New Jersey, with nine cases each, and Massachusetts with four), along with California ($n = 7$), Washington, and Utah ($n = 5$ each), dominated the citations to jury-relevant research, making up the majority of the citations (39 of 66). This owes, in part, to significant debates about juror reactions to eyewitness evidence and to death penalty jurisprudence that occurred among high court members in most of those states. By contrast, citations to *LHB* were far less common among states in the South (with just two cites from Texas and only one jury cite in Tennessee, Alabama, and Georgia). As was true for U.S. appellate courts, sometimes a single justice (e.g., Alan B. Handler, now retired, in New Jersey) authored multiple opinions or dissents that used *LHB* research. Again, because I searched on the use of just one journal, I can make no claims about whether some regions or some justices tend to be particularly open to social science research more generally, but the suggestive patterns are nonetheless intriguing.

Ecological Validity

Detailed attention to ecological validity in state supreme court cases was even rarer than in the federal appellate cases. By far the most common pattern was a straightforward citation to an article in support of an assertion—for example, that the defense had presented an empirically based argument, but the court was rejecting it, as in *People v. Welch* (1999). In *Welch*, after restating defense claims that jury instructions inadequately defined mitigation and citing work by Haney and Lynch (1994), concluded,

> As stated earlier, "[w]e presume that jurors comprehend and accept the court's directions." . . . The presumption that the jurors in this case understood and followed the mitigation instruction supplied to them is not rebutted by empirical assertions to the contrary based on research that is not part of the present record and has not been subject to cross examination. . . . We accordingly reject defendant's claim. (*People v. Welch*, 1999, p. 773, citations in original omitted)

Other times courts used *LHB* citations supportively, particularly when announcing new rules, such as overturning a ban that had prevented experts from testifying about eyewitness accuracy (see *Commonwealth v. Walker*, 2014: from Pennsylvania; *State v. Copeland*, 2007: from Tennessee; *State v. Guilbert*, 2012; *State v. Outing*, 2010, concurring: both from Connecticut), changing evidentiary standards regarding eyewitness testimony (*State v. Henderson*, 2011: from New Jersey), or calling for a special jury instruction on eyewitness evidence (*State v. Cabagbag*, 2012: from Hawaii; *State v. Henderson*, 2011: from New Jersey; *State v. Mitchell*, 2012: from Kansas). Much like Justice Sotomayor's dissent in *Perry*, dissenters also drew on *LHB* in a straightforward way. For example, in *State v. Lawrence* (2007), Justice Katz of Connecticut argued in dissent for new rules that would require the prosecution to prove "beyond a reasonable doubt" (rather than by the preponderance of the evidence) that a confession was obtained voluntarily. He wrote that the majority's confidence in jurors to properly weigh conflicting evidence about a confession and to consider such conflicts in arriving at a verdict "plainly has been discredited by several scholarly studies" (2007, p. 201), adding,

> Statistics have shown not only that juries are unable to identify false confessions, but that they regularly base their verdicts on such confessions despite other evidence pointing to innocence. . . . Mock jury studies have shown that confession evidence has greater impact than eyewitness testimony, character testimony and other forms of evidence. See [citation to Kassin & Neumann, 1997]. These studies demonstrate that jurors are unable to detect false confessions because of the commonsense expectation of self-serving behavior in others and the accompanying

disinclination to believe that a person would falsely confess. [Citation to Kassin & Gudjonsson, 2004]; see also [Kassin & Sukel, 1997] (mock jury study demonstrating that false confession increased conviction rate even when jury recognized it as coerced, court ruled it inadmissible and jurors claimed it did not affect verdict). (*State v. Lawrence*, pp. 201–203)

In other words, in most opinions, the justices do not dwell extensively on methodology. Judges accept or reject the findings in ways that accord with their conclusions about the case.

Consistent with results for the federal appellate courts, two arenas sparked commentary about ecological validity: prior record effects and death qualification. Both topics generated extensive commentary, one because the majority and the dissent disagreed about the legal change and the value of social science; the other because a high court discussed social science results in ways that ensured a death penalty verdict would not be disturbed. In *People v. Allen* (1988), a Michigan case, the court considered the convictions of five defendants convicted in separate trials (consolidated into one review). The majority overturned the convictions of three of the defendants on the grounds that the prior conviction evidence, presented to impeach the testifying defendant's credibility, was more prejudicial than probative. A footnote then cited Wissler and Saks (1985) to dispute the dissent's contention that jurors use prior convictions to determine only credibility. A few pages later, the majority cited the study again to note the inefficacy of limiting instructions, summarizing that the severity of the prior crime (murder vs. perjury) affected only conviction rates but not credibility ratings.

The dissenting opinion by Justice Boyle critiqued the methodology of the Wissler and Saks (1985) study, calling it a "public opinion survey," a study based on "observations of 160 persons approached in Laundromats, supermarkets, bus terminals, and private homes who were asked to determine guilt or innocence of a hypothetical defendant from a two-page case summation" (*People v. Allen*, 1988, pp. 685–686). After detailing the study's results in tabular form to highlight that numerically few people changed verdicts in each condition (1988), Justice Boyle concluded: "The number in the sample is so low, the margin for error so high, and the conditions so removed from those in an actual jury trial, that the majority cannot be serious in placing any reliance on this slender reed" (Footnote 20). (This same judge also critiqued Kalven and Zeisel, 1966, marshaling the data to suggest that misusing prior record evidence occurs infrequently.) Because of the dissent's critique, the majority opinion included the following:

> We do not agree with [the dissent's] conclusions, but welcome their critique of these materials as social science experiments cannot serve as the primary basis for judicial decision. Many fundamental principles of our

> jurisprudence are based on assumptions of human behavior that have never been, and in most cases cannot be, scientifically tested. We also note that the rule we modify today, and that the dissent urges us to leave as is, was the result of assumptions about jury behavior and the effectiveness of limiting instructions that were accompanied by relatively little analysis or study. The studies cited are nevertheless relevant, support our view, and deserve consideration. In citing them, however, we do not suggest that the amendment of MRE 609 is based solely upon them. (*People v. Allen*, 1988, p. 579–580)

This back and forth, with its detailed engagement with a study's results, was rare, and seemed prompted entirely by the strong disagreement over the need for changes in the law governing admission of prior record evidence. Wholesale changes in law from high courts based on social science results are themselves infrequent, with changes in the eyewitness arena a notable exception. As noted earlier, some state high courts have recently changed rules on evidentiary standards, thereby allowing experts to testify on eyewitness reliability, or they have altered jury instructions; such changes were buttressed, in part, by *LHB* research (see, e.g., *State v. Henderson*, 2011). For purposes of this review, the significant point is that in the eyewitness cases, such changes occurred with little to no substantive critique of the underlying research on jury decision making. The reasons for this difference are likely multifaceted, but notably the sheer amount of research available on eyewitness memory makes it far less likely that a justice could label any single eyewitness study a "slender reed" (*People v. Allen*, 1988, Footnote 20).

Death qualification emerged as the second area to generate extensive commentary on methodology, and in these instances, the state high courts rejected any need for a change in law. A majority opinion in *State v. Griffin* (1999), a case in which a defendant appealed her conviction because her jury was death qualified, critiqued survey-based research from the *LHB* symposium on death qualification (Haney, 1984a) for failing to involve an "actual, or even a simulated, jury experience" (p. 705) and rejected the Cowan et al. (1984) mock jury study as not being based on jurors from Connecticut and failing to capture the lengthy voir dire that occurs in capital trials.

The most extensive critique of social science as it relates to the death penalty occurred in *State v. Addison* (2013). The lengthy opinion upheld the death sentence of the single occupant of New Hampshire's death row, an African American man convicted of murdering a White police officer while trying to evade capture for other crimes. Part of the appeal concerned the results of a pretrial hearing in which the defense had attempted to have the death penalty barred entirely, arguing not only for the ill effects of death qualification but also on the grounds that it was racially biased. The trial court's hearing in April 2008 included evidence on the issues of race and death qualification, with the defense experts including Mahzarin Banaji and Sam Sommers, together with William Bowers and Wanda Foglia of the Capital Jury Project. Rogers Elliott and Ebbe Ebbesen, critics of death qualification research (see Elliott, 1991; Elliott & Robinson, 1991; Konečni, Ebbesen, & Hock, 1996), testified for the State.

The state high court upheld the trial court's rejection of both arguments, announcing that the trial judge's decision was the result of "several carefully explained reasons" (*State v. Addison*, 2013, p. 609). One reason was that all the research offered was, in the judge's view, "fundamentally flawed" (*State v. Addison*, 2013, p. 609). Specifically, the trial court judge explained that mock jury studies, including those on race and decision making, have the "major disadvantage" of studying "mock juries rather than real juries" (*State v. Addison*, 2013, p. 607). The Capital Jury Project, involving studies of real jurors, was "weakened by methodological flaws," including a long delay before jurors were interviewed and the limits of self-reports, small sample sizes, the dated nature of the data, and the fact that no participants came from New Hampshire (*State v. Addison*, 2013, p. 605). By contrast, studies of the race Implicit Association Test (IAT)—used to suggest racial bias among the predominantly White jury pool—had generated New Hampshire-based samples, totaling over 1,000 people; nonetheless, the trial court noted that IAT results had not been linked to sentencing by mock jurors and, according to State's experts, offered only moderate predictive validity. The IAT research also did not incorporate deliberation or "procedural safeguards" that courts use. Finally, archival studies of actual capital cases (e.g., Baldus & Woodworth, 2003) "suffer from a fundamental problem that an unrecorded variable may have caused or contributed to the racial disparities" (2013, p. 608).

Thus, to recap the reasoning supported by this high court: One cannot trust mock jury studies because such work does not reflect the experience of real jurors. However, studies of real jurors can be ignored unless they have large sample sizes, omit no variable or case characteristic that might—somehow, some way—affect results, and reflect results from jurors residing in a small northeastern state. Although IAT researchers have amassed large sample sizes from New Hampshire, and such work does point to implicit biases against African Americans in the population, the work can be rejected because it was not part of a mock jury study—which, of course, could be ignored in any case (see earlier). The treatment of social science research in *State v. Addison* (2013) leads one to conclude that there are, in essence, no existing social science data of any kind that would lead the court to acknowledge systematic flaws in how capital juries are selected or in how they make decisions. In other words, although perhaps this case evidences a concern for ecological validity, more likely it furthers—just as *Lockhart v. McCree* (1986) did—the "myth of the definitive study" (Thompson, 1989, p. 202).

DISCUSSION

According to this review, citations to *LHB* studies in appellate court opinions are infrequent, but rarer still are statements from the courts that unrealistic, mock jury methods have doomed the relevance of the social science. Although ecological validity concerns cannot be safely ignored, the review points to areas (e.g., eyewitness research) that have seen recognition come slowly, buttressed in part by symmetry between actual cases and simulation results. Finally, results have suggested that the death penalty remains an area in which courts are particularly critical of research, but that does not mean that all areas will suffer the same fate.

Since its founding, *LHB* has appeared in just over 160 opinions in either the U.S. Supreme Court, U.S. Courts of Appeals, or State Supreme Courts; more than half of these appearances supported claims about the jury. Given the thousands of cases these courts hear each year, *LHB* makes its way into only a tiny number of opinions. At the same time, low numbers do not mean no influence, particularly when one looks at dissenting and concurring opinions, in which a subset of judges or justices use social science to point out different ways of interpreting the case before them. Haney (1993) lamented the dissent-heavy pattern of citations to psychology as evidence of a lack of influence. Although lacking precedential power, dissents and concurrences should not be dismissed as irrelevant. They may, for instance, lay the groundwork for future views. Jury-relevant work from *LHB* was used, for example, in the dissent of *State v. McClendon* (1999), a Connecticut case that barred expert testimony on eyewitnesses; a similar citation appeared in the concurrence of *State v. Outing* (2010), which urged overturning such bars, something finally accomplished in *State v. Guilbert* (2012).

This review also points to a number of topics that seem ripe for further development. For example, *LHB* studies on the influence of prior record information and joinder emerged in multiple state high court opinions and several appellate court rulings; one state high court even used an *LHB* mock jury study to buttress its conclusion that state admissibility rules of evidence on prior convictions should change (*People v. Allen*, 1988). Jurors' views on the insanity defense, their treatment of scientific evidence (e.g., DNA results), and reactions to expert testimony about counterintuitive social science results (e.g., confessions) also emerged in multiple cases, as did assertions about procedural issues such as the effects of juror questioning and decision making surrounding the peremptory challenge. The U.S. Supreme Court and U.S. Circuit Courts each produced an opinion suggesting the need for more data on how jurors react to "off-stage" facets of a trial (Rose, Diamond, & Baker, 2010), such as the presence of officers in the gallery (*Holbrook v. Flynn*, 1986), or to potentially suggestive details (a visible stun belt; *Stephenson v.*

Wilson, 2010). All these areas vary in how well developed they are currently, but for nearly all, the scientific basis for understanding these issues can certainly move beyond the older, sometimes "classic" studies courts tend to cite. The citations, particularly those from recent cases, suggest that courts continue to struggle with issues of interest to jury scholars.

Notably, several state high courts used *LHB* articles to either call for a special instruction on eyewitness evidence or to overturn a state ban on allowing expert witnesses to testify in such cases. None of these cases went on at length about the unrealistic nature of the simulations used in eyewitness research, nor did they dwell on the design of studies demonstrating that jurors give great weight to eyewitness evidence. To be sure, eyewitness research faces ecological validity concerns (Penrod & Bornstein, 2006), but in recent years, the eyewitness literature has had two particular advantages that may have helped further its effects on the courts. First, the field as a whole—if not the particular question of how jurors treat eyewitness testimony—has developed a deep scientific database; this depth, in turn, permitted experts to produce heavily cited review papers that offer consensus views on the empirical support for conclusions in the area and suggestions for best practices (e.g., Wells et al., 1998, appeared in nearly all the state cases suggesting a need for a change in practice). No such equivalent "white paper" exists in the jury literature, but one can reasonably ask, "Why not?" Particularly with more research, areas such as the risks of joinder or prior record evidence, pretrial publicity, problems with peremptory challenges, or perhaps even the value of permitting juror questions may be areas in which a group of jury scholars could produce a consensus document designed to support a specific legal change that scholars believe would help the quality or experience of jury decision making.

Second, the tragedy of so many documented wrongful convictions demonstrably linked to eyewitness error gives the simulated findings, particularly with respect to claims about jurors, real-world relevance. Apart from pointing out the power of confession evidence (another topic that has produced a "white paper" summary; Kassin et al., 2010), wrongful conviction studies have not identified aspects of jury decision making itself or jury procedures that are problematic but remediable with new trial procedures, new evidentiary rules, or new instructions. No review has found, for example, that wrongful convictions are disproportionately likely to occur in cases with high pretrial publicity or when jurors are not allowed to ask questions at trial. It is unlikely we would ever see such a clear-cut result, and it is possible that any remedies proposed (e.g., routine change of venue) are impractical. But scholars in the field should consider looking intensively at the one or two issues that they believe could be developed in depth, produce a consensus document, and point to practical and significant ways to improve the jury decision-making context. Given the importance of "general acceptance" under prevailing standards for admission of expert evidence (*Daubert v. Merrell Dow Pharmaceuticals*, 1993; *Frye v. U.S.*, 1923), consensus documents published in peer-reviewed journals such as *LHB* may have particular resonance with courts; unlike amicus briefs, they are not encumbered by specific issues and complicated fact patterns associated with a single case.

Although my review finds that ecological validity concerns are infrequent, this should not be interpreted to mean that jury researchers can safely ignore the need to do so-called "Stage 2 research" (Diamond, 1997), in which ideas are tested in realistic situations with jury-eligible subjects. I limited my analysis to a single peer-reviewed journal, and results should be generalized to an analysis of law review articles, which judges may be more comfortable citing and critiquing. More significant, I have counted only citations; courts may well express ecological validity concerns by simply ignoring research. In addition, some of the citations occurred in cases in which the party making an argument supported by social science lost the claim, with the court offering only broad statements about not giving credence to the study or studies cited (e.g., *People v. Welch*, 1999). Whether ecological validity concerns shaped such conclusions is unknowable because the reviewing court did not explain the basis for its rejection in detail. Finally, some judges perhaps used more subtle tactics to convey a reluctance to trust results—for example, putting quotation marks around terms such as "jurors." Interestingly, in at least one case (*Exxon Shipping v. Baker*, 2008), this tactic was applied to well-funded research that had attempted to achieve some measure of ecological validity (e.g., a community sample, deliberation; see Hastie et al., 1998). This, together with the low total number of citations to jury-relevant *LHB* research ($n = 7$ cases), offers some support for the notion that the U.S. Supreme Court, in particular, tends to put up high bars to recognizing mock jury research.

The recent New Hampshire high court decision in *State v. Addison* (2013) indicates that when it comes to death penalty jurisprudence, the bars for all types of research seem impossibly high. Appellate courts have long indicated "death is different" (e.g., Abramson, 2004). Plausibly, jury scholars should likewise not rest generalizations about the openness of courts to empirical research on the fairly extreme conclusions drawn in cases such as *Lockhart v. McCree* (1986) or its progeny. With a few exceptions (e.g., in New York State, *People v. LaValle*, 2004), high courts seem exceedingly reluctant to be the source of changes to, including the wholesale abolition of, the death penalty. Empiricism on the death penalty is far from useless, and indeed, decision-making challenges for jurors in death penalty cases may be a ripe topic for a consensus statement from jury scholars. Nonetheless, researchers conducting such work must commence with realistic expectations. It is remarkably difficult to move any one particular court, reviewing any one particular (and typically gruesome or high-profile) crime, to dramatically reform or end this practice. The goal in this or any jury area should be to have large amounts of high-quality scholarship at the ready when appropriate influence opportunities arise. As in policymaking, the perfect should not be the enemy of the good.

REFERENCES

Abramson, J. (2004). Death-is-different jurisprudence and the role of the capital jury. *Ohio State Journal of Criminal Law, 2*, 117–164.

Allen, M., Mabry, E., & McKelton, D. (1998). Impact of juror attitudes about the death penalty on juror evaluations of guilt and punishment: A meta-analysis. *Law and Human Behavior, 22*, 715–731. http://dx.doi.org/10.1023/A:1025763008533

Bailey, W. C. (1977). Imprisonment v. the death penalty as a deterrent to murder. *Law and Human Behavior, 1*, 239–260.

Baldus, D. C., & Woodworth, G. (2003). Race discrimination in the administration of the death penalty: An overview of the empirical evidence with special emphasis on the post-1990 research. *Criminal Law Bulletin, 39*, 194–226.

Bell v. Bell, 512 F.3d 223 (2008).

Bersoff, D. N. (1986). Psychologists and the judicial system: Broader perspectives. *Law and Human Behavior, 10*, 151–165. http://dx.doi.org/10.1007/BF01044566

Bersoff, D. N. (1987). Social science data and the Supreme Court: Lockhart as a case in point. *American Psychologist, 42*, 52–58. http://dx.doi.org/10.1037/0003-066X.42.1.52

Boehnert, C. E. (1989). Characteristics of successful and unsuccessful insanity pleas. *Law and Human Behavior, 13*, 31–39. http://dx.doi.org/10.1007/BF01056161

Bordens, K. S., & Horowitz, I. A. (1985). Joinder of criminal offenses: A review of the legal and psychological literature. *Law and Human Behavior, 9*, 339–353. http://dx.doi.org/10.1007/BF01044475

Bornstein, B. H. (1999). The ecological validity of jury simulations: Is the jury still out? *Law and Human Behavior, 23*, 75–91. http://dx.doi.org/10.1023/A:1022326807441

Bray, R. M., & Kerr, N. L. (1979). Use of the simulation method in the study of jury behavior: Some methodological considerations. *Law and Human Behavior, 3*, 107–119. http://dx.doi.org/10.1007/BF01039151

Breau, D. L., & Brook, B. (2007). 'Mock' mock juries: A field experiment on the ecological validity of jury simulations. *Law & Psychology Review, 31*, 77–92.

Brewer, M. B. (2000). Research design and issues of validity. In H. T. Reiss & C. M. Judd (Eds.), *Handbook of research methods in social and personality psychology* (pp. 3–16). New York, NY: Cambridge University Press.

Brigham, J. C., & Bothwell, R. K. (1983). The ability of prospective jurors to estimate the accuracy of eyewitness identifications. *Law and Human Behavior, 7,* 19–30. http://dx.doi.org/10.1007/BF01045284

Brown v. Farwell, 525 F.3d 787 (2008).

Carroll, J. S., Kerr, N. L., Alfini, J. J., Weaver, F. M., MacCoun, R. J., & Feldman, V. (1986). Free press and fair trial: The role of behavioral research. *Law and Human Behavior, 10,* 187–201. http://dx.doi.org/10.1007/BF01046209

Catterson, C. (2006). Changes in appellate caseload and its processing. *Arizona Law Review, 48,* 287–299.

Cavoukian, A., & Heslegrave, R. J. (1980). The admissibility of polygraph evidence in court: Some empirical findings. *Law and Human Behavior, 4,* 117–131. http://dx.doi.org/10.1007/BF01040487

Coleman, B. L., Stevens, M. J., & Reeder, G. D. (2001). What makes recovered-memory testimony compelling to jurors? *Law and Human Behavior, 25,* 317–338. http://dx.doi.org/10.1023/A:1010607401492

Commonwealth v. Walker, 92 A.3d 766 (2014).

Connolly, T. (1987). Decision theory, reasonable doubt, and the utility of erroneous acquittals. *Law and Human Behavior, 11,* 101–112. http://dx.doi.org/10.1007/BF01040444

Cooper, J., Bennett, E. A., & Sukel, H. L. (1996). Complex scientific testimony: How do jurors make decisions? *Law and Human Behavior, 20,* 379–394. http://dx.doi.org/10.1007/BF01498976

Costanzo, S., & Costanzo, M. (1994). Life or death decisions: An analysis of capital jury decision making under the special issues sentencing framework. *Law and Human Behavior, 18,* 151–170. http://dx.doi.org/10.1007/BF01499013

Cowan, C. L., Thompson, W. C., & Ellsworth, P. C. (1984). The effects of death qualification on jurors' predisposition to convict and on the quality of deliberation. *Law and Human Behavior, 8,* 53–79. http://dx.doi.org/10.1007/BF01044351

Cutler, B. L., Penrod, S. D., & Dexter, H. R. (1990). Juror sensitivity to eyewitness identification evidence. *Law and Human Behavior, 14,* 185–191. http://dx.doi.org/10.1007/BF01062972

Daubert v. Merrell Dow Pharmaceuticals, 509 U.S. 579 (1993).

Deffenbacher, K. A., & Loftus, E. F. (1982). Do jurors share a common understanding concerning eyewitness behavior? *Law and Human Behavior,* 6, 15–30. http://dx.doi.org/10.1007/BF01049310

Diamond, S. S. (1997). Illuminations and shadows from jury simulations. *Law and Human Behavior, 21,* 561–571. http://dx.doi.org/10.1023/A:1024831908377

Douglas, K. S., Lyon, D. R., & Ogloff, J. R. P. (1997). The impact of graphic photographic evidence on mock jurors' decisions in a murder trial: Probative or prejudicial? *Law and Human Behavior, 21,* 485–501. http://dx.doi.org/10.1023/A:1024823706560

Eisenberg, T., LaFountain, N., Ostrom, B., Rottman, D., & Wells, M. T. (2002). Juries, judges, and punitive damages: An empirical study. *Cornell Law Review, 87*, 743–782.

Elliott, R. (1991). Social science data and the APA: The *Lockhart* brief as a case in point. *Law and Human Behavior, 15*, 59–76. http://dx.doi.org/10.1007/BF01044830

Elliott, R., & Robinson, R. J. (1991). Death penalty attitudes and the tendency to convict or acquit: Some data. *Law and Human Behavior, 15*, 389–404. http://dx.doi.org/10.1007/BF02074078

Epstein, L., & Clarke, C. E. (2010). Academic integrity and legal scholarship in the wake of *Exxon Shipping*, Footnote 17. *Stanford Journal of Law and Policy, 21*, 33–51.

Epstein, L., & King, G. (2002). The rules of inference. *The University of Chicago Law Review, 69*, 1–133. http://dx.doi.org/10.2307/1600349

Exxon Shipping Co. v. Baker, 554 U.S. 471 (2008).

Fitzgerald, R., & Ellsworth, P. C. (1984). Due process vs. crime control: Death qualification and jury attitudes. *Law and Human Behavior, 8*, 31–51. http://dx.doi.org/10.1007/BF01044350

Fontaine, G., & Kiger, R. (1978). The effects of defendant dress and supervision on judgments of simulated jurors: An exploratory study. *Law and Human Behavior, 2*, 63–71. http://dx.doi.org/10.1007/BF01047503

Frazier, P. A., & Borgida, E. (1988). Juror common understanding of the admissibility of rape trauma syndrome evidence in court. *Law and Human Behavior, 12*, 101–122. http://dx.doi.org/10.1007/BF01073120

Frye v. U.S., 54 App. D.C. 46 (1923).

Greene, E., & Dodge, M. (1995). The influence of prior record evidence on juror decision making. *Law and Human Behavior, 19*, 67–78.

Greene, E., & Loftus, E. F. (1985). When crimes are joined at trial. *Law and Human Behavior, 9*, 193–207. http://dx.doi.org/10.1007/BF01067051

Grigsby v. Mabry, 758 F.2d 226 (1985).

Gross, S. R. (1984). Determining the neutrality of death-qualified juries: Judicial appraisal of empirical data. *Law and Human Behavior, 8*, 7–30. http://dx.doi.org/10.1007/BF01044349

Haney, C. (1984a). Death qualification [Special issue]. *Law and Human Behavior, 8*(1–2).

Haney, C. (1984b). On the selection of capital juries: The biasing effects of the death-qualification process. *Law and Human Behavior, 8*, 121–132. http://dx.doi.org/10.1007/BF01044355

Haney, C. (1993). Psychology and legal change: The impact of a decade. *Law and Human Behavior, 17*, 371–398. http://dx.doi.org/10.1007/BF01044374

Haney, C., & Lynch, M. (1994). Comprehending life and death matters: A preliminary study of California's capital penalty instructions. *Law and Human Behavior, 18*, 411–436.

Haney, C., & Lynch, M. (1997). Clarifying life and death matters: An analysis of instructional comprehension and penalty phase closing arguments. *Law and Human Behavior, 21*, 575–595. http://dx.doi.org/10.1023/A:1024804629759

Hans, V. P., & Ermann, M. D. (1989). Responses to corporate versus individual wrongdoing. *Law and Human Behavior, 13*, 151–166. http://dx.doi.org/10.1007/BF01055921

Harris v. Thompson, 698 F.3d 609 (2012).

Hastie, R., Schkade, D., & Payne, J. (1998). A study of juror and jury judgments in civil cases: Deciding liability for punitive damages. *Law and Human Behavior, 22*, 287–314. http://dx.doi.org/10.1023/A:1025754422703

Hazelwood, D. L., & Brigham, J. C. (1998). The effects of juror anonymity on jury verdicts. *Law and Human Behavior, 22*, 695–713. http://dx.doi.org/10.1023/A:1025711024462

Heuer, L., & Penrod, S. (1988). Increasing jurors' participation in trials: A field experiment with jury notetaking and question asking. *Law and Human Behavior, 12*, 231–261. http://dx.doi.org/10.1007/BF01044383

Heuer, L., & Penrod, S. (1994). Juror notetaking and question asking during trials: A national field experiment. *Law and Human Behavior, 18*, 121–150. http://dx.doi.org/10.1007/BF01499012

Holbrook v. Flynn, 475 U.S. 560 (1986).

Honts, C. R., & Perry, M. V. (1992). Polygraph admissibility: Changes and challenges. *Law and Human Behavior, 16*, 357–379. http://dx.doi.org/10.1007/BF01044774

Jones, S. E. (1987). Judge- versus attorney-conducted voir dire: An empirical investigation of juror candor. *Law and Human Behavior, 11*, 131–146. http://dx.doi.org/10.1007/BF01040446

Kagehiro, D. K., & Stanton, W. C. (1985). Legal vs. quantified definition of standards of proof. *Law and Human Behavior, 9*, 159–178. http://dx.doi.org/10.1007/BF01067049

Kalven, H., & Zeisel, H. (1966). *The American jury*. Boston, MA: Little, Brown.

Kassin, S. M., Drizin, S. A., Grisso, T., Gudjonsson, G. H., Leo, R. A., & Redlich, A. D. (2010). Police-induced confessions, risk factors, and recommendations: Looking ahead. *Law and Human Behavior, 34*, 49–52. http://dx.doi.org/10.1007/s10979-010-9217-5

Kassin, S. M., & Gudjonsson, G. H. (2004). The psychology of confessions: A review of the literature and issues. *Psychological Science in the Public Interest, 5*, 33–67. http://dx.doi.org/10.1111/j.1529-1006.2004.00016.x

Kassin, S. M., & McNall, K. (1991). Police interrogations and confessions: Communicating promises and threats by pragmatic implication. *Law and Human Behavior, 15*, 233–251. http://dx.doi.org/10.1007/BF01061711

Kassin, S. M., & Neumann, K. (1997). On the power of confession evidence: An experimental test of the fundamental difference hypothesis. *Law and Human Behavior, 21*, 469–484. http://dx.doi.org/10.1023/A:1024871622490

Kassin, S. M., & Sukel, H. (1997). Coerced confessions and the jury: An experimental test of the 'harmless error' rule. *Law and Human Behavior, 21*, 27–46. http://dx.doi.org/10.1023/A:1024814009769

Keeten v. Garrison, 742 F.2d 129 (1984).

Klassen, D., & O'Connor, W. A. (1988). A prospective study of predictors of violence in adult male mental health admissions. *Law and Human Behavior, 12*, 143–158. http://dx.doi.org/10.1007/BF01073122

Konečni, V. J., Ebbesen, E. B., & Hock, R. R. (1996). Factors affecting simulated jurors' decisions in capital cases. *Psychology, Crime & Law, 2*, 269–297. http://dx.doi.org/10.1080/10683169608409784

Littlejohn v. Trammel, 714 F.3d 817 (2013).

Lockhart v. McCree, 476 U.S. 162 (1986).

Loftus, E. F. (1986). Ten years in the life of an expert witness. *Law and Human Behavior, 10*, 241–263. http://dx.doi.org/10.1007/BF01046213

Luginbuhl, J., & Middendorf, K. (1988). Death penalty beliefs and jurors' responses to aggravating and mitigating circumstances in capital trials. *Law and Human Behavior, 12*, 263–281. http://dx.doi.org/10.1007/BF01044384

McAuliff, B. D., Kovera, M. B., & Nunez, G. (2009). Can jurors recognize missing control groups, confounds, and experimenter bias in psychological science? *Law and Human Behavior, 33*, 247–257. http://dx.doi.org/10.1007/s10979-008-9133-0

McCabe, J. G., Krauss, D. A., & Lieberman, J. D. (2010). Reality check: A comparison of college students and a community sample of mock jurors in a simulated sexual violent predator civil commitment. *Behavioral Sciences & the Law, 28*, 730–750. http://dx.doi.org/10.1002/bsl.902

Miller-El v. Dretke, 545 U.S. 231 (2005).

Neuschatz, J. S., Lawson, D. S., Swanner, J. K., Meissner, C. A., & Neuschatz, J. S. (2008). The effects of accomplice witnesses and jailhouse informants on jury decision making. *Law and Human Behavior, 32*, 137–149. http://dx.doi.org/10.1007/s10979-007-9100-1

Otto, A. L., Penrod, S. D., & Dexter, H. R. (1994). The biasing impact of pretrial publicity on juror judgments. *Law and Human Behavior, 18*, 453–469.

Penrod, S. D., & Bornstein, B. H. (2006). Generalizing eyewitness reliability research. In R. C. L. Lindsay, D. Ross, D. Read, & M. Toglia (Eds.), *Handbook of eyewitness psychology: Vol. II. Memory for people* (pp. 529–556). Mahwah, NJ: Erlbaum.

People v. Allen, 429 Mich. 558 (1988).

People v. Lavalle, 3 N.Y.3d 88 (2004).

People v. Welch, 20 Cal 4th 701 (1999).

Perry v. New Hampshire, 132 S. Ct. 716 (2012).

Pezdek, K., Avila-Mora, E., & Sperry, K. (2010). Does trial presentation medium matter in jury simulation research? Evaluating the effectiveness of eyewitness expert testimony. *Applied Cognitive Psychology, 24*, 673–690. http://dx.doi.org/10.1002/acp.1578

Pickel, K. L. (1995). Inducing jurors to disregard inadmissible evidence: A legal explanation does not help. *Law and Human Behavior, 19*, 407–424. http://dx.doi.org/10.1007/BF01499140

Posner, R. (2014). *Economic analysis of the law* (9th ed.). Austin, TX: Wolters Kluwer.

Rose, M. R. (1999). The peremptory challenge accused or race or gender discrimination? Some data from one county. *Law and Human Behavior, 23*, 695–702. http://dx.doi.org/10.1023/A:1022393506784

Rose, M. R., & Diamond, S. S. (2008). Judging bias: Juror confidence and judicial rulings on challenges for cause. *Law & Society Review, 42*, 513–549. http://dx.doi.org/10.1111/j.1540-5893.2008.00350.x

Rose, M. R., Diamond, S. S., & Baker, K. M. (2010). Goffman on the jury: Real jurors' attention to the "offstage" of trials. *Law and Human Behavior, 34*, 310–323. http://dx.doi.org/10.1007/s10979-009-9195-7

Schklar, J., & Diamond, S. S. (1999). Juror reactions to DNA evidence: Errors and expectancies. *Law and Human Behavior, 23*, 159–184. http://dx.doi.org/10.1023/A:1022368801333

Schuller, R. A., & Vidmar, N. (1992). Battered woman syndrome evidence in the courtroom: A review of the literature. *Law and Human Behavior, 16*, 273–291. http://dx.doi.org/10.1007/BF01044770

Shannon v. U.S., 512 U.S. 573 (1994).

Silver, E., Cirincione, C., & Steadman, H. J. (1994). Demythologizing inaccurate perceptions of the insanity defense. *Law and Human Behavior, 18*, 63–70.

Skeem, J. L., Louden, J. E., & Evans, J. (2004). Venirepersons's attitudes toward the insanity defense: Developing, refining, and validating a scale. *Law and Human Behavior, 28*, 623–648. http://dx.doi.org/10.1007/s10979-004-0487-7

Sommers, S. R., & Norton, M. I. (2007). Race-based judgments, race-neutral justifications: Experimental examination of peremptory use and the Batson challenge procedure. *Law and Human Behavior, 31*, 261–273. http://dx.doi.org/10.1007/s10979-006-9048-6

State v. Addison, 165 N.H. 381 (2013).

State v. Cabagbag, 127 Haw. 302 (2012).

State v. Copeland, 226 S.W.3d 287 (2007).

State v. Griffin, 251 Conn. 671 (1999).

State v. Guilbert, 306 Conn. 218 (2012).

State v. Henderson, 208 N.J. 208 (2011).

State v. Lawrence, 282 Conn. 141 (2007).

State v. McClendon, 248 Conn. 572 (1999).

State v. Mitchell, 294 Kan. 469 (2012).

State v. Outing, 298 Conn. 34 (2010).

Steadman, H. J., & Morrissey, J. P. (1981). The statistical prediction of violent behavior: Measuring the costs of a public protectionist versus a civil libertarian model. *Law and Human Behavior, 5*, 263–274. http://dx.doi.org/10.1007/BF01044942

Stephenson v. Wilson, 619 F.3d 664 (2010).

Tanford, S., Penrod, S., & Collins, R. (1985). Decision making in joined criminal trials: The influence of charge similarity, evidence similarity, and limiting instructions. *Law and Human Behavior*, 9, 319–337. http://dx.doi.org/10.1007/BF01044474

Thompson, W. C. (1989). Death qualification after *Wainwright v. Witt* and *Lockhart v. McCree*. *Law and Human Behavior, 13*, 185–215. http://dx.doi.org/10.1007/BF01055923

Thompson, W. C., Cowan, C. L., Ellsworth, P. C., & Harrington, J. C. (1984). Death penalty attitudes and conviction proneness: The translation of attitudes into verdicts. *Law and Human Behavior*, 8, 95–113. http://dx.doi.org/10.1007/BF01044353

Thompson, W. C., & Schumann, E. L. (1987). Interpretation of statistical evidence in criminal trials: The prosecutor's fallacy and the defense attorney's fallacy. *Law and Human Behavior, 11*, 167–187. http://dx.doi.org/10.1007/BF01044641

Trujillo v. Sullivan, 815 F.2d 597 (1987).

U.S. v. Amaya-Manzanares, 377 F.3d 39 (2004).

U.S. v. Blagojevich, 614 F.3d 287 (2010).

U.S. v. Chischilly, 30 F.3d 1144 (1994).

U.S. v. Gomez, 712 F.3d 1146 (2013).

U.S. v. Hardy, 643 F.3d 143 (2011).

U.S. v. Lewis, 787 F.2d 1318 (1986).

U.S. v. Johnson, 892 F.2d 707 (1989).

U.S. v. Johnson, 970 F.2d 907 (1992).

U.S. v. Owens, 682 F.3d 1358 (2012).

U.S. v. Richardson, 233 F.3d 1285 (2000).

U.S. v. Smithers, 212 F.3d 306 (2000).

Wainwright v. Witt, 469 U.S. 412 (1985).

Weekley v. Jones, 76 F.3d 1459 (1996).

Weiten, W., & Diamond, S. S. (1979). A critical review of the jury simulation paradigm: The case of defendant characteristics. *Law and Human Behavior, 3*, 71–93. http://dx.doi.org/10.1007/BF01039149

Wells, G. L., Small, M., Penrod, S., Malpass, R. S., Fulero, S. M., & Brimacombe, C. A. E. (1998). Eyewitness identification procedures: Recommendations for lineups and photo spreads. *Law and Human Behavior, 22*, 603–647. http://dx.doi.org/10.1023/A:1025750605807

Wissler, R. L., & Saks, M. J. (1985). On the inefficacy of limiting instructions: When jurors use prior conviction evidence to decide on guilt. *Law and Human Behavior*, 9, 37–48.

Young v. Conway, 698 F.3d 69 (2012).

III

SYNTHESIS AND FUTURE DIRECTIONS

11

SUGGESTED DO'S AND DON'TS FOR FUTURE JURY RESEARCH: A SWAN SONG

NORBERT L. KERR

I became involved in my first jury study (Davis, Kerr, Atkin, Holt, & Meek, 1975) over 40 years ago, in 1972, working as a greenhorn research assistant in the lab of the late James H. Davis (whose many significant contributions to our understanding of juries and other interesting groups are worthy of special note and praise; e.g., see Kerr & Tindale, 2012). Like many young scholars, I got turned on to the study of juror and jury behavior and to the possibility that such work might contribute to an ideal of justice. Over the past 40 years, I have never lost that enthusiasm or hope and have spent a fair fraction of my professional life delving into the jury's mysteries. I am now close to full retirement and so do not have quite the same vested professional interest in the future of the field that many do. Still, I care about that future and have some opinions (mostly contrarian ones, I am afraid) about how that future should be pursued. Thus, I am honored and gratified to have my thoughts included in this volume and for the opportunity to offer a "swan song."

http://dx.doi.org/10.1037/0000026-012
The Psychology of Juries, M. B. Kovera (Editor)

As you may know, a swan song (according to Wikipedia, 2016) is

> a metaphorical phrase for a final gesture, effort, or performance given just before death or retirement. The phrase refers to an ancient belief that swans (*Cygnus* spp.) sing a beautiful song in the moment just before death, having been silent (or alternatively, not so musical) during most of their lifetime. (para. 1)

To be frank, I have not been conspicuously silent during my professional lifetime, so some of my advice will sound familiar to some of you. But allow me to sing my piece, and then I will leave it to the reader to decide whether my song is a beautiful one or just the hissing of an old bird (or a bit of each).

It is an old saw for messengers to say, "I've got good news and bad news; which do you want to hear first?" My advice about future jury research will take the form of some proscriptions (don'ts) and prescriptions (do's), and for a variety of reasons (including a desire to conclude on an assertive and positive note), let us start with the don't verses of my swan song.

DON'T REFLEXIVELY INCLUDE DELIBERATING JURIES IN RESEARCH

My experience as an author, reviewer, and editor has shown that a lack of data on deliberating juries is a common criticism of research on individual juror behavior. Consequently, in nearly every such published study one will find—buried in a litany of the paper's limitations—an acknowledgment (often an apology) that the results obtained on jurors might not replicate in deliberating juries and that follow-up studies using juries would be needed before one could have any real confidence in the ecological validity of those results. Similarly, I believe it is widely (and accurately) held that a research proposal that includes juries has, all else being equal, better prospects for funding than a comparable one that focuses on individual juror behavior. It may sound a bit strange coming from someone whose empirical work has focused more on the study of juries than on jurors, but I believe that this common viewpoint is not well justified.

For the moment, suppose we are genuinely interested in jury rather than juror behavior. If it were just as easy to do a study on juries as it was on jurors, there could be little objection to a preference or insistence on jury (vs. juror) research. But of course, it is not as easy. In experimental studies, for example, it is far more difficult and costly to obtain a dozen participants to get a single data point than it is to obtain a single participant. One needs different and more elaborate labs and equipment to contain and observe groups (especially larger groups such as the traditional 12-person jury). Studies that include deliberation are, of necessity, longer than those that do not. And the content analysis of mock jury deliberation is notoriously labor intensive. Field studies of actual jury behavior carry additional difficulties that are logistical (e.g., getting access to the courts and the juries), legal (e.g., legal prohibitions from direct observation of jury deliberations), and methodological (e.g., controlling for differences among the unique cases each actual jury hears; relying on retrospective reports, sometimes from a small subsample of the jury). So, all else being equal, it is far less costly and difficult to mount a study of individual juror decision making than a comparable study of jury decision making. If the resources available for such research were infinite, that would not matter, but, of course, they are finite (and, sadly, scarce). So one argument is that we can get more "bang for our buck" (i.e., do more research on more questions of interest) by studying jurors instead of juries.

But even granting this efficiency argument, a preference or insistence on jury (vs. juror) research might still be based on another reasonable premise—that group behavior does not always mimic individual behavior (e.g., Baron & Kerr, 2003; Davis, 1969; Forsyth, 2013; Tindale, Smith, Dykema-Engblade, & Kluwe, 2012)—and hence the generalizability of the latter to the former is an important external validity question. The most obvious (albeit costly) way to address it is empirically—either (a) study juries from the get go, or (b) if one only has resources to do less costly juror research, insist on replication with juries before having any confidence in the ecological validity of that juror research.

However, I would argue that it is more efficient and more informative to use our scarce resources to develop and substantiate powerful predictive models of jury decision making that apply across a wide domain of contexts (i.e., types of trials, sizes of juries, populations of jurors). Such models can make it possible to predict with some confidence how juries would behave from knowing how jurors behave. If we had confidence in the predictive validity of this model, we could take effects observed in a study of jurors (e.g., the distributions of conviction vs. acquittal by jurors in a condition with a physically attractive vs. a physically unattractive defendant; Efran, 1974) and estimate the likely effect that would have been observed in deliberating juries (i.e., the corresponding, predicted distributions of convictions and acquittals by juries in the two defendant-attractiveness conditions). In this way, theory (viz., the predictive model) could bridge the gap between what we had observed in jurors to what we might reasonably expect to observe among juries. And potentially, this could be done for any juror phenomenon for which the predictive validity of that theory could be reasonably assumed.

A strong argument can be made that for criminal trials with few verdict alternatives (e.g., single-count criminal cases with a reasonable doubt standard of proof that require a simple guilty vs. not guilty verdict), we already possess such a predictive model (e.g., Davis, 1973; Kerr & MacCoun, 2012; Stasser, Kerr, & Davis, 1989). Research on actual juries (e.g., Devine, Buddenbaum, Houp, Stolle, & Studebaker, 2007; Kalven & Zeisel, 1966; Zeisel & Diamond, 1978) converges with substantial mock jury research (e.g., Devine, 2012; MacCoun & Kerr, 1988; Stasser, Kerr, & Bray, 1982; Stasser et al., 1989) to suggest a stochastic, predictive model that accurately predicts jury verdict distributions. That model has three key features: (a) initial large-majority factions nearly always prevail; (b) hung juries become more likely as initial dissensus in the jury increases (e.g., there is no large-majority faction initially, as when the jury begins deliberation with an equal split of 6G/6NG); and (c) absent initial large majorities, factions favoring acquittal, are relatively more likely to prevail than equally large factions favoring conviction (a "leniency asymmetry" effect).

There are various ways of formalizing such a predictive model (e.g., MacCoun, 2012; Penrod & Hastie, 1979), but for several reasons (its substantial empirical base, its clarity for illustrating the issues at hand, and frankly, because of my familiarity with it) I will do so using Davis's (1973) social decision scheme (SDS) model (see Stasser, 1999, for a summary of that model). For our present purposes, the core of that model is the SDS matrix, *D*. Its rows specify all the possible ways an r-person jury can begin deliberation; for example, for a 12-person jury, there are 13 such "distinguishable distributions," those presented in the first two columns of Table 11.1. There are as many columns as there are group decision alternatives—so, three columns if we attempt to predict hung juries as well as convictions and acquittals (Models 3 and 4 in Table 11.1), two columns if we disregard hung juries and simply attempt to predict jury convictions versus acquittals (Models 1 and 2 in Table 11.1).

The entries in a *D* matrix represent the predicted probability that a jury beginning deliberation with a particular split will eventually reach each possible jury alternative. So, to illustrate, consider Model 4 at the far right of Table 11.1. Davis and colleagues (1975) found this decision scheme to provide the most accurate prediction (among 13 alternative schemes competitively tested) for a diverse sample of mock juries (of sizes six vs. 12; deliberating under a unanimous vs. two-thirds majority decision rule). This simple decision scheme predicts that whenever two thirds or more of the jury supports a verdict at the start of deliberation, the jury will ultimately reach that verdict (see the first five rows and the last five rows of the Model 4 *D* matrix). And it predicts that juries beginning deliberation without any such supermajority would always hang (see the sixth through eighth rows). As one can see, Model 4 captures the first two features of the generic jury prediction model described earlier (viz., large majorities prevail and more evenly split juries are more likely to hang), but not the third feature (i.e., for Model 4, submajorities

TABLE 11.1
Plausible Social Decision Schemes for 12-Person Criminal Juries Facing a Dichotomous, Guilty/Not Guilty Choice

Initial Juror Split		Model 1		Model 2		Model 3			Model 4		
G	NG	G	NG	G	NG	G	NG	H	G	NG	H
12	0	1.000	0.000	1.000	0.000	1.000	0.000	0.000	1.000	0.000	0.000
11	1	0.997	0.003	1.000	0.000	0.992	0.003	0.005	1.000	0.000	0.000
10	2	0.987	0.013	1.000	0.000	0.972	0.013	0.015	1.000	0.000	0.000
9	3	0.957	0.043	1.000	0.000	0.935	0.042	0.023	1.000	0.000	0.000
8	4	0.865	0.135	0.670	0.330	0.835	0.130	0.035	1.000	0.000	0.000
7	5	0.615	0.385	0.431	0.569	0.578	0.362	0.060	0.000	0.000	1.000
6	6	0.316	0.684	0.192	0.808	0.281	0.609	0.110	0.000	0.000	1.000
5	7	0.118	0.882	0.126	0.874	0.111	0.829	0.060	0.000	0.000	1.000
4	8	0.032	0.968	0.060	0.940	0.031	0.934	0.035	0.000	1.000	0.000
3	9	0.010	0.990	0.000	1.000	0.010	0.967	0.023	0.000	1.000	0.000
2	10	0.003	0.997	0.000	1.000	0.003	0.982	0.015	0.000	1.000	0.000
1	11	0.001	0.999	0.000	1.000	0.001	0.994	0.005	0.000	1.000	0.000
0	12	0.000	1.000	0.000	1.000	0.000	1.000	0.000	0.000	1.000	0.000

Note. Model 1 is based on Kerr and MacCoun's (2012; Figure 3b) bBOP fitting of Devine et al.'s (2007) data for 92 real juries' verdicts (excluding hung juries). Model 2 is a modification of Model 4, excluding hung juries and with leniency asymmetry in sub-two-thirds-majority splits estimated from MacCoun and Kerr's (1988) meta-analysis of mock jury studies. Model 3 is a modification of Model 1, adding estimates of hung jury probabilities estimated from Zeisel and Diamond's (1978; Graph 1, p. 505) freehand interpolation of Kalven and Zeisel's (1966, p. 489) data. Model 4 is Davis's (e.g., Davis et al., 1975) "two-third majority wins, hung otherwise" D matrix. G = guilty; H = hung; NG = not guilty.

for acquittal are no more likely to prevail than comparable submajorities for conviction). There were hints of such a leniency asymmetry in Davis et al.'s (1975) data (e.g., the second best fitting model included such an asymmetry; cf. their Table 3), but because the trial they used was so lopsided (78% of jurors favored acquittal), there were just too few closely split juries to detect it.

Subsequent mock jury research has provided consistent evidence for such a leniency asymmetry and has also suggested that it is a result of the reasonable doubt standard of proof (which prescribes that defendants be given the benefit of jurors' doubts about guilt; see MacCoun & Kerr, 1988). Model 2 in Table 11.1 simplifies and improves on Davis's Model 4 in two ways: (a) it drops hung juries as an outcome to be predicted, and (b) it incorporates the leniency asymmetry found in MacCoun and Kerr's (1988) meta-analysis of mock jury studies. MacCoun and Kerr obtained meta-analytic estimates for the entries for the fifth (8G/4NG), seventh (6G/6NG), and ninth (4G/8NG) rows. Those are inserted into Model 2, and the intermediate rows (the sixth and eighth rows) are estimated by averaging the values in the adjacent two rows. So, for example, Model 2 predicts that among evenly split (6G/6NG) mock juries that reach a verdict, most (~80%) will acquit. By now there is substantial empirical evidence suggesting that Model 2 (or something rather similar to it) can accurately predict mock jury conviction rates from mock juror conviction rates in criminal trials.

There are far fewer data with actual juries to test the predictive accuracy of something such as Model 2, although what does exist routinely replicates the first two features of the generic model. There has been a bit of controversy about whether the leniency asymmetry that is so clear in mock juries might be absent in actual juries (e.g., see Devine, Buddenbaum, et al., 2007; Devine, Olafson, et al., 2004; Sandys & Dillehay, 1995). However, there was a coding bias in the prior studies examining actual juries, and when this bias is eliminated, a (somewhat attenuated) leniency asymmetry is evident in the real jury data (Kerr & MacCoun, 2012). For example, Model 1 in Table 11.1 presents the *D* matrix that best fits the verdict data for 92 actual juries studied by Devine et al. (2007). This estimation eliminates the aforementioned coding bias and uses MacCoun's (2012) bidirectional balance of pressures or bBOP model to both get a full estimation of the function relating juror to jury preference and to smooth minor irregularities across the observed data (see Kerr & MacCoun, 2012, for details). I suggest that Model 1 (or something similar to it) could accurately predict actual jury conviction rates from something rarely available in real criminal trials, juror predeliberation conviction rates.

The attentive reader may notice that there is yet another *D*, Model 3, in Table 11.1. It supplements Model 1 by trying to predict hung juries as well. The entries in the third column of Model 3's *D* were estimated from Zeisel and Diamond's (1978; Graph 1, p. 505) freehand interpolation of Kalven and Zeisel's (1966, p. 489) data, with the entries in the remaining columns based on Model 1's corresponding entries. In principle, something similar could be attempted for Model 2, but because the likelihood of hung mock juries seems to depend strongly on how much time they are given to deliberate (vs. the nearly unlimited time actual juries are given; Kerr, 1981), it is hard to estimate them well, beyond assuming that they would be larger values (hung juries more likely in mock juries, the basis for Models 2 and 4) than those shown in the final column of Model 3 (based on actual jury behavior).

When one visually compares these different *D* matrices, the similarities are far more striking than the differences. Yes, the asymmetry leniency in Model 1 (based on actual juries' data) is less pronounced than the same asymmetry in Model 2 (based on mock or simulated juries' data), but do these isolated and small differences really matter when it comes to using jurors' verdict data to predict juries' verdict data? To begin to explore this issue, I compared the predictions of Models 1 and 2 (see Figure 11.1). In Figure 11.1, the *x* axis represents the rate at which individual jurors might convict (ranging from a proportion of 0.0 guilty votes to 1.0). The *y* axis represents the corresponding rates at which juries convict. The solid line shows what would happen if jury deliberation had no effect on conviction rates; in SDS terms, this is the prediction of a proportionality *D*, where the likelihood of a faction prevailing is equal to its relative frequency (e.g., 8G/4NG split juries would

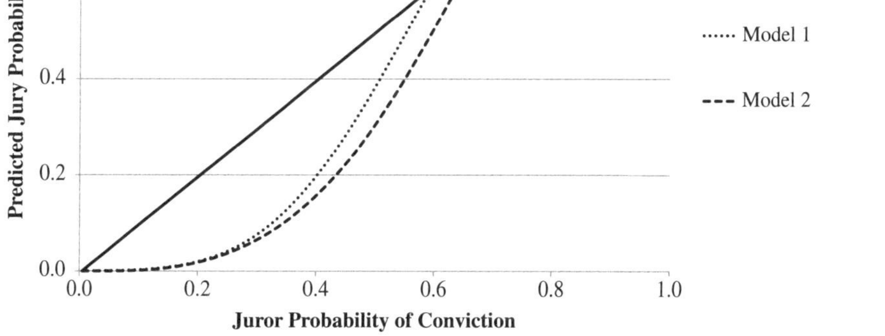

Figure 11.1. Model 1 and Model 2 predictions of jury conviction for all possible juror conviction rates.

convict two thirds of the time). This model is presented here as a useful, symmetric baseline. The long-dashed curve shows the jury conviction rates predicted by Model 1. The short-dashed curve shows the predictions of Model 2. As one can see, there is not much difference between the models' predictions. They both predict polarization of verdicts (Myers & Kaplan, 1976)—when juror conviction rates are low, jury rates are lower still; when juror conviction rates are sufficiently high, jury rates will be higher still. The leniency asymmetry is evident—for example, when juror opinion is evenly split, they both predict that juries are relatively more likely to acquit than to convict.

Earlier I suggested that having such models would make it possible to make reasonable estimates of the magnitude of jury effects if we knew the magnitude of an effect among jurors. Suppose we did a study of the effects of defendant attractiveness on mock juror verdicts, and the conviction rate for the unattractive defendant was 8% higher than for the attractive defendant. The first thing that Figure 11.1 tells us is that the size of the corresponding effect among juries will depend on the overall (i.e., averaged across conditions) juror conviction rate. If that overall rate is extreme (say, lower than 20% or higher than 80%), the jury effect would be smaller than the juror effect. So, for example, suppose the overall conviction rate was 18% and our 8% juror effect reflected a conviction rate of 14% in the attractive defendant condition versus 22% in the unattractive defendant condition. Model 2 (based on mock jury data) would predict a conviction rate of 0.6% in the attractive defendant condition and 2.6% in the unattractive condition, a net jury-level effect of ~2.5%. The results would be quite similar had one preferred Model 1; the corresponding figures would be high attractive = 0.7%, low attractive = 2.9%, net effect of ~2.8%. However, if the overall conviction rate had been moderate, both Models 1 and 2 would predict the opposite, with larger effects in juries than in jurors. For example, if the overall juror conviction rate were 50%, with condition rates of 46% and 54%, Model 2 would predict that the 8% difference at the juror level would become a ~14% difference among juries. Under Model 1, the 8% juror effect would be predicted to produce a jury effect of ~17%. The key point is that knowing how some independent variable of interest affected juror verdicts, we can use plausible and empirically validated prediction models (such as Model 1 and Model 2) to make educated guesses about what we would have observed in juries deliberating that same trial. And because the most plausible predictive models (my candidates are in Table 11.1) do not differ that much from one another, our educated guesses are not likely to differ much if we prefer one such model (e.g., Model 2) to another (e.g., Model 1).

Incidentally, the small differences there become smaller still as one considers smaller juries. The interested and motivated reader can explore (and, I suggest, confirm) my sweeping conclusions him- or herself with any of the Models in Table 11.1 (or with some alternative plausible model of his or her devising) with an Excel worksheet that carries out the relevant calculations, posted online at http://www.msu.edu/user/kerr/Jury/SDS.Jury Predictions.xlsx.

Caveats

My conclusion—that less costly juror research may often be sufficient to answer the same research questions about juries—carries a few caveats. Obviously, some such research questions are only relevant at the jury level (e.g., the effects of unanimous vs. nonunanimous jury decision rules, C. E. Miller, 1989; effects of jury deliberation polling procedures, Tindale, Nadler, Krebel, & Davis, 2004). And one has to assume that the same model that has made accurate jury predictions in some or many other situations will do as well in a novel situation of interest. So, it is at least conceivable that there are some kinds of trials or jury populations in which the generic, three-feature model advanced here breaks down to some degree for some feature(s). For one example, there is far less evidence of what *D* should look like for a civil trial using a preponderance of evidence instead of a reasonable-doubt standard, and what little does exist (e.g., Kalven & Zeisel, 1966; MacCoun & Kerr, 1988, Experiment 2) has suggested it may not show any leniency (i.e., prodefendant) asymmetry.

The SDS model also implicitly assumes that jurors have all the relevant information available to deliberating jurors and evaluate and integrate it much as deliberating jurors do. There are situations in which these assumptions might not hold. For example, Sommers (2006) provided evidence that certain lines of argumentation that arise and are influential in mixed-race juries are never pursued in all-White juries. Such evidence need not require the abandonment of the three-feature generic *D*s of Table 11.1, but some tweaking (e.g., in Sommers's situation, the leniency asymmetry should be stronger for mixed-race than for all-White juries). And others (e.g., Kaplan & Miller, 1978) have argued that deliberating juries put relatively more emphasis on relevant, legally permissible evidence versus irrelevant, impermissible information (e.g., jurors' attitudes toward the attorneys), resulting in generally weaker extralegal biases among juries than among jurors. Although most of the evidence seems to contradict the latter prediction (see Kerr, MacCoun, & Kramer, 1996; Kerr, Niedermeier, & Kaplan, 1999), there might be some kinds of juror biases that juries effectively police and attenuate. Again, though, if these can be described and well understood, the *D* models may be appropriately modified to handle such cases.

Finally, the available predictive models may be sufficient for simple cases and judgments (one charge, two verdict option, reasonable doubt standard), but they have not yet been sufficiently developed or tested to handle other more complicated trials (e.g., involving multiple charges, lesser included offenses) or nonverdict jury judgments (e.g., damage awards in civil trials, sentencing recommendations in capital trials). Again, I would recommend that we devote more of our scarce resources to the development of more general and complex predictive models, rather than reflexively studying juries in any and all more complex trial situations.

DON'T WORSHIP THE IDOL OF MUNDANE REALISM

The most common method used in prior jury research is the experimental simulation study (e.g., Chapter 9, this volume), and the modal simulation is unrealistic in several regards (when compared with actual jury trials; Bornstein, 1999). For example, the mock jurors are likely to be college students rather than drawn from a population more representative of actual jurors (which would be older, less well-educated, etc.); the stimulus trial is often fictional and nearly always much briefer than a real trial; the stimulus trial is almost never a live presentation in a courtroom, only occasionally a realistic (e.g., video version) representation of a real trial, and likely to be a brief written summary of evidence and testimony; certain features of a real trial, such as voir dire and jury instructions, are often omitted; the juror and jury judgments obtained are sometimes other than those real jurors would make (e.g., ratings of guilt rather than verdicts, recommended sentences); jury deliberation is often absent and, when present, nearly always limited in length; and in nearly all simulation studies, the juror judgments made have been inconsequential (i.e., mock jurors are aware that a guilty verdict will not result in any punishment for any actual defendant). Consequently, a persistent theme in discussions about jury research has been the need for more field research (where issues of realism do not arise) or for greater realism in simulation research (e.g., Diamond, 1997; Dillehay & Nietzel, 1980; Konečni & Ebbesen, 1979; G. R. Miller, Fontes, Boster, & Sunnafrank, 1983; Mitchell, Walker, & Monahan, 2011; Wiener, Krauss, & Lieberman, 2011). Rather similar prescriptions are advocated in this volume (e.g., see Chapters 7, 8, and 9). Although granting the desirability of more realistic jury research, it would be a serious mistake to insist reflexively on high degrees of realism in future jury research.

Before proceeding, I should offer a brief note on terminology. Aronson and Carlsmith (1968) distinguished between two kinds of realism in experimental research. *Mundane realism* refers to the extent to which the experimental context is similar to some real context of interest. *Experimental realism* refers to whether the experimental context feels real to the participant—that is, it engages him or her to exhibit the same basic psychological processes that would be engaged were the context a natural or "real" one. A jury simulation study that takes place in a courtroom would hence be more mundanely realistic than one that took place in a laboratory. A jury simulation study that engaged the same concerns and reactions felt by jurors in an actual courtroom would be more experimentally realistic than one that did not, regardless of the research setting. Aronson and Carlsmith argued (and I agree) that they are not the same thing and that in most cases, achieving high experimental realism is more important than achieving high mundane realism. With few exceptions (e.g., Chapter 9, this volume), I believe that most of the calls for greater realism in jury research are calls for greater mundane realism.

My colleague Robert Bray and I have developed this argument at length elsewhere (Bray & Kerr, 1979, 1982; Kerr & Bray, 2005), so I will only summarize a few key points here. First, there is little theory or data suggesting that juror or jury behavioral phenomena are either quantitatively or qualitatively different in relatively less versus more realistic research settings. This is not just an appeal to ignorance—that we do not have the evidence, so it must not exist. Rather, there are several attempts to explore whether, when, and how specific aspects of simulation verisimilitude might moderate juror and jury phenomena of interest (for reviews, see Bornstein, 1999; Kerr & Bray, 2005). Most impressive in this regard is Bornstein's (1999) analyses of studies comparing student versus nonstudent mock jurors. In only one of 26 studies did this variable (student/nonstudent sample) moderate the effect of some other variable, and in that study (Cutler, Penrod, & Dexter, 1990), it did so for only two of the 10 independent variables studied. On the basis of such analyses, Bornstein concluded that there was "strong evidence that factors at trial affect students and nonstudents in the same way" (p. 80). Likewise, it appears to be the exception rather than the rule that other mundane realism variables (e.g., more realistic stimulus trial, jury vs. juror verdicts) show such moderation effects (Kerr & Bray, 2005).

Again, if there were no real costs entailed by doing more realistic research, there could be little objection to making research as realistic as possible (at least when the primary concern was with actual jury behavior per se). But there are substantial costs (e.g., in using a live vs. videotaped trial, accessible and inexpensive student participants vs. a representative sample of jurors, using courtrooms vs. laboratories). Realism costs. By insisting on high realism in a world of finite resources for our research, we ensure that there will be less research done.

But the costs are not only tangible costs of research logistics. Achieving greater realism nearly always involves a loss of experimental control and, consequently, greater threats to the internal validity of the research (Runkle & McGrath, 1972). The most realistic option available—field studies of actual juries—rarely permits one to draw clear and confident causal inferences because there are just too many factors that cannot be controlled. Hence, high realism not only means that less research will be done but also that less internally valid research will be done.

There are a number of counterarguments to my argument. One common one is that unrealistic jury research will have far less impact than more realistic research. It is suggested that lay, legal, and policy-setting audiences will be better convinced by more realistic research—or conversely, that such audiences will more readily dismiss the findings of less realistic research. A second, related counterargument is that more realistic research will reduce the risks of ecological invalidity of the findings of such research, and hence those findings can be applied to real juries in real courtrooms with more confidence. For both reasons, some suggest (e.g., G. R. Miller et al., 1983) that the advantages of more realistic research (e.g., impact, ecological validity) more than compensate for any costs (e.g., internal validity, the sheer amount of research).

The second counterargument reflects a common but fallacious assumption—that one can establish the ecological validity of a finding (i.e., its generalizability to a particular setting or ecology of interest, in our case, to real jury behavior) by maximizing the similarity between the conditions of one's research and the conditions arising in the real-world setting of interest. It is widely assumed that ecological validity depends primarily on how realistic the research is. There is a kernel of truth in this assumption—all else being equal, the fewer the differences between a research setting and any particular real-world setting of interest, the fewer reasons to hesitate in generalizing findings in the former to the latter. But the assumption I am objecting to goes further—it suggests that high realism is necessary and sufficient to ensure ecological validity. It is neither (for extended discussions, see Bray & Kerr, 1982, Kerr & Bray, 2005). Phenomena observed under quite unrealistic conditions are often quite informative about what occurs in the real world (e.g., research on carcinogenic effects in lab animals can be revealing about cancer risks in humans), and phenomena observed in highly realistic settings can be misleading about what happens in some or most other corners of the real world.

To illustrate the latter point, consider the question of whether permitting jurors to discuss a case before jury deliberation biases the eventual jury verdict. Two excellent field studies of civil juries in Arizona (Diamond, Vidmar, Rose, Ellis, & Murphy, 2003b; Hannaford, Hans, & Munsterman, 2000) explored this question among actual juries for a large and reasonably representative sample of real cases. In one (Hannaford et al., 2000) random assignment was used to determine which juries were permitted predeliberation discussion. Although there were some intriguing hints, the overall rate of proplaintiff verdicts did not differ materially between the juries permitted versus prohibited predeliberation discussion. Now, by the common "realism = ecological validity" reasoning, we ought to be reassured by such highly realistic research that permitting such discussions would be a benign, nonbiasing innovation in jury trials. The studies also documented that this innovation is also quite popular among judges, attorneys, and (especially) jurors (who understandably chafe under the usual prohibition of predeliberation discussion with others).

Recently, I conducted a highly unrealistic jury simulation study on the same question (Kerr, 2009). I found that the evidence jurors heard after a mid-trial discussion had a stronger impact on their civil trial verdicts than the evidence they heard before such discussions; juries prohibited from engaging in such discussions showed no such effect. The most plausible interpretation of the results was that such discussions caused juries to focus on the evidence heard since the last discussion and to treat evidence presented earlier as having already been covered by the previous discussion. So, for example, in trials with strong defense cases (presented primarily in the latter half of the trial), there would be a prodefense bias in juries permitted predeliberation discussion (a bias which would be absent had such discussions been prohibited). These preliminary results suggest that the innovation of predeliberation discussions, although popular, might well not be benign.

My point is not that the field studies were flawed in some way. They were conducted meticulously, and their authors made the most of what could be done in the field. But they could not (as the authors themselves readily acknowledged) do what could be done in a well-controlled (and unrealistic) lab experiment—for example, manipulate factors of interest (e.g., strength of evidence before and after discussion), reduce variability due to trial differences, and make sure that all those who were permitted to engage in pretrial discussion actually did so. Hence, they were not well suited to detect certain effects of interest. Future research should eventually settle the issue of just how malignant or benign predeliberation discussion is. But if the bias I observed in my study turns out to be reliable and robust, it would have been a mistake to rely too heavily on the realism of the initial research to settle that issue.

What about the other counterargument—that those who govern the jury system will be unconvinced by unrealistic research. There certainly are many examples of appellate judges discounting the findings of juror and jury research on the grounds of its artificiality (see Chapters 9 and 10, this volume) and evidence (Kovera & McAuliff, 2000; McAuliff & Groscup, 2009) that at least some trial judges and jurors also mistrust evidence that is based on less realistic research. It is quite unclear whether this is a fixed and principled insistence on realistic research or a flexible, unprincipled but convenient means of discounting unwelcome results (e.g., see Ellsworth, 1988; Kerr, 1986; Studebaker et al., 2002). Such questions arise when the same justices who reject (too artificial) science when it contradicts their view of a legal dispute readily embrace (equally artificial or otherwise flawed) science that supports their view in another dispute. Yes, legal policy makers want and prefer realistic research, but I suggest that they will also dismiss realistic research if it does not also give them what they want substantively (see Redding & Reppucci, 1999).

Caveats

I am not advising that we disvalue more realistic research; I am advising that we not invariably prefer it, regardless of investigators' resources, research objectives, or the current state of knowledge. The best route to reliable knowledge is via converging operations and methods. There may be instances in which most of what we know about some aspect of jury behavior is based on research that is highly unrealistic; more realistic research might then be viewed as the most useful next step in achieving such convergence (Diamond, 1997). Given its high cost, I would also argue that the value of more realistic research increases when there is good reason to believe that there is actually "something there" (i.e., a reliable phenomenon to study). But because of its lower cost and greater internal validity, it will often be more unrealistic research that will initially convince us that there probably really is something there (Diamond, 1997).

DO BE SELECTIVE ABOUT JUROR AND JURY RESEARCH QUESTIONS

Selecting one's research question is, in many ways, like selecting a romantic partner. Both are matters of opportunity, personal taste, personal resources, and the odd workings of chance. And for both, deliberate choice, after carefully weighing the pros and the cons, is usually the exception rather than the rule. To the extent that we do exercise some rationality and free will in both areas, it may be useful to consider some of those pros and cons and to be selective.

I would like to suggest four features that might make a research question relatively more attractive to those of us interested in studying juror and jury behavior. In doing so, I assume that most of us are motivated, at least partially, to improve the ways actual juries function—for example, to make juries more efficient, to increase the rate of accurate verdicts, and to reduce the impact of personal biases that undermine that accuracy. In short, most of us would like our research to have some impact on the working institution of the trial jury. I suspect that we can have more impact if we follow four simple guidelines when choosing our research questions.

Choose Research Questions That Inform Legal Controversies

Obviously, there is likely to be more impact—more research funding, more attention to findings, more application of those findings—when people in the legal community care about an issue. And they are most likely to care when there is some active dispute on that issue.

Choose Research Questions That Are Relevant to Proposed Innovations

Although legal institutions and procedures are notoriously slow to change, sometimes the need for change is evident. In the case of the jury, nearly everyone agrees that there have to be better ways of helping jurors deal with trial complexity, making judicial instructions comprehensible to jurors, making jury service less burdensome, minimizing the impact of patently extralegal considerations (e.g., defendant gender, race, or age) on jury verdicts, and so forth. Research that helps the legal system choose the best ways to innovate—that is, what's most effective, most efficient, and least likely to bring unwanted side effects—is more likely to have some impact. Kurt Lewin famously noted that "the best way to understand something is to try to change it" (Greenwood & Levin, 1998, p. 19). As his own (e.g., Lewin, 1947) and much other work shows, trying to solve a real, practical problem is a great way to challenge old ideas and get new ones.

Choose Research Questions That Examine the Law's More Implausible Assumptions About Human Behavior

Of course, there is no shortage of implausible assumptions (e.g., jurors instructed to disregard testimony can do so, jurors exposed to prejudicial pretrial publicity can proceed as if never exposed to it, jurors can make judgments of guilt without considering the likely consequences of their verdicts). Our training and knowledge as social scientists make us better qualified to recognize and empirically check such assumptions. Moreover, when we have strong theoretical and/or empirical grounds for questioning the plausibility of some legal assumption, the odds of success in our research increase—we are more likely to find ourselves operating in the context of justification and confirmation than in the context of discovery and exploration.

Choose Research Questions That Help Develop or Test Psychological Theory

I have heard some complain that jury research has been too preoccupied with psychological theory and too little concerned with answering applied questions. There is a kernel of truth to this position. For example, sometimes our research on juries completely ignores legal realities (e.g., asking mock jurors to sentence defendants when, in most instances, actual juries play no role in sentencing) in ways that limit the utility of our findings (Kerr, 1978). But on the whole, this position is misguided. Both the history of science and our training should have taught us the value of good theory—for organizing what we observe, for directing where we look, for filling in holes in our knowledge, and for understanding when and why some cause will have some effect. For all these reasons, Lewin (1952) was correct when he famously asserted, "There is nothing as practical as a good theory" (p. 169). By "good" theory, I mean not only valid theory (that survives repeated attempts at disconfirmation, resulting in what Lakatos, 1978, called "progressive research programmes") but also theory with broad and deep implications for a wide range of behaviors and contexts. Not all theory is good theory; some theoretical questions turn out to be purely "academic" questions (in the most pejorative sense of the word).

It might be illustrative to focus on a couple of research questions that satisfy all these criteria, one an old, much-researched question and one a newer, not-much-researched question. The former is the question of whether the size of the jury matters, precisely the question that was being addressed in my first jury study (Davis et al., 1975) conducted back in the early 1970s. I can take no credit for choosing the question—that was my advisor, Jim Davis's, wise choice. And I doubt that Jim chose it because it nicely fit the list of desiderata I propose here. As suggested earlier, many other factors probably entered in, including (a) personal taste: Jim was fascinated with the experimental study of small groups, and a study of jury size matched that interest well; and (b) available resources: Jim had access to the extensive labs and huge subject pool of the University of Illinois Department of Psychology required to undertake such a massive study. But, in retrospect, the question does nicely fit my list. The U.S. Supreme Court's ruling in *Williams v. Florida* (1970) rejecting the argument that the Constitution's guarantee to a trial by jury required a 12-person jury both opened the door to the innovation of smaller (less expensive) juries and created a legal controversy (both within and without the Court) about whether such an innovation would have undesirable, unintended consequences (e.g., for jury representativeness, for thorough jury deliberation, for ultimate jury verdict). The Court majority's conclusion—that the size of the jury really should not matter—attracted Jim's interest in part because of its implausibility.

There had been multiple prior demonstrations that group size affected group behavior (e.g., Davis, 1969; Shaw, 1971; E. J. Thomas & Fink, 1963). Some of those findings supported the thrust of *Williams v. Florida* (1970). For example, participation in discussion had been shown to be more uniform and universal in smaller groups than in larger groups (e.g., Stephan & Mishler, 1952), a beneficial result of reducing jury size. Other findings were incongruent with *Williams*. For example, conformity research (Asch, 1952) showed that having support for one's position helps those holding minority positions resist the pressures of the majority, and all else being equal, social support is relatively more likely in a larger jury than a smaller one. Even an elementary grasp sampling should have shown the justices that smaller juries would be less representative juries (e.g., be less likely to include members of cognizable minority groups; Lempert, 1975). For these and other reasons, it was not much of a gamble to undertake research to show that jury size did matter. And the effect of group size had genuine theoretical significance. As noted earlier, one of the key parameters of the SDS model is the size of the group; comparisons of different sized juries provided a perfect opportunity to test the SDS model's theoretical predictions on the effect of group size. Finally, this research question also reflected the odd workings of chance. The *Williams* ruling was handed down in 1970, just as Davis (1973) was formalizing his thinking on the SDS model. Although that early study certainly did not settle the question, it arguably did have some impact, becoming part of a literature that eventually led the Supreme Court in *Ballew v. Georgia* (1978) to impose some limits on the shrinking of the jury.

As noted earlier, I have recently done some research on the effects of permitting jurors to discuss a case before deliberations (Kerr, 2009). In this instance, the choice of research question was mine, and I was drawn to the question precisely because it satisfied all my proposed desiderata. The idea of permitting such discussion has been prominent among a number of innovations proposed to "modernize" the jury (including such innovations as permitting jurors to question witnesses, allowing jurors to take notes during the trial, routinely providing full transcripts to the jury; Munsterman, Hannaford-Agor, & Whitehead, 2006). Because there are many good arguments both for sticking with tradition (and barring such discussions) and for bucking tradition (and permitting such discussions), there is some legal controversy surrounding the question (Diamond, Vidmar, Rose, Ellis, & Murphy, 2003a).

Given findings in several literatures, such as the effects of early commitments on information evaluation and eventual decisions (e.g., Cialdini, 2006; Klayman & Ha, 1987) or the effects of social validation on one's opinions (e.g., Festinger, 1954; Wittenbaum, Hubbell, & Zuckerman, 1999), the fundamental assumption underlying this proposed innovation—that jurors' verdicts will not be affected by permitting predeliberation discussions—struck me as implausible (even after seeing the early empirical returns that tended bear out this assumption; Diamond et al., 2003b; Hannaford et al., 2000). Moreover, the question has broad theoretical significance, beyond its applied significance for the jury. Juries are not the only decision-making group that is charged with giving all relevant evidence equal and fair consideration and for which the evidence that is available to the group early tends to support a different choice than the evidence that is available late. Hence, research on this question in juries could contribute materially to theory and knowledge on related questions (e.g., group's overreliance on shared information; Stasser & Titus, 2003). It is probably much too early to judge whether research on this question will eventually have an impact (e.g., lead to a more cautious and empirical approach to jury reform), but the fact that it seems to meet all my desiderata gives me more optimism that it will.

Caveats

More important than all of my suggested desiderata for choosing one's research question is that you find the question interesting. You are more likely to give your best thinking, your best efforts, and your true commitment to questions that you have a passion for, regardless of how interesting or important others might find it. Or, as Shakespeare aptly wrote,

> No profit grows where is no pleasure ta'en:
> In brief, sir, study what you most affect.
>
> (*Taming of the Shrew*, Act 1, Scene 1)

Of course, to the degree that you want your research to have an impact, it may not be enough that you are personally convinced it is interesting, even if that might motivate your best work. You may also have to be able to convince others (the research funders, the journal editors, the legal policy makers) that it is interesting, but I would venture that having a genuine passion for your question is usually an excellent starting point for convincing others.

Another common criticism of jury research is that it sometimes is "tilting at windmills"—in quixotic attempts to win battles that are not worth fighting for a number of reasons (e.g., because the relevant legal issues have apparently already been settled, existing practice is too well-established to be altered by our scientific efforts, or existing practice is based less on the answers to empirical questions than on weighing competing values). For example, before *Lockhart v. McCree* (1986), it made sense to study whether death-qualified juries are more conviction prone than death-unqualified juries. But after the U.S. Supreme Court decided in *Lockhart* to discount a substantial and converging research literature that unequivocally demonstrated that conviction is more likely with death-qualified juries, it might well be viewed as a waste of time and effort to add to that literature. In a world of limited research resources, there is some wisdom in this advice. However, some legal issues that are seemingly settled and invulnerable to new empirical evidence deserve to be challenged. Whether it is settled policy in the United States to excuse all jurors with reservations about the death penalty from capital trial juries, one has to stick one's head in the sand to conclude that such a policy does not result in juries more likely to convict (precisely in those trials in which the burden of proof on the prosecution should be its greatest). So, even though adding new research evidence on this question might be viewed as quixotic, it could contribute eventually to changing a bad policy.

In this vein, I am inspired by the efforts of several colleagues (e.g., see Chapter 6, this volume) to promote the use of the jury in countries where it has never been used before. The existing means of settling legal disputes in these nations are well entrenched. Nevertheless, these colleagues have persisted in doing research that is informing an important debate and is gradually increasing receptiveness to the use of lay participation in trials. So, considerations of maximizing short-term impact should be tempered with considerations of maximizing impact in the long run on big, important questions. For the latter, I would nominate the following as windmills worth tilting at:

- In light of the evidence showing how poorly attorneys can perceive favorable versus unfavorable jurors during voir dire (e.g., Kerr, Kramer, Carroll, & Alfini, 1991; Olczak, Kaplan, & Penrod, 1991; Otis, Greathouse, Kennard, & Kovera, 2014) and the clear potential for excluding certain classes of jurors (e.g., African American jurors in venires in which they constitute a small minority; Sommers & Norton, 2008), should peremptory challenges be eliminated or curtailed?
- Given the manifest advantages (e.g., McCrystal, 1977; G. R. Miller, Bender, Florence, & Nicholson, 1974) for eliminating irrelevant or prejudicial testimony, for giving judges more time to consider attorney objections, for streamlining trial presentation, and for providing a more complete trial record for appellate courts, should carefully edited video recordings of trials replace live trials?

DO DEVELOP AND TEST FORMAL MODELS OF JUROR AND JURY BEHAVIOR

Earlier I called for jury research that helped develop or test psychological theory, broadly conceived. For those of us interested in the jury, there is additional value added for theory that applies specifically to the tasks given jurors and juries—first and foremost to reaching verdicts but also to subtasks that are instrumental for reaching verdicts (e.g., judging witness credibility, story construction and evaluation, opinion revision following diagnostic information, leader/foreperson selection and behavior). In particular, the field would profit from concerted efforts to test, extend, and improve on extant models of individual juror decision making (e.g., the story model: Pennington & Hastie, 1993; Bayesian models: Schum & Marti, 1993; signal detection models: Kerr, 1993; E. A. Thomas & Hogue, 1976) and of jury decision making (e.g., the SDS model: Davis, 1973; the social judgment scheme model: Davis, 1996; the social transition scheme model: Kerr, 1981, 1982; the social interaction sequence model: Stasser & Davis, 1981; the DICE/JUS model: Penrod & Hastie, 1980, and Hastie, Penrod, & Pennington, 1983; the bBOP model: MacCoun, 2012). The basic virtues of good theory—for organizing what we have observed, for stimulating new research, for directing where we look next, for filling in holes in our knowledge, and for aiding our understanding of when and why people behave as they do—are amplified when that theory has a sharp focus on the people, contexts, and behaviors of primary interest.

Earlier I suggested some characteristics that help make a behavioral theory a "good" one. For all these and other reasons, I would like to give special emphasis to theories that are highly formalized in their structure, such as mathematical or computational models. The special virtues of such formal theories have been well articulated elsewhere (e.g., Abelson, 1967; Hastie & Stasser, 2000; Rosenberg, 1968) and include greater precision in theoretical structure and implications, less likelihood of internal inconsistency, more precise prediction, and the possibility of exploring (both theoretically and empirically) the effect of model parameters. The scientific study of juries is a relatively new enterprise, but from my perspective (of a swan waddling down an exit ramp), we have gotten more "bang for our buck" from such formal theories than from less well-formalized theories and still less from atheoretical empirical work. The yield of 40-plus years of research using Davis's formal SDS model (e.g., Kerr, Stasser, & Davis, 1979; Kerr & Tindale, 2012; Levine, 1999; Parks & Kerr, 1999; Stasser et al., 1982, 1989; Tindale et al., 2004) can serve as one persuasive illustration.

TO MAXIMIZE IMPACT, DO AND DISSEMINATE MAXIMALLY GOOD SCIENCE

I will confess that I am, at heart, a basic researcher who happens to be interested in juries. The primary and immediate goal of my jury work has not been to have an impact on the jury system but rather simply to contribute to knowledge. My training and experience have counseled reliance on scientific methods to achieve that goal. Even if maximizing impact is one's primary goal, I believe it is still good advice to strive to do the best science possible. By that,

I do not mean invariably preferring any one method (e.g., tightly controlled laboratory experimentation) to any other (e.g., descriptive field research). Rather, I mean carefully and pragmatically using every useful scientific tool—logical, methodological, statistical, and theoretical—at our disposal.

This strategy also means that we resist the idea that when it comes to having an impact in the real world, there is a single best method. Runkle and McGrath (1972) suggested that the notion of a best method for any research question is a siren song. They identified eight generic research strategies (that even included the nonempirical strategies of developing formal theory or using computer simulations; see Figure 11.2) and noted that each of these

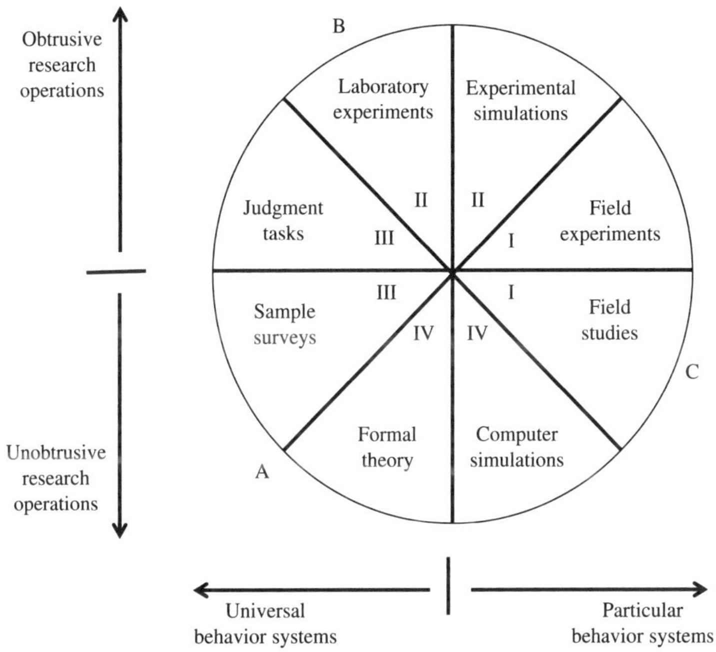

I. Settings in natural systems
II. Contrived and created settings
III. Behavior not setting dependent
IV. No observation of behavior required

A. Point of maximum concern with generality over actors
B. Point of maximum concern with precision of measurement of behavior.
C. Point of maximum concern with system character of context

Figure 11.2. The research strategy circumplex model. From *Research on Human Behavior: A Systematic Guide to Method* (p. 85), by P. J. Runkle and J. E. McGrath, 1972, New York, NY: Holt, Rinehart and Winston. Copyright 1972 by Janet W. McGrath. Reprinted with permission.

has inherent strengths and weaknesses. By opting for one you always gain something (e.g., maximum realism in field research, maximum representativeness of respondents in survey research, maximum control and precision of measurement in laboratory research), but you inevitably do so at the cost of something else. We are always on the horns of a multihorned dilemma when choosing our research strategies, and there is no choice that avoids all the horns. The best one can do is make the most of the strengths offered by your choice of strategy and then hope that you or others can obtain converging evidence in additional research that uses other strategies with different strengths. We make the most convincing case through the convergence or triangulation of what we learn with these different, flawed methods, not by putting most or all of our eggs into a single or a few flawed methodological baskets.

Doing the best science also means being cautious about risking our reputation for objectivity through too-close collaboration with the partisan advocates within adversarial legal systems. I am not criticizing jury consultants or expert witnesses (at least not when the goal is to contribute the tools and findings of science to make sure that each side in a legal dispute can present its strongest possible case), nor those who point out the value of close collaboration between scientists and courtroom advocates (e.g., see Chapter 3, this volume). I am only saying that in studying the jury, as in any other scientific inquiry, we are more likely to learn something useful and to be able to persuade others of its utility when our motive in undertaking our research is to learn what is true rather than what might be most useful to one or the other side of some legal dispute.

Koehler and Meixner (Chapter 7, this volume) have suggested that when it comes to persuading those who determine jury policy (e.g., trial and appellate judges, attorneys, legislators, court administrators), we should give them what they want. Koehler and others in this volume have suggested (correctly, I believe) that "what they want" is research that is as realistic as possible (of course, if possible they also want findings that confirm their prior opinions). But I suggest that rather than giving scientifically naive audiences what they want, we have to try to shift what they want from the evidence that feels most familiar to them to the best scientific evidence we can provide. This goal can be achieved, although not quickly, through both general and more targeted efforts to increase scientific literacy—in short, through education. To the degree that we can identify policymakers who are more receptive to the utility of scientific evidence for the jury, we should try to disseminate and explain our findings to them first rather than to do so indiscriminately or to those who strongly prefer tradition or intuition over scientific evidence when it comes to understanding and improving the jury system.

A SWAN SONG CODA

When it comes to music, beauty is in the ear of the listener. After hearing my swan song, you might well agree with Samuel Taylor Coleridge that

> Swans sing before they die—
> 'twere no bad thing
> Should certain persons die
> before they sing.

I hope that there were at least a few true notes in my long-winded song.

Medawar (1981) in his *Advice to a Young Scientist* said,

> Any scientist of any age who *wants to make important discoveries must study important problems*. . . . It is not enough that the problem is "interesting"—almost any problem is interesting if it is studied in sufficient depth. . . . No, the problem must be such that it *matters* what the answer is—whether to science generally or to mankind. (p. 13)

Those of you who have chosen the problem of unraveling the mystery of juries can at least be confident that your problem is both interesting and important.

REFERENCES

Abelson, R. P. (1967). Mathematical models in social psychology. *Advances in Experimental Social Psychology, 3*, 1–54. http://dx.doi.org/10.1016/S0065-2601(08)60341-X

Aronson, E., & Carlsmith, M. (1968). Experimentation in social psychology. In G. Lindzey & E. Aronson (Eds.), *The handbook of social psychology* (2nd ed., Vol. 2, pp. 1–79). Reading, MA: Addison Wesley.

Asch, S. E. (1952). *Social psychology*. http://dx.doi.org/10.1037/10025-000

Ballew v. Georgia, 435 U.S. 223 (1978).

Baron, R. S., & Kerr, N. L. (2003). *Group process, group decision, group action* (2nd ed.). Buckingham, England: Open University Press.

Bornstein, B. H. (1999). The ecological validity of jury simulations: Is the jury still out? *Law and Human Behavior, 23*, 75–91. http://dx.doi.org/10.1023/A:1022326807441

Bray, R. M., & Kerr, N. L. (1979). Use of the simulation method in the study of jury behavior: Some methodological considerations. *Law and Human Behavior, 3*, 107–119. http://dx.doi.org/10.1007/BF01039151

Bray, R. M., & Kerr, N. L. (1982). Methodological issues in the study of the psychology of the courtroom. In N. L. Kerr & R. M. Bray (Eds.), *The psychology of the courtroom* (pp. 287–323). New York, NY: Academic Press.

Cialdini, R. B. (2006). *Influence: How and why people agree to things*. New York, NY: Morrow.

Cutler, B. L., Penrod, S. D., & Dexter, H. R. (1990). Juror sensitivity to eyewitness identification evidence. *Law and Human Behavior, 14*, 185–191. http://dx.doi.org/10.1007/BF01062972

Davis, J. H. (1969). *Group performance*. Reading, MA: Addison Wesley.

Davis, J. H. (1973). Group decision and social interaction: A theory of social decision schemes. *Psychological Review, 80*, 97–125. http://dx.doi.org/10.1037/h0033951

Davis, J. H. (1996). Group decision making and quantitative judgments: A consensus model. In E. H. Witte & J. H. Davis (Eds.), *Understanding group behavior: Vol. 1. Consensual action by small groups* (pp. 35–59). Hillsdale, NJ: Erlbaum.

Davis, J. H., Kerr, N. L., Atkin, R. S., Holt, R., & Meek, D. (1975). The decision processes of 6- and 12-person mock juries assigned unanimous and two-thirds majority rules. *Journal of Personality and Social Psychology, 32*, 1–14. http://dx.doi.org/10.1037/h0076849

Devine, D. J. (2012). *Jury decision making: The state of the science*. New York: New York University Press.

Devine, D. J., Buddenbaum, J., Houp, S., Stolle, D. P., & Studebaker, N. (2007). Deliberation quality: A preliminary examination in real juries. *Journal of Empirical Legal Studies, 4*, 273–303. http://dx.doi.org/10.1111/j.1740-1461.2007.00089.x

Devine, D. J., Olafson, K. M., Jarvis, L. L., Bott, J. P., Clayton, L. D., & Wolfe, J. M. T. (2004). Explaining jury verdicts: Is leniency bias for real? *Journal of Applied Social Psychology, 34*, 2069–2098. http://dx.doi.org/10.1111/j.1559-1816.2004.tb02691.x

Diamond, S. S. (1997). Illuminations and shadows from jury simulations. *Law and Human Behavior, 21*, 561–571. http://dx.doi.org/10.1023/A:1024831908377

Diamond, S. S., Vidmar, N., Rose, M., Ellis, L., & Murphy, B. (2003a). Inside the jury room: Evaluating juror discussions during trial. *Judicature, 82*, 54–58.

Diamond, S. S., Vidmar, N., Rose, M., Ellis, L., & Murphy, B. (2003b). Juror discussions during civil trials: Studying an Arizona innovation. *Arizona Law Review, 45*, 1–82.

Dillehay, R. D., & Nietzel, M. T. (1980). Constructing a science of jury behavior. In L. Wheeler (Ed.), *Review of personality and social psychology* (pp. 246–264). Beverly Hills, CA: Sage.

Efran, M. G. (1974). The effect of physical appearance on the judgment of guilt, interpersonal attraction, and severity of recommended punishment in a simulated jury task. *Journal of Research in Personality, 8*, 45–54. http://dx.doi.org/10.1016/0092-6566(74)90044-0

Ellsworth, P. C. (1988). Unpleasant facts: The Supreme Court's response to empirical research on capital punishment. In K. C. Haas & J. A. Inciardi (Eds.), *Challenging capital punishment: Legal and social science approaches* (pp. 177–211). Newbury Park, CA: Sage.

Festinger, L. (1954). A theory of social comparison processes. *Human Relations, 7,* 117–140. http://dx.doi.org/10.1177/001872675400700202

Forsyth, D. R. (2013). *Group dynamics* (6th ed.). Boston, MA: Cengage Learning.

Greenwood, D. J., & Levin, M. (1998). *Introduction to action research: Social research for social change.* Newberry Park, CA: Sage.

Hannaford, P. L., Hans, V. P., & Munsterman, G. T. (2000). Permitting jury discussions during trial: Impact of the Arizona reform. *Law and Human Behavior, 24,* 359–382. http://dx.doi.org/10.1023/A:1005540305832

Hastie, R., Penrod, S., & Pennington, N. (1983). *Inside the jury.* Cambridge, MA: Harvard University Press.

Hastie, R., & Stasser, G. (2000). Computer simulation methods for social psychology. In H. T. Reis & C. M. Judd (Eds.), *Handbook of research methods in social and personality psychology* (pp. 85–114). New York, NY: Cambridge University Press.

Kalven, H., & Zeisel, H. (1966). *The American Jury.* Boston, MA: Little, Brown.

Kaplan, M. F., & Miller, L. E. (1978). Reducing the effects of juror bias. *Journal of Personality and Social Psychology, 36,* 1443–1455. http://dx.doi.org/10.1037/0022-3514.36.12.1443

Kerr, N. L. (1978). Severity of prescribed penalty and mock jurors' verdicts. *Journal of Personality and Social Psychology, 36,* 1431–1442. http://dx.doi.org/10.1037/0022-3514.36.12.1431

Kerr, N. L. (1981). Social transition schemes: Charting the group's road to agreement. *Journal of Personality and Social Psychology, 41,* 684–702. http://dx.doi.org/10.1037/0022-3514.41.4.684

Kerr, N. L. (1982). Social transition schemes: Model, method, and applications. In H. Brandstatter, J. H. Davis, & G. Stocker-Kreichgauer (Eds.), *Group decision making* (pp. 59–80). London, England: Academic Press.

Kerr, N. L. (1986). Social science and the Supreme Court. In M. F. Kaplan (Ed.), *The impact of social psychology on procedural justice* (pp. 56–79). Springfield, IL: C. C. Thomas.

Kerr, N. L. (1993). Stochastic models of juror decision making. In R. Hastie (Ed.), *Inside the juror: The psychology of juror decision making* (pp. 116–135). http://dx.doi.org/10.1017/CBO9780511752896.007

Kerr, N. L. (2009, October). The effects of pre-deliberation jury discussion: New empirical evidence. In N. L. Kerr (Chair), *Current research at the social psychology/law interface.* Symposium presented at the meeting of the Society of Experimental Social Psychology, Portland, ME.

Kerr, N. L., & Bray, R. M. (2005). Simulation, realism, and the study of the jury. In N. Brewer & K. Williams (Eds.), *Psychology and law: An empirical perspective* (pp. 322–364). New York, NY: Guilford Press.

Kerr, N. L., Kramer, G. P., Carroll, J. S., & Alfini, J. (1991). On the effectiveness of voir dire in criminal cases with prejudicial pretrial publicity: An empirical study. *The American University Law Review, 40,* 665–701.

Kerr, N. L., & MacCoun, R. J. (2012). Is the leniency asymmetry really dead? Misinterpreting asymmetry effects in criminal jury deliberation. *Group Processes & Intergroup Relations, 15*, 585–602. http://dx.doi.org/10.1177/1368430212441639

Kerr, N. L., MacCoun, R. J., & Kramer, G. P. (1996). Bias in judgment: Comparing individuals and groups. *Psychological Review, 103*, 687–719. http://dx.doi.org/10.1037/0033-295X.103.4.687

Kerr, N. L., Niedermeier, K. E., & Kaplan, M. F. (1999). Bias in jurors vs. bias in juries: New evidence from the SDS perspective. *Organizational Behavior and Human Decision Processes, 80*, 70–86. http://dx.doi.org/10.1006/obhd.1999.2855

Kerr, N. L., Stasser, G., & Davis, J. H. (1979). Model-testing, model-fitting, and social decision schemes. *Organizational Behavior & Human Performance, 23*, 399–410. http://dx.doi.org/10.1016/0030-5073(79)90006-0

Kerr, N. L., & Tindale, R. S. (2012). Scientific inquiry on how groups decide: The Davisonian approach. *Group Processes & Intergroup Relations, 15*, 577–584. http://dx.doi.org/10.1177/1368430212455119

Klayman, J., & Ha, Y. (1987). Confirmation, disconfirmation, and information in hypothesis testing. *Psychological Review, 94*, 211–228. http://dx.doi.org/10.1037/0033-295X.94.2.211

Konečni, V. J., & Ebbesen, E. B. (1979). External validity of research in legal psychology. *Law and Human Behavior, 3*, 39–70. http://dx.doi.org/10.1007/BF01039148

Kovera, M. B., & McAuliff, B. D. (2000). The effects of peer review and evidence quality on judge evaluations of psychological science: Are judges effective gatekeepers? *Journal of Applied Psychology, 85*, 574–586. http://dx.doi.org/10.1037/0021-9010.85.4.574

Lakatos, I. (1978). *The methodology of scientific research programmes: Philosophical papers* (Vol. 1). http://dx.doi.org/10.1017/CBO9780511621123

Lempert, R. O. (1975). Uncovering "nondiscernable" differences: Empirical research and the jury size cases. *Michigan Law Review, 73*, 643–708. http://dx.doi.org/10.2307/1287721

Levine, J. M. (1999). Transforming individuals into groups: Some hallmarks of the SDS approach to small group research. *Organizational Behavior and Human Decision Processes, 80*, 21–27. http://dx.doi.org/10.1006/obhd.1999.2852

Lewin, K. (1947). Group decision and social change. In T. Newcomb & E. Hartley (Eds.), *Readings in social psychology* (pp. 330–344). New York, NY: McGraw-Hill.

Lewin, K. (1952). *Field theory in social science: Selected theoretical papers by Kurt Lewin.* London, England: Tavistock.

Lockhart v. McCree, 476 U.S. 162 (1986).

MacCoun, R. J. (2012). The burden of social proof: Shared thresholds and social influence. *Psychological Review, 119*, 345–372. http://dx.doi.org/10.1037/a0027121

MacCoun, R. J., & Kerr, N. L. (1988). Asymmetric influence in mock jury deliberation: Jurors' bias for leniency. *Journal of Personality and Social Psychology, 54*, 21–33. http://dx.doi.org/10.1037/0022-3514.54.1.21

McAuliff, B. D., & Groscup, J. L. (2009). Daubert and psychological science in court: Judging validity from the bench, bar, and jury box. In J. L. Skeem, K. S. Douglas, & S. O. Lilienfeld (Eds.), *Psychological science in the courtroom: Consensus and controversy* (pp. 26–52). New York, NY: Guilford Press.

McCrystal, J. L. (1977). The promise of prerecorded videotaped trials. *American Bar Association Journal, 63*, 977–979.

Medawar, P. (1981). *Advice to a young scientist.* New York, NY: Basic Books.

Miller, C. E. (1989). The social psychological effects of group decision rules. In P. Paulus (Ed.), *Psychology of group influence* (2nd ed., pp. 327–356). Hillsdale, NJ: Erlbaum.

Miller, G. R., Bender, D., Florence, T., & Nicholson, H. (1974). Real versus reel: What's the verdict? *Journal of Communication, 24*, 99–111. http://dx.doi.org/10.1111/j.1460-2466.1974.tb00396.x

Miller, G. R., Fontes, N. E., Boster, F. J., & Sunnafrank, M. J. (1983). Methodological issues in legal communication research: What can trial simulations tell us? *Communication Monographs, 50*, 33–46. http://dx.doi.org/10.1080/03637758309390152

Mitchell, G., Walker, L., & Monahan, J. (2011). Beyond context: Social facts as case-specific evidence. *Emory Law Journal, 60*, 1109–1155.

Munsterman, G. T., Hannaford-Agor, P., & Whitehead, G. M. (2006). *Jury trial innovations.* Williamsburg, VA: National Center for State Courts.

Myers, D. G., & Kaplan, M. F. (1976). Group-induced polarization in simulated juries. *Personality and Social Psychology Bulletin, 2*, 63–66. http://dx.doi.org/10.1177/014616727600200114

Olczak, P. V., Kaplan, M. F., & Penrod, S. (1991). Attorneys' lay psychology and its effectiveness in selecting jurors: Three empirical studies. *Journal of Social Behavior & Personality*, 6, 431–452.

Otis, C. C., Greathouse, S. M., Kennard, J. B., & Kovera, M. B. (2014). Hypothesis testing in attorney-conducted voir dire. *Law and Human Behavior, 38*, 392–404. http://dx.doi.org/10.1037/lhb0000092

Parks, C. D., & Kerr, N. L. (1999). Twenty-five years of social decision scheme theory. *Organizational Behavior and Human Decision Processes, 80*, 1–2. http://dx.doi.org/10.1006/obhd.1999.2850

Pennington, N., & Hastie, R. (1993). The story model for juror decision making. In R. Hastie (Ed.), *Inside the juror: The psychology of juror decision making* (pp. 192–222). http://dx.doi.org/10.1017/CBO9780511752896.010

Penrod, S., & Hastie, R. (1979). Models of jury decision making: A critical review. *Psychological Bulletin, 86*, 462–492. http://dx.doi.org/10.1037/0033-2909.86.3.462

Penrod, S., & Hastie, R. (1980). A computer simulation of jury decision making. *Psychological Review, 87*, 133–159. http://dx.doi.org/10.1037/0033-295X.87.2.133

Redding, R. E., & Reppucci, N. D. (1999). Effects of lawyers' socio-political attitudes on their judgments of social science in legal decision making. *Law and Human Behavior*, *23*, 31–54. http://dx.doi.org/10.1023/A:1022322706533

Rosenberg, S. (1968). Mathematical models of social behavior. In G. Lindzey & E. Aronson (Eds.), *The handbook of social psychology* (2nd ed., pp. 179–244). Reading, MA: Addison Wesley.

Runkle, P. J., & McGrath, J. E. (1972). *Research on human behavior: A systematic guide to method*. New York, NY: Holt, Rinehart and Winston.

Sandys, M., & Dillehay, R. C. (1995). First-ballot votes, predeliberation dispositions, and final verdicts in jury trials. *Law and Human Behavior*, *19*, 175–195. http://dx.doi.org/10.1007/BF01499324

Schum, D. A., & Marti, A. W. (1993). Formal and empirical research on cascaded inference in jurisprudence. In R. Hastie (Ed.), *Inside the juror: The psychology of juror decision making* (pp. 136–174). http://dx.doi.org/10.1017/CBO9780511752896.008

Shaw, M. (1971). *Group dynamics*. New York, NY: McGraw-Hill.

Sommers, S. R. (2006). On racial diversity and group decision making: Identifying multiple effects of racial composition on jury deliberations. *Journal of Personality and Social Psychology*, *90*, 597–612. http://dx.doi.org/10.1037/0022-3514.90.4.597

Sommers, S. R., & Norton, M. I. (2008). Race and jury selection: Psychological perspectives on the peremptory challenge debate. *American Psychologist*, *63*, 527–539. http://dx.doi.org/10.1037/0003-066X.63.6.527

Stasser, G. (1999). A primer of social decision scheme theory: Models of group influence, competitive model-testing, and prospective modeling. *Organizational Behavior and Human Decision Processes*, *80*, 3–20. http://dx.doi.org/10.1006/obhd.1999.2851

Stasser, G., & Davis, J. H. (1981). Group decision making and social influence: A social interaction sequence model. *Psychological Review*, *88*, 523–551. http://dx.doi.org/10.1037/0033-295X.88.6.523

Stasser, G., Kerr, N. L., & Bray, R. M. (1982). The social psychology of jury deliberations: Structure, process, and product. In N. L. Kerr & R. M. Bray (Eds.), *The psychology of the courtroom* (pp. 223–256). New York, NY: Academic Press.

Stasser, G., Kerr, N. L., & Davis, J. H. (1989). Influence processes and consensus models in decision-making groups. In P. Paulus (Ed.), *Psychology of group influence* (2nd ed., pp. 279–326). Hillsdale, NJ: Erlbaum.

Stasser, G., & Titus, W. (2003). Hidden profiles: A brief history. *Psychological Inquiry*, *14*, 304–313. http://dx.doi.org/10.1080/1047840X.2003.9682897

Stephan, F. F., & Mishler, E. G. (1952). The distribution of participation in small groups: An exponential approximation. *American Sociological Review*, *17*, 598–608. http://dx.doi.org/10.2307/2088227

Studebaker, C. A., Robbennolt, J. K., Penrod, S. D., Pathak-Sharma, M. K., Groscup, J. L., & Devenport, J. L. (2002). Studying pretrial publicity effects: New methods for improving ecological validity and testing external validity. *Law and Human Behavior*, *26*, 19–41. http://dx.doi.org/10.1023/A:1013877108082

Swan song. (2016). In *Wikipedia*. Retrieved from http://en.wikipedia.org/wiki/Swan_song

Thomas, E. A., & Hogue, A. (1976). Apparent weight of evidence, decision criteria, and confidence ratings in juror decision making. *Psychological Review*, *83*, 442–465. http://dx.doi.org/10.1037/0033-295X.83.6.442

Thomas, E. J., & Fink, C. F. (1963). Effects of group size. *Psychological Bulletin*, *60*, 371–384. http://dx.doi.org/10.1037/h0047169

Tindale, R. S., Nadler, J., Krebel, A., & Davis, J. H. (2004). Procedural mechanisms and jury behavior. In M. Brewer & M. Hewstone (Eds.), *Applied social psychology* (pp. 136–164). Malden, England: Blackwell.

Tindale, R. S., Smith, C. M., Dykema-Engblade, A., & Kluwe, K. (2012). Good and bad group performance: Same process—different outcomes. *Group Processes & Intergroup Relations*, *15*, 603–618. http://dx.doi.org/10.1177/1368430212454928

Wiener, R. L., Krauss, D. A., & Lieberman, J. D. (2011). Mock jury research: Where do we go from here? *Behavioral Sciences & the Law*, *29*, 467–479. http://dx.doi.org/10.1002/bsl.989

Williams v. Florida, 399 U.S. 78 (1970).

Wittenbaum, G. M., Hubbell, A. P., & Zuckerman, C. (1999). Mutual enhancement: Toward an understanding of the collective preference for shared information. *Journal of Personality and Social Psychology*, *77*, 967–978. http://dx.doi.org/10.1037/0022-3514.77.5.967

Zeisel, H., & Diamond, S. S. (1978). The effects of peremptory challenges on jury and verdict: An experiment in a federal district court. *Stanford Law Review*, *30*, 491–531. http://dx.doi.org/10.2307/1228114

CONCLUSION: THE FUTURE OF JURY RESEARCH

MARGARET BULL KOVERA

Throughout this volume, leading jury scholars have identified what they view as gaps in our knowledge of jury behavior and have made recommendations for closing these gaps. For some of the authors, the gaps are substantive. Researchers have failed to pursue certain important lines of inquiry that would flesh out our understanding of jury behavior, including the role of trial advocacy in trial outcomes, the effects of race on juror behavior and decisions, the effects of the group context on juror decision making, and how jury decisions stack up against those rendered by judges. Moreover, our knowledge about lay participation in legal decision making is relatively U.S.-centric, neglecting how procedural differences in lay decision participation in other countries around the globe may moderate the general principles of jury decision making that scholars have identified. Certainly there are other substantive areas in need of scholarly attention from jury researchers. How do we identify those other areas?

http://dx.doi.org/10.1037/0000026-013
The Psychology of Juries, M. B. Kovera (Editor)

For other authors in the volume, gaps in our knowledge sometimes arise from the types of methods we choose to study jury behavior, especially more tightly controlled experiments that may fail to simulate a real juror's task in any meaningful way. However, even strong advocates for ecological validity, including some of the authors of chapters in this volume, still recognize that there may be circumstances in which less realistic methods are preferable or at least tolerable. But how do we determine when it is important to value verisimilitude in our methods and when might it be less important? In the remainder of this chapter, I attempt to synthesize the viewpoints of the authors of this volume, making recommendations for jury scholars, novice and more expert alike, about how to choose interesting and important research questions and what methods might be best to test those questions. I end by making a few recommendations for directions that jury researchers might fruitfully pursue in the future. By no means is this list exhaustive, but it provides a starting point for the development of a research agenda for future jury researchers.

RECOMMENDATIONS FOR CHOOSING JURY RESEARCH QUESTIONS

In the first six chapters of this volume, each of the authors makes recommendations for areas of inquiry that have been relatively neglected by jury researchers and that need additional attention. Kerr (Chapter 11) likened selecting a research question to selecting a romantic partner, suggesting that idiosyncratic variables such as opportunity, interest, resources, and chance will govern selection. Although he is correct that there are idiosyncratic variations in whom people select as romantic partners, there are also fairly well-articulated standards of beauty and attractiveness. These standards may change over time and cultures, but they exist. Similarly, it is likely that there would be some agreement about whether certain research questions are more interesting than others. Three approaches to choosing empirical jury research questions consistently emerged across the contributions to this volume:

Choose research questions that help develop or test psychological theory.

In their respective chapters, Norbert L. Kerr (Chapter 11) and Lora M. Levett and Dennis Devine (Chapter 1) reminded us of the importance of developing and testing models that could describe and predict both juror and jury decision making across a wide variety of cases and contexts. As Kerr noted, good theory provides a framework for organizing past research findings and for identifying gaps in our existing knowledge. The model of individual juror and group jury decision making described by Levett and Devine is an example of the type of theorizing that can help researchers identify holes in the literature and develop new hypotheses that, if tested, can produce findings that will fill those gaps. In addition, Jennifer S. Hunt (Chapter 4) illustrated that drawing on basic theory from the subdisciplines of psychology can also serve the purpose of organizing a research literature and illuminating its gaps, in this case the literature on the effects of race on jury decision. Drawing on social psychological theory, she argued that jury researchers have primarily studied race effects as if there is only a Black–White dichotomy, neglecting to study variables such as within-race variations in phenotypic appearance and their effects on juror decisions (cf. Eberhardt, Davies, Purdie-Vaughns, & Johnson, 2006) and the effects of within-race cultural differences. Whether theory is specifically developed to explain jury behavior or borrowed from other subdisciplines within psychology, it has the potential to direct researchers to important questions worthy of their attention.

Study the effects of system variables.

The contributors to this volume often proposed questions that tested the effects of variables that were under the control of players in the justice system. For example, Christina A. Studebaker (Chapter 3) urged researchers to study the effects of the strategies that attorneys choose when deciding how to present trial evidence in a way that best serves their client. Valerie P. Hans and her colleagues (Chapter 6) argued for studying how citizens evaluated the legitimacy of different systems of lay participation. In contrast, authors generally did not identify research on *estimator variables*—variables that cannot be controlled by the litigants or the court—as interesting to pursue unless research on the variables might provide some theoretical insight or were paired with some type of system variable or intervention, such as when Jennifer S. Hunt (Chapter 4) advocated for studying procedural interventions that would reduce racial bias in jury decisions.

Gary Wells (1978) first proposed this estimator-system variable framework to guide eyewitness researchers toward investigations of variables that would provide more useful information, but the framework can be adapted for use by jury researchers who are interested in applied—rather than theoretical—questions. In the context of jury research, *estimator variables* are those variables that influence the verdicts (e.g., defendant characteristics, witness characteristics) but are not under the control of the litigants or the judicial system. Understanding how estimator variables operate in the jury setting may be useful for predicting when it would be helpful for a defendant to accept a plea bargain or a plaintiff to accept a settlement, but studying them will not provide evidence about how to improve justice because they are not mutable. In contrast to estimator variables, *system variables* are characteristics of the trial that are under the control of the litigants or the court. Although estimator variable research may prove useful to attorneys, litigants, and trial consultants who endeavor to predict how juries are likely to decide a particular case, system variable research is more likely to produce findings that improve the quality of the decisions that jurors render, influence policy, and increase the justice that defendants and victims receive. There may be exceptions to this preference for system variable research, but the exceptions will most likely be interesting because they are testing whether there is empirical evidence for legal assumptions about human behavior (discussed later) or because the research tests whether a court procedure—a system variable—interacts with an estimator variable to influence jury decisions. Examples of these exceptions include whether jurors can put aside racial biases when making decisions (testing a legal assumption) or whether judicial instructions can reduce the effects of defendant race or gender on juror decisions (an estimator × system variable interaction).

Choose research questions for which the findings will be interesting, whether or not the hypotheses are supported.

In addition to suggesting that jury researchers should design studies that develop and test theory, Norbert L. Kerr (Chapter 11) argued that they should choose questions that provide evidence to inform legal controversies, test the effects of proposed innovations, and examine whether legal assumptions about human behavior are accurate. The beauty of these guidelines for choosing questions is that the findings will be interesting whether or not they support the hypothesis being tested. The field of psychology is currently plagued by failures to replicate accepted findings (Open Science Collaboration, 2015), and concerns have been raised about researchers' use of questionable research practices—known as "*p*-hacking" (Simmons, Nelson, & Simonsohn, 2011)—to increase the likelihood that they will find effects that are statistically significant at $p < .05$. It is interesting to know whether legal assumptions about human behavior are accurate or whether procedural innovations will work. Sometimes legal assumptions will be accurate or procedural innovations will prove effective; sometimes assumptions will not be accurate or innovations will not have their intended effect. Either way, the findings will be interesting. Thus, these types of questions, in addition to providing important information about jury functioning, do not incentivize *p*-hacking. Many of the suggestions for future research proposed by contributors to this volume fall under this category of research questions, including the suggestions that we test the legal assumptions that deliberation improves juror memory (Hirst & Stone, Chapter 2) and that judges are better decision makers than are jurors (Robbennolt & Eisenberg, Chapter 5) or that we test the effects of different methods of legal advocacy (Studebaker, Chapter 3).

RECOMMENDATIONS FOR CHOOSING JURY RESEARCH METHODS

Readers of this volume might come to the conclusion that jury researchers are more successful at posing new areas of inquiry than they are at settling deep-seated differences in preferences for different methodologies. The contributions to this volume reflect the division in the field about the relative importance of different types of validity, with some authors emphasizing the importance of ecological validity or verisimilitude (Koehler & Meixner, Chapter 7; Krauss & Lieberman, Chapter 8) and others emphasizing the importance of internal validity (Kerr, Chapter 11). And although everyone agrees that the ability to generalize research findings to real cases is important, there is disagreement over the extent to which ecological validity is required to achieve generalizable findings. Despite these differences, there are a few common themes running through the discussions of how to choose a methodology when designing jury research.

Evaluate the need for high ecological validity on a case-by-case basis.

Several contributors to this volume argued that the importance of ensuring that jury studies have high ecological validity is dependent on the goals of the researcher conducting the studies. These authors argued that high ecological validity is less essential when researchers are focused on making theoretical contributions about basic psychological processes in decision making but more essential when scholars conduct research intended to identify procedures that would improve the legal system or when they wish to influence legal audiences with their work (Koehler & Meixner, Chapter 7; Krauss & Lieberman, Chapter 8). Although these authors argued that researchers with more applied goals should be careful to maximize ecological validity, they noted that there may be exceptions to this general rule—for example, in cases in which it is unlikely that the effects of manipulated variables would differ as a function of variations in ecological validity. Thus, whether a researcher should aim to maximize the ecological validity of a given study depends on the theoretical versus applied nature of the research question and the likelihood that variations in ecological validity would moderate the influence of variables that are central to the hypotheses being tested.

In addition to these recommendations, I would also argue that ecological validity may be more important for jury research examining estimator variables—variables that cannot be controlled by the players in the legal system—than it is for research investigating the influence of system variables. Some scholars have argued that external validity is more important for making point predictions rather than supporting theoretical conclusions (Anderson & Bushman, 1997). Estimator variables are more likely to be used solely for making predictions about whether the variable will influence litigants' likely success at trial (a point prediction) than are system variables. Moreover, estimator variables in the real world may naturally covary with other estimator variables in ways that are not well captured in laboratory experiments, another argument for maximizing ecological validity when studying this type of variable.

It is interesting to note that one of the primary reasons for calling for ecological validity—the need to appeal to the courts—may have no real traction according to Mary R. Rose's (Chapter 10) analysis of appellate court's discussions of jury research. She found that courts rarely if ever mention ecological validity as a concern. The editors and peer reviewers of jury research also appear less concerned by low ecological validity than by low internal validity (Krauss & Lieberman, Chapter 8). Finally, Brian H. Bornstein (Chapter 9) found few interactions between variables capturing variations in ecological validity (e.g., nature of sample, trial modality) and the variables researchers manipulated to test hypotheses. Despite these empirical findings suggesting that legal and scholarly audiences may be less concerned by ecological validity than we once thought, it would be wise for researchers to consider the importance of maximizing ecological validity for each jury study they conduct, given the goals of the research and the likely interaction of methodological features of the study with the manipulated variables.

Maximize internal validity to the best of your ability.

Norbert L. Kerr (Chapter 11, under the heading "To Maximize Impact") encouraged jury researchers to "do the best science possible." The survey data presented by Daniel A. Krauss and Joel D. Lieberman (Chapter 8) suggest that those responsible for evaluating the scholarly contributions of jury research value internal over external validity. Maximizing internal validity is important for two reasons. The first, most obvious reason is that maximizing internal validity ensures that one can draw causal conclusions about the effects of manipulated variables on outcome measures such as verdict, ruling out alternative explanations for those effects. Second, and perhaps less obvious, maximizing internal validity is necessary for establishing external validity of findings because a study cannot have external validity unless it has high internal validity.

At its core, external validity is a question of whether the relationships among variables discovered in one setting, with one sample, at one time are the same relationships present in other settings, other populations, at other times (Cook & Campbell, 1979). If a study provides no information about causal relationships among variables, there is nothing to generalize (Anderson & Bushman, 1997; Banaji & Crowder, 1989). It is true that some reviewers may complain about the low ecological validity of some internally valid jury simulations, but it would be improper to conclude that the findings from low ecologically valid trial simulations are not externally valid because there have been demonstrations in other areas of inquiry, namely, aggression, that ecologically invalid research findings can generalize to real-world settings (Anderson & Bushman, 1997). Besides, the data from Krauss and Lieberman's (Chapter 8) survey of editors and reviewers suggests that jury researchers likely would be successful publishing their work if they ensured that they were asking interesting questions about jury behavior using methods that ruled out alternative explanations for their findings.

Include behavior as an independent or dependent variable in jury research.

Unlike the preceding recommendations, this suggestion is based on my reading of the body of research on the jury rather than on statements made by other contributors to this volume, yet I believe it remains worthy of note. Despite a firm footing in the discipline of psychology, the science of behavior, there is relatively little behavior to be found in most jury research. Other than a small number of studies that include deliberations in their designs, it is hard to find studies that include a behavioral manipulation of the independent variable or that collect information about behavior as dependent variables. Psychology and law is not alone in its neglect of behavior in its laboratory experiments. Social psychologists have also noted that if one were to define behavior from looking at what constitutes behavior in the pages of the *Journal of Personality and Social Psychology*, one might be left with the impression that behavior consists of self-reports, computer keystrokes, and pencil markings (Baumeister, Vohs, & Funder, 2007). An intentional decision to infuse behavior into our experimental paradigms might broaden the questions we are asking beyond those that can be studied with convenient paradigms consisting of reading written trial summaries and circling numbers on a questionnaire.

Take, for example, the research on scientific jury selection. For decades, scholars of jury selection have searched for demographic, personality, and attitudinal variables that will predict verdict, primarily by correlating participants' responses to questions about their personal characteristics, their behavioral tendencies, or attitudes with their responses to questions evaluating the trial evidence or collecting their verdicts (Kovera & Austin, 2016). This particular area of inquiry has stagnated, perhaps in part because few, if any, variables predict verdicts across a variety of trial contexts. And the singular focus on identifying predictors of verdict has perhaps distracted scholars from studying jury selection in the context of a social interaction among the judge, the attorneys, and the venirepersons. Some research has examined whether the social interaction between the judge and venirepersons influences juror responses to voir dire questions (Jones, 1987) or their verdicts (Crocker & Kovera, 2010), and I imagine that there are many other areas of jury research that may benefit from an infusion of behavior into the research design.

DIRECTIONS FOR FUTURE RESEARCH

Test new models of jury decision making.

Devine's (2012) director's cut model of jury decision making makes predictions for both individual and group decision-making processes. However, many of the hypotheses derived from this model remain untested. When subjected to empirical scrutiny, will Devine's model hold up? Does it describe individual juror decision making better than Pennington and Hastie's (1988, 1991) story model? Certainly, the director's cut model is less parsimonious than the story model, so it would have to provide a better description of juror decision making to prove to be a better alternative.

Even if Devine's (2012) model of individual decision making outperforms the story model in its explanatory power, the question remains whether the model will also explain decision making of lay participants in systems other than that of the United States. Devine's model categorizes jurors on the basis of their belief in the story offered by the prosecution/plaintiff. In inquisitorial justice systems, in which the trial procedure is structured to seek truth rather than to provide adversaries a chance to argue their version of events, the role of the prosecution/plaintiff story in jurors' decisions may be less prominent. Finally, it is not clear that categorizing jurors on the basis of their belief in the prosecution/plaintiff story, a primary predictor in the Devine model, would be useful for understanding jury decision making in some Asian countries in which jurors are convicting 98% or more of the defendants who face trial. In these systems, almost every juror would likely fall into the believer category (as opposed to doubters, mullers, or puzzlers), and the lack of variability would result in this categorization of jurors providing little explanatory power.

Study systems of lay participation around the globe.

As exemplified in the earlier discussion, if there is to be a complete understanding of how laypeople make legal decisions, it is crucial that researchers begin to extend the focus of their research to systems around the globe rather than exclusively studying how jurors in the United States make decisions in the context of their system. This U.S.-centric approach causes researchers to neglect interesting psychological questions such as how groups with mixed expertise on a topic (in the case of mixed tribunals, differences in legal knowledge) collaborate to arrive at a jointly agreed on decision based on a single set of facts. Hans and her colleagues (Chapter 6) argued that research on global systems of lay participation in legal decisions should take a comparative approach and is better suited to empirical methods more likely to be used by sociologists (e.g., surveys, interviews) than by many psychologists who study the jury (e.g., experiments, jury simulations). Although it is true that questions of whether new systems of lay participation in several Asian countries are perceived to be legitimate by the citizenry are better suited to nonexperimental methods, the differences between these systems and the U.S. system raise a number of interesting questions about how jurors with differing status (professional judges vs. lay jurors) both deploy and respond to attempts at informational and normative influence. As argued by several contributors to this volume, most jury research questions are best answered using multiple methods, and this area of inquiry is unlikely to be an exception.

Examine the effects of consequentiality and other methodological variables on jury decisions.

Bornstein (Chapter 9) noted that there still is relatively little research examining the extent to which methodological variables moderate the influence of experimental manipulation. Although there is somewhat more research addressing the potential influence of sample type (student vs. community members or real empaneled jurors) than other potential methodological moderators (e.g., consequentiality, trial modality, trial length), the findings to date do not provide a consistent picture of whether or when sample type moderates juror decisions (Bornstein, Chapter 9; Koehler & Meixner, Chapter 7). And as these authors noted, there is almost no research addressing whether the lack of consequences associated with participants' decisions in jury simulation studies—which is a seemingly immutable disadvantage to simulations—alters their decision making. The high-stakes nature of real trials, with serious potential consequences for defendants, including payment of large monetary awards or a loss of freedom, are difficult to capture in simulations, but we could do better than we have. Scholars exploring other areas of inquiry in psychology and law, namely, those studying confessions, have managed to develop paradigms that simulate the consequences that suspects experience if they confess to a crime, including crimes they did not commit (Madon, Guyll, Scherr, Greathouse, & Wells, 2012; Russano, Meissner, Narchet, & Kassin, 2005). With concerted effort, jury researchers should be able to develop paradigms that simulate—at least to a greater extent than we have to date—the consequentiality of jurors' decisions.

FINAL NOTE

As the chapters in this volume make evident, jury research is plentiful and has tackled many interesting questions. Yet much remains to be done. By tackling important questions, whether they be theoretical or applied in nature, and using the best methods for studying the research question posed, jury researchers will be poised to contribute vital data about basic psychological processes underlying decision making and about applied issues facing the courts. With these data, courts will be able to make evidence-based decisions about procedural changes that will improve the justice that litigants receive.

REFERENCES

Anderson, C. A., & Bushman, B. J. (1997). External validity of "trivial" experiments: The case of laboratory aggression. *Review of General Psychology, 1*, 19–41. http://dx.doi.org/10.1037/1089-2680.1.1.19

Banaji, M. R., & Crowder, R. G. (1989). The bankruptcy of everyday memory. *American Psychologist, 44*, 1185–1193. http://dx.doi.org/10.1037/0003-066X.44.9.1185

Baumeister, R. F., Vohs, K. D., & Funder, D. C. (2007). Psychology as the science of self-reports and finger movements: Whatever happened to actual behavior? *Perspectives on Psychological Science, 2*, 396–403. http://dx.doi.org/10.1111/j.1745-6916.2007.00051.x

Cook, T. D., & Campbell, D. T. (1979). *Quasi-experimentation: Design and analysis issues for field settings*. Chicago, IL: Rand McNally.

Crocker, C. B., & Kovera, M. B. (2010). The effects of rehabilitative voir dire on juror bias and decision making. *Law and Human Behavior, 34*, 212–226. http://dx.doi.org/10.1007/s10979-009-9193-9

Devine, D. J. (2012). *Jury decision making: The state of the science*. New York: New York University Press.

Eberhardt, J. L., Davies, P. G., Purdie-Vaughns, V. J., & Johnson, S. L. (2006). Looking deathworthy: Perceived stereotypicality of Black defendants predicts capital-sentencing outcomes. *Psychological Science, 17*, 383–386. http://dx.doi.org/10.1111/j.1467-9280.2006.01716.x

Jones, S. E. (1987). Judge- versus attorney-conducted voir dire: An empirical investigation of juror candor. *Law and Human Behavior, 11*, 131–146. http://dx.doi.org/10.1007/BF01040446

Kovera, M. B., & Austin, J. L. (2016). Juror bias: Moving from assessment and prediction to a new generation of jury selection research. In C. Willis-Esqueda & B. H. Bornstein (Eds.), *The witness stand and Lawrence S. Wrightsman, Jr.* (pp. 75–94). http://dx.doi.org/10.1007/978-1-4939-2077-8_6

Madon, S., Guyll, M., Scherr, K. C., Greathouse, S., & Wells, G. L. (2012). Temporal discounting: The differential effect of proximal and distal consequences on confession decisions. *Law and Human Behavior, 36*, 13–20. http://dx.doi.org/10.1037/h0093962

Open Science Collaboration. (2015). Estimating the reproducibility of psychological science. *Science, 349*, aac4716. http://dx.doi.org/10.1126/science.aac4716

Pennington, N., & Hastie, R. (1988). Explanation-based decision making: Effects of memory structure on judgment. *Journal of Experimental Psychology: Learning, Memory, and Cognition, 14*, 521–533. http://dx.doi.org/10.1037/0278-7393.14.3.521

Pennington, N., & Hastie, R. (1991). A cognitive theory of juror decision making: The story model. *Cardozo Law Review, 13*, 519–558.

Russano, M. B., Meissner, C. A., Narchet, F. M., & Kassin, S. M. (2005). Investigating true and false confessions within a novel experimental paradigm. *Psychological Science, 16*, 481–486.

Simmons, J., Nelson, L., & Simonsohn, U. (2011). False-positive psychology: Undisclosed flexibility in data collection and analysis allows presenting anything as significant. *Psychological Science, 22*, 1359–1366. http://dx.doi.org/10.1177/0956797611417632

Wells, G. L. (1978). Applied eyewitness-testimony research: System variables and estimator variables. *Journal of Personality and Social Psychology, 36*, 1546–1557. http://dx.doi.org/10.1037/0022-3514.36.12.1546

INDEX

ABOUT THE EDITOR

Margaret Bull Kovera, PhD, is Presidential Scholar and a professor of psychology at John Jay College of Criminal Justice, City University of New York. She received her BA and PhD in psychology from Northwestern University and the University of Minnesota, respectively. She is a Fellow of the American Psychological Association, the Association for Psychological Science, the American Psychology–Law Society (APLS), and the Society for the Psychological Study of Social Issues. She is a past president of APLS and the editor-in-chief of *Law and Human Behavior.* Dr. Kovera received the Saleem Shah Award for Early Career Achievement in Psychology and Law and the APLS Outstanding Teacher and Mentor Award.